EC LAW

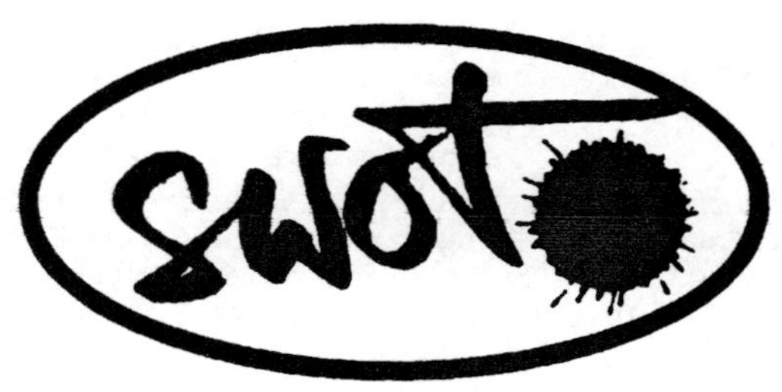

EC LAW

Third Edition

Nigel G. Foster

BA, LLM, Dip.German

Senior Lecturer in Law, Cardiff Law School,
University of Wales
Director, Law and German Degree

Series Editor: C.J. Carr, MA, BCL

OXFORD
UNIVERSITY PRESS

OXFORD

UNIVERSITY PRESS

Great Clarendon Street, Oxford OX2 6DP

Oxford University Press is a department of the University of Oxford.
It furthers the University's objective of excellence in research, scholarship,
and education by publishing worldwide in

Oxford New York

Auckland Bangkok Buenos Aires Cape Town Chennai
Dar es Salaam Delhi Hong Kong Istanbul Karachi Kolkata
Kuala Lumpur Madrid Melbourne Mexico City Mumbai Nairobi
São Paulo Shanghai Taipei Tokyo Toronto

Oxford is a registered trade mark of Oxford University Press
in the UK and in certain other countries

Published in the United States
by Oxford University Press Inc., New York

A Blackstone Press Book

© N Foster 1993
First published 1993
Second edition 1995
Third edition 2000

The moral rights of the author have been asserted
Database right Oxford University Press (maker)

All rights reserved. No part of this publication may be reproduced,
stored in a retrieval system, or transmitted, in any form or by any means,
without the prior permission in writing of Oxford University Press,
or as expressly permitted by law, or under terms agreed with the appropriate
reprographics rights organization. Enquiries concerning reproduction
outside the scope of the above should be sent to the Rights Department,
Oxford University Press, at the address above

You must not circulate this book in any other binding or cover
and you must impose this same condition on any acquirer

British Library Cataloguing in Publications Data

A record for this book is available from the British Library

Library of Congress Cataloguing in Publications Data

Data applied for

ISBN 1-84174-110-8

3 5 7 9 10 8 6 4 2

Typset by Style Photosetting Limited, Mayfield, East Sussex
Printed in Great Britain
on acid-free paper by
Biddles Ltd, Guildford and King's Lynn

CONTENTS

CONTENTS

PREFACE

In writing this book it has been necessary to be selective in the material included. It is not possible, given the constraints of the aims of the SWOT series, to go into all details or provide extensive case law coverage. Whilst this type of book is not comprehensively welcomed by all academic staff, the continued pressure on universities caused by the expansion in numbers, which appears at the time of writing to be continuing, means that not all students will have access to all the materials we as teachers consider they should consult. More positively, many students benefit greatly from consulting a more accessible introduction to a topic before getting stuck into a main text. Hence, I believe these books serve a vital role in legal education, apart from their use as a revision guide closer to assessment.

The topics that have been included are those likely to be common to the majority of European Community law courses (even if called European Union law courses). The text does not cover individual topics comprehensively because the information provided is intended to cover the principal points and as the basis for answering typical questions. Areas covered are most aspects of institutional and procedural law and the substantive law topics of free movement of goods and persons, competition law and sex discrimination law.

The major change for this edition is the entry into force of the Treaty of Amsterdam on 1 May 1999. While the Treaty made few significant changes in substance, its greatest impact on the study of Community law is probably the re-numbering of the EC and TEU Treaties, which will be a thorn in the side of EC law students (and teachers, for that matter!) for many a year. Although new numbering now applies, the old numbering must still be learnt as all previous case law will refer to old numbering only and, as some cases take up to 13 years to final judgment on appeal before the ECJ, the problem will remain a current one for at least the next decade.

The policy adopted in this book is to refer predominantly but not exclusively to the new numbers followed by the old numbers in brackets, e.g., Art 234 (old 177). For the most part, even when referring to pre-Amsterdam case law or legislative provisions, the new number will be given first although this may not be technically correct. Occasionally, when close attention to the old numbers and content of provision is essential, the old numbers will be retained but that this will be made clear, e.g., old Art 5 (now 10). It is hoped confusion may thus be avoided.

My thanks go to colleagues: Robin Churchill and Phil Fennell for permission to use a number of questions formulated jointly and severally for tutorial, essay and exam questions used on the courses on European law and Community law since 1983. Thanks also to my wife for additional help and my children, Lynsey and Alexander, for mostly understanding why I'm not always around to play. Thanks also to Blackstone staff.

For errors and omissions, I am solely responsible. I would be grateful to be advised of any errors discovered and also any general comments in respect of coverage, treatment or any other aspect of the book.

Nigel Foster
Pontprennau, Cardiff
January 2000

TABLE OF CASES

Cases have been arranged in alphabetical order.

INTRODUCTION

The purpose of this book is to provide a study guide and revision aid — a before-and-after book. It is not a textbook with full explanations and cannot fulfil that role. I assume that additional reading from a comprehensive text and other support reading will be undertaken.

The information is good for all forms of assessment including examinations and coursework and can also be used as preparation for tutorial discussions. Whilst modularisation, which is taking place in many but not all universities, will affect the structure of many courses on EC/EU law, the essential requirements and skills of question-answering remain the same.

In this book I have condensed a huge area of law into a short guide and included only the material necessary to obtain a basic grasp of Community law topics, while attempting not to over-simplify it. Inevitably this has the result that only a framework or overview of many cases and areas of the law has been given. It is an introduction to the basic principles of stated law, and therefore there is no speculation on how the law might develop in the future or how future cases may be decided. It is an attempt to summarise the past and provide a picture of the present, not the future.

The cases referred to are the leading cases in Community law: where one serves as an adequate example of the point or principle of law, rather than two or more, then just one is employed. In any event, later cases often summarise the development of the law until then, and often provide précis of earlier cases and judgments.

Case numbers or key words concerning the subject matter are given in the text to avoid confusion with similarly titled cases, for example the million-and-one cases against Italy, and because not all cases are always referred to by their full name but by an abbreviated form. The abbreviated case name is also included in the alphabetical list of cases.

The book is designed to be used during the course and as a refresher at the time of revision, when it will no doubt prove most useful, when you simply do not have the time to do all the extensive reading that should have been done months before. However, it is not written with a view to providing cram notes only, so do use it alongside your other study materials during the course of the year.

Although there are some example questions and answers included in chapters 3 to 11, these are not intended to be learned by heart. Before the questions indicate how particular points are answered in context, there is a reasonable amount of general discussion in each of the chapters. In some instances the answers provide only a framework and not complete answers, although for others a complete answer will be given. The idea is to show you what is required for certain questions and how to structure your responses, and not simply to answer them for you. By doing the latter you might not understand what was required and be tempted to learn the answer provided and repeat it in an examination, whatever the actual question asked, thus failing to answer the question set. Indeed, in order to provide full answers I would have to repeat much of the information given in the earlier parts of the chapters. It seems better instead to refer you to this information for you to adapt to the particular answer. Some examples of this will be given but you need to develop this skill for the examination. In fact, supplying complete answers to each question may further be counter-productive in that you may be dismayed by the amount of material and the fact that you would never be able to provide that in an examination. However, I have included one or two examples of full answers to demonstrate what is meant and which will prove more useful for those answering term or course work essays. These complete answers are possible because I am aware of what is required from the question. In an exam such answers would probably attract marks of 75 per cent or more — so don't be put off!

COMMON ABBREVIATIONS

AG	Advocate General
CAP	Common Agricultural Policy
CFI	Court of First Instance
CFSP	Common foreign and security policy
CJHA	Cooperation in the fields of justice and home affairs
CMLR	Common Market Law Reports
COREPER	Committee of Permanent Representatives
Court of First Instance	The Court of First Instance of the European Communities
Court of Justice	The European Court of Justice
EC	European Community/ies
ECA	European Communities Act 1972
ECB	European Central Bank
ECHR	European Convention on Human Rights
ECJ	European Court of Justice
ECR	European Court Reports
ECSC	European Coal and Steel Community
EEA	European Economic Area
EEC	European Economic Community
EFTA	European Free Trade Association
EIB	European Investment Bank
EMU	Economic and Monetary Union
EP	European Parliament
ERTA	European Road Transport Agreement
ESCB	European System of Central Banks
EU	European Union
EURATOM	European Atomic Energy Community
GATT	General Agreement on Tariffs and Trade
IGC	Intergovernmental conference
MEP	Member of the European Parliament
OEEC	Organisation for European Economic Cooperation
PLC	Public Limited Company
QMV	Qualified majority voting
SDA	Sex Discrimination Act
SEA	Single European Act
TEU	Treaty on European Union

1 GENERAL STUDY AND EXAMINATION TECHNIQUES

INTRODUCTION

Some of the advice in this chapter is repeated in chapter 2 and elsewhere in the volume. This may be irritating if you read this book from cover to cover, but I do not think this is the approach you will adopt. You are more likely to dip into the book as and when you need, therefore it is necessary to assume that you might not have read this chapter before looking at the other chapters. As a consequence, basic information will be repeated wherever the context demands it.

During the course of your studies and as you approach exam time, you will no doubt be receiving advice from many sources, not all of which will be the same. Given that, who is to say that my advice is any better than other people's advice? As with other people's advice it is based largely on experience: mine is based on my experience taking examinations at degree, post-graduate and a number of other levels, and from 17 years of experience of the problems, difficulties and successes of students. This doesn't mean to say this will coincide with the experience of others, or that what may work for one person will necessarily work for another. I am loath, therefore, to give full and detailed advice of 'the best way' to learn and pass exams and so I will provide just some pointers on the way.

THE PURPOSE OF COURSES

The main aim of a course of study is the teaching of the source and the rules of a particular subject area, the development of these rules, how they are applied in cases and how you should apply those rules. In respect of Community law there are more specific aims considered in chapter 2.

Your principal aim will be to pass the assessment, which for the majority of students studying Community law — whether for a degree, a professional qualification or on any other type of course — is usually in the form of a three-hour (but sometimes more or less), unseen examination at the end of the course, although modularisation may bring an increase in other forms of assessment, notably dissertations or similar extended pieces of work. The object of your study, nevertheless, should be the compilation of a comprehensive set of notes from which you are able to revise in preparation for the examination, or as the basis or starting point for other assessment.

There are, of course, other objectives for you, such as learning the information itself and for use in your chosen career; however, you can succeed in acquiring that knowledge and still fail the course.

Whilst the three-hour examination clearly has faults as a system of assessment, unless there is a radical change in thinking of the core subjects, it is likely to remain the most prominent form of assessment. There is a kinder form of assessment for those who do not cope well with the exam format but who have nevertheless worked hard and have understood the information. This involves assessing a student's work during the year, usually through extended pieces of written work, such as 5,000-word essays. Unfortunately, the increased financial constraints on education mean that this alternative may have to give way to the economically cheaper and administratively easier form of assessment, which is the closed book examination paper. In most cases, therefore, the material to be learned must be reduced to fit this format.

For most of you Community law will be taken as a second- or third-year subject and the exam result will count towards the class of honours of your degree. No doubt you want to get the best result in this and all other subjects to achieve the best result overall. Even if, in a few, rare cases, it is a first-year subject and does not count towards the final result, you will nevertheless wish to increase your chances of a comfortable pass. While the courses you are taking provide the necessary legal material, very few assist you in the technique of applying that material effectively when it is most needed, in the examination. Chapters 1 and 2 and the sample questions and answers are intended to help you in this.

COURSE STUDY

Lectures

One definition of a lecture is the process or art of transferring the notes of one person to the notes of many others, without their passing through the minds of either. This should obviously be avoided from both points of view. The objective from the lecturer's standpoint should be the conveying of basic knowledge and understanding of particular areas of law in a digestible form. Lectures should provide guidance to introduce and reinforce the understanding of a topic by a selective approach to the legal material.

Most lecturers provide lecture handouts containing a summary or list of the essential points of a lecture, case references, and often the text of legislative provisions. These handouts vary in scope, but clearly the more comprehensive they are the less you will have to write. This doesn't mean to say that you can switch off, you should concentrate on the lecture instead.

Attending Lectures

Lecture preparation   Lectures can save you an awful lot of effort, all the more so if they are not your first contact with the subject. Advance reading for lectures will make the subject matter more intelligible and permit you to listen to the context and arguments put forward, rather than being the first time you encounter the information.

Making notes   It would be usual for a lecturer to begin by introducing the material to be covered and the main points or themes that will be developed during the course of the lecture. If not contained in the handout, this will enable you to make a note of the headings under which you can make your notes and references to cases and legislative provisions.

It should be clear that a good set of notes is essential for revision later in the year, but notes taken in lectures should not be a copy of every word spoken. They are not supposed to provide the sole source of revision work, they should form the foundation for further reading, which may also be necessary for tutorial work.

You should try to listen to what is being said and to record brief notes to summarise in as few words as possible the key points of the lecture rather than a complete transcript of the lecture. The idea is to cover the topic with a minimum of notes. Concentrate, therefore, on the structure of the lecture as a guide to the law and development of law in a particular subject. This is better than making a longer set of notes but without ever fully concentrating on the words spoken. Too many students try to write down every single word and end up with reams of indiscriminate notes while, at the end of the lecture, having little idea of what was said. I have tried to explain this in lectures, but even as I am saying 'You have no need to write every word', pens are furiously writing out 'You have no need to write every word'! I say 'No, stop writing a moment, please, and listen!', and the words appear on the pages: 'No, stop writing a moment, please, and listen'! Well, perhaps not quite as bad as that, but somewhere near.

Summaries in your own words are important because they provide good practice at being able to formulate the material for yourself, as is necessary to answer questions competently. In order to reformulate material you have to understand it; in doing so you will be learning it.

While lecturers' styles vary, you will learn when a particular lecturer expects items to be noted by a direct statement, or a change in pace and emphasis of delivery or if actual quotes from provisions or cases are read out.

Much of what has been said in lectures will usually be reinforced in tutorials. It may therefore be useful to leave space in your notes for later amendments and additions to be made without having to rewrite the notes, perhaps using only one side of the paper, although I admit this may be environmentally objectionable but we are not quite at the stage whereby we can type lectures directly into the laptops we take into the lecture theatre. I guess it will happen at some stage, though!

Use of legislation collections in lectures You may find it helpful to take a legislation collection into the lectures with you. This will enable you to refer directly to the provisions being discussed. It should not be necessary to try to record provisions referred to verbatim, but just accurately to cite the provision. This in turn allows you to listen and understand the explanation or interpretation, rather than worrying about trying to write down every single word of the provision. Leave an appropriate space in your notes for insertion of the precise wording later.

Cases in lectures You may come across various approaches to cases by lecturers, from providing a detailed and technical treatment of cases as case studies of particular legal points or developments to general overviews. Or lectures may be a commentary upon developments in the law in general terms, with no specific mention of the details of particular decisions. Some lecturers will expect prior reading of the textbooks or cases to be undertaken, and some require back up reading after the lecture. Both may be unrealistic expectations of what the majority of students will do in reality, but I can only advise that if an overview technique is employed you may not understand or get as much out of the lectures if you do not back it up with your own reading of the cases.

Work after lectures Try to re-read your notes soon after the lecture and when the lectures on a particular topic are finished, because you might need to tidy up your notes. Not every point made in the lecture may be understood fully at the time, therefore you should highlight any such points in your notes so that you can fill any gaps and clarify any difficulties while they are still fresh in your mind, either by questions to your lecturer or tutor, or by your own research. To leave them might result in your not even remembering that there was a problem.

The optimum time to read the textbooks and articles which have been referred to, is probably when the lectures on a particular topic are finished. You will need a coherent set of notes to prepare for tutorials, if these are intended to cover the topic. If not, then the textbooks should be consulted to consolidate your notes and understanding for revision purposes.

INDIVIDUAL STUDY

Textbooks

Textbooks are intended to provide all the basic information necessary to understand the law on a particular topic, and should include a consideration of issues which are difficult or controversial. They should be read to clarify any ambiguities and difficulties you have, to expand on points referred to in lectures and to prepare for tutorials. Notes need only be taken either to fill in any gaps in your own previous notes or your understanding, or to assist you in answering the questions and problems set for tutorial discussion.

You will find no lack of cases in most textbooks — far more than are absolutely essential for either an understanding or a demonstration of a particular topic. This is because textbook writers tend to include every possible case or reference, even where the case does not take the principle of law any further but is merely a further or later example of its application, in order to give complete coverage of the topic.

Reading Cases

Normally it will not be enough for you to read only the headnote of a case, because it is too brief and may give the wrong impression. Therefore, unless your tutor says that reading the headnote is enough, you should read the whole case.

In order to assist an understanding of cases, particularly long and complex ones, case notes or annotations can be consulted. If not referred to in lecture or tutorial handouts, these can be looked for in the leading legal periodicals on the particular subject or in general indexes to legal periodicals. Case notes are short notes, between two and 10 pages long, giving concise details of the facts, legal issues and decision, and provide a clear insight into the case. They may also point out the implications that the decision may have for the future. It may be helpful, indicating the principal aspects of the case, to read the case note before you tackle the decision in the law report.

Articles in Legal Journals

There is little point in making detailed notes on an article to begin with. Read the article to understand what the writer is saying and whether it is useful to your understanding of the topic or for preparation for tutorials. It may be necessary to read it a second time, however, and to make notes of the principal points raised.

Use of Highlighting Pens

Do not use these too much! I have seen some articles and cases which look as if the highlighting pen was the size of a wallpaper brush — either that, or the student has a paint dip in which the whole of the article has been immersed! The end result is that the article glows as if it were toilet paper washed up near Sellafield or from Chernobyl. I have even seen some examples where, following the paint job, further highlighting using different colours or underlining has then been employed to emphasise the really important sentences. Be discriminatory, because otherwise there is little point in going to the expense of purchasing highlighting pens. If you only photocopy rather than making your own notes — and I have seen many examples of this — then making your own marginal notes is far more constructive.

Photocopying Material

Speaking of photocopies, consider carefully both the amount of time and money you spend on this. The time would be better spent in the library, reading, understanding and making your own notes from the recommended material. You may find you don't need to photocopy particular articles as they are of only incidental relevance for the tutorial, so do yourself a favour and read the material first. You may find that by reading it and making notes you may no longer need to photocopy it. This has a number of advantages — it could save a lot of time, it provides necessary practice in reading and concentrating on finding the material information from academic articles, and the money saved from not photocopying various materials could buy you a decent textbook on the subject.

Photocopying is not a substitute for learning. Bringing photocopies of all the recommended reading into a tutorial is not preparation. Even if you have gone through it and highlighted relevant parts, it does not order the material in your mind, sufficient to address the tutorial questions and discussion or for revision purposes.

SEMINARS AND TUTORIALS

The terms 'tutorials' and 'seminars' are used here synonymously to mean small group teaching of between six to 12 students, and unfortunately these days often more.

Purpose

Seminars and tutorials are extremely important in a degree course and should be used constructively. This requires diligent preparation beforehand. They provide opportunities for you to contribute during class, and you may be called on to enter into a discussion or to suggest an answer.

Tutorials enable you to consolidate your understanding of a relatively small part of the syllabus. They should provide all those involved with the chance to discuss points of difficulty and an opportunity to test their understanding of the subject under consideration.

Resource pressures will continue to hit most institutions of higher education, and tutorials will inevitably become larger and less frequent. You should therefore make the most of the opportunity provided by tutorials; the alternative is that you will have to work more without guidance.

Unfortunately, many students, if allowed, are prepared either to let the discussion be conducted by the tutor and one or two others, or for it to turn into a different sort of lecture. It is unfair to go to a tutorial meeting not properly prepared and, in effect, work off the backs of others and, even if you can make lots of notes from other students' contributions, if you haven't prepared, you will probably not understand them.

Tutorial Preparation and Tutorial Work

Tutorials can probably be divided into two broad categories: those which seek to expand on the material covered in lectures and act to test the understanding of that information, and those which raise new topics not previously covered in the lecture series.

Tutorial preparation varies considerably between students. There are those who try to rely entirely on lecture notes and/or masses of photocopied material, and who hope to find the answers by leafing through them while in class. Others do masses of reading but fail to spend any time answering the questions. If asked a question by the tutor they have to resort to turning over page after page of copious notes to find the case, article or point in question, or anything! Then, there are those who attempt to answer questions on insufficient information or work, and those who do neither but hope to get by.

Certainly read through your lecture notes before preparing the tutorial on the topic. If you have previously re-read and supplemented them, you will benefit when it comes to preparing tutorial questions because you will have already acquired a knowledge relevant to most tutorial questions, as they often arise directly from the teaching programme. You should, therefore, have more time for thinking about the tutorial problems instead of having to treat them as a completely new and isolated piece of work for which you have to prepare the questions set from scratch.

Issues or questions on a tutorial sheet often reflect the approach adopted in the examinations on a particular topic, and it is common practice for past examination questions to be used as a basis for tutorial questions. Your aim should be to cover enough material in order to understand and discuss the issue raised, but to avoid becoming tied down by points of unnecessary detail or general background information.

Most of you will have read a substantial amount of material in preparation. However, the major shortcoming in preparation is the failure to apply the information acquired to the issues set for discussion, or to know how to tackle the problem under discussion.

Where the tutorial explores more fully points discussed in lectures, your tutor is likely to be looking for an understanding of the law and a willingness to discuss some of the more difficult aspects of the law. If you work from the lecture sheets and the provisions of law and cases which have been indicated previously on the lecture sheets, all the essential information for the basis of the tutorial work has been provided. Where the tutor covers a topic not dealt with in the lectures, you will need to prepare a basic set of notes from a textbook, preferably an introductory text. This will allow you to identify the leading cases and difficulties which form part of the topic and will give you a base from which to prepare the tutorial. The tutorial sheet should direct you to the important aspects of the area and further reading.

Lastly, a few hours' work at the end of a topic will allow you to tidy up your notes while the materials are fresh in your mind. This will save you a lot more work later on, especially during the crucial revision period which is being reduced along with the academic year.

COURSE WORK

Most courses include written work consisting of two to four pieces per year, some of which may count towards an overall assessment, but most course work is not included as a part of the final result. This essay writing should be used as an opportunity to prepare for the examination, as essays call for closer study of particular issues. Course work, whether assessed or not, is worth doing well. Effort put into essays and a review of the comments on them are a useful aid for revision, particularly where the topic of the essay reappears in some form in the examination.

The comments made in respect of the sample questions and answers apply equally to course work. Course work will clearly give you more scope to spell out your views unless a deliberate policy of imposing strict word limits has been applied to get you to produce concise answers more suitable as revision for exams.

As an alternative to course work, class tests may be set which may comprise a series of questions or be the equivalent of a mini exam in which one answer must be written from two to four questions set within the time of a lecture or tutorial slot. If this is the case in your course, then the advice here about examinations will also be useful for preparation and the approach of this book be more appropriate.

REVISION FOR EXAMINATIONS

Revision Preparation

There is a distinct limit to the amount of material which can be written in an examination. This may favour the student who has done the minimum and is capable of writing only a limited but sufficient amount. Other students work hard throughout the year but underachieve in the examinations. If you have studied consistently during the year your task will be a lot easier than that of those with incomplete notes because they have not attended classes regularly, or than that of those with a mass of unedited material.

Whichever category applies to you, the most important requirement for revision is a coherent set of notes from which to work. You must read through all your lecture and seminar notes to ensure that you have a complete set. If you have not, the first task will be to produce a set of concise notes prior to the revision period. You may find it necessary to rewrite parts of your notes in order to reduce them to a manageable size for revision purposes. Revision rewriting can be useful, and even if you are short of time you ought to compile your own set of notes to revise from. It is not time wasted — as one of the best ways of remembering anything is to write it down.

This section concentrates on two issues: what to revise and how to revise. Having decided what to revise, you can concentrate on how to revise most effectively. There is first some preparation that must be undertaken before either of these can be achieved, and which will also help you decide what to revise.

What to Revise

Exam content   An internally set and marked examination, which is the case in nearly all degree examinations, would generally reflect fairly accurately what has been taught during the year. Examinations are usually set within the confines of a published syllabus issued at the beginning of the course. Hence the basic exam content will inevitably arise from the syllabus content, but the exam need not cover all of the syllabus. While there is no guaranteed way of knowing when a topic will appear in an examination, there are a number of indicators which can help you decide what might appear and what you choose to revise.

First of all, list the topics in your course. Assuming that you have worked steadily during the year, you should have a series of separate and identifiable topics within the subject area and can probably identify about 10 topics which might justify an examination question. There may be some topics which are so important that there will always be a question on them, so you should consult past papers for evidence of how often the syllabus topics have appeared previously.

Other indicators are: the number of lectures spent on topics during the teaching of your course; the topics covered in the tutorials and essays during the course of the year; whether certain matters were topical in the particular year, e.g., in Community law the changes which have been introduced by Maastricht or the Treaty of Amsterdam; and finally, but only possibly, the research interests or recent publications of the lecturers involved.

One point which may go some way towards consoling you is that examiners do not normally try to catch you out and are unlikely to examine on something that has not been covered during the year. They would usually try to ensure that all the issues on the paper have been covered on the course.

Revision content   If you opt to revise selectively there is the crucial choice of revision subjects to decide. Having compiled a list of the probables, you need to decide how many and which ones you are going to revise. Revision of between 50 to 80 per cent of a syllabus would cover most students' plans; some will revise 100 per cent. I did about 75 per cent, but I have known some to go below 50 per cent. This really is a gamble, and also depends on the way the exam paper is set, i.e., whether you are forced to answer particular questions from separate sections. In such a case you are advised to revise a higher percentage of the syllabus.

Most degree examinations will involve a straight choice of three to five questions from between 9 to 15 set. Decide which topics you know well and are confident in, and those areas in which you are weak. If there are not enough of the former, then more work is required on one or more topics falling into the latter group.

Although law subjects are usually split into a number of topics, this is done to ease the presentation of the material into manageable bites. In reality there is a lot of overlap which may be repeated in the examination, so be prepared for the mixed question in making your decision as to how many topics to cover. Past papers will be the best evidence of this unless the course lecturer and examiner has changed for this year or advises a change.

How to Revise

Revision should not be too passive, and there are two things to avoid:

(a)   mechanically underlining or highlighting passages which, although making the words prominent on a page, will be of little help if most of a page is emphasised;

(b)   the photocopying of masses of material and trying to read it for revision instead of your own edited or distilled notes.

Revision can be carried out either by subject or by topic. The preference is yours but also depends on the amount of time between examinations. If all are close together, variation may help: if spread out, revision by subject may be better to ensure even coverage of your subjects.

Methods to assist you include reciting the material out loud, and if it helps pacing the room at the same time because material continually recited tends to stick in the mind; it encourages activity and aids concentration, or at least stops you falling asleep. You might also get fit at the same time. However, don't let it be too mechanical or you won't really be learning anything.

Another active alternative is to rewrite the notes continually. As they became more and more familiar, rewriting becomes unnecessary; it becomes possible to slim down the notes to major headings, or key words and case law or just the titles will prompt your memory.

Practice for the examination   Some time ought to be spent during revision in the analysis of past questions and drafting possible answers. Practice at question answering is extremely important. The questions can be selected from a range of questions on topics in tutorial sheets, essay titles and past examination papers.

There is no need to write all the answers in full, but you may wish to practise writing complete answers to some of the questions within the amount of time permitted. In general, it is sufficient to draw up a plan of what you would include if the questions were set in an examination. Do this without reference to notes, but check later to see that you covered most, if not all, of the points. However, don't be too discouraged if there are questions in past examination papers which cause you difficulty or which you are unable to answer comprehensively.

A planned introduction to each of the topics which you have learned could prove useful, but do not attempt to prepare model answers to be written regardless of the actual question or form of it. Prepare topics within a flexible framework so that you can cope with different sorts of questions on the same topic. Even though the actual questions on a particular topic could vary enormously, often a concise introduction could form a common opening to a range of questions on a particular topic. The advantages are that it saves time and prepares you and the examiner for what follows. Additionally, definitions can be prepared, such as those for direct effects and direct applicability.

While the accurate citation and acknowledgement of authors is not necessary or expected in examinations, it is nevertheless always welcome and helps to demonstrate your mastery of the material.

Length of revision period Most students use part, if not most, of the Easter vacation and the summer term/second semester up to the exams. Depending on the particular form of modularisation and/or semesterisation which has been adopted at your institution, the teaching period may vary, exams may take place at other times during the course of the academic year, or the period set aside for revision may differ. However, I would advise you not to skip the last tutorials or lectures. You might learn something to your advantage, even if you have already decided not to revise the subject matter of the last topic.

To help plan your revision time, a revision timetable can prove very useful — but preferably not the 'Rimmer' variation for devotees of 'Red Dwarf', which ends up taking a lot of time in constructing and redrafting it, leaving little for the revision itself.

The timetable should cover the whole of the revision period and the time you have between the examinations. This enables you to divide your time between various subjects and concentrate more on weaker areas, if necessary. Carefully prepared, it ensures you will have done the optimum amount necessary for the exams.

When you revise, i.e., early in the morning or late at night, is according to your personal clock, and I can give little advice here. Whether you are an early starter or a late reviser, try not to overdo it and get plenty of exercise between periods of revision. The examination period is physically as well as mentally demanding and you need to be fit to get through it without too much detriment to your health. That can follow later, when the exams are over and you celebrate your success!

EXAMINATIONS AND ASSESSMENTS

The frequency of examinations and number per subject will vary now more than ever between institutions as various forms of modularisation and semesterisation are introduced. This will not, however, remove the need for you to give an examination your best shot first time round. Whilst some courses may go over to other forms of assessment, exams are still likely to be a very much used form of assessment and the better mark in each exam, the better your overall degree classification will be. As EC law is one of the core subjects it is more likely that the unseen examination will continue to be the most usual form of assessment in this subject. Hence then the need to be prepared both in subject knowledge and exam technique.

Most examiners, unless they are particularly nasty specimens, want you to pass the examination. They will give you marks for making a particular point but are not likely to take marks away because you haven't made it. Your course director or lecturer will usually be the person who sets your examination paper, and he or she will be much more interested in finding out whether you have understood the principles of law, can apply them to a given factual situation and make some critical analysis, if required.

The Examination

At the start, allow time to read over the paper as a whole, to select the questions you intend to attempt and to understand what the questions are actually requiring in an answer. However, some papers are quite lengthy and a thorough reading of the questions could take 10 to 15 minutes. A compromise is to find a question that you are confident about and can get on with, but don't spend too long on it. Finish it, if you can, before the allotted time. When you have finished the first question you will be in a better frame of mind to read the rest of the paper and choose the remaining questions.

General examination technique You should be able to establish the rubric in advance of the examination; if not, ask before you enter the exam hall. In that way, the particular requirements of the exam will not be a shock. Alternatively, and in any case, if you can see the rubric on the examination paper while waiting to start, read it before the start.

The rubric informs you about the length of time allowed for the examination, the structure of the examination, how many questions to answer, whether there are compulsory questions and, in the case of a sectioned examination paper, how many questions should be answered from each section. Unless the contrary is stated, you may assume that all the questions on a paper carry equal marks.

The Most Important Rule in Respect of the Exam

You must attempt all the questions required of you! To help you do this you must work out the amount of time you can spend on each answer and stick to it.

Omitting to follow this golden rule of examination technique leads to more failures or drastically lower marks than anything else. It is particularly frustrating and annoying to see it happen, because it is avoidable! You are throwing away valuable marks that could make a crucial difference in the standard of your pass, or the difference between a pass and a fail and may ultimately lead to a lower degree classification. Unless your other answers are exceptional, you are far more likely to pick up more marks by starting a new question than by spending additional time on the others.

If you find that you are reaching your time limit for an answer, leave plenty of space and move on to the next question. You can always come back later to finish the question if you have sufficient time. As a last resort, when time has virtually run out, you can include brief notes of what you would have written had time permitted, or refer to your plan as the continuation of the answer or the answer itself. This is, however, a poor second to the proper planning of your time!

The second most important rule   Make sure you answer the question set and not one that you would have liked the examiner to set. Questions in examinations and other pieces of work rarely, if ever, take the form 'Write all you know about', but this is often the form of answer produced. Thus regurgitation of all you know on a topic should be avoided. Instead you must adapt the material you have revised to suit the demands and requirements of the question being asked. Practice questions at revision time will help prepare you to do this.

Read every question at least twice before starting to answer it, and make sure you have not misread a vital word or the instruction, or even missed out a complete line in your eagerness or anxiety to get on with the answer.

Types of Questions

Certain requirements are considered by the examiner when constructing questions. Essay questions are intended to get you to discuss the points of law arising, especially the controversial points and new developments, and to give overviews of the whole topic. Problem questions try to get you to apply provisions and principles of law to factual circumstances. The better answer will also be expected to highlight legal developments and discuss particular difficulties or ambiguities in the application of the law.

Essay questions often involve the citation of an extract from a judgment, an academic article, an official report or, less frequently, a legislative provision. Sometimes a statement is not attributed to any of these sources, which usually means that the examiner has devised this statement. While essay questions often appear to be easier than problem questions, you should read them carefully to avoid mistakes which may be apparent only when your answer has been completed.

'Explain', 'comment', 'evaluate' and 'discuss' are all similar terms which require more than a descriptive answer. They require you to give reasons, to put the comment or quote into context and to show the influence on the development of the law, or require you to show the strengths and weaknesses of alternative points of view.

Planning Answers

Although you will be anxious simply to get on and start writing, take time to plan an answer. Plans are not only helpful in terms of the content of your answers, but may also assist enormously in achieving a sensible structure and balance. They will allow you to relax a little and will ensure that your answer, when it is written, will be far more comprehensible to the person marking your script, i.e, the examiner.

A plan should enable you to answer coherently and according to a considered structure, to ensure that all the main points are covered and to avoid excessive time spent on one point or in repetition.

Essays The plan should begin by breaking down the question into its different requirements, unless the statement is short and straightforward. Next, try to define any words or phrases which need further explanation. The part of your plan which identifies the legal issues involved in the question may be useful as the basis for the introduction to your answer.

Essay-type questions, by their nature, can require coverage of a much wider range of material than problem questions. The answers can also be much broader and it is often difficult to determine clearly the line between what is relevant to an answer and what is not. The only rule of thumb that can be given here is to advise you to pose the question, when considering whether to include additional information, 'Does it assist in answering the question?' If the answer is 'not really', then don't bother!

Legal problems As you re-read the question, the factual issues, legislation and relevant case law which spring to mind should be noted briefly. The plan is often formed as you jot down the facts which give rise to the legal issues to be resolved.

After identifying the area of law, the material facts and specific provisions which appear relevant to the problem, apply the provisions of law to the facts. It may be that you can draft at least a provisional answer at this stage. It is likely, however, that you will then be required to cite relevant cases to assist you in coming to a conclusion on the matter, or to confirm your conclusion and to demonstrate how the courts have previously resolved the matter. Apply the principles adopted in those cases to the facts or statements in the question. If there is inconsistency between cases you should distinguish these cases from each other, commenting on whether or not the distinction could affect the application of law in the problem at hand. For years now, I have suggested a simple perhaps even simplistic mnemonic/acronym to help remember this technique: FLAC. Facts, Law (either provisions of legislation or principles of law), Application of the law to facts and the Conclusions or Consequences. Write it down at the top of the answer sheet and it will help you get at least a basic order for your answer. In citing cases, don't be concerned if you can't remember their full names or any part of their names, but indicate by a brief description the case you mean. In most cases this will be acceptable, as it is the principle of law which is important and not the names of cases. The names are merely convenient labels by which we identify cases, thus other forms of identification must be acceptable.

Difficulties may well be caused in problems involving two or more potential parties. Make notes for each, which, if they prove to coincide, will allow you to answer for two parties at the same time.

This plan should be used as the basis for your answer. No doubt as you write your answer further relevant material will be remembered which can be incorporated. Always start your answer on a clean page and leave plenty of space, even a clear page, between your answers. Whilst this may not be the most environmentally friendly advice, it is examiner and examinee friendly. This allows you to add any comments you remember later, rather than having to search for a space to leave a message for the examiner that the rest of your answer is at the back of the answer book, or trying to cram notes into the margin (these are often close to impossible to read). Completing a last answer in note form should be adopted only as a last resort.

The Use of Statutory Materials in the Examination Room

Some institutions allow statutory materials to be referred to during the examination. One real advantage is that there is no need to concentrate too heavily on memorising statutory provisions while revising. It leaves you more time to consider the application and interpretation of the law, rather than having to waste time on the regurgitation of particular provisions. It also makes it pointless to reproduce the whole of a legislative provision in an answer if the examiner knows that you have it in front of you during the examination. Indeed, there is no need for such reproduction, even if statutory materials are not allowed to be used in the examination.

However, to ignore the legislative provisions completely prior to the examination means you will be unfamiliar with them and will probably waste time finding the relevant provisions, e.g., some candidates, when provided with materials, seem to spend an inordinate amount of time browsing or flicking through them during the examination. If you can, try to treat these materials as a last resort or as a mental crutch which you can fall back on should your memory fail you. There is no compulsion to look at them at all, but you may still need to cite specific parts when using a particular provision to support your answer.

Open-book examinations, where you are able to take in other materials as well, are less common and vary considerably as to the materials that the candidate is allowed to use during the examination and as to the time allowed to complete the examination. You still have to revise and prepare thoroughly for the examination and should not rely on finding the information while in the exam hall. These exams are a hybrid of the closed-book examination and assessment, but still require a structured answer at the end of the day. If they take the form of exam papers which can be taken away and the answers handed in at some specific later date, they can be regarded as assessed work, considered next.

Assessed Course Work

Many courses allow for some form of assessed work, whereby a set number of pieces of work completed throughout the year will be credited towards a final mark or completely replace the examination. The approach to assessed work builds on much of what has previously been said, with the addition of a few special points. For example, the question must be read correctly, the essay still needs to be planned, and submission dates and length limits must be observed (as must time limits in exams).

Many assessment questions are in fact taken from old examination papers, but you are, of course, now concentrating on specific aspects of the law and will be expected to deal with them in depth. The preparation thus requires a wide range of reading of texts and articles from which you need to make careful notes.

A particular consideration is the need to be accurate with your citation of work you have consulted and from which you have reproduced paragraphs. Make notes and citations of all items read. Detail the name of the book or article, the author, publisher, date of publication and place of publication and, most importantly, the page number(s). These are required if you use any of the material directly, or if you find you need to go back to the original for more information or clarification. It is good practice, even if not required, to provide a bibliography of the materials that you have used in answering the question, but don't refer vaguely to lecture notes.

You may be required to submit more than one copy of your work, and, increasingly, this must be typed or printed. Most institutions should, however, issue their own notes of guidance for the specific form required. If not, you must ascertain this information from the person setting the assessed work.

2 INTRODUCTION TO, AND THE STUDY OF, COMMUNITY LAW

GENERAL INTRODUCTION TO COMMUNITY LAW

The Community Legal Order

The various aspects of the Community legal order will be considered in detail later, only a brief overview being given here.

The Community has its own legislative bodies — the Council and the European Parliament (EP) which are able to promulgate legislation, although the Council enjoys the lion's share. This legislation is independent of the Member States and has priority over the laws of the Member States. The Community has its own executive — the Commission — and judicial powers are exercised by the European Court of Justice (ECJ or the Court of Justice) and by the Court of First Instance (CFI). The laws produced provide not only the Member States but also Community citizens and legal persons with rights and duties.

A brief mention will also be made here in respect of the terms 'European Union' (EU) and 'European Community' (EC) as their use can be confusing. They will also be considered in chapter 3. 'European Union' was brought in by the Treaty on European Union (TEU) (the Maastricht Treaty) and describes the extension by the Member States into additional policies and areas of cooperation. The EU consists of three pillars comprising the existing Communities (the three original treaties), a common foreign and security policy and cooperation in the fields of justice and home affairs, although some changes to these pillars have been made by the Treaty of Amsterdam, which will be considered later, the pillars remain essentially intact.

'European Community' is the new term for the European Economic Community (EEC), but now is generally accepted as referring to the three original treaties as well. As the Court of Justice has very little jurisdiction over the two new pillars, European Community law courses are not likely to consider the second and third pillars in any depth. Most courses will continue to study EC law, as contained in the EC Treaty only and not consider the parts of the EU outside of the EC Treaty. The term 'Treaty on European Union' (TEU) is synonymous with the Maastricht Treaty. Both terms are widely used and are interchangeable. It is important to be aware of this.

The Community has competence for the Member States in some external affairs, such as concluding agreements with third countries.

Community Law

The study of Community law is not just the study of another subject area which follows the same or similar patterns as other legal subjects. The institutional and procedural laws of the Community, as well as the substantive laws, are quite different from those of the common-law systems in England and Wales or Ireland, so they must be regarded as a completely new topic for study. The EC Treaty, as amended, is the principal basis of all of these elements of Community law. It is not a static Treaty or body of law, but is amended from time to time as the Member States agree, as can be seen from the Single European Act (SEA), the Maastricht Treaty (TEU) and most recently by the Treaty of Amsterdam.

At the time of the founding of the Communities and the drafting of the treaties, legal models were sought on which to base the general form of the legal system for the Communities. There were no Member States from common-law jurisdictions, and it was therefore to be expected that the Community legal system would broadly resemble a civil law system and take many examples from the French and German legal systems, e.g., much of the procedure of the courts is based on French administrative law, as are actions for damages under the second paragraph of Art 288 (old 215).

The establishment of a framework treaty, which provides broad principles or aims, also reflects the way in which civil law countries approach legislative enactment with codified law. They commence with general abstract principles, as in the Preamble and Arts 2 and 3 of the EC Treaty. The Treaty even includes a form of good faith clause in respect of Art 10 (old 5), something with which lawyers from civil law countries are quite familiar.

The rest of the EC Treaty, although putting the broad aims into greater detail, is still an outline for the areas of law the Member States agreed should be included. It provides, for example, the basic legal regime for free movement of goods and workers, competition law and agriculture. Some sections are more detailed than others. Free movement of goods has required little secondary legislation, whereas competition law and agriculture have been subject to considerable legislative addition. Thus, for the most part, the Treaty requires completion by detailed regulations and directives. These areas can be and have been added to, e.g., environmental and consumer protection by the SEA and new policy areas introduced by Maastricht, notably economic and monetary union and health and safety and industry policies.

Incidentally, all Treaty Article references in this volume are to the EC Treaty, and where appropriate to the predecessor EEC treaty, unless where otherwise stated.

Finally, gaps and ambiguities in the legislation and in the interpretation of it are filled by the Court of Justice, and thus a body of case law arises.

Community law can be divided broadly into three main components: institutional law, procedural law and substantive law.

Institutional law   This is in effect, and is sometimes called, the constitutional law of the Community.

Institutional law concerns the structure or constitution of the Communities, the regulation of the main institutions and other bodies of the Community, the sources of Community law and the special concepts of Community law, including supremacy and direct effects. Institutional law also concerns the relationship of the institutions as between themselves and the relationship of the Community with the Member States and its external relations with other countries and international organisations. The institutions are involved in the legislative and budgetary processes, and as this relationship alters in time, disputes which seek to define the boundaries of the powers and duties of the institutions and their relationship to each other, give rise to increasing amounts of case law.

In this area, the role of the Court of Justice has been fundamental to the development of the Community. The Court has been called upon many times to adjudicate inter-institutional disputes and those between institutions and Member States. It is becoming increasingly involved as the institutions seek to protect their powers or legally extend them, e.g., the Court of Justice has cautiously assisted the EP in pressing for and gaining increased democratic power in the Community.

The Court of Justice has been instrumental in the development of the legal system because of its judicial activism. Its pronouncements on the status and effects of the provisions of Community law have resulted in the establishment and development of the most fundamental and leading principles of Community law, including direct effects, supremacy and general principles.

This is an expanding area of Community law, as exemplified by the changes wrought by the SEA and the TEU to the EC Treaty which expand the areas of competence of the Community and alter the power relationship in the Community by, for example, providing the EP with greater legislative power.

Procedural law   This is sometimes referred to as the administrative law of the Community, and is also called judicial review or judicial control in the Community. It is concerned with the various actions that can be taken by the institutions, Member States and natural and legal persons. These generally involve the enforcement of rights against the Community institutions, the Member States and individuals. Procedural law covers a range of remedies: direct actions at the level of the Community, and indirect actions involving the national courts as well, considered in chapters 5 and 6.

Procedural law is clearly concerned with the details of actions before the courts, all of which must be based on a specific provision within the Treaties and must therefore comply with the legal requirements of the provision. The Court of Justice is often its most restrictive in this area in terms of upholding the right or ability of individuals to challenge acts of the Community. The admissibility barriers that have to be overcome by individuals for actions under Arts 230, 232 and 241 (old 173, 175 and 184) are considerable. Actions referred to the Court of Justice from the national courts are for the most part much more favourably received.

Substantive law   Substantive law concerns the legal rules which carry out the broad policy areas of law agreed under the Community Treaties. It can be distinguished from the law relating to the institutions and the procedural law of the Community. Substantive law is largely secondary law and takes effect predominantly in the Member States and not at the Community level, despite its primary base in Treaty articles.

The substantive law of the Community is also described as economic law, or the law of the economy of the Community, and even European Community private law. However, this is not a particularly meaningful label as the concept of economic law varies from state to state and between political systems. Additionally, this simplistic tag may not explain the attitude of the Community, as expressed by the Court of Justice, to the substantive law of the Community, and suggests it is concerned only with the economic considerations of the Community and not with wider concerns which may be relevant. The Community is quite clearly, as demonstrated by the Preamble and opening Articles to the EC Treaty, particularly as amended by the Treaty of Amsterdam, concerned with far more than the setting up of a regulatory framework for limited aspects of the economies dealing only with free trade rules. Examples which reflect purely economic integration or cooperation would be agreements between the EFTA and GATT countries, who only want the economic trade rules. The eventual aims of the Community have been the subject of much discussion, especially in respect of the Maastricht Treaty. Although not expressed directly, the phrase 'An ever closer union' in the original EEC Treaty is accepted by many to indicate the long-term aim, or goal or desire for political union or federation. It has been repeated in the text of the Treaty agreed at Maastricht.

Economic integration is to be achieved by two main methods: negative and positive integration. *Positive integration* is the formulation of common policies, e.g., agriculture, transport and competition, and *negative integration* is the removal of barriers, most notably discrimination on the grounds of nationality, but especially in respect of the free movement of the factors of production.

There is a large and increasing number of areas of substantive law which now arise from the Community Treaties and subsequent intergovernmental agreements. These have been increased by the Maastricht Treaty. These chapters will deal with only four topics, however, all of which were part of the original policies of the Community and are covered in most courses on European Community law, the Bar examinations and in Law Society core subject requirements.

Those included are the free movement of goods, the free movement of workers and persons, competition law and sex discrimination law. The first three, at least, are centrally concerned with the achievement of the economic goals of the Community, but it is open to argument whether the concerns, and thus the law, in these areas have been promulgated only for economic ends, or whether there are other concerns and aims of the Communities to be taken into account. The general question to be asked is whether there was also an intent for these laws to achieve social aims, or whether it is just because these economic laws were seen to impact so strongly at the social level in the Member States that this view may now be taken.

The 'freedoms' are clearly part of the wider aims of the Community, as expressed in the Treaty Preamble, Arts 2 and 3, which seek to establish economic and social integration amongst the Member States, progression towards which is achieved by the forging of common policies and the establishment of the free movement of certain factors. By freeing the basic factors of production it is hoped that economic development or expansion will be promoted throughout the Community. The four fundamental factors are the freedom of movement of goods, persons, services and capital.

Competition and social policy, under which is sex discrimination, fall outside the four freedoms. Competition was, along with agriculture, a policy of the Community, whereas sex discrimination is included as a part of social law.

There is often an overlap of areas of substantive law which is both inevitable and necessary in the context of the internal market. The fundamental freedoms that must be observed by the Member States could never be effective without the ability to ensure that private firms are not able to erect their own barriers to trade by cartels. Hence, competition rules are essential to ensure the effectiveness of the laws on the free movement of goods and vice versa. Additionally the prohibition on discrimination, both in terms of nationality and sex, also imposes itself in the other areas of substantive law where appropriate, e.g., free movement of persons and free movement of goods.

The Court of Justice has for a long time referred to the support that must be given to the four freedoms of the Community, which it regards as fundamental elements or cornerstones of the Community, and will do its best to uphold them. It will interpret the Community rules of law generously, i.e., wherever possible it will try to uphold the Community rules in the face of national legislation. The exceptions or derogations which the Member States are allowed in some of the provisions are interpreted narrowly against the Member States. The aim is to give the greatest possible effect to Community rights and less scope to Member State derogations which, if allowed free rein, would undermine the aims of the Community.

THE METHODOLOGY OF COMMUNITY LAW

The Community legal system, like the civil law systems, is a deductive system, therefore the adopted approach to the application of the law is from the general to the particular. This means starting with general laws (the Treaty or code) and becoming increasingly particular, through secondary legislation and then case law, in order to reach a conclusion in a given case. Deductive law concerns the application of enacted law in all future situations, to be supplemented by case law only where necessary. The common-law approach, in contrast, is the gradual development and build up of rules of law from the particular situations or cases to establish a general rule. The cases give rise to a general principle of law, and this is known as inductive reasoning.

Applied to resolving legal disputes, the result in a particular case is also achieved by working from the general to the particular, i.e., from the broad framework Treaty rules, which may often include the Preamble and Arts 2, 3, 10 (old 5), and 12 (old 6), to the relevant provisions of the specific chapter or title of the Treaty, any secondary legislation on the topic and the relevant case law on the interpretation and application of the provisions. As will be considered in the following chapters, the interpretation techniques of the Court of Justice also follow the approach of considering the general aims to help decide particular cases. The Court of Justice will often make reference to the Preamble and general provisions of the Treaty to justify a particular decision. It applies law in the scope of the Treaty as a whole, in the light of the basic aims and objectives of the Treaty and the specific legislation. For example, in respect of Art 2, see *Mr and Mrs F v The Belgian State* concerning social security, *Europemballage and Continental Can v Commission* in respect of Art 3, and the *Von Colson* case which was very strongly argued on the basis of Art 10 (old 5) EC. A more recent case is *Francovich*, which was argued strongly on the basis of Art 10 (old 5) to provide state liability for the failure of the Member State to implement a Directive when it was held not to give rise to direct effects.

Article 12 (old 6) EC, which was Art 7 EEC, the general prohibition on discrimination on the grounds of nationality, is also relevant to all areas of Community law. It is used as a general tool of the Court of Justice to reach just results in particular circumstances which might not be reached by the application of more specific provisions. For example, it has been used to extend the law in respect of vocational training and fees for education, as can be seen in the cases of *Blaizot, Humbel, Lair, Brown,* and *Gravier,* amongst others.

THE FORM OF LEGISLATION IN THE EUROPEAN COMMUNITIES

Treaties

The primary form of legislation in the Communities are the various treaties, the most notable of which is the EC Treaty, otherwise referred to as the Treaty of Rome. The two other original treaties, the European Coal and Steel Treaty (ECSC) and the European Atomic Energy Treaty (EURATOM), have since been added to by the Acts of Accession, providing details for the enlargement of the Communities by new Member States. The most important additional treaties are the Merger Treaty, the Single European Act, the Treaty on European Union (the Maastricht Treaty) and the Treaty of Amsterdam, all of which have amended the original treaties. The ECSC Treaty is due to expire on 23 July 2002 and its provisions will probably be merged into the EC Treaty.

The treaties of the Communities, with the exception of the ECSC Treaty, are drawn up in all the official languages of the Communities, all of which are equally authentic. Any difficulties which arise from the fact that different meanings may, despite all attempts, arise between languages is usually overcome by the Court of Justice applying the teleological interpretation of the spirit of the provision rather than the letter.

The treaties are described as self-executing, in that no further action need be taken by a Member State to incorporate or transform the treaty into the national legal order once it has ratified the treaty. Some Member States, such as the UK, may need an introductory Act to mark formally the presence of the treaty, but would not reproduce the text of the treaty into a national Act. Further details of what is meant by 'self-executing' can be found in chapter 4.

The treaties are framework treaties in that they lay down broad guidelines for the pursuit of certain agreed aims and objectives. They do not provide extensive details for the implementation of these policies, which is left, for the most part, to secondary legislation of the Community or failing that to the Court of Justice who will rule on what was intended by the Treaty provision. For example, although the EC Treaty broadly provides that workers should be guaranteed freedom of movement in the Communities, it did not define, nor indeed did any secondary legislation define, what was meant by worker. It was thus up to the Court of Justice to provide definitions of what it considered should be included in the definition of worker in the Community context.

Secondary Legislation

In the Communities secondary legislation arises entirely subject to the authority, higher rank and procedures provided for in the treaties. They consist of Regulations, Directives and Decisions, further details of which are explained in chapter 4.

THE FORM AND REPORTING OF JUDGMENTS OF THE EUROPEAN COURT OF JUSTICE

The Form of Judgments

The report is drafted first of all in the language of the case, which is chosen by the parties or the defending Member State from the eleven official languages following the entry of Finland and Sweden to the Communities. The internal working documents of the court and its deliberations are, however, conducted in French, its working language. The full report, as required by the Rules of Procedure of the Court, comprises a brief summary of judgment, followed by the report for the hearing drawn up by the Judge-Rapporteur containing the facts and procedure, and a summary of the arguments of the parties. The next part of the report contains the opinion of the Advocate-General, although this does not form an official part of the report. The final part contains both the reasons or grounds for the judgment, presented in numbered paragraphs, and finally, the usually very succinct single ruling of the Court. (See also the sections on the Court in chapter 3.)

The Reporting of Cases

There is only one official set of reports of cases emanating from the Court of Justice and the Court of First Instance. These are the European Court Reports which are cited as ECR and proceeded by the year of publication. These are published in all of the official languages. These are divided into Part I, containing the judgments of the European Court of Justice, Part II containing the judgments of the Court of First Instance and ECR-SC containing staff cases which are no longer automatically translated into all of the official languages. However, publication of cases in these reports is severely delayed by two to three years, largely as a result of the translation requirements into the official languages, and alternative reports must be consulted if the full text is required. The principal alternative, which reports cases soon after judgment, is the Common Market Law Reports, cited as CMLR, which provide reports in English not only of the judgments of the Community courts but also of cases from the national courts of other Member States which have considered or applied important points of Community law or which have demonstrated the attitude of the national courts to such Community concepts as supremacy or direct effect.

As a further alternative, the Court of Justice produces shorter notes of judgments and opinions in the form of a series entitled 'The proceedings of the Court of Justice and Court of First Instance of the European Communities'. The stated aim is to provide much quicker information on case decisions and the work of the Court. These are not authentic, although they may be quoted providing the source is stated. They are often the first written statement available giving a summary of the reasons for a particlar decision and should be available in your college or university library. Summaries of cases can also be found in the *Official Journal*, and on the internet recent case law can be found at: http://europa.eu.int/eur-lex/en/index.html.

STUDYING COMMUNITY LAW

Many of the comments made in this chapter will repeat much of what was said generally in chapter 1. This does no harm as they are worth repeating. This time, however, the comments are made in the context of Community law.

How does the system of Community law affect the study and, more importantly, the examination of Community law? Awareness of the type of system should underpin the whole approach to the study and exposition of Community law. The assumptions of common-law subjects or approach are not always valid here. The study of Community law must be put in the context of the background of the Community, i.e., its history and development. Community law study is not like most subject courses of national law, where a lot of background has already been covered in general or first-year subjects dealing with the legal system or constitutional law or other basic or core courses. EC law is a completely new system to learn and a lot of background reading must be undertaken. In many EC courses, the whole system is studied in one course, in others it may be split into its various components. Whichever form, at the start this may be daunting and confusing, because there are many new terms or buzzwords, or 'Eurojargon', to learn, especially in the areas of the sources of law, general principles, the free movement of goods and the economic terms of the common market. A selection would include: *acquis communautaire*, comfort letters, comitology, contemporaneity, COREPER, democratic deficit, direct applicability, dominant positions, ECOSOC, horizontal direct effects, indistinctly applicable, intergovernmentalism, Ioannina compromise, Maastricht, principle of equivalence, proportionality, qualified majority voting, rule of reason, subsidiarity, supranationalism, teleological. If you understand all of these and can place them in context, you have already come a long way towards understanding the Community and Community law. Perhaps you could test yourself now, when you first read this, and then shortly before your examination. If you are unsure, especially close to the examination, the answers can be found by looking them up in the index at the end of this book.

Community Law Courses

The basic aims of Community law courses are likely to include consideration of its historical origins and the development of the Community and Community law in the wider political, economic and social contexts; the rules governing the institutions, especially within the above framework; and the relationship between Community law and Community courts and national law and national courts, judicial remedies and a number of areas of the substantive law of the Communities.

While the objectives of Community law courses may differ in various institutions, I would generally expect that lecturers would have broadly similar expectations of what the students should have learned or be capable of at the end of the course. The course would probably be designed to provide information concerning the present composition, powers and functions of the institutions and how these aspects have developed over time, so that you are able to criticise these aspects and suggest improvements, especially in relation to the other institutions and recent changes. In respect of the Community legal system, you should be able to explain how the law applies to, and may be invoked by, individuals, to discuss the conflict and resolution of the conflict between Community law and national laws, especially in the national courts, and to discuss the range of judicial remedies in the Community legal order and the procedures involved. You should therefore be able to resolve factual problems involving these remedies, highlighting any particular difficulties which have arisen in the jurisprudence of the Court of Justice and/or national courts.

Lastly, in terms of substantive law, you should be able to discuss the basic aims of the Community in the areas considered and the basic framework of the Treaty provisions and subsequent legislation adopted by the Community, the relevant case law of the Court of Justice and its impact on the legal developments in the areas considered, and be able to apply this information to resolve factual problems and to suggest solutions.

The Approach of this Volume

The study of Community law in this volume follows much the same pattern as discussed above. First, the Treaty aims and main provisions will be outlined, then specific articles in particular parts of the Treaty which outline the Community policy will be considered. Where, as is the case in most areas, there is secondary legislation, this will be summarised and the relevant provisions discussed.

Thus, the general approach to Community law means starting with the EC Treaty. For a complete answer one would even need to start with the general provisions of the Treaty. This means the Preamble and Arts 2, 3, 10 (old 5) and 12 (old 6). These act as guidelines to the objectives of the Treaty and Community, they demonstrate the aims that subsequent legislation is designed to achieve and, more to the point, they are referred to by the Court of Justice and can serve as powerful justifications or grounds for the Court to decide in a particular way.

The Study of Community Legislation

That there is a great deal of legislation to consider should come as no surprise if you already have viewed the topics that will be covered on your course. The extensive coverage of EC law courses must necessarily involve a considerable amount of legislation. Therefore it is necessary to be selective. For the most part, this selection will already have been made for you by your lecturers. Clearly the provisions of the EC Treaty are of most importance, but not all of them. There is also a great deal of secondary legislation, especially, but not exclusively, in the substantive law areas.

What you actually learn and what you may just need to be aware of or have reference to, depends on the attitude of your particular course of study, or college or university, to legislation collections and cases and materials books. Many of you will be able to take into written unseen examinations a copy of one of the collections of EC legislation currently available. There are a number of collections available at the moment (the fact that one also carries the names of Foster and Blackstone would not influence me in the slightest, honest!). However, given that you are probably allowed a choice between these volumes, if necessary you could take advantage of cheaper, old editions, as it is not so much what you choose, but how you use it. The disadvantages of old editions speak for themselves because they are, by their very nature, not up-to-date. You will have to be aware of any changes if you have bought a secondhand legislation collection. Only you can decide whether the saving of a few pounds is worthwhile. If in doubt, save yourself the anguish and buy the latest edition. What is important, is that you should obtain a copy of EC legislation early in the academic year and use it throughout for reference in the lectures and in tutorials/seminars. You will find that by examination time you will know what legislation is important and, more to the point, will already be familiar with it. This avoids frantic searches through the legislation in the examination hall, usually accompanied by an expression of panic, in the desperate pursuit of anything vaguely relevant to your answer. This is not only a waste of time, it is hardly conducive to establishing the relaxed but concentrated frame of mind necessary for tackling the questions, so be prepared!

For those of you who cannot take legislation or legislation collections into the examination, it is even more important to discern which are the legislative provisions it is necessary to know, and the earlier the better. In this case you will be forced to be selective, because even if it is not necessary to learn by rote every single word, you must be able to paraphrase with precision, so as not to distort the meaning or intent of the particular provision.

The Study of Case Law

Since there are many cases which involve the same subject matter, the textbooks do not always choose the same decisions as examples, and authors may try to liven up what can be regarded as a fairly dull area of Community law by citing the more interesting cases, including blow-up-dolls, sex shops, unlawful killings and prostitutes, amongst others. Only occasionally will a new case deal with anything novel, although there are many new cases. Most of them are simply variations on themes of previous cases. The examples cited in this book may or may not, therefore, reflect those covered by the textbooks or your course in EC law. My advice here is, when in doubt, or to try to cut down the number of cases that have to be learned or revised, use the examples given by your course lecturers. This does not invalidate the specific cases used here or in other texts. What is important are the interpretations and application of law reached, and these remain valid regardless of the actual case used. Some cases are clearly important and cannot be disregarded, for example, *Van Gend en Loos* and *Costa v ENEL*. If you do not know why these two cases are so significant, then get reading!

Read, where you can, the cases themselves, but certainly make use of the case notes, before and after reading the case itself, if necessary. Although, where the subject matter is difficult, in the areas of competition law and free movement of goods in particular, the cases can be quite lengthy, Community law cases are normally reasonably short. The judgments are usually very concise, so much so that the reasoning behind them is not always obvious. If this is the case, then it will be necessary to read the opinion of the Advocate-General. However, the Court is not obliged to follow either the Advocate-General's opinion or reasoning in reaching its decision, e.g., as in *Van Gend en Loos*; therefore, in order to understand the decision fully, a case note may be the only answer.

While not recommended, it may be possible to learn Community law from a really small core of cases, perhaps about 30–40, because many cases which have arisen from a substantive law problem have resulted in the leading principles and developments in Community institutional and procedural law. A suggested list — and one which, like the Eurojargon above, may be used as a sort of checklist — would probably include the following cases: *Van Gend en Loos, Leonesio v Ministero dell'Agricoltura e delle Foreste, Ratti, Verbond v The Netherlands, Costa v ENEL, Simmenthal, Internationale Handelsgesellschaft, Foglia v Novello, CILFIT, Von Colson, Francovich, Factortame* (more than one), *Plaumann, Töpfer,* the *Isoglucose* cases, *Lütticke, International Fruit v Commission, Codorniu, Commission v Italy (Art Treasures), Schöppenstedt, Denkavit, Dassonville, Cassis de Dijon, Prantl, Keck, Defrenne v SABENA, Marshall, Van Duyn, Barber, Van Binsbergen, Reyners, Säger, Gebhard, ICI v Commission, Consten and Grundig, United Brands, Continental Can.* This list is by no means exhaustive and I am not advocating that you should concentrate on these cases alone, but as a minimum these are cases of which you should be aware as they are the leading cases. If you remember the meaning of these cases it is likely that they will remind you of further cases which develop the principles, such as *Marleasing* and *Kolpinghuis* in respect of *Von Colson* or the cases which go on to clarify or expand previous judgments such as those which followed the *Barber* or *Factortame* cases. Do you know all of the listed cases, what they are about, the area of Community law, and the decision and principle of law of which they are examples? If not, look them up in the case list.

Cases and Materials Books

Cases and materials books, of which there are two or three good examples given in the bibliography at the end of the volume, can be useful in providing handy source materials on the leading provisions of law and cases, especially where library facilities are scarce. The increase in student numbers, of which you will no doubt be aware on your courses, without the proportionate additional funding for facilities will inevitably mean library stocks must suffer and you will find it extremely difficult to get hold of basic materials in the library. In such circumstances a cases and materials book may well prove to be a worthwhile purchase. I know that your finances are far from inexhaustible, but to ease the burden consider sharing the cost of books with two or three other students taking the same courses, rotating the books as you need them. This means you can have access to all the recommended books on a course without the full cost — but try not to fall out over the books, please!

Course Work

For general comments about lectures and tutorials, see the appropriate sections in chapter 1.

Reading to prepare for lectures and tutorials on Community law courses will often be recommended from the specialised European law journals. The leading Community law journals are: *European Law Review*, the *Common Market Law Review*, *Legal Issues of European Integration*, and the *European Journal of International Law*. In addition, leading UK law journals also include developments in Community law, sometimes in separate up-dating sections. See, amongst others, ICLQ, LQR, *Public Law* and the *Modern Law Review*.

The European Union itself also publishes a great deal of general information and specialist documents. Check to see whether your library has a European Documentation Centre. If so, become familiar with its layout and holdings — it may prove useful, especially in respect of assessed work. And there is, of course, the Internet, or WWW, which is a massive source of material. Try starting at http://europa.eu.int/.

THE GENERAL APPROACH TO COMMUNITY LAW QUESTIONS

Essays

(a) Identify the area of law which is being dealt with in the question to hand; even if not explicit, this is usually obvious.

(b) Determine what the question is asking you. This may sound trite, but if you do not interpret it correctly your answer may be close to worthless. Therefore you must try to dissect the question or de-construct it, i.e., break it into parts to determine what is necessary to provide the answer to the question. A couple of examples will help:

Example 1.   Is it the case that 'the doctrine of the supremacy of Community law is a logical if not necessary inference from Community treaties'?

This clearly concerns supremacy, and most questions would require you to define the subject matter of the question, unless this is done as a part of the question and you are required to discuss the given definition. So, with the above question, you need to state clearly and concisely what you understand by the phrase 'the doctrine of the supremacy of Community law'.

You are then asked whether 'it is the case that [it] is a logical if not necessary inference', and you have to determine exactly what this cryptic part of the question is demanding as an answer. It suggests the supremacy of Community law is (i) logical, but that it is not (ii) a necessary inference from the treaties. You must address both these contentions.

Although the word 'logical' appears first, I would start by addressing the part about the inference, because this more directly requires you to consider the Treaty provisions and follows the deductive approach outlined above. It also appears to me to make sense to consider whether the Treaties do provide for supremacy, before having to consider the logic of whether Community law is supreme. So, you must consider whether the Treaties provide for supremacy. The question has already hinted that this is not expressly to be found in the Treaty, i.e., there is no article which clearly states that Community law is supreme. On a direct reading of the Treaty you might not necessarily infer that Community law is supreme.

You are thus led to consider whether Community law supremacy is logical from the Treaty. Without going into the details here, you clearly are required to consider any provisions which logically demand supremacy. While you could attempt to determine this yourself by an analysis of provisions, it would be far easier — and is what the question is driving at — if you were to look to the institution which has already done this for you in its case rulings, i.e., the Court of Justice in the cases of *Van Gend en Loos*, *Costa* v *ENEL* and *Simmenthal*, amongst others.

Example 2.   'Though the Community Treaties indicate either indirectly or by implication an intention that Community law should be paramount over the law in each Member State, they contain no express provision to that effect. For the present, therefore, this question is in practice largely dependent on the constitutional law of each Member State.' Discuss.

This is a similar question, in that it also covers supremacy; but it is also concerned with the Member States' law and not just Community law.

The parts to be addressed are the indirect or implied intention of the Treaties for supremacy of Community law and the fact that there is no express provision. This requires a discussion of any Treaty articles which would lead to this conclusion and the rulings of the Court of Justice which confirm this. This is really just another formulation of the first example given.

The question then suggests that because supremacy is not express, the Member States' constitutional laws determine supremacy. You are then required either to confirm this with examples, or to refute it by reference to Court of Justice rulings, i.e., the issue to be addressed is whether Community law supremacy is determined according to national constitutional laws?

See chapter 5 for full consideration of these questions.

(c)   Once you have identified the principal issues, these will form the sections in your answer. In your plan, set out the issues which arise from the above, i.e., what information must now be supplied, just as I have shown.

A certain amount of general discussion might be welcome, depending on the approach adopted in your particular course and the subject matter of the question. This should be clear from the content of the lectures and whether any background discussion was given. This might include discussion of the motives for the inclusion of particular areas or provisions in the Treaty, or the general economic background or theory in competition law, for example.

The degree of detail included would depend on the emphasis given in your particular course to these general considerations and the type of question to be addressed. Clearly, in term essays and assessed essays these general points should be covered in reasonable detail. In exam essay answers, the available time will determine the amount of detail.

(d)   When the issues to be addressed are clear, set out the legal regime which is relevant to the question, i.e., the relevant legislative provisions. A complete answer would make reference to the general provisions of the Treaty. This sets the problem and answer in context, and it allows you to determine what you think the result should be even before any hard law is referred to. Start with the Preamble, determine whether the subject matter is referred to in Arts 2 and 3, and investigate whether there are specific Treaty articles on the matter. If there are, outline these!

See the examples in the following chapters, especially those in the substantive areas of law such as the free movement of persons. For instance, in the case of questions on the free movement of workers, reference should first be made to the Treaty Preamble and Arts 2 and 3 — in particular, reference to the abolition, as between Member States, of obstacles to freedom of movement for persons. Then, in respect of the free movement of workers, it would be useful to outline briefly the scope of rights given by Art 39 (old 48) EC and secondary legislation, i.e., Regulation 1612/68 and Directives 64/221 and 68/360. There is usually no need to rewrite in full the actual provisions, and a summary of their scope should be acceptable.

(e)   Lastly, the discussion itself can take place and be completed with a paragraph summarising the main conclusions.

Problem Solving

The problem questions are usually designed to test whether the basic concepts of Community policy and law have been understood, and how the rights given by the Treaty and secondary legislation have been interpreted and expanded by the ECJ in particular, given situations.

(a)   The general approach to problem solving is first to identify the area of law. Again, as with essays, this is usually, but not always, obvious, especially with mixed questions which may cover two or three topics in Community law. Next, the mnemonic I suggested in chapter 1 applies (FLAC), identify the factual issues or particular problems arising from the situation provided in the problem. Then discuss the general applicable legal regime and the specific provisions to set the context of the problem as succinctly as possible, as was discussed above. Apply the legislative provisions and case law on the provisions to the issues, and come to conclusions on each issue. By setting out the problems and issues of an answer, a form of plan has already been established, which can be the basis of a separate plan but could easily be incorporated into a couple of opening paragraphs to provide a complete and structured answer.

One of the most common mistakes made in answering problem questions in Community law is adopting a common-law approach, i.e., looking at the facts of a case and saying 'This looks like, e.g., the *Marshall* case', and attempting to apply the decision or, as common-law lawyers would call it, the *ratio decidendi* of the case to the facts to reach a conclusion: 'Well, there was this other case in which it was decided X; therefore the result in this case is also X.'. No mention is made of the EC Treaty or secondary Community legislation, as if the *Marshall* case existed in a vacuum or was common law. The approach is, of course, one learned while studying common-law subjects such as contract and tort, where there is often no statute law to which to refer. In Community law this is clumsy and wrong, i.e., the outcome may not be a simple application of previous judgments. See the different results of cases involving the EP and Council under Art 230 (old 173) and two cases arising under the Art 288 (old 215) action for damages, *Plaumann* and *Lütticke*. Follow it through — first the legislation and then the case law. The result might well be the same in most cases, but it cannot be guaranteed. The common law approach completely disregards the policy considerations inherent in Community law, which can at times lead to results not entirely clear from a straight application of the relevant legislation or case law conclusions. See, for example, in the area of the free movement of workers, the cases of *Lair* and *Brown* in deciding whether those studying can obtain benefits as workers or the case of *P v S and Cornwall CC* in sex discrimination law.

To repeat, start with the identification of the factual issues which must be resolved by the application of provisions of law from a certain area of Community law.

(b)   The next step is to see whether there is any secondary legislation on the matter. Your course of study should have revealed all of this to you and none of the actual provisions should come as a surprise. It would be far too late to start a search for relevant legislation in any subject area of EC law in the examination, if you are allowed to take legislation materials into the exam. Frantic, last minute searches for something (anything!) on the subject are not likely to produce a good answer or, more to the point, the right frame of mind to be able to produce a competent answer in an exam. You should therefore make yourself familiar with the principal secondary legislative provisions during your course of study, or at least at the time of your consolidation and revision of your course notes. So get a legislation book or materials book and use it throughout the course of the year.

(c)   At this stage of answering a question it may be possible to reach a conclusion on the legal position in a particular problem based only on the legislation, but usually you will need case law to iron out any uncertainties or ambiguities, or simply to back up your conclusion and demonstrate how the Court of Justice has decided the matter in cases with similar subject matter. In most cases the question would be designed with some of the case law in mind, in order to test your knowledge of areas of Community law. It is only at this stage, however, that case law should come into the discussion: it should not fill the opening lines of your answer. I promise you, it all makes much more sense doing it this way. I could think of many analogies to demonstrate the disadvantages of the latter form of approach, e.g., using case law first is not seeing the wood for the trees. Take an overview and work your way slowly into the problem; see the shape of the wood/answer first and then concentrate on the individual trees/details of the answer.

In particular problems, the choice of relevant cases can be more problematic. Despite the fact that there is a certain number of leading cases in EC law — surprisingly few when counted — particular ones will have been referred to in your course. However, the textbooks may favour different cases as examples of the interpretation of the same legal provision. Often the choice of one case as against another makes little difference, even if was not one cited on your course. The golden rule here is make sure that any case cited concerns the same legal provision or the same legal issue in dispute, e.g., the considerations employed in determining whether a particular forum is one capable of making references to the Court of Justice for the purposes of Art 234 (old 177). I have given the cases of *Nordsee* v *Nordstern* and *Broekmuelen* as examples, whereas I note that the cases of *Vaassen, Politi* v *Italy* and *Dreher* v *Italian Finance Administration* are used elsewhere.

Some cases have been used by the Court of Justice by way of analogy between similar provisions in the EEC (and now EC) and ECSC Treaties. Only follow the lead of the Court of Justice in this respect. Similarity of fact is less important than similarity of provision. These general guidelines will be demonstrated clearly in the sample questions and answers in the following chapters. Please note, however, this is not a questions and answers book and only one or two sample questions per chapter or topic are provided rather than a full range of questions designed to cover all aspects of each topic. If further example questions are required, it is recommended that one of the available question-and-answer books is consulted.

Where the citation of one case will suffice to answer the point under consideration in a problem question, use one and not any more, especially those which simply repeat the same principle. Only if you have time to spare can you indulge in the luxury of citing all the cases applicable to a certain area. In fact, later cases often do this for you by referring back to the developing law in the area. However, certain leading cases are fundamental and should be used in preference to later ones, e.g., *Van Gend en Loos, Costa* v *ENEL,* and *Ratti.* These should be recognised during the course of study.

Other comments in respect of revision and examination technique can be found in chapter 1.

3 *THE COMMUNITIES: LEGISLATIVE AND BUDGETARY PROCEDURES*

INTRODUCTION

It has already been stressed in chapter 2, but is worthwhile repeating here
that a study of Community law cannot be made without having a reasonable idea about the background and development of the Communities
against which to compare and judge present-day developments. This
chapter will provide a brief overview of this history and development but
must be supported by further reading, especially by those who have not
previously acquired any knowledge of the Communities. Particularly
important are the power struggles between the institutions which are the
hallmark of any truly dynamic process of constitutional evolution.

THE HISTORY AND DEVELOPMENT OF THE COMMUNITIES

Origins

Although there had been ideas to unify Europe before the Second World
War, it was only afterwards that they found fruition. This was prompted
by the horrific events and the devastation of Europe during the war.
Political and economic cooperation and development between nations was
regarded as crucial to replace the economic competition which was viewed
as a major factor in the outbreak of wars between European nation states.
The first forms of cooperation concentrated on these aspects and led to the
foundation of the United Nations in 1945, the Organisation for European
Economic Cooperation (OEEC) in 1948, and NATO and the Council of
Europe in 1949.

The direct impetus for the Communities came in the form of a plan proposed in 1950 by the French Foreign Minister Robert Schuman, in conjunction with the research and plans of Jean Monnet, to link the French and German coal and steel industries. These industries which were vital in waging war would be taken out of the hands of the nation states and put under the control of a supranational body. This would not only help economic recovery, but would also remove the disastrous competition between the two states. It was aimed at making future war not only unthinkable but also materially impossible. The plan was deliberately left open for other European countries to join in its discussions.

The UK, at that stage, was also keen to see a united Europe but, despite the seeming enthusiasm of Winston Churchill evidenced by his call to create 'a kind of United States of Europe' at a speech at the University of Zürich in 1946, Britain did not envisage a role as a key participant and was reluctant to involve itself, even in the negotiations. It had at the time a historical legacy which involved quite different economic and social ties, including the Empire and then Commonwealth and the Atlantic alliance, all of which featured strongly in the war recently won. These ties of security and common language are often overlooked, but played no small part in the attitude of Britain to Europe in the immediate post-war years. Britain also regarded its status as remaining a world power, whose sovereignty and independence could not be compromised by membership of such an organisation.

Belgium, The Netherlands and Luxembourg (the 'Benelux nations') saw the benefits to be gained from membership and integration, and Italy also considered it to be in its interest to join. So six nations went on without the UK to sign the European Coal and Steel Community Treaty (ECSC) in 1951 which came into force in 1952. The Benelux nations then proposed that rather than limiting the integration to two industries, the member nations should integrate the whole of their economies. Following a conference, the Spaak Report was prepared to consider the establishment of an Economic Community and an Atomic Energy Community for energy and the peaceful use of nuclear power. Britain was again invited to participate but withdrew after minimal participation and instead with Austria, Switzerland and other nations set about establishing the European Free Trade Association (EFTA) in 1958, which involved no further supranational or political aims than a common market for goods.

In 1957, the Treaties of Rome were established, setting up the European Economic Community (EEC) and the European Atomic Energy Community (EURATOM). At first all three Communities had their own institutions but a shared court. These were merged in 1965 by the Merger Treaty, the provisions of which have been incorporated into the present treaties. The EEC Treaty was, and now as the EC Treaty is the most important, especially in terms of its scope.

The ECSC Treaty, established for 50 years only, will expire in 2002. In the absence of clear information at this stage, it is presumed the industries will then be governed by the EC Treaty.

The Basic Objectives of the Communities

Initial aims and the integration debate   The EEC Treaty was aimed at the establishment of a common market and the progressive approximation of the economic policies of the Member States.

The general aims included the creation of the common market, which was to be achieved by abolishing obstacles to the freedom of movement of all the factors of production, namely goods, workers, providers of services, and capital. The Treaty also provided for the abolition of customs duties between the Member States and for the application of a common customs tariff to imports from third countries. There were to be common policies in the spheres of agriculture and transport, and a system ensuring that competition in the common market was not distorted by the activities of cartels or market monopolists. An embryonic social policy and regional policy also appeared

A debate commenced early in the discussions and life of the Communities — which has continued — about whether the Communities were supposed to integrate only in the specific areas as originally set out in the EEC Treaty, largely relating to free trade, or whether something more dynamic was intended. Many terms have been used to describe these developments. It was originally considered that because there was success in certain policies, this would automatically lead to a spillover from one area to another which would result in increasing integration. This is termed 'functional integration', or 'neo-functionalism' or 'federalism'. In fact it was considered that in order for the original policies to work properly there would have to be continuing integration. Thus, sector-by-sector integration and the process of European integration was regarded as an inexorable process. For example, common tariffs and the establishment of the common market would lead to exchange rates being stabilised to ensure that production factors and costs in the Member States were broadly equal. This in turn would require monetary union to be established to ensure exchange rates did not drift apart, and this would make it necessary for full economic union to be achieved so that the value of different components of the common currency would not be changed by different economic and fiscal policies in different countries. This economic integration would also mean that political integration would follow.

Intergovernmentalism, supranationalism or federalism?   These terms are employed to describe the form of integration undertaken by the Communities. 'Intergovernmentalism' is the normal way in which international organisations work. Their decisions require unanimity and are rarely enforceable without it; even then, they will be enforceable only between the signatory states and not by the citizens of those states. 'Supranationalism' describes the fact that the decision-making is made at a new and higher level than that of the Member States themselves, and that such decisions replace national rules. 'Federalism' may be the argued goal of the Communities if the aims are not limited to the distinct policies thus far agreed. In order to make the goal of the Communities more acceptable, the term 'a closer union' has been used in both the EEC Treaty (now the EC Treaty) and the TEU. It is unclear whether it refers to federalism or something short of that. While the Community does operate on the supranational level, it does not signify an inevitable move to federalism. Only as future developments unravel, will its final destination become clearer.

Wherever the Community is going, a number of significant developments have already taken place which are steps on that path.

Significant developments

Widening of the Communities   A change of mind by the UK occurred in 1961, when the Conservative government under Harold Macmillan applied for membership of the Communities. The reasons for previously not joining, i.e., world power status and direct links with most of the world, had been weakened by the economic demise of the UK, the Suez débâcle and the continuing conversion of the Empire into a Commonwealth of independent states. Trade patterns were shifting towards Europe and the Atlantic alliance was less prominent. Britain had observed the much faster economic progress made by the six, and this as much as anything else provoked the desire for membership. Whether Britain was ever interested in the entire Community package is not clear.

Britain now had to bargain from the outside and its application was vetoed by Charles de Gaulle, the French President, as was the 1967 application by the Labour government under Harold Wilson. President de Gaulle's opposition to the potentially distorting influence of the UK in the Community was clearly expressed at the time. In 1970, however, the application by the Conservative Prime Minister, Edward Heath, was successful, and in 1973 the UK joined the Communities, as did Ireland and Denmark, mainly because of their trade dependency on the UK. A second expansion took place in 1981 when Greece joined, and a third expansion when Spain and Portugal joined in 1986. A smaller automatic expansion took place in 1990 with the unification of Germany, and lastly the Community was joined by Austria, Finland and Sweden on 1 January 1995, bringing the total number of members to 15. Once again the Norwegian electorate chose to reject membership in a referendum held in November 1994.

The Community was spawned in the aftermath of World War II. For membership, states exchanged some sovereignty and monetary contribution for security, the stability of democratic nationhood and economic progress. It is argued that Britain did not need the first two benefits and the third proved illusory in the 1970s and 1980s, hence the view that the bargain was not a good one for Britain. These considerations seem ever to present themselves in relation to the membership of the UK in the Community.

Further expansion of the Communities is under consideration. Since the TEU, the criteria for membership have been much more clearly spelled out Article 49 (old O) of the TEU provides that 'Any European State which respects the principles set out in Art 6(1) (old F) may apply to become a member of the Union'. These principles are liberty, democracy, respect for human rights and the rule of law. Applications are currently pending with Cyprus, the Czech Republic, Estonia, Hungary, Poland and Slovenia selected as the first in line for membership. Further applications are being considered from Bulgaria, Latvia, Lithuania, Romania, Slovakia, and Turkey. The Council rejected an application from Morocco because they did not regard it as a European State. The change of Government in Malta has revitalised its application but the rejection by the Swiss of membership of the European Economic Area (EEA) in 1992 has put its application on hold Nevertheless, there is a potential increase to 29 Member States. Indeed there are not many European States left to apply, only Iceland, Norway. Liechtenstein, Monaco, the remnants of Yugoslavia and Albania and perhaps parts of the former Soviet Union.

All new States are required to accept and adopt the entire body of community law as contained in the treaties, conventions and agreement with third countries, secondary legislation and in the judgments of the European Court of Justice. This is termed in eurojargon the *'acquis communautaire'* and this requirement is now enshrined in Art 2 (old B) of the TEU

Deepening of the Communities   Initially, the Communities were very successful in achieving the aims set out and in promoting economic growth in the Member States in contrast with countries such as the UK. The dismantling of customs duties was achieved by the original six Member States before the target date set down in the EEC Treaty. Additionally, the competition policy and the common agricultural policy, successful in terms of guaranteeing production but the object of criticism ever since because their price support mechanisms have generated over-production, are both regarded as successes. However, following this initial period, the brake was put on the Commission, and consequently the Communities, by de Gaulle in 1965. The Commission proposed that the Communities should move to a system of own resources, combined with the proposal that the Council should move to majority voting as envisaged in the Treaty and that the Parliament should have more control over the expenditure of the Communities. These proposals were vetoed by de Gaulle, however, who, when the other Member States were not opposed, adopted a policy of non-attendance of the Community institutions by the French representatives, which became known as the 'empty chair boycott'.

The compromise which was agreed to bring the French back was the infamous Luxembourg accords, adopted to break the deadlock. These basically provided that where a vital national interest of any Member State was at stake, that Member State could veto a proposal in Council. Member states were left to define a vital interest. Thus, until the demise of de Gaulle in 1969, the planned moves were prevented. It resulted in stagnation in the decision-making process and considerable expressions of dissatisfaction at the slow pace at which the goals of the EEC were being achieved.

The basic problem was the near inability of the Member States to reach decisions on Community legislation. This stemmed partly from the Luxembourg accords but also from the doubling of the members of the Community between 1973 and 1985. Trying to obtain the unanimous agreement of all 12 members at times proved to be impossible. In particular, the concerns were the time taken by the Community institutions to make new laws; the amount of work the Council was faced with, partly because particular provisions were presented many times as the Commission made amendments; the lack of representative democracy in the decision-making process of the Community, and the delays experienced by litigants to the Court of Justice. Thus some change had to be brought about.

Some adjustments had been made in the form of amendments to the original Treaties, but these were of a limited nature. They included the Merger Treaty of 1965, which merged the three political institutions of the Communities (the Court of Justice had always served all three). More significant, but restricted to a specific process, was the increase in the powers of the EP in the budgetary process by the budgetary treaties of 1970 and 1975. Accession treaties dealt specifically with the details of accession of the new Member States and how these affected the composition of the institutions, for example.

Many official inquiries were conducted by the different Community institutions, and a number of areas where improvements were required had already been identified by various reports in the lifetime of the Communities. Amongst these were: the Vedel Report of 1972, with proposals by the Commission to strengthen the powers of the EP; the Tindemans Report on 'European Union' in 1976; the Report of the Three Wise Men in 1979; the Spierenburg Report in 1979; the Stuttgart European Council, Columbo/Genscher Initiative of 1983; and the EP publication 'Draft Treaty of the European Parliament establishing the European Union'. All of these, especially the last, helped develop the climate for the eventual changes brought about by the Single European Act (SEA), the Treaty on European Union (the Maastricht Treaty) and the Treaty of Amsterdam.

The Single European Act

The Dooge Committee set up the Intergovernmental Conference in 1985, to discuss the decision-making of the Council of Ministers, the legislative powers of the EP, the executive power of the Commission, the policy areas of the Community and the delays before the Court of Justice. The SEA was the product of that conference and came into force in the EEC in May 1987. Despite its name, it is a true amending treaty agreed by the Member States. The preamble of the SEA states that it is 'a step towards European Union'. It amended the EEC Treaty in several important respects, perhaps most importantly, the change of the legislative process affecting 10 Treaty articles and generally the extension of the Community's competence and concern in new policy areas. The SEA's influence in four important areas is noted below. While the Treaty on European Union and the Treaty of Amsterdam have replaced or removed some matters and further amended the EEC Treaty in respect of the same matters, the changes brought about by the SEA are still worth noting.

The internal market and '1992'   The SEA set a new date of 31 December 1992 for the completion of the internal common market, which originally should have been achieved by 1 January 1970. This was simply a priority date set by the Commission, by which time measures, which should have been completed earlier, should be finalised.

The internal market is defined in Art 14 (old 7a) EC as comprising 'an area without internal frontiers in which the free movement of goods, persons, services and capital is ensured in accordance with the provisions of this Treaty'. In 1985, the Commission identified 279 areas in which directives or other provisions were considered necessary to complete the internal market. By the end of October 1992, 282 directives had been proposed and drafted. By the end of December 1992 all but 18 had been adopted by the Council.

Economic and social cooperation   Articles 158–162 (old 130a–130e EEC), as amended, provided that the Community shall develop and pursue its actions leading to the strengthening of its economic and social cohesion. In particular, the Community must aim at reducing disparities between the various regions and the backwardness of the least-favoured regions. Various funds have been set up: the European Regional Development Fund, to help redress regional imbalances between various areas of the Communities by financing infrastructural development; the Social Fund, to finance employment initiatives; and the European Investment Bank, which operates as a commercial bank, lending money to finance projects in the promotion of which the Community has an interest.

Research and technology   Article 163 (old 130f) of the EC Treaty declared the Community's aim of strengthening the scientific and technological basis of European industry and encouraging it to become more competitive at international level. Articles 163–173 (old 130f–130p) set out the framework for the pursuit of research and development cooperation.

Environmental protection   Article 174(1) (old 130r(1)) set out the objectives of Community action relating to the environment. They are (i) the preservation, protection and improvement of the environment; (ii) contribution towards protecting public health; and (iii) a prudent and rational utilisation of human resources. Article 174(2) (old 130r(2)) provided that action shall be based on the principles that preventive action should be taken, that damage should as a priority be rectified at source, and that the polluter should pay.

Community action aimed at the protection of the environment is subject to the principle of 'subsidiarity' set out in Art 174(4) (old 130r(4)).

The SEA also made formal the position of the European Council, introduced political cooperation, qualified majority to the Council, the co-operation procedure in law making and measures towards monetary union, paved the way for the Court of First Instance and increased Commission powers, all of which are considered in the appropriate sections below.

The European Economic Area

In October 1991, the EFTA Member States of Austria, Finland, Iceland, Norway, Sweden, and Switzerland, and now joined by Liechtenstein, signed an agreement with the EEC on the creation of the European Economic Area (EEA). This subjects the EFTA Member States to the Community rules on the internal market and competition. They will not be represented in the Community institutions and will take no part in the decision-making processes of the Community, but they will be subject to all Community law relating to the Single Market as defined by the Court of Justice. Following the Swiss rejection, as a result of their referendum in December 1992, the remaining six States went on to sign the agreement in March 1993 to come into force on 1 July 1993. However, following the entry to the Community of Austria, Finland and Sweden — Iceland, Norway and Liechtenstein are now the only remaining EFTA members of the EEA, none of which now have membership applications pending. Switzerland remains outside both the EC and the EEA but has an application for membership of the EC on hold.

The Maastricht Treaty on European Union

It was realised very soon after the signing of the SEA that it was only part of the answer and it was further argued that what was really required were further institutional changes and the adoption of common monetary and fiscal policies. The SEA had made future changes possible. The intergovernmental conferences took place to debate these, and the Maastricht Treaty was agreed in February 1992 and was due to come into force on 1 January 1993, but the process was thrown into confusion, however, by the rejection of Maastricht by a slim Danish majority in a referendum, the economic crises in some Member States and the delays in the UK and in Germany in finalising ratification. The Edinburgh Summit in December 1992 agreed to allow the Danes to opt out of participation in stage III of the Economic and Monetary Union, the single currency, and the defence arrangements of Maastricht. Guidelines were also agreed on what was meant by subsidiarity under the new Art 5 (old 3b) of the EC Treaty. The interpretation of this difficult concept provides that the Community should only act where it has the power to do so, where the objective can only be achieved best at the Community level and where the action is proportionate to the aims. However, quite who decides this will inevitably provide much scope for conflict. For details see the Bulletin of the EC, No. 12, 1992.

The main changes, set out as objectives in Arts 1–10 (old A–I) of the Maastricht Treaty, are the increase and further development of policy areas, the plan to move to a single economy and monetary union with a single currency, and more political cooperation, especially in the areas of foreign policy, security, home affairs and justice (Arts 11–45 (old J–K)). The EEC Treaty name is amended to represent the changes that have taken place, to read the European Community (EC).

The new term, the European Union, is introduced under Art 1 (old A). However, quite where it is applicable seems to cause some confusion. 'European Union' describes the extension by the Member States into additional policies and areas of cooperation. The Union consists of three pillars comprising the existing Communities (the three original treaties), a common foreign and security policy (CFSP) and cooperation in the fields of justice and home affairs (CJHA) in all contexts. European Community law remains the term to describe the law governing the EC Treaty and is what most courses on the European Union/Community will cover.

European Union law does exist but is very limited. This will be discussed further in the section on the present structure of the Union and Treaties below. 'European Community' is the new term for the European Economic Community. As the Court of Justice has very little jurisdiction over the two new areas outside the European Community, it is misleading to speak of European Union law in all contexts. Some parts of the Treaty, such as decision-making, already amended by the SEA and the TEU, have been subject to further amendment and replacement by the Treaty of Amsterdam. The TEU also started a trend which was continued at Amsterdam in the attachment to the treaties of numerous protocols and declarations which help in many cases to define further some provisions of the treaties and outline the reservations of some Member States. For the most part these will not be considered in any detail in courses on EU or EC law. The TEU also set up a timetable for the revision of the Treaties by providing that a new intergovernmental Conference (IGC) be set up in 1996. It was given the objectives of proposing changes to reform the institutional structure in preparation for enlargement, to consider the role of the individual in relation to the Union and to review the common foreign and security policy, especially in respect of the rights of the free movement of persons. The IGC lasted until June 1997 when the Treaty of Amsterdam was drafted. It was signed by all Member States in October 1997 and following a slow but less troublesome ratification by all Member States, entered into force on 1 May 1999.

The Treaty of Amsterdam

Whilst not as dramatic as the changes brought about by the TEU, the Treaty of Amsterdam did introduce a number of changes. Unfortunately, some of these have considerably complicated the structure of the Union and the Treaties. A clear failure was the lack of significant institutional reform (scheduled for another IGC which commenced in Brussels in February 2000) needed prior to any increase in the number of Member States.

The Agreement on Social Policy, previously lying outside of the Treaty structure has been accepted now by all 15 Member States and incorporated into the EC Treaty in the new Arts 136–145 (old 117–122).

A new section on employment has been introduced under Arts 125–130 (old 109n–109s) EC which provides that the Member States can develop co-operative ventures to combat unemployment.

Part of the Justice and Home Affairs pillar concerned with the free movement of persons moves within the EC Pillar (see Arts 61–63 (old 73i–73k) EC and Art 29 (old K.1) TEU). Furthermore, the European Union is to incorporate the Schengen agreement on the elimination of all border controls for 13 States, but not for the UK nor Ireland and there are some special provisions for Denmark. The institutional reforms were far more modest. The legislative procedures have been reduced and amended with the result that the European Parliament's powers are modestly increased and the number of Commissioners was capped at 20, both of which will be considered further below.

The Treaty of Amsterdam has also added more protocols. Again for the most part these will not be considered in any detail in courses on EC law. If in doubt, ask.

Finally, the various changes to the treaties were consolidated and this led to new renumbered versions of the EC and European Union Treaties. I'm afraid you will have to learn to live with both new and old numbering, as any cases commenced before 1 May 1999 will refer to the old numbering. Further confusion may be added because the TEU has had its letters converted into numbers, hence, you need to take real care with the Article numbers and origin, i.e., EC or TEU Treaty.

As a result of Amsterdam, the Union is now a much more complex entity and will continue to evolve. The next section will try to set out a brief overview of the revised structure. And, as the Community evolves further, so also will the debate continue as to what sort of Community the Member States and citizens of Europe want: an economic club or an emergent political federation or confederation?

The Revised Structure of the EU and the Treaties

The EU still comprises three pillars, albeit modified. It also retains broadly the division between the supranational EC pillar and the intergovernmental nature of the other two, but this, I'm afraid has also been altered.

The first pillar, the EC pillar has been revised and expanded further by Amsterdam. The basic structure of the old EEC Treaty has been retained but expanded to include monetary union, a section on employment, an increased in the provision on the general free movement of persons on top of the policy extensions previously effected by the TEU. The objectives of the Union are revised in Art 3 EC:

(a)   the prohibition, as between Member States, of customs duties and quantitative restrictions on the import and export of goods, and of all other measures having equivalent effect;

(b)   a common commercial policy;

(c)   an internal market characterised by the abolition, as between Member States, of obstacles to the free movement of goods, persons, services and capital;

(d)   measures concerning the entry and movement of persons as provided for in Title IV;

(e)   a common policy in the sphere of agriculture and fisheries;

(f)   a common policy in the sphere of transport;

(g)   a system ensuring that competition in the internal market is not distorted;

(h)   the approximation of the laws of Member States to the extent required for the functioning of the common market;

(i)   the promotion of coordination between employment policies of the Member States with a view to enhancing their effectiveness by developing a co-ordinated strategy for employment;

(j)   a policy in the social sphere comprising a European Social Fund;

(k)   the strengthening of economic and social cohesion;

(l)   a policy in the sphere of the environment;

(m)   the strengthening of the competitiveness of Community industry;

(n)   the promotion of research and technological development;

(o)   encouragement for the establishment and development of trans-European networks;

(p)   a contribution to the attainment of a high level of health protection;

(q)   a contribution to education and training of quality and to the flowering of the cultures of the Member States;

(r)   a policy in the sphere of development cooperation;

(s)   the association of the overseas countries and territories in order to increase trade and promote jointly economic and social development;

(t)   a contribution to the strengthening of consumer protection;

(u)   measures in the spheres of energy, civil protection and tourism.

The principle of subsidiarity has been given heightened prominence in Art 5 (old 3b) with further details on its application in protocol 30 attached to the Treaty of Amsterdam.

The second pillar on common Foreign and Security Policy (Arts 11–28 (old J.1–J.18) TEU) has been modified in terms of its decision-making process and now allows for the possibility of abstentions, providing consensus is achieved by the other States. This pillar remains outside the jurisdiction of the ECJ.

The third pillar is now called 'Provisions on Police and Judicial cooperation in Criminal Matters' as a result of the transfer to the EC pillar of provisions concerned with the free movement of persons (Arts 61–63 (old 73i–73k) EC). The Schengen agreement has now been incorporated into the Union as a Protocol. The role of the Western European Union has been strengthened under Amsterdam as the military wing of the majority of the Member States.

Part of the complication is that the parts that have moved to EC are subject to less progressive law-making procedures with unanimity by the Council and less of a role for the European Parliament. In contrast the decision-making procedures of the third pillar, previously exclusively intergovernmental, now allow for the possibility of more flexible decision making by some of the Member States (but not all). Whilst this inevitably complicates the overall picture, it may allow a coming together in the future of the three pillars and thus satisfy the critics of the development of pillars two and three along intergovernmental lines. See Arts 40–44 (old K.12–K.16) TEU and Art 11 (old 5a) EC. Depending on the degree of attention given to this topic in your particular course, you may have to consult a much more detailed explanation of the changes in one of the leading texts, such as Weatherill and Beaumont, *EU Law*, 3rd edn, pp. 17–32, as it is really beyond the scope of this introductory text, which concentrates on EC Law.

THE COMMUNITY INSTITUTIONS

Article 7 (old 4) of the EC Treaty states that the tasks entrusted to the Community shall be carried out by these institutions: a European Parliament, a Council, a Commission, a Court of Justice and a Court of Auditors. These institutions serve all three present Communities as a result of the Merger Treaty of 1965 and also now, as a result of Art 3 (old C) of the TEU, serve the European Union. Article 7 (old 4) requires each institution to keep within the limits of the powers conferred on it by the Treaty.

Article 7 (old 4) further states that the Council of Ministers and the Commission shall be assisted by an Economic and Social Committee and a Committee of the Regions acting in an advisory capacity (Art 7(2) (old 4(2))). The detailed provisions governing the institutions are set out in Part 5 of the Treaty, and each section begins with an article outlining the general functions of the institution in question.

The SEA provided for the addition of the Court of First Instance and formalised the position of the European Council.

The Maastricht Treaty added the Court of Auditors to the list of principal institutions, provided for the establishment of the European Investment Bank (EIB) in Art 9 (old 4b) to the EC Treaty (as amended), and provided for the creation of the European System of Central Banks (ESCB) and a European Central Bank (ECB) in Art 8 (old 4a). The complete review of the institutions which should have taken place when the Treaty of Amsterdam was being negotiated has been postponed to an IGC which should take place no later than one year before the number of Member States is due to increase to 20 according to a protocol on the institutions attached to the Treaty of Amsterdam. This commenced in February 2000.

The Council of Ministers

Despite the changes brought about to the legislative processes by the various Treaty amendments, the Council remains the main legislative organ of the Communities. Its tasks, composition and functions are outlined in Arts 202–210 (old 145–154) EC. It consists of representative Ministers of the Member States, depending on the subject-matter under discussion. Foreign Ministers attend the general Council and Agriculture or Finance Ministers, for example, attend the specialist Councils.

Article 202 (old 145) imposes on the Council of Ministers the duty of ensuring the coordination of the general economic policies of the Member States, and confers upon it the power to take decisions and to delegate to the Commission.

The Council has the final power of decision for the adoption of legislative proposals made by the Commission except in matters governed by the co-decision procedure which provides the European Parliament (EP) with a final right of veto, as outlined under Art 251 (old 189b) of the EC Treaty and considered below in the section on legislative procedures. Depending on the particular treaty provision under which legislation is enacted, it may have to consult the EP and the Economic and Social Committee and/or the Committee of the Regions, or following the measures introduced by the SEA, TEU and the Treaty of Amsterdam, co-operate or co-decide with the EP. It reaches its decisions by voting, but the majority required differs depending on which treaty article the legislative proposal is based. Article 205 (old 148) provides for a simple majority, a qualified majority or unanimous voting. In 1965, the Council was due to move from unanimity in all cases to qualified majority voting, often shortened to QMV, for certain subject areas of the Treaty. This was objected to by President de Gaulle of France and the ensuing dispute led eventually to a boycott of the institutions by the French members. It was only resolved when a compromise, called the Luxembourg Accords or Luxembourg Compromise was reached. This was essentially an agreement to disagree but provided that, where a Member State identified a very important national interest, all the Member States should try to reach a unanimous decision, rather than that Member be overruled. The six Member States could not, however, agree on the consequence of a failure to agree but the conclusion, which was certainly that of the French and generally accepted, was that an objecting member state effectively had a veto over the decision. The legal position of the Accords was uncertain, but despite the provision in the Treaty for majority and qualified majority voting, the Council denied itself for many years this ability. Successive enlargements and the difficulties in reaching a consensus led the Council to realise that it could no longer make progress only using unanimity. Thus, particularly after the Treaty revisions of the SEA and TEU, the Council has moved slowly but significantly to using QMV in more and more areas. So much so, that the continued validity of the Luxembourg Accords had been brought into doubt. However, the Treaty of Amsterdam appears to have not just revived the possibility of the Accords being a valid agreement on which to rely, but to provide the essence of the Luxembourg compromise with a firm foundation within the EC Treaty. Article 11(2) (old 5a(2)) provides that if a Member State, for important and stated reasons of national policy, objects to the other Member States seeking to pursue a matter of closer cooperation, the Council shall not take a vote on that matter but may request that the matter be referred to the European Council for a decision by unanimity. At present it is impossible to tell what effect this provision will have or indeed if it will ever be used. For the moment QMV is being slowly extended and it is proposed for the next IGC in 2000 that it be extended further.

QMV works as follows. Article 205 (old 148) provides that each Member State has a number of votes crudely in proportion to the size of the population. France, Germany, Italy and the UK have ten; Spain eight; Belgium, Greece, the Netherlands and Portugal five; Austria and Sweden four; Denmark, Ireland and Finland three; and Luxembourg two. It doesn't take much to realise that Luxembourg with a population of c. 600,000 and two votes fares much better than Germany with a population of c. 81 million and 10 votes. This system was due to be revised for the Treaty of Amsterdam but the decision was put off until the next ICG. In voting under QMV, rather than a simple majority of States being able to pass a decision, a certain majority of votes has to be achieved from the combination of the blocks of votes of the Member States. The qualified majority is 62 votes from a possible total of 87. If voting on a proposal which has been introduced by the Council rather than the Commission, a minimum of 10 Member States must have voted in favour. A blocking majority of 26 votes will prevent a proposal from being passed.

Unfortunately, a further gloss must be added to the voting systems because prior to the last enlargement, the UK and initially Spain became concerned that with a greater number of States, a blocking minority would be harder to achieve as it required more votes and thus more countries. Thus, another voting compromise was agreed at the European Summit held in Ioannina in Greece (and now called the Ioannina Compromise). This provides that if a proposed legislative measure is opposed by Member States having between 23 and 25 votes, the Member States must try to reach an agreement, regardless of what the Treaty actually says, by a minimum of 65 votes. That is rather than the 62 only as required formally by the Treaty. This compromise too has now been formalised in the Community legal order both in a 1994 Decision (1994 OJ L105/1, as amended) and in a declaration attached to the Final Act of the Treaty of Amsterdam. This too will be subject to revision at the next IGC. Hence then two compromises have to be taken into account when considering the voting system of the Council.

Apart from the form of voting which is specified in particular articles throughout the Treaty, the Council also has general powers to enact legislation. Article 93 (old 99) empowers the Council of Ministers, acting unanimously to adopt provisions for the harmonisation of legislation concerning turnover taxes, excise duties and other forms of indirect taxes (VAT) to the extent that such harmonisation is necessary to ensure the functioning and establishment of the internal market. Article 94 (old 100) provides for the approximation of laws not catered for by any of the specific parts of the Treaty and requires unanimity by the Council and Art 95 (old 100a), originally introduced by the SEA, provides that the Council shall act by a qualified majority on proposals which have as their object the establishment and functioning of the internal market. Article 308 (old 235) provides that the Council may enact measures to attain the objectives of the Community. Both the TEU and the Treaty of Amsterdam have extended the Treaty articles which require QMV rather than unanimity on the part of the Council.

In matters coming within the second and third pillars of the Union, the Council votes by unanimity but with the allowance under Justice and Home Affairs matters that some Member States may abstain from the vote but equally not be bound by the agreed measure.

In order to assist the work of the Council, which does not meet permanently, the Committee of Permanent Representatives (COREPER) was established, consisting of representatives of the Member States who may be part of the ambassadorial delegation or other civil servants on secondment (see Art 207 (old 151) EC). This body was brought in to reduce the workload of the Council, to balance the result of the delegation of decision making power to the Commission and to sift the Commission proposals. Additionally, Management Committees were also set up to supervise the delegation of power to the Commission, and are considered in further detail below. Furthermore, the TEU made formal the existence and position of the general secretariat to the Council under Art 207(2) (old 151(2)) EC.

The Council of Ministers is chaired by a Presidency which is held by each of the Member States in turn, as determined by Council Decision 95/2. Thus ministers from these and the head of government or State chairs the Council meetings or summit for a period of six months. You may come across the term *Troika* used in conjunction with the Council. This merely describes the situation where to provide continuity in policy, the current President and both the previous and succeeding Presidents act in conjunction, particularly in the pursuit of international relations.

The European Council   The European Council, which is not an institution of the Union, arose from the summit meetings of the heads of state and government of the Member States, who met from time to time to discuss matters outside the formal scope of the Community treaties and provide impetus for the Community or act in response to international crises.

Article 2 SEA placed the European Council on a legal basis and formalised European political cooperation in the areas of foreign policy consultation and cooperation and monetary cooperation.

These moves have been further formalised and brought into the European Union framework by Art 4 (old D) of the Maastricht Treaty, which states that the European Council shall provide the Union with the necessary impetus for its development and shall define the general political guidelines. The European Council will now be required to meet twice a year to discuss the progress of the union and to report to the EP on an annual basis. Whilst it could, the practice is that it does not act as the Council of Ministers of the EC.

Decision making by the European Council is strictly by unanimity as it is purely an intergovernmental organisation. The European Council formally appoints the Presidents of the Commission and the European Central Bank. The President of the Commission now attends European Council meetings.

The Commission

The Commission, the executive of the Community, was given the sole right as the proposer of legislation under the original treaties, although this was in effect partially circumvented by the Council and European Council. It has its own powers of decision-making, under Arts 81 and 86 (old 85 and 90) and is able to exercise powers delegated to it by the Council of Ministers, now regulated by Decision 87/373.

The composition, tasks and functions of the Commission are determined by Arts 211–219 (old 155–163) EC. It presently consists of 20 members, made up of two from France, Germany, Italy, Spain and the United Kingdom, and one each from the other Member States. The Commission President is nominated unanimously by the Member States and subject to EP approval. The President and the Member States then nominate the other 19 Commissioners and the entire Commission is then subject to the approval of the EP (see Art 214 (old 158)). The term of office is for a renewable period of five years. They are required to act independently (Art 213 (old 157)). Following the TEU, only one or two Vice-Presidents can be elected. The Commission can be removed by a vote of censure by the EP but only collectively (Art 201 (old 144)). The method of appointment of the Commission was revised under the Treaty of Amsterdam, as noted above, but was employed before coming into force by the European Council when the entire Commission resigned on 15 March 1999 following a damning report of an independent Committee of experts appointed by the EP. This exposed serious fraud, cronyism and incompetence on the part of individual Commissioners. Resignation of the entire Commission was the only way to oust the culpable Commissioners. A new Commission was approved by the EP in September 1999.

Although no further reform has yet taken place, a Protocol was attached to the Treaty of Amsterdam which proposed to limit to one the number of Commissioners from each State. It is now likely to be subject to more extensive reform than previously proposed.

The Commission has four main tasks. Article 211 (old 155) imposes the general duty of ensuring the proper functioning and development of the common market and the following four specific duties:

(a)   To ensure that the provisions of the Treaty and the measures taken by the institutions under them are applied. The Commission is described as the guardian or watch-dog of the Communities, because it is given the task of prosecuting breaches of the Treaty by Member States under Art 226 (old 169), by other institutions under Art 230 (old 173), and by individuals under various provisions of the Treaty and secondary legislation, e.g., Regulation 17 in respect of competition.

(b)   To formulate recommendations or deliver opinions on matters dealt with in the Treaty, if it expressly so provides or if the Commission considers it necessary. Here the Commission is acting as the initiator of legislation.

(c)   To have its own power of decision and to participate in the shaping of measures taken by the Council of Ministers and by the EP in the manner provided for in the Treaty, as a legislator under delegated powers.

(d)   To exercise the powers conferred on it by the Council of Ministers for the implementation of the rules laid down by the latter, thus acting as the executive of the Communities.

The Commission is regarded as the most federal institution of the EC, due largely to its independence from direct national influences.

The European Parliament

Originally this was called the Assembly and consisted of members nominated from the Member State governments. It was arguably more aptly named at that time, because it is not a true parliament consisting of two chambers and a head of state but is only one chamber. However, the term 'Parliament' was used by its members from an early date, and particularly following the direct election of its 518 members for the first time in 1979. The term arguably carries more prestige and attracts greater respect from the public. Consequently the SEA, in Art 3(1), provided legal recognition of the Assembly's decision to call itself the European Parliament, and this is clearly confirmed by Art 189 (old 137) EC, as amended. The EP is governed by Arts 189–201 (old 137–144) of the EC Treaty and has enjoyed a significant increase in its powers and functions under the Maastricht Treaty and more limited changes under the Treaty of Amsterdam.

Legislative powers   Before the SEA, the EP had largely advisory and consultative powers under old Art 137 EEC, which provided that the Assembly 'shall exercise the advisory and supervisory powers which are conferred on it by this Treaty'. The Treaty specified only 17 instances where the EP had to be consulted. Under its advisory role, certain provisions of the Treaty required that the EP be consulted before a decision could be adopted by the Council (see old Arts 54 and 235 EEC). Its participation in the legislative process was increased by the conciliation procedure of 1977, the introduction of the cooperation procedure by the SEA and by the introduction of the co-decision or parliamentary veto procedure under Art 251 (old 189b) EC by the TEU, considered separately below. The assent of the EP is a prerequisite to the accession of new Member States and to the entry of the Community into international and association agreements (Arts 300, 310 (old 228, 238) EC and Art 49 (old O) TEU). However, its legislative role is still limited, to such an extent that the term 'democratic deficit' is used to describe this state of affairs. (But see the Maastricht and Amsterdam changes, below.)

Control of the Executive   The EP also has a general role in the scrutiny of the work of the Council and Commission by its ability to question the Commission under Art 197 (old 140) and through discussion of the Commission's reports under Art 200 (old 143). It is able to censure the Commission by a two-thirds majority vote to remove the Commission, but only in its entirety and not individual Commissioners (Art 201 (old 144)). The Treaty of Amsterdam now requires that the nominated President of the Commission is approved by the EP and then the whole Commission as nominated by the Member States in conjunction with the President of the Commission is subject to the approval of the EP (see Art 214 (old 158)). Following the pressured resignation of the Commission in March 1999 and the appointment of a new Commission under this procedure in September 1999, this could well be an area subject to further control after the next IGC. Until the new Commissioners are approved, the censured Commissioners remain in office.

Budgetary powers   The EP had more extensive budgetary powers under the Budgetary Treaty of 1975, which gave the Parliament a greater say over the Community's budget, including the power to reject it, which it did in 1979 and 1984 (see Art 272 (old 203) and text below). The 1979 rejection was partly the consequence of the increase in democratic legitimacy gained by the EP as a result of being directly elected in that year for the first time.

Rights to litigate   Although the EP was not named as one of the privileged applicants for the purposes of taking actions under Arts 230 and 232 (old 173 and 175) EC, the Court of Justice has held in the 'Transport' case (*European Parliament v Council*) that it is able to bring an action for failure to act under Art 232 (old 175); and while it does not have a general right of challenge under Art 230 (old 173) (*European Parliament v Council (Comitology)*), it has the right to take action to protect its own prerogative powers (*European Parliament v Council (Chernobyl)* and *European Parliament v Council (Students Residence Directive)*). This latter right is now confirmed in the amended Act 230 (old 173) EC. Acts of the EP can also be challenged under Art 230 (old 173) (see *Les Verts v European Parliament* and *Council v European Parliament (Budgetary Procedure)*). The TEU has also amended Arts 230 and 232 (old 173 and 175) to specify that the acts or omissions of the EP can be challenged under the usual conditions.

In Edinburgh, December 1992, the European Council agreed to increase the number of members of the European Parliament to 567 from 1994 to reflect German unification and in the light of the enlargement of the Community by the entry of Austria, Finland and Sweden, it has been increased to 626. This remains the number of Members of the European Parliament (MEPs) presently but the Member States agreed in the Amsterdam Treaty, with an eye on the situation following the next expansion, to set the number of MEPs to a maximum of 700. As a result Art 189 (old 137) was amended.

The TEU gave the EP a more extensive role in the legislative process. Article 192 (old 138b) empowers it to take part in the adoption of Community Acts, under Art 251 (old 189b) by giving its consent (co-decision) or under Art 252 (old 189c) by delivering an advisory opinion (cooperation). It also entitles it to request the Commission to submit proposals which the EP considers necessary for the implementation of the EC Treaty (Art 192 (old 138b)). Art 190(4) (old 138(3)) requires a common system of election to be set up for the election of the next EP. While all Member States, including the UK, have used PR voting systems, this is still not a common system. Under Art 193 (old 138c), the EP may also set up, on the vote of a quarter of its members, a temporary watch-dog committee of inquiry to investigate alleged contraventions or maladministration in the implementation of Community law, except where the matter is *sub judice*. Article 194 (old 138d) formalises the right of Community citizens to petition the EP. Article 195 (old 138e) provides the right of Community citizens to complain to an ombudsman, appointed by the EP, about the maladministration of the Community institutions, with the exception of the judicial activities of the Community courts.

These additional powers should go some small way towards correcting the democratic deficit in the Community mentioned above. However, the EP has been given additional tasks under the EU third pillar but these are rights to be consulted only on legislative proposals made by the Member States (see Arts 39 and 42 (old K.11 and K.14) TEU). A protocol to the Treaty of Amsterdam seems also to have settled the vexed question of the seat of the EP but probably only to the satisfaction of the Member States directly involved. The EP is destined to be forever in transit between the plenary sessions in Strasbourg and Brussels and its secretariat in Luxembourg.

The European Court of Justice

Composition and general functions Article 220 (old 164) EC outlines the general function of the European Court of Justice (ECJ), which is to ensure that in the interpretation and application of the Treaty the law is observed. Originally this court had exclusive jurisdiction over Community law but it has now been joined by the Court of First Instance.

The Court of Justice, which has its seat in Luxembourg, consists of 15 judges and eight advocates-general, although up to October 2000 it has nine advocates-general. These are nominated and appointed by unanimous agreement by the governments of the Member States. They must be chosen from persons whose independence is beyond doubt and who possess the qualifications required for appointment to the highest judicial office in their own countries (Arts 221–223 (old 165–167)).

Judgments of the Court of Justice are delivered in a single ruling, and Art 2 of the Statute of the Court provides that before taking up judicial office, each judge shall, in open court, take an oath to preserve the secrecy of the Court's deliberations. Arguments in favour of the single opinion of the Court are that it supports the authority of the Community Court and the new legal system. It helps to build up a new European law and avoids reliance on the laws of particular States. It also provides for more authoritative decision-making for the future. Arguments against are that it often results in terse and cryptic judgments, with little evidence of reasoning, it stifles true legal argument, and it may inhibit judges and the development of law. To some extent these criticisms may be countered by the provision and activity of advocates-general.

The role of the advocates-general is to assist the Court by giving an opinion, with complete independence and impartiality, on the legal issues of a case which will be examined in depth, and to review critically the jurisprudence of the Court on the subject. It is a mandatory requirement that the opinion of an advocate-general be heard before judgment is given. Although this opinion is not binding on the Court, it carries weight and adds to the development of Community law. Thus an opinion of the advocate-general acts like a first instance decision, subject to an automatic and instant appeal. The advocates-general can adopt a public view or the parties' views but cannot be bound to present any particular view.

The Court has been divided into chambers of three, five or seven judges to help expedite the business of the court (Art 221 (old 165)).

The TEU introduced an amended Art 221 (old 165) which reduces the occasions when the Court may need to sit in plenary session, i.e., when a Member State or Community institution that is a party to an action requests plenary jurisdiction.

Jurisdiction   The Court's jurisdiction is limited by the treaties to the area of the Member States and to giving interpretations on disputed rules under the EEA Treaty and opinions on proposed international agreements and Treaties. A judgment of the Court can have consequences and effects outside that area, e.g., *ICI* v *Commission (Dyestuffs)* in which the ICI head office, then outside the territory of the Community, was fined through subsidiaries based in the EEC.

The Court's jurisdiction can be divided in a number of ways. One way is to look at the broad types of actions available under Community law and adjudicated by the Court. This also considers the parties to the actions. Here three main categories can be established. One considering actions taken against the Member States, then actions concerned with the review of acts of the Community institutions and a third category consisting the preliminary rulings under Art 234 (old 177) of the Treaty. Certain other aspects of the Court's work, such as interim measures and appeals from the Court of First Instance stand outside of such a division and have to be considered separately. One can also consider the way in which the Court is acting, such as a constitutional court when considering the powers of the institutions and Member States or the relations between them. It acts as an administrative court in cases of judicial review of acts of the institutions. It acts as an appeal court in hearing cases from the Court of First Instance. It also acts to determine the scale of fines against those offending competition law and also the Member States when they breach Community law obligations and as such therefore acts as a kind of criminal law court.

The jurisdiction can also be divided into the following two categories:

(a)   direct judicial control, whereby the Court interprets a rule and applies it to decide the case itself; and

(b)   indirect judicial control, whereby the court interprets and rules on the validity of provisions, not the subject of a direct action before the Court.

This jurisdiction is mainly concerned with ruling on matters at the request of national courts.

Direct actions are also termed 'the contentious jurisdiction' of the Court. The Court ensures the legal exercise of the Community legislative and executive powers by the Community institutions by Arts 230–232 (old 173–175) and by Art 241 (old 184), concerning the judicial review of legally binding acts. The Court ensures respect of the Community obligations by the Member States via Arts 226–228 (old 169–171), and by individuals via various articles scattered throughout the Treaty, e.g., Art 83(2)(a) (old 87(2)(a)) and Regulation 17/62 concerned with competition policy. Articles 235 and 288 (old 178 and 215), second paragraph, confer non-contractual (delictual) jurisdiction, and Art 236 (old 179) gives the Court of Justice jurisdiction over staff cases. The Court may exercise preventative judicial control to block the conclusion of an envisaged agreement between the Community and a third state or an international organisation, if it is considered incompatible with the EC Treaty (Art 300 (old 228)). It can also be called upon to adjudicate in contractual disputes between Community institutions and contractual partners if called to do so under an arbitration clause in a contract (Art 238 (old 181)).

Indirect judicial control is exercised by the preliminary ruling proceeding of Art 234 (old 177), whereby references are made from the courts of the Member States, and under Art 241 (old 184) for applications by individuals before either the national courts or the Court of Justice.

Finally, the Court's jurisdiction has been extended by the Treaty of Amsterdam and it has been given the power to consider disputes arising between Member States under the third pillar of the Union. Member States may also decide whether to accept the court's jurisdiction to accept preliminary rulings on limited aspects of the decisions and measures taken under that pillar (see Art 35 (old K.7) TEU).

Interpretation   The European treaties and some of the secondary legislation are framework measures which often require considerable amplification and interpretation. This has given a wide scope to the Court of Justice to engage in judicial activism. Notable judgments are those concerned with what are now fundamental decisions of the Court including direct effects, supremacy and the liability of the Member States. Hence, the Court has played a crucial role in the development of the Community legal order and the Communities themselves.

The style of interpretation is described as 'teleological', in that the Court tries to determine, in the light of the aims and objectives of the treaties and legislation, what was intended and what result would assist those goals. The Court often refers to the 'spirit' of the Treaty and Community to come to a particular conclusion. These methods are applied in addition to the usual array of methods of interpretation found in the Member States' legal systems.

The Court of Justice often refers to the Preamble and general provisions of the Treaty to assist it in reaching decisions, notably Arts 2, 3, 10 (old 5) and 12 (old 6).

Precedent   While there is no formal system of precedent, the Court tries, as do courts in civil law jurisdictions, to maintain consistency in its judgments. Past decisions are often cited in court, and do therefore carry some persuasive, rather than any formal, authority.

The Court of First Instance

The SEA provided for the setting up of a Court of First Instance (CFI) to relieve the case load of the Court of Justice (now governed under Art 225 (old 168a) EC with the detailed rules provided in Decision 88/591). The Court of First Instance has 15 members, one of whom may act as an advocate-general where considered necessary in complex cases. The Court is divided into chambers of three and five judges. In 1999, it decided that for simple cases a single judge could decide the matter.

The Court of First Instance commenced operation on 1 September 1989. Its jurisdiction was initially limited to the areas of staff cases, actions under Arts 50 and 57 to 66 ECSC, actions against the Community institutions arising under Arts 230 and 232 (old 173 and 175), and competition policy. It has now been expanded by the TEU under Art 225 (old 168a) EC to allow any area of jurisdiction to be transferred with the exception of Art 234 (old 177) references. By Council Decisions 93/350 and 94/149 jurisdiction has been extended to hear all actions brought by natural and legal persons and related damages claims under Arts 230 and 232 (old 173 and 175). The procedure allows appeals on points of law only to the Court of Justice. Three grounds are given:

(a)   lack of competence by the court;

(b)   breach of procedure; and

(c)   the infringement of a Community provision or rule of law by the Court, or an error in the interpretation or application of law.

Despite the optimism and low numbers of appeals in the early years, the continued increase in the numbers of cases being lodged at the CFI and the large numbers of cases which were transferred to it by the Court of Justice, the overall backlog of cases pending judgment before the CFI and the Court of Justice has increased dramatically. In 1998, there were over 1,000 cases pending before the CFI and another 300 plus before the Court of Justice. Exacerbating this problem is the increase in the time taken to reach judgment in all types of action. Clearly, further and more radical reform of the Court and its rules is needed. The Member States, however, declined to transfer the power to amend these to the Court when the Treaty of Amsterdam was being negotiated.

THE LEGISLATIVE PROCESS

In order to try to resolve various problem areas, such as the democratic deficit, expansion of Member States and voting arrangements in the Council, there have been a number of Treaty amendments both increasing and complicating the legislative procedures. The Treaty of Amsterdam has, at last, made an attempt to rein in the prolixity and complexity of these procedures. Some time will be required to see if the emergent picture is any clearer.

The Original Consultation Procedure

A limited number of Treaty articles (17) provided that the Council was required to consult the EP before coming to a decision on Community secondary law. However, on receipt of that opinion the Council could proceed to ignore it and override any view given by the EP. In *Roquette* and *Maizena* v *Council* in 1980, the Court of Justice annulled a regulation because the Council had failed to consult or obtain the opinion of the EP before it passed the legislation. Furthermore, in *European Parliament* v *Council* (1992), the Court annulled a regulation which had been amended by the Council without a further consultation of the EP taking place. This procedure only applies now to the C.A.P. and non-express powers under Art 308 (old 235).

The Conciliation Procedure

This was introduced by the Joint Declaration of the Council, Commission and EP in 1975, as a result of the view that although the EP had no say over compulsory expenditure in the budget, it should nevertheless be given an opportunity to participate in the decisions concerning substantial compulsory expenditure. The procedure can be enacted by either the EP or the Council. The EP is able to give its opinion, but this may be disregarded by the Council. Whilst it still may exist on paper, it no longer features as a legislative process.

The Cooperation Procedure

This was introduced under Arts 6 and 7 SEA, which amended the old Art 149 EEC to establish a form of first and second reading and set time limits for the process of legislation in the policy areas noted above, largely affecting the internal market. Under the TEU this was re-enacted under Art 252 (old 189c) EC and is of far less importance now under the Treaty of Amsterdam.

After the Council has received a proposal from the Commission and the opinion of the EP, it adopts a common position on the basis of a qualified majority vote (Art 205 (old 148) EC: 62 out of a total of 87 votes). Then, rather than proceed immediately to decide on the matter, as it would have done under the old consultation procedure, this common position is sent to the EP which has three months in which to act. It can approve the proposal, do nothing — in which case the Council can adopt the common position by a simple majority vote — or reject the common position. Where the EP rejects it the Council can nevertheless adopt it, but only if it does so within three months and by a unanimous vote. Lastly, if the EP makes amendments, the Commission must re-examine the proposal and resubmit it to the Council within one month. The Council then has three months to act. It can adopt it by a qualified majority, amend it by unanimity, or do nothing (in which case the proposed measure will lapse). This complex procedure was the subject of much criticism. At Amsterdam, the Member States agreed to transfer all policy areas under this procedure to the co-decision procedure, with the exception of EMU which was beyond the remit of discussions and thus amendment at Amsterdam.

The Co-Decision Procedure

Article 249 (old 189) EC has been amended by the TEU to provide that the EP shall act jointly with the Council and Commission in the legislative process. Extended into many more areas and simplified by the Treaty of Amsterdam, this is now the most often employed legislative procedure in the Treaty.

The Art 251 (old 189b) co-decision procedure, ultimately allows the EP to reject a legislative proposal. After the EP has given its opinion on a legislative proposal, the Treaty of Amsterdam now allows it to be adopted if the EP has proposed no amendments or the Council accepts any amendments, otherwise the Council shall adopt a common position by a qualified majority. The EP can, within three months, either approve it or take no decision, in which case the Council can adopt the measure. Alternatively, the EP can reject or amend the proposal by an absolute majority. If it amends the proposal, the Council can, within three months, approve those amendments by a qualified majority; but if the Commission has issued a negative opinion on the amendments, the Council can only approve by unanimity. If the Council does not accept the amended proposal the matter is referred to a new Conciliation Committee to attempt to achieve a compromise within six weeks. If a joint text is approved, the Council and EP may adopt the provision together within six weeks. If there is no agreement, the Council must confirm its position within six weeks and the EP may finally reject it within six weeks by an absolute majority. The Council no longer has the power to override the EP at the last stage but ultimately the EP can veto legislation only rather than force its opinion through.

The Assent Procedure

This was introduced by the SEA whereby the EP's assent is required by the Council in respect of membership applications to the EU and international and association agreements: Art 49 (old O) TEU and Arts 310 and 300(3) (old 238 and 228(3)). In the event of disagreement, the EP has a veto.

THE LEGAL BASE FOR LEGISLATIVE PROPOSALS

The legal base used for legislation is fundamental to the relative powers and ability of the other institutions to affect the content of Community law because it decides which of the above legislative procedures must be used. The use of qualified majority voting in the Council of Ministers is extremely important to the Commission, which stands a better chance of having proposals accepted by a majority rather than by all Member States. The extreme views can thus be ignored rather than taken into account at the draft stages.

The legal base is also vital to the level of participation of the EP in the legislative process. These consequences result because it is possible to base measures on more than one Treaty provision, due to the fact that the subject-matter can straddle different areas of the Treaty. Hence, there is clear ground for differences of opinion as to which is the correct Treaty base to use. The EP has not refrained from challenging the Council for the use of the incorrect legal base and regularly brings cases before the Court of Justice (see e.g., *European Parliament v Council* (case 22/96)). However, given the simplification of the legislative procedures by the Treaty of Amsterdam and the change of legal bases for many provisions in favour of the EP, it might not be such an important issue in the future.

Measures for the single market require majority voting in the Council. Therefore, the Commission is trying to exploit the provisions of the Treaty by introducing as much legislation as possible under Art 95 (old 100a), whereas the Council has argued the proposals should have as their legal base other articles requiring unanimity. See, as an early example and one likely to be in materials books, the case of *UK v Council* (the 'Hormones' case), concerned with the old Art 100 which required unanimity and old

Art 43 under which the measure was adopted requiring only a qualified majority. This was objected to by the UK but held to be appropriate by the Court of Justice.

In the 1992 case of *European Parliament v Council*, the EP successfully challenged the adoption of Directive 90/366 on the residence of students, which the Council adopted under Art 308 (old 235) (requiring only consultation) rather than under old Art 7 (which would require the cooperation procedure to be used). The Directive was annulled and has been re-enacted.

A further case to focus on the issues raised above is *Commission v Council (Re Titanium Dioxide Directive)*. The Council adopted a directive on the basis of the old Art 130s (now 175) as an environmental measure, which then required unanimity and only consultation of the EP, despite the protests of the EP at the time. The Commission argued it should have been adopted using old Art 100a (now 95) as a single market measure, which then required QMV and the cooperation procedure instead. While the Court of Justice acknowledged that both could be a valid base, the use of old Art 130s instead of old Art 100a deprived the EP of its greater role in the legislative process. Even if both were used, as suggested by the Council, it would still have to decide unanimously and thus overrule any opinion objections of the EP.

In a similar challenge, in *Commission v Council (Waste Directive)* (case C-155/91), to a waste Directive 91/156, adopted under old Art 130s (now 175) by the Council, the Commission challenged it on the basis that Art 100a (now 95), in respect of the internal market, should have been used as the legal base. On this occasion, the Court disagreed and held that the protection of the environment stated in the Directive was the real reason and not the free movement of waste. Therefore, the challenge by the Commission was rejected.

A further case concerned the adoption by the Council, in June 1993, of a Directive specifying a maximum working week, albeit with the ability of workers to work longer voluntarily. The UK, which was opposed to this, was unable to veto the proposal as it was introduced under the Health and Safety of Workers provision under the old Art 118a (now 138) of the EEC Treaty, which required only a qualified majority in the Council. The UK formally requested the ECJ in April 1994 to annul the Directive in *UK v Council* (case C-84/94), arguing that it would have been more appropriate to base the measure on Art 308 (old 235) or 94 (old 100) either of which would have required unanimity on the part of the Council thus allowing the UK the chance to veto the measure. The Court of Justice was, however, satisfied with the choice of old Art 118a.

The view of the Court of Justice is essentially that the democratic process which now involves the EP demands that where two legal bases are available requiring differing procedures, the one allowing the EP the greater role must be used so as not to deprive the EP and the Community of its democratic right, unless it can be shown the matter is primarily more concerned with a particular Treaty base.

DELEGATION

Prior to the SEA, the only article of the EEC Treaty which dealt with delegation was Art 211 (old 155), which provided: 'In order to ensure the proper functioning and development of the common market, the Commission shall . . . exercise the powers conferred on it by the Council for the implementation of the rules laid down by the latter.'

Delegation can be in the form of wide discretionary powers, and may include legislative as well as administrative regulations and directives. It may, however, be subject to confirmation or limits, or to rules laid down by the delegating authority, or the delegating authority may retain the right to rescind the decision. This last right is usually subject to a time limit within which the delegating authority must act. A system of committees was set up to supervise the exercise of delegated power, whereby the Council has retained control over the delegated power.

Delegation and the management committees were considered by the Court of Justice as early as 1958. In *Meroni v High Authority*, the Court stressed the necessity of preserving the balance of power in the institutional structure of the Communities as envisaged by the Treaties, and which would therefore not allow the delegation of discretionary powers involving policy decisions. In the *Koster* case of 1972, the delegation to the Commission under the management committee procedure was challenged, it being alleged that the procedure disturbed the institutional balance of the Community contrary to the Treaty and undermined the independence of the Commission. The Court of Justice observed the management committee could not itself take decisions but merely gave options of implementation, therefore the power balance was not disturbed. Thus, provided the empowering legislation is adopted by the procedures envisaged by the Treaty, the details can be delegated to the Commission. The Court of Justice further held in the case of *Rey Soda* of 1975 that implementing powers under Art 211 (old 155) must be interpreted widely, especially under the common agricultural policy where actions must often be taken on a day-to-day basis.

SEA Amendments

The SEA amended Art 202 (old 145) EEC by adding a third indent, which provided that 'The Council may impose certain requirements in respect of the exercise of these powers', and further provided the Council's right to reserve to itself implementing powers. Consequent on this, Decision 373/87, known as the 'Comitology Decision', was adopted to determine principles and rules governing the system of management committees. The Decision provides for three standard committee types: advisory committees, management committees (which have two procedural variants providing greater powers of decision for the Commission) and regulatory committees (which require positive approval of the decisions by the committee). The committees consist of representatives of the Member States and a non-voting Commission chair.

In the case of *Commission v Council* (case 16/88), concerning the Commission's power of implementation under Art 274 (old 205), the Council delegated power to conclude certain contracts to the Commission, subject to a management committee procedure. The Commission argued that implementation under Art 274 (old 205) concerning budgetary procedure was not subject to management committees. The Court of Justice held that as the powers were also legislative in character, they were validly subject to the management committee procedures.

It is argued that since the formalisation of the procedure, too much power has been given to the committees and is consequently lost from the Commission and EP. The system allows the Council to withdraw delegated powers at any time when decided by the committee. The EP attempted to challenge the 'Comitology Decision' *European Parliament v Council* (case 302/87), particularly because the Council failed to state in which circumstances particular procedures would apply, but the challenge failed due to inadmissibility of the direct challenge by the EP.

The Commission has further powers of its own under Art 81(3) (old 85(3)) competition law exemptions and Art 86 (old 90) State aids.

THE BUDGETARY PROCESS

As a result of the delay of the introduction of the system of own resources owing to the objections of French President de Gaulle in 1965–66, own resources and a revised budgetary procedure were not introduced until 1970, when the EP was given the last word on non-compulsory expenditure. The procedure for determining expenditure is governed by Arts 272 and 273 (old 203 and 204) EC, as amended by the Budgetary Treaty of 1975 and the Council Decision of 1994 (94/728) on own resources and Council Decision 94/729 on Budgetary Discipline. Two forms of expenditure are categorised: compulsory and non-compulsory. Compulsory expenditure is that automatically arising from or forming the inevitable consequence of Treaty obligations to third parties. Non-compulsory expenditure covers the expenditure required in respect of the institutions and that which is not obligatory under the Treaty, and largely applies to the social and regional funds.

The Procedure

The Commission proposes the first draft and the maximum increase for non-compulsory expenditure, which the Council and EP are unable to exceed. The Council then prepares the draft budget by a qualified majority. It is sent to the EP, who may approve it within 45 days, in which case it will be adopted. Alternatively, the EP can modify or amend the non-compulsory expenditure in the draft and return it to the Council.

Modifications can be made by the EP in respect of compulsory expenditure, which can be rejected by the Council by a qualified majority. Ultimately, however, the EP cannot interfere with compulsory expenditure which includes the common agricultural policy and thus consumes between 65 to 80 per cent of the total budget.

Amendments can be made by a majority to non-compulsory expenditure such as the regional and social funds. These draft budgets can be modified by the Council by a qualified majority within 15 days. The draft is returned to the EP, which can modify it within 15 days by a majority and at least three-fifths voting. The EP can then either adopt or reject the budget under Art 272(8) (old 203(8)), as it did in 1979 following the direct elections and again in 1984. In such cases the one-twelfth rule automatically applies until the dispute is resolved, whereby the Commission is provided with one-twelfth of the previous year's money per month.

OTHER COMMUNITY BODIES

The Court of Auditors

Expenditure is audited by a special body — the Court of Auditors — established under the 1975 Budgetary Treaty and Art 276 (old 206) EC. It is required to give the Commission a discharge if the expenditure is correct (Art 276 (old 206)).

The TEU promotes this body to a full institution of the Community under Arts 7 (old 4) and 246–248 (old 188a to 188c) EC.

The Economic and Social Committee

This was introduced to serve in an advisory role to represent various sectional interests, such as consumer groups, trade unions, education, and must be consulted for the adoption of certain legislation as determined by the Treaty, although its opinion once received may be safely ignored by the Council. Its members are appointed in a personal capacity along national lines by the Council. It is governed by Arts 7 (old 4) and 257–261 (old 193–197) EC.

The Committee of the Regions

Established by the TEU (Arts 263–265 (old 198a–198c) EC), this is also an advisory body set up to represent regional and local bodies which must be consulted for the enactment of certain legislation (see Arts 149, 151 and 157 (old 126, 128 and 130) EC).

QUESTIONS

This chapter, in dealing with such a wide range of subjects, inevitably gives rise to a very wide area of questions, the particular type of which will be determined by the emphasis given to the topics in your courses. I have sought, therefore, to include only sample questions and framework answers to cover these areas. Direct questions on the history and development of the Communities would be rare, because the answers could only be very descriptive and not, therefore, particularly suitable for the level of examination you are taking. Questions tend to be concentrated on the institutions, and in particular on the interrelationship of these institutions in the legislative and other processes of the Community. However, depending on the treatment in your course, a question along the lines of the first one here may be asked.

1.   Explain Britain's changing attitude to the Communities.

This is looking for a historical analysis, not just of Britain's attitude but also of the developments of the Communities as well. Britain's attitude originally was a direct response to the setting-up of the Community, and as developments took place to the Communities, so further reactions from Britain were prompted.

The answer could be divided into time periods to help in the presentation; however, such divisions are often artificial, and which the facts do not always fit comfortably into them. Periods could include the 1950s and the setting-up of the Community; the 1960s and Britain's failed application attempts; the 1970s when Britain entered but had second thoughts; and the 1980s to date and the intermittently hostile relations of the UK with the rest of Europe but some movement closer together as a result of the landslide Labour victory in the May 1997 General Election.

The answer should thus include a brief outline of the setting-up and the historical developments of the Communities and, in particular, the reasons for this, e.g., the economic reconstruction of Europe following the Second World War, the elimination of harmful national jealousies spurred on by economic competition, and the promotion of economic and political stability, especially in the face of the rising Soviet threat. The establishment of the Communities was not intended to exclude the UK, and should not have done so except that the UK chose not to participate at this stage. You should highlight the views expressed by the British Prime Minister, Winston Churchill, at the end of the war and then the reasons why Britain declined to take part, e.g., the Empire and Commonwealth, its perceived world role, the Atlantic alliance, trade patterns. Once the Communities had been formed, it did prompt Britain to organise the setting up of EFTA.

The next period to discuss is the later attempts of the UK to enter, the reasons for this — mainly concerned with its economic success and fortress Europe views — and the vetoes by French President de Gaulle and the reasons for these.

The UK joined in 1973, so the reason for this successful third attempt must be considered, as must the timing of the entry. In this decade the UK renegotiated entry terms and held a referendum on membership. The timing of the entry coincided with the world oil crisis and economic recession.

In the 1980s the first part of the decade was occupied with the wrangles over the British budget, which hindered progress on other matters in the Community and did not engender relaxed relations with Britain's partners in the Community. These wrangles were settled in 1984. Furthermore there has been the UK's reluctance to join the other partners in monetary union and the social policy, both of which need to be considered. Lastly, the discussions and agreements of Maastricht could be mentioned, in particular the opt-outs which were negotiated.

The change of Government in the UK on 1 May 1997 saw a change in the relationship with Europe with the new Labour Government announcing soon afterwards the intention to sign up to the social chapter, which was carried through soon afterwards, and generally to take a more participatory role in Europe. The UK opposition to monetary union seems to have been removed although uncertainty remains as to when the UK might join. Difficulties over the ban on the export of British beef products also means that the UK was unwillingly isolated in Europe. These two aspects, amongst others, do not aid the integration of the UK with the other European Union members despite the change of outlook on Europe of the UK Government. The fact that the UK will not commit itself to joining the Euro must still leave room for doubt in the minds of some, although there is certainly no serious talk of withdrawal these days.

Much of the explanation for Britain's attitude lies, naturally, in the realm of politics rather than law, in a strict sense. The degree to which this is there covered in your course will determine whether such questions will be set in an examination and the detail required in your answer.

To conclude, you could include a paragraph trying to summarise Britain's attitude over the four decades, although, it has to be said, this is no easy matter, as it is a complex of many concerns and influences. Whether Britain is a reluctant or just a hesitant partner is itself still unclear. Britain's continued attitude to the Community might provide further evidence.

2. 'As far as its legislative and budgetary procedures are concerned, the EC is neither efficient nor democratic.'

(a) What features, if any, in the powers and the decision-making procedures of the Council and European Parliament support the above statement?

(b) What reforms would you advocate which would meet these criticisms?

This question is quite complex because it is in three parts. It could easily be that the first, the quotation, could be a question in its own right. If it was, although the basis of the question and answer would be the same, the amount of emphasis or detail would need to change. I will point this out as I go through the question, as an example of how material can be adapted to suit different formulations of questions which cover the same topic area.

The first part of the question The first part can be broken down to determine what issues must be considered. You must consider the legislative and budgetary procedures, i.e., they must be described as concisely as possible because there is a lot more of the question to answer. If the first part was a full question, then you would provide a detailed description of the budgetary and legislative procedures as they are today. For the longer question, because specific features of these procedures will be considered in the answer to (b), they need only be outlined briefly at this stage.

The legislative procedure at present follows four forms including the limited power of assent — the original consultation, the cooperation first introduced by the SEA and the co-decision or parliamentary veto power introduced by the TEU. You should provide a brief summary of each one, e.g., under its advisory role, certain provisions of the EC Treaty required that the EP be consulted before a decision could be adopted by the Council (see Arts 52 (old 63) and 308 (old 235)). The *Isoglucose* cases confirmed the EP had to be consulted but that the EP's opinion can be ignored. The conciliation procedure which gives the EP an opinion on proposals involving heavy expenditure still exists on paper but cannot really be considered to be a self-standing procedure.

The co-operation and co-decision procedures are described in the text above.

The budgetary procedure is governed by Art 272 (old 203) EC, as amended by the Budgetary Treaty of 1975, and the Council Decisions of

1994 (94/728 and 94/729) on own resources should also be described in brief as noted in the text above.

Having basically described the two procedures, you must then address the issues that, in respect of the two procedures, the EC is neither efficient nor democratic. The quotation implicitly limits this to the procedures by the words 'as far as its . . . procedures are concerned'. As a full question, you must determine if this is correct by critically reviewing the procedures at this stage. The longer question requires you to do this in respect of selected features.

In respect of efficiency, you would discuss the delays in the legislative procedure, the fact that there are a number of procedures depending on the Treaty article and that the procedures are becoming more complex and — as evidence of this you could point to the stagnation of the legislative process in the 1970s and 1980s — the fact that the Council could not cope with the amount of work necessary and had to devise ways in which decision-making power could be delegated but control retained.

The question of democracy is easier to address. It clearly points to the role of the EP as the only directly elected body, but which has only a minor role in the legislative process, and to the question of delegation to committees controlled by the Council and not the EP. This whole argument is described as the 'democratic deficit' in the Community, i.e., because the EP is the only democratically elected element, in order to maintain the democratic right or justification for European laws the legislative processes must include greater participation by the EP. If this democratic deficit is real, then something needs to be done.

The second part of the question The second part of the question (2(a)) requires you to look more closely at 'features' in the powers and decision-making procedures of the Council and the EP to support the criticism of the first statement. You must therefore describe the powers of the two institutions in the two processes and outline any features which you consider do support the view expressed or, if you consider there are no such features, you must take the view that the procedures are efficient and democratic, but you will have to explain why. There are two ways to tackle this part. The first would be to look at features of the Council in the legislative procedure and in the budgetary procedure, and also at the features of the EP in the legislative procedure and in the budgetary procedure. The second way would be to consider the features of the procedures as a whole as they are the result of the interaction of the EP and the Council. While both would be valid, I would prefer the second approach because it would be more succinct and thus neater.

The powers of the Council are basically set out in Art 202–210 (old 145–154) EC. The Council disposes of Community legislation initiated by the Commission and is the main legislator. The power of the EP is set out in Arts 189–201 (old 137–144) and 251–252 (old 189b–189c). EC Article 189 (old 137) provides that it shall 'exercise the powers conferred upon it by this Treaty'. The Treaty originally specified only 17 instances where the EP has to be consulted. There have been a number of changes to the legislative participation of the EP to date. EP budgetary powers stem from the Treaty of July 1975, plus the Joint Declaration of 1982.

Next you need to outline the features in the procedures which show that the EC is neither efficient nor democratic. The limited role played by the EP in making Community law, the fact that at present four procedures exist and the slowness of the procedures should all be discussed. In particular, it should be noted that the cooperation procedure applied to only a limited number of Treaty articles, even less after the Treaty of Amsterdam being restricted to EMU only. There is no time limit on the first reading, which may act in the Council's favour if it does not wish to proceed, and that the EP enjoys at best only a power of veto in the co-decision procedure. In respect of the budget, the EP can affect non-compulsory expenditure only to a set maximum and, although it can reject the whole budget, the Community then employs the one-twelfth rule, so that the Community is not brought to a grinding halt.

The third part of the question   To help you in this part (2(b)), the reforms put in effect under the Maastricht Treaty and the Treaty of Amsterdam should be considered to determine whether these have answered the criticisms before suggestions for further reform are made.

The criticisms of Maastricht are that the power of co-decision still does not go very far and gives the EP only a negative power of veto, and Art 251 (old 189b) still applies to only limited specific areas. The EP's ability under Art 192 (old 138b) to request the Commission to make legislative proposals in areas of Community policy is also uncertain, in as much as it is not clear whether it can insist that a proposal is made. The changes introduced by the Treaty of Amsterdam, whilst welcome and beneficial to the EP, are also limited. They increase the use, and streamline the co-decision procedure. The Treaty also extends the areas in which the assent of the Parliament is to be required to incorporate the structural and cohesion funds. However, these do not actually increase the level of participation of the EP and its ability to insist on particular measure and thus do little to reduce the democratic deficit and make the Union more democratic.

Whatever other reforms you suggest will depend on your views as to whether the Community is inefficient or undemocratic, or whether Maastricht or Amsterdam has improved the situation, i.e., does it answer the democratic deficit? Your suggested reforms might be to increase the EP's powers to give it an equal power of decision-making and an equal say in the approving of the budget, and generally to speed up the procedures, but it would not do simply to state this. You must say how this is to be done and the consequences for the other institutions. Any increase in the powers of the EP has to be at the expense of some other organisation, not the national parliaments but the Council of Ministers and/or the Commission.

This final section is probably the hardest to prepare for, in that it really requires you to have read particular suggestions during your course, such as the EP's own Draft Treaty on European Union, rather than to try to consider reforms in the exam. Although good suggestions will pick up a few extra marks, they are not the major part of the answer, and is not worth spending an excessive amount of time trying to think up reforms.

You may be asked questions relating to the general role of the Court of Justice in respect of its contribution to the Community and the legal order. Two examples are given below, to which only framework answers will be provided here. However, it should be noted that, as with other questions on the institutions, these questions also require answers that will inevitably be rather descriptive. This makes it difficult to obtain very high marks as the comments made must be very original.

3.   Evaluate the role played by the Court of Justice, including the advocates-general, in the development of the Community legal order.

This question can be split into three or four parts: the role of the Court of Justice; the role of the advocates-general; and how the Court and the advocates-general have assisted the Community legal order.

The role of the Court of Justice is defined in Art 220 (old 164) EC and has been considered above (p. 60). The detail you include here will depend on the coverage in your course and whether, for example, you have considered in detail the Protocol to the Court of Justice. Similarly, the role of the advocates-general is initially prescribed in the Treaty, Art 222 (old 166), and further details can also be found above.

The Court of Justice has assisted the foundation of the Community legal order by the establishment and development of leading principles of Community law, such as direct effects, supremacy and State liability. Here you would need to cite the cases in which these doctrines were established. The Court has helped to support democracy in the Community by its case rulings in actions concerning the rights of the Community institutions and notably the EP, e.g., *European Parliament* v *Council (Students Residence Directive)*.

The advocates-general have also helped in the development of Community law, largely in their detailed research for cases involving comparative research of the laws of Member States, which has led at times to the introduction of national legal principles into the Community legal order, e.g., in the case of *Transocean* the principle of *audi alteram partem* was introduced.

You would need to provide a number of further examples of the Court's and advocates-general's very active roles in the judicial process. This might then lead you on to a discussion about judicial activism by the ECJ and whether this is to be welcomed or indeed should be allowed to play a role in the development of the European Community and Union. Some Member States have taken great exception to some of the bolder judgments of the Court of Justice. So much so that it was originally on the agenda of the Amsterdam ICG that the Court's role was to be reviewed, however, in the end this did not take place.

Alternatively, the question may combine looking at the contribution of the Court of Justice to the Community legal order and the establishment of leading doctrines.

4.   'The decisions of the European Court of Justice in *Van Gend en Loos* and *Costa* v *ENEL* constitute the foundation stones of the new legal order represented by the European Communities.' Discuss.

This question concerns direct effects and supremacy, and you may have recognised the term 'new legal order' as coming from the case of *Van Gend en Loos*: '. . . the Community constitutes a new legal order of international law for the benefit of which the states have limited their sovereign rights, albeit in limited fields, and the subjects of which comprise not only Member States but also their nationals'. Clearly you must discuss the actual decisions in the two cases cited, say why they are foundations of the new legal order and what the new legal order is.

First, the brief factual circumstances must be outlined and the pleadings of the parties. In the case of the national authorities in these cases, both were looking for a solution along normal national or international law lines which would not involve them in having to recognise the claims of the other parties. Thus the rulings of the Court of Justice should be employed to show how the two cases are indeed the first to establish the leading principles of Community law. This is where quotations from the cases would be of immense use. From *Costa* v *ENEL* I have selected two passages which clearly show the view of the Court of Justice:

By contrast with ordinary international treaties [under] the EEC Treaty . . . the Member States have limited their sovereign rights and have created a body of law to bind their nationals and themselves . . . .

It follows . . . that the law stemming from the Treaty . . . could not . . . be overridden by domestic legal provisions, however framed, without being deprived of its character as Community law and without the legal basis of the Community itself being called into question.

The concept of the new legal order can be expanded, and its consequences for the Member States and individual Community citizens, by demonstrating how the Court built further on the foundation cases in subsequent cases.

5.   A Directive which bans certain nitrate fertilisers, for reasons of concern over seepage into the water table and the desire to achieve a common market in similar products, has been adopted by the Council. However, due to the protests of two Member States, influenced by the farming lobbies in their countries, the Directive was adopted under Art 175(2) (old 130s(2)) by the Council, despite the Commission proposal that either Art 37 (old 43) or Art 95 (old 100a) should be used as the base and the protests by the EP that only Art 95 (old 100a) should have been used. As a result of the insistence in Council by the two Member States, the Directive will not come into force for four years, and its requirements will then be phased in over 10 years.

What are the consequences of the use of these different legal bases for the institutions concerned, and what would be the likely outcome of an action by the Commission or the European Parliament challenging the Council for basing the Directive on Art 175(2) (old 130s(2)).

This is a question dealing with the topical issue of the legal base of Community legislation. It is really part problem and part essay, as it asks you specifically to provide a consideration of general issues in your answer.

You will need to consider which institutions are concerned and why, and how they are affected by the use of the three legal bases given in the problem. I think it would also be useful to state generally that the use of different legal bases in the Treaty determines which particular legislative procedure is employed in enacting the provision. This in turn determines the extent of the role played by the various institutions. Thus you are required to consider each of the provisions given to state which procedure is required:

Article 37 (old 43) concerns the power to enact legislation for the common organisation of the Community market in agricultural products. Legislation can be enacted under it by a qualified majority in Council, which must consult the EP, i.e., the consultation procedure.

Article 95 (old 100a) was originally introduced by the SEA in order to complete the single market, and thus concerns the adoption of measures which have as their object the establishment and functioning of the internal market. This article provides that such measures must be adopted by a qualified majority in Council in co-decision with the EP, i.e., the procedure under Art 251 (old 189b) as introduced by the TEU.

Article 175(2) (old 130s(2)), introduced by the SEA and amended by the TEU, concerns the enactment of provisions under the Community environmental policy which even after Amsterdam still require unanimity in the Council and only consultation of the EP.

Next, you should determine which institutions are concerned and why. The choice of a certain legal base is important here to all the actors involved: to the Member States, the Council, the Commission, and the EP. Each of these could be considered briefly in turn.

The Member States are represented in Council by the relevant Ministers of the national governments. They are thus subject to whatever political pressures are present in the Member States, and the degree to which this is important depends on the strength of the government concerned and on the strength of the pressure groups and lobbies who might object to certain legislative proposals. In some Member States the farming lobbies are very influential and the governments in these Member States may therefore wish to take their protests into account. If these States are a minority in Council, the consequence for the Member States is that if any other base is used not requiring unanimity to enact legislation, they would not be able to veto the measure or at least water down the requirements significantly. Hence, the use of Art 175(2) (old 130s(2)) in this situation is vital. An example of where a Member State has taken an action to try to protect such an interest is *UK v Council* (the 'Hormones' case).

The Commission may wish to see a proposal go through on a majority vote if one or two nations object. The Treaty base will affect the content of the proposals in that, if they know a qualified majority vote applies, then they can ignore the objections of the extreme views in Council as these will be outvoted. They need not water down proposals to take into account all views, in case the measure is not adopted at all. See *Commission v Council (Erasmus)*. Hence then in this case, as far as the Commission is concerned, the use of either Art 37 (old 43) concerned with agriculture, or Art 95 (old 100a) measures for the single market would achieve what they wanted.

The EP is clearly concerned, as the base adopted affects its level of participation. Its opinion in the consultation procedure can be ignored by the Council, whereas at least under Art 95 (old 100a) and measures for the single market the co-decision procedure is more likely to reflect the views of the EP.

Lastly, in this part it would be worth mentioning that the Council might continue to prefer to use Art 175(2) (old 130s(2)) because as a body it retains full, unshared power in the legislative process. Other bases weaken its position as a Community institution.

The last part of the question requires an answer as to whether the Commission and EP could do anything to challenge the decision by the Council to use Art 175(2) (old 130s(2)) rather than the other suggested provisions. Here an action on the grounds of Art 230 (old 173) may be undertaken by the Commission which is a privileged applicant (see chapter 6), and the EP, which can use Art 230 (old 173) under certain circumstances, e.g., it has the right to take action under Art 230 (old 173) to protect its own prerogative powers (*European Parliament* v *Council (Chernobyl)* and *European Parliament* v *Council (Students Residence Directive)*). See especially *Commission* v *Council (Re Titanium Dioxide Directive)*.

The view of the Court of Justice is essentially that the democratic process which now involves the EP demands that where two legal bases are available requiring differing procedures, the one allowing the EP the greater role must be used so as not to deprive the EP and the Community of its democratic right. In the light of the case law, it is quite likely the Court will find in favour of the Commission and/or the EP and annul the directive enacted under Art 175(2) (old 130s(2)) but see now the case of *Commission* v *Council (Waste Directive)* in which the Court of Justice decided on the basis of the primary ground for the enactment of the legal provision. In this case two grounds are cited pointing to two different provisions. In such a circumstance the previous decisions of the Court may be followed.

Other exam questions may concern the role and legality of the management committee and procedures, the budget or legislative procedures in further detail, or focus on the powers and rights of the EP, the Council or the Commission separately.

FURTHER READING

Boyle, B., 'The Democratic Deficit of the European Community' (1993) 46 Parliamentary Affairs pp. 458–477.

Boyron S., 'The consultation procedure: has the Court of Justice turned against the European Parliament?' (1996) 21 EL Rev 145.

Bradley, K., 'Comitology and the Law; Through a Glass Darkly' (1992) 29 CML Rev 693.

Craig, P. and Harlow, C., (eds), *Lawmaking in the European Union* (Kluwer, 1998).

Dashwood, A., 'The Limits of Community Competence' (1996) 21 EL Rev 211.

Foster, N., 'The New Conciliation Committee under Article 189b EC' (1994) 19 EL Rev 185.

Franklin, M., *Britain's Future in Europe* (Pinter Press, 1990).

George, S., *Politics and Policy in the European Community*, 3rd edn (Oxford: Oxford University Press, 1996).

Hartley, T., 'Constitutional and Institutional Aspects of the Maastricht Treaty' (1993) 42 ICLQ 213.

Lane, R., 'New Community Competences under the Maastricht Treaty' (1993) 30 CML Rev 939.

Lodge, J. (ed.), *The European Community and the Challenge of the Future*, 2nd edn (Pinter Press, 1993).

Nicholls, A., 'Britain and the EC: the historical background' in Bulmer et al., *The UK and EC Membership* (Pinter Press, 1992).

Nugent, N., *The Government and Politics of the European Community*, 3rd edn (Macmillan, 1994).

Pinder, J., *European Community: the Building of a Union* (Oxford: Oxford University Press, 1991).

Raworth, P., 'A timid step forwards: Maastricht and the democratisation of the European Community' (1994) 19 EL Rev 16.

4 *THE FORMS OF COMMUNITY LAW*

INTRODUCTION

This chapter concerns the forms of law employed in the Community, from the Treaties and secondary legislation to the doctrines and principles of law developed or employed by the Court of Justice. The order in which the material is covered may not correspond with the standard texts on Community law, but the main aspects are nevertheless covered.

The primary source of Community law consists of the three original constitutional Treaties, as amended by a number of subsequent Treaties, and agreements of the Member States, including the Accession Treaties of the new members, the Merger Treaty, the Budgetary Treaty and the SEA. The Maastricht Treaty on European Union both extensively amends the original Treaties and is a constitutional Treaty in its own right significantly increasing the scope of the European Communities into the European Union. More recently is the Treaty of Amsterdam which makes further amendments both significant and minor. One of the more significant changes is the re-numbering of the articles which was done because, after a series of amendments to the numbering, it was agreed that the numbering was getting *somewhat out of hand*, e.g., with Articles such as old Arts 130a to 130o. On the plus side, it makes it easy to oversee; on the down side, it is inevitable that for years to come, both the old and new versions will have to be learned.

A secondary source of Community law is the legislative measures enacted by the Community institutions in the form of regulations, directives and decisions, all of which should conform to their treaty base.

An additional source of law arises from the international agreements entered into by the Community on behalf of the Member States, or those where the Community has taken over the competence of the Member States as agreed. Notable are *Association* agreements, the GATT agreements and the Lomé Conventions between the Member States and many Third World nations.

Lastly, there are the judicial developments of the Court of Justice, whose case law includes the establishment of the doctrines of direct effects and supremacy and the introduction of a number of general principles of law.

THE TREATIES

Upon the accession of Member States to the Community, all of the provisions of the Treaties automatically become part of the generally binding law of the Member States and are applicable not only to the Member States but also to the citizens of those countries. This form of law is known as directly applicable law, and also as self-executing law. It does not rely on the way in which the Member State has incorporated it for its validity. The leading case of *Van Gend en Loos* is confirmation that Community law is also the legal concern of individuals and not just the Member States, and that Treaty provisions are capable of direct effects whereby they can be relied upon by individuals before their national courts provided they satisfy the criteria for direct effects, considered further below.

Additionally, at the level of the Community there are international Community agreements, which are provided for under Art 293 (old 220), e.g., the Brussels Convention on Jurisdiction and Enforcement of Judgments in Civil and Commercial Matters and the Rome Convention on Contractual Obligations.

Mention must also be made now of the various Protocols which have been added the Treaties, particularly by the Maastricht and Amsterdam Treaties. These provide interpretations of Treaty provisions or supplements to them and have the same status as the Treaties themselves. Article 311 (old 239) provides that the Protocols form an integral part of the Treaty.

The Treaties can only be changed by an intergovernmental conference of all the Member States unless, as is increasingly the case, opt-outs are negotiated for certain Member States.

THE LEGISLATIVE ACTS OF THE COMMUNITY INSTITUTIONS

The legislative acts of the Community are provided for by Art 249 (old 189) EC, which empowers the institutions to create legislation, three forms of which are binding. These are regulations, directives and decisions. Furthermore, they can make recommendations or deliver opinions.

Article 249 (old 189) provides:

A regulation shall have general application. It shall be binding in its entirety and directly applicable in all Member States.

> A directive shall be binding, as to the result to be achieved, upon each Member State to which it is addressed, but shall leave to the national authorities the choice of form and methods.
>
> A decision shall be binding in its entirety upon those to whom it is addressed.
>
> Recommendations and opinions shall have no binding force.

Regulations

Article 249 (old 189) declares regulations to be directly applicable. They are also described as self-executing because of the way they take effect in the Member States. They are general provisions of legislation applicable to all rather than specific to individuals or groups. Regulations are detailed forms of law so that the law in all Member States is exactly the same.

They become legally valid in the Member States without any need for implementation. In fact, it was held in *Leonesio* (case 93/71) that Member States cannot subject the regulation to any implementing measures other than those required by the Act itself. There may, however, be circumstances where the Member States are required to provide implementing measures to ensure the effectiveness of the regulation, as in the 'Tachograph' case *Commission v UK*.

According to Arts 253–254 (old 190–191) regulations shall state the reasons on which they are based and refer to any proposals or opinions which were required. Failure to do so may lead to their annulment following an action under Art 230 (old 173). Regulations must be published in the *Official Journal* and enter into force on the date given or on the 20th day following publication if no date is given.

Directives

Directives set out aims which must be achieved but leave the choice of the form and method of implementation to the Member States. This was done to ease the way in which national laws could be harmonised in line with Community law, and gives the Member States a wider area of discretion to do this. If, for example, a Member State considers that the existing national law is already in conformity with the requirements of a new directive, then it need not do anything, apart from the requirement now in many directives that the Member State must inform the Commission of how the directive has been implemented.

Member States are given a period in which to implement directives, which can range from one year to five or more, depending on the complexity of the subject matter and the urgency for the legislation. Directives are required to state the reasons on which they are based (Art

253 (old 190)) and those addressed to all Member States are now required to be published in the OJ according to the amended Art 254 (old 191) EC.

Although they are not directly applicable, in that they are automatic and general in application and give rights without further implementation, directives have been held to give rise to directly enforceable rights in specific circumstances, where they have not been implemented or have been implemented incorrectly, considered below in the section on direct effects.

Decisions

Decisions are binding and enforceable acts of law which are usually addressed to Member States, or to specific individuals, e.g., the Commission addresses Decisions to individuals under competition and anti-dumping law to declare whether their action is in breach of the competition law rules.

Article 249 (old 189) is not exhaustive of the legally binding acts which can be created by the institutions, and the Court of Justice has held that it can review all measures taken by the institutions, whatever their nature and form, which are designed to produce legal effects. Thus such acts need not stem from the specific acts listed in Art 249 (old 189). See the *Noordwijks Cement Accord* and *Commission* v *Council (ERTA)* cases.

Even a press release has been found to have legal effects in *UK* v *Commission* (case C-106/96) and was consequently annulled for lacking a legal base.

Recommendations and Opinions

These non-legally binding acts have not been questioned in the Court of Justice as to their actual validity, but can be taken as persuasive statements of policy which should comply with the aims of the Treaties and Communities overall, see in this context *Grimaldi* v *Fonds des Maladies Profession-nelles* (case C-322/88).

Procedural Requirements

Article 253 (old 190) of the Treaty requires that the binding acts of institutions shall state the reasons on which they are based and shall refer to any proposals or opinions which were required to be obtained. In practice this means the Treaty base must also be cited. Failure by the institutions to comply with these requirements will give rise to grounds for judicial review of the measure under Art 230 (old 173). For example, it was held in *France* v *Commission* (case C-325/91) that there was a requirement to state the Treaty base, without which the measure is void.

Publication

Article 254 (old 191) provides the rules concerning the publication of the various acts. Regulations, directives and decisions adopted under Art 251 (old 189b) must be signed by the Presidents of the EP and the Council and published in the OJ. Directives addressed to all Member States must also be published. They become valid on the specified date, in the absence of which they come into force on the twentieth day following publication. Other directives and decisions take effect on the date of notification given in the acts, although these are also invariably published in the *Official Journal*.

Agreements with Third Countries

Articles 300 and 310 (old 228 and 238) cater for the conclusion of agreements with countries associated with the Member States and international agreements to be reached with other third countries. Such agreements bind the Member States. In the *Haegemann* v *Belgium* case, an agreement between the Community and Greece was held to be binding on the Member States even though such agreements are not envisaged by Art 249 (old 189). see also the cases of *International Fruit* (case 21–24/72) and *Kupferberg* (case 104/81).

Judicial Developments

The Treaties are largely framework constitutional treaties and require substantial supplement. Much of this arises in the form of the secondary legislation of the Community, but this also needs to be interpreted. There is thus much scope for activity on the part of the Court of Justice.

The Court of Justice has determined that the Treaty and secondary legislation must be interpreted and applied according to the scheme of the Treaty as a whole, and in the light of the broad principles of the Preamble and Arts 2, 3, 10 (old 5) and 12 (old 6), to achieve the result required for the Community. The resulting case law or jurisprudence encompasses a wide variety of law. It is not simply restricted to the interpretation of words or phrases from legislative provisions, but has led to the development of some of the most fundamental doctrines and principles of Community law, including direct effects, supremacy, state liability the development of general principles of Community law and the application of outside general principles. This law as developed by the Court of Justice in cases before it, is quite clearly a source of Community law.

GENERAL PRINCIPLES

General principles have been used to assist the Court of Justice in the interpretation and application of Community law, and by the parties to assist them in challenging the Community institutions or law and the actions of the Member States in the application of Community law. They are also referred to in actions for damages against the Community institutions.

The Community and Court of Justice were morally, if not legally, obliged to observe fundamental human rights, especially those upheld in the constitutions of Member States. The *Internationale Handelsgesellschaft* case showed the potential for conflict and ultimate harm to the Community legal order if the Community failed to uphold human rights provisions. No self-respecting legal system in Europe could ignore, or be seen to be ignoring, such ideologically important rights as these.

Some general principles are imported into the legal system from external sources, whereas others have been developed by the Court of Justice from the Treaty, which has supplied the basis for principles coinciding with the general principle of non-discrimination. This applies in respect of nationality and sex, and has been developed into a general principle of equality and non-discrimination. The specific fundamental principles of Community law established by the Treaty, such as the fundamental freedoms, specific rights and more recently, subsidiarity, are not counted as general principles.

General principles from external sources include those contained in particular provisions of other legal systems, in particular the constitutions of Member States, or the European Convention of Human Rights (ECHR) and the many rules of natural justice found in common law or in written form in some Member States. These general rules of application can be found in one form or another in most, if not all, of the Member States.

The Justification of the Use of General Principles

There are three Treaty articles which provide some justification for the Court of Justice to introduce general principles into the Community legal order.

Article 220 (old 164) is a general guideline set by the Treaty for the functioning of the Court of Justice. It states, 'The Court of Justice shall ensure that in the interpretation and application of this Treaty the law is observed'. This is taken to mean the law outside of the Treaty. Article 220 (old 164) has been invoked to introduce very many different general principles of law, most notably human rights.

More specifically, two further articles of the Treaty mandate the court to take account of general principles of law. Article 230 (old 173) refers to the infringement of any rule of law relating to the application of the Treaty as one of the grounds for an action to challenge the validity of Community law, and Art 288 (old 215), concerned with damages claims, specifically allows the settlement of claims by the Community on the basis of the general principles of the laws of the Member States.

Since the last two are specific to the claims raised under those Treaty articles, they are not really the focus of our concern. They do, however, serve to reinforce the Court of Justice's claim that it can rely on general principles as a source of law in the Community legal order.

The Source of the General Principles

General principles can arise from the national constitutions, principles of natural law or justice, or international law and agreements, e.g., the ECHR. Sometimes the actual articles of the ECHR are referred to directly, as in the *Hauer* and *R* v *Kent Kirk* cases.

The public law and legal systems of Germany and France — and now the UK — have had a considerable impact on the supply of general principles for the Community legal order. The principles which form a source of Community law need not be present in all of the Member States legal systems, nor indeed in a majority. The Court of Justice will often conduct a comparative review of whether or in what form the principle exists in some or all of the Member States.

Often, too, it is the nationality of the advocate-general and judges in the case which may be particularly influential in the introduction of a certain principle into the Community legal order. The advocates-general from particular countries are more easily able to identify the principles, which may be common in one form or another in a number of the Member States, and are thus more likely to introduce these principles to the Court of Justice. For example, the Latin maxim *'audi alterem partem'* was introduced by the British advocate-general in *Transocean Marine Paint Association* v *Commission*. He argued that in the absence of the affected party being allowed to present their view on the condition, the Commission's decision would be in breach of a general principle of law, clearly applicable in the UK and other legal systems.

Article 6(2) (old F(2)) of the TEU obliges the European Union to respect the articles of the ECHR and those human rights common to the Member States as general principles of Community law. Any applicant States joining the European Union are now obligated by Art 49 (old O) TEU to have respect for human rights and any Member State which seriously and persistently offends human rights may have its rights under the Treaties suspended by the other Member States under a new provision in Art 7 TEU.

Categories of General Principles

General principles are sometimes classified into broad groupings. While this is probably not particularly useful because of the diversity of principles and the degree of overlap, it may aid the study and revision of the principles if they are introduced in groups. I have therefore divided them into three groups concerned with (i) basic human rights, (ii) equality and (iii) procedural rights; however, it must be stressed that the categories are not watertight and there is considerable overlap. Indeed, some principles may be differently organised by different authors. Don't worry, it is the principles themselves that are important and not the categorisation.

Human or fundamental rights   While there is no specific catalogue of rights in the EC Treaty, some isolated articles do give rights which either coincide with general principles or which have helped in the development of general principles. These are Arts 2 (concerned with social protection, the standard of living and quality of life), Arts 3 and 39 (old 48) (dealing with the free movement of persons), Arts 12, 34 and 39(2) (old 6, 40 and 48(2)) (concerned with discrimination), Art 43 (old 52) (social security) and Art 141 (old 119) (equal pay). Apart from these unconnected articles, no specific set of obligations is imposed by the Treaty on the Community institutions to guarantee individual rights of citizens. This apparent lack of commitment was in turn reflected in the decisions of the Court of Justice when faced with arguments or pleas raised by litigants based on basic or human rights. Hence, the early case law of the Court of Justice presents the view of a Community unsympathetic to the fundamental human rights of individuals. (See *Stork* v *High Authority* and *Sgarlata* v *Commission*, in which arguments based on individual rights were clearly rejected in favour of upholding Community law.) This position can be contrasted with the then six Member States' positions regarding human rights.

Following the Second World War, Western European nations were more than ever ideologically committed to the concept of protecting human rights. The German and Italian constitutions were rewritten with very strong commitments to basic rights. By 1955, all the original members of the EEC, except France, had ratified the ECHR. In the face of this the Court of Justice could not maintain its unsympathetic stance and adopted from the late-1960s a new response, which was seen clearly in the case of *Stauder* v *City of Ulm*. A German citizen protested that his fundamental right of human dignity, protected by Art 1 of the German Grundgesetz (its Basic Law or Constitution), was being infringed by having his name on the coupon when claiming cheap butter released by the Community. The Court of Justice held that the Community measure did not require his name and had not prejudiced his fundamental rights which were 'enshrined in the general principles of Community law and protected by the Court'. In a number of cases the Court reaffirmed its statement that fundamental rights form part of the general principles based on constitutional traditions of Member States.

The conversion of the Court of Justice was not entirely free from difficulties, in that the courts of some Member States clearly regarded the statements as rhetorical and reserved the right to ignore Community law which infringed national constitutional rights guarantees. (See, for example, *Internationale Handelsgesellschaft*, later reversed in *Wünsche Handelsgesellschaft*, considered below.)

After the French ratification of the ECHR in 1974, the Court of Justice also referred to the ECHR as an example of the Member States' commitment to fundamental rights. See, for example, the cases of *Nold* v *Commission* and *Rutili* v *Minister for the Interior*. Encouragement also came from the Joint Declaration by Community Institutions on Fundamental Rights, 5 April 1977, which stressed the importance of national constitutions and the ECHR. In *Hauer* v *Land Rheinland-Pfalz*, the Court of Justice considered for the first time, and in some detail, a provision (Art 1 of Protocol 1) of the ECHR to help it decide the case. Although it recognised the right of property in the case, the exercise of it was subject to overriding Community interests. Thus, despite recognition of the fundamental rights, cases have usually been resolved on the basis either of Community law applying or the rights being subject to limitations mainly of the Community interest.

In *R* v *Kent Kirk*, a fine by a UK court based on a UK Order was held to infringe the principle of non-retroactivity, because the Order was supposedly validated by later Community legislation despite the current infringement of a Community regulation. The Court of Justice held such an action violated the principle of non-retroactivity of criminal law enshrined in Art 7 ECHR and now a principle of Community law. In *UNECTEF* v *Heylens et al.*, the Court of Justice was able to declare that 'free access to employment is a fundamental right which the Treaty confers'. In *Wachauf*, the Court of Justice extended its support of fundamental rights by holding that the actions of Member States in implementing Community measures must also comply with the requirements of human rights provisions.

While it has been the subject of discussion for many years, there are at present no plans for the European Union to join as a signatory to the ECHR, although the European Council Presidency Conclusions of 3 and 4 June 1999 proposed to establish the Community's own catalogue of fundamental human rights and to attach these to the Treaties.

As noted, Art 6 (old F) of the TEU requires the Union to respect fundamental human rights as contained in the ECHR as part of the general principles of Community law and any applicant States joining the

European Union are now obligated by Art 49 (old O) TEU to have respect for human rights and any Member State which seriously and persistently offends human rights may have its rights under the Treaties suspended by the other Member States under a new provision in Art 7 TEU.

Equality and non-discrimination   While this principle is specifically catered for in the EC Treaty under Art 12 (old 6) (the general non-discrimination article), Art 141 (old 119) (on the grounds of sex), Art 34(2) (old 40(3)) (in respect of the common agricultural policy) and Art 39(2) (old 48(2)) (for the free movement of workers), it is also a general principle recognised by the Court of Justice. It applies in all areas of Community law, especially to the fundamental freedoms. For example, in *Razzouk and Beydoun v Commission*, the Court of Justice held that a Commission decision, which discriminated between men and women in relation to certain pension payments, should be annulled as being contrary to the fundamental right of equal treatment of the sexes.

The principle was again applied in *Bergmann v Grows-Farm* ('the skimmed milk powder case'), where the Court of Justice held that a scheme to force animal feed producers to incorporate skimmed milk powder in animal feed discriminated against non-dairy farmers. It was also applied to religious discrimination in *Prais v Council*, although on the facts, involving a Community competition for a post held on a Jewish religious festival, the Council was held not to have breached the general principle of equality. It was nevertheless held by the Court of Justice that, wherever possible, Community employees and citizens should have the general principle of non-discrimination in respect of religious freedom upheld in their favour.

The Community has moved further towards the development of a general principle of equality or at least non-discrimination in an amendment made to the EC Treaty by the Treaty of Amsterdam. Article 13 (old 6a) provides that the Council may take appropriate action to combat discrimination based on sex, racial or ethnic origin, religion or belief, disability, age or sexual orientation. To the date of writing, no action has been taken under this provision.

Rules of natural justice and procedural law   A number of principles are closely associated with administrative law principles, also classified under the rules of natural justice. These can be found in differing forms in the Member States' legal systems, as common-law rules in the UK, or as a part of the constitution in Germany (see Arts 101–104 of the Grundgesetz). Sometimes these rights are also referred to as defence rights.

(a)   The right to judicial review   A general right to have decisions reviewed by a court exists. The Court of Justice bases its view on the constitutions of

the Member States and notably on Art 6 ECHR, dealing with a fair and public hearing, and Art 13 ECHR, dealing with the provision of an effective judicial remedy. See *Johnston* v *Chief Constable of the RUC* and *UNECTEF* v *Heylens*. In the latter case, the Court of Justice had already determined that free access to employment was a fundamental right in the Community. It thus becomes essential that there must be a remedy of a judicial nature against any decision of a national authority refusing the benefit of that right. The *UNECTEF* case also established that the duty to give reasons was a general principle to be recognised in the Community legal order.

The Latin maxim *'audi alterem partem'* — the right for both parties to present their cases — was held to be a general principle in *Transocean Marine Paint Association* v *Commission*. The Court of Justice held also in the case of *Kuhner* that where a person's rights were affected, that person must be given the opportunity to make his or her views known and the right to be heard must be upheld. This may also be termed 'the right to a hearing'.

(b) Confidentiality or legal privilege In the case of *AM & S* v *Commission*, the company refused to hand over certain documents during a raid by Commission officials on AM & S under the rules on competition law, on the ground that by doing so the principle of legal privilege would be breached. The Court of Justice held the principle was recognised in the Community legal order, provided it was in relation to or in preparation for a client's defence, and it must be between a party and an independent lawyer. The *National Panasonic* (case 136/79) and *Hilti* (case T-30/89) cases are also concerned with privilege.

(c) Legal certainty The basic concept underlying legal certainty incorporates a number of ideas concerned with the boundary between legality and illegality, or lawfulness and unlawfulness, which should be marked clearly in advance. Additionally, the existence of sanctions or punishment for the breach of the rule or overstepping the boundary should be reasonably ascertainable; not the exact punishment, but at least the type and scope or range of punishment applicable. As such, the principle of proportionality is included in this category. Textbooks differ in their classification of general principles, and proportionality may be classified as a distinct and separate principle (see below). This is not really important — the point is that it is nevertheless recognised as a general principle by the Court of Justice and is often quoted in cases to defeat the arguments of the Member State or Commission.

Legal certainty thus includes the sub-concepts of legitimate expectations, protection of vested rights, proportionality and non-retroactivity. It was first acknowledged by the Court of Justice in *Defrenne* v *SABENA (No. 2)*, and was later confirmed in the *Barber* v *Guardian Royal Exchange* case to support the Court's argument that the judgment could not be retroactively effective.

(d) Non-retroactivity This principle is seen in its purest form in the cases of *R v Kent Kirk* and *Barber* (considered above) and is firmly established as a general principle of Community law. Legislation should not impose punishments retroactively or be the legal base for punishments, particularly with regard to criminal sanctions.

The case of *Public Prosecutor v Kolpinghuis Nijmegen* is also a very good example of the principle being cited by the Court of Justice in defence of the rights of the individual. In this case it was used to protect the company from being prosecuted by the Dutch authorities on the strength of Community law, where the Netherlands had failed to implement it correctly into national law.

Civil or non-criminal law retroactivity may also occur when a person's actual rights or expected rights are altered, re-defined or totally removed. Thus the principle of non-retroactivity may take on more subtle forms in civil law application, to solve the difficulties created by the alteration or withdrawal of rights by Community legal measures.

(e) Legitimate expectation or vested rights Legislation is presumed not to be retroactive unless the purpose of the measure would otherwise be undermined; but the legitimate expectations of affected parties must be observed, hence it is easy to overlap this with non-retroactivity.

In *Sugar Export v Commission*, a regulation was enacted by the Commission on 30 June 1976 which removed the right of sugar exporters to cancel licences previously granted. 1 July 1976 was set as the date of entry into force, but the regulation was not published until 2 July 1976. Sugar Export applied for a cancellation on 1 July 1976 but was at first refused by the Commission. The Court of Justice interpreted the regulation as coming into force on 2 July 1976, and held while there was no intention of retroactivity, the rights vested in the applicant, to apply on 1 July 1976, must be protected. The principle was confirmed by the Court of Justice in *Töpfer v Commission* (case 112/77).

In *Commission v Council (Staff Salaries Case)*, the principle was employed in different circumstances when the Council adopted a three-year experimental period for a system of staff salary payments but changed this after only nine months. Despite the view that the Council could not bind itself as such, the Court of Justice held the employees had a reasonable or legitimate expectation that the Council would abide by its decision.

(f) Proportionality This embodies the concept that the punishment should fit the crime and no more, or must be reasonable under the circumstances.

It puts the question to the relevant authority of whether the same result could be achieved by other methods or means less harmful to the party concerned. So in the Community context, it means that individuals should not be restricted by actions beyond those necessary in the public or Community interest, and any fines or punishment must be in proportion to the seriousness of the breach. It occurs frequently throughout all areas of Community law, and especially with regard to the internal market. It was invoked in the cases of *Internationale Handelsgesellschaft, Rutili* and *R v Pieck* in respect of the free movement of persons, and in *Commission v Germany (Beer Purity)* in relation to the free movement of goods. The case of *R v Intervention Board for Agricultural Produce ex parte Man* serves as a very good example. A company was required to give a security deposit to the Intervention Board when seeking a licence to export sugar outside the Community. The applicant was then late, but only by four hours, in completing the relevant paperwork. The Board acting under a Community Regulation, declared the entire deposit of over one and a half million pounds to be forfeit. The court held that the automatic forfeit of the entire deposit in the event of any failure was too drastic in view of the function of the system of export licences, i.e., it was disproportionate to the aims.

The principle of proportionality has now been given statutory recognition under Art 5 (old 3b) of the EC Treaty which provides 'Any action by the Community shall not go beyond what is necessary to achieve the objectives of this Treaty'.

(g)   Recent developments   In keeping with a system of law in which case law is regarded as important and can supply legal principles which become general principles to be applied in future cases, new principles can arise. Subsidiarity is a general principle which, although existing in its own right previously, was deliberately introduced into the Community by the TEU and is now contained in Art 5 (old 3b) EC, which provides that the Community shall take action, in accordance with the principle of subsidiarity, only if and insofar as the objective of the proposed action cannot be sufficiently achieved by the Member States and can only be better achieved by the Community. As this concerns the relationship with the Member States and until we see the Court of Justice being required to tackle this, it will be dealt with in the next chapter which concerns the impact of Community law on the Member States.

Other case law developments are taking place. Good faith received support as a general principle of Community law in the case of *Steff-Houlberg Export*, concerned with the recovery of exports refunds which had been found to have been unduly paid. The export company were not responsible for the breach of rules and had acted in good faith. Under national law and also in view of the time elapsed, the refunds should not be recoverable. The ECJ held this to be the position under EC law also.

DIRECT APPLICABILITY AND DIRECT EFFECTS

The Distinction between Direct Applicability and Direct Effects

'Direct effects' were described by Judge Pescatore as the infant disease of Community law, which I take to mean something which everyone growing up in the Community legal system must experience. Judging from my own initial difficulties, and observing the sufferings of many students over the years, this experience is not often a pleasant one, and is an experience which, if one is subjected to prolonged exposure, can re-occur in later life, as may be detected in some attempts to clarify this 'infant disease'. These concepts and the distinction are, however, fundamental to the study and understanding of the nature of Community law. I shall try to relieve that suffering as much as possible by the following explanation and demonstrate that these two concepts are to be distinguished.

The doctrine of direct effects is a judicial development of the Court of Justice. It is very closely connected to and very often confused with, direct applicability; however, there are fundamental differences between the two concepts. Direct effects play a central role in the Community legal order because of their link with the application and enforcement of Community law in the courts of the national legal systems, and are therefore very much related to supremacy of Community law. Unfortunately, the terminology of the Court of Justice and of many of the national courts has not been consistent. This has added greatly to the difficulty in understanding these concepts. Very often they do not use the term 'direct effects' but use 'direct applicability' instead, but in the sense that the provision gives rise to rights enforceable by individuals before the national courts.

Direct effects were sometimes considered to be a sub-concept of direct applicability, or direct applicability to be a prerequisite for direct effects. The Court of Justice has spoken of regulations which are directly applicable but which by their very nature can have direct effect in the *Verbond* and *Grad* cases, which suggests this is automatically the case. In *Grad* it also stated that the ability of an individual to invoke a decision before a national court leads to the same result as would be achieved by a directly applicable provision of a regulation, again as if to suggest the concepts are the same. Hence the confusion!

I consider this to be such an important topic that careful and further study at this stage may alleviate greater suffering and panic during revision, when you need it least. Two of the earliest articles on the subject, which I consider to be clear and succinct, are: L. Brinkhorst, in a case note on the *Grad* and *SACE* decisions, in (1971) 8 CML Rev 380, and A. Easson, 'The direct effect of EEC directives' (1979) 28 ICLQ 319.

Direct Applicability

Direct applicability, a term previously recognised in international law, should be used to describe the way in which some provisions of Community law have legal validity in the Member States. It is therefore a mode of incorporation of law which is generally or universally binding. The term 'self-executing' is also often used to describe such law, in that such law itself establishes its validity in the host State.

In the EC, 'directly applicable' is specifically mentioned in Art 249 (old 189), concerning regulations which shall have general application and shall be directly applicable. The Member States are obliged not to transform Community regulations into national legislation, except where necessary under the legislation. See the cases of *Commission* v *Italy (Slaughtered Cows)* and *Commission* v *UK (Tachographs)*. The term applies additionally in respect of Treaty articles, as these also satisfy the requirement of directly applicable law by their automatic validity in the Member States following the simple ratification of the Treaty, because the Articles themselves are not actually transformed into national law. They are generally binding in that they can also obligate individuals.

Direct Effects

'Direct effects' is the term given to judicial enforcement of rights arising from provisions of Community law, which can be upheld in favour of individuals in the courts of the Member States. To be capable of direct effects a provision must satisfy the criteria established by the Court of Justice, i.e., that the provision should be clear and precise, unconditional, should not require implementing measures by the State or Community institutions, or leave room for the exercise of discretion by the Member State or Community institutions. If these requirements are satisfied, it gives rise to a right which is enforceable in the national courts. In *Van Gend en Loos* it was held that the institutions of the Community are endowed with sovereign rights, the exercise of which affects not only Member States but also their citizens, and that Community law is capable of conferring rights on individuals which become part of their legal heritage.

Whereas 'directly applicable' applies only to regulations and Treaty articles, 'direct effects' can arise from all forms of legislative provision.

Direct effects have been declared by the Court of Justice in a series of cases in respect of Treaty articles, regulations, directives, decisions and provisions of international agreements to which the Community is a party.

Treaty articles   The case of *Van Gend en Loos* is the leading Community law case in respect of Treaty articles. It concerned the imposition of a customs tariff by Holland, contrary to Community law. The defendant customs authorities argued that as the Treaty article was addressed to the Member State, it could not be enforced by individuals. The Court of Justice rejected this and held the provision, Art 25 (old 12), was suited by its nature to produce direct effects.

In order to be capable of giving rise to direct effects an article must satisfy the criteria noted above. The Court of Justice not only enabled private parties to defend their rights, but was also able to add to the enforcement of Community law by individuals in the case where Member States had failed to comply and the Commission had not taken any action.

The case of *Alfons Lütticke GmbH* v *Hauptzollamt Saarlouis* (1965) was an early demonstration of the difference between articles of the Treaty which could give rise to direct effects and those incapable. The case declared that old Art 95 (now 90) satisfied the criteria so as to give rise to direct effects but that old Art 97 did not. (Article 97 has been repealed under Amsterdam.) Old Art 95 (now 90) stated: 'No Member State shall impose, directly or indirectly . . . any internal taxation of any kind . . .'. Old Art 97 stated: 'Member States . . . may, in the case of internal taxation . . ., establish average rates . . .'.

Direct effects have been found to arise from many Treaty articles. Such articles often obligate not just organs of the state, as in a vertical relationship, but other individuals too, in particular, in the Community context, employers. It was confirmed by the Court of Justice that employers are obligated to comply with the requirements of a Treaty article, and other individuals may enforce corresponding rights directly against the obligated party who has failed to comply with Community law. In this case the resultant rights are termed 'horizontal direct effects'. The first case to confirm this was that of *Defrenne* v *SABENA (No. 2)*, in which the rights of an air hostess to equal pay, guaranteed under Art 141 (old 119) EC, were upheld against the employing airline, SABENA, who were in breach of the obligation.

Article 12 (old 6) EC, a very general clause imposed on the Member States, was also found to be capable of horizontal direct effects in the case of *Walrave and Koch*, but Art 10 (old 5) was held in *Hurd* v *Jones* not to give rise to direct effects.

Regulations While regulations are clearly directly applicable by reason of Art 249 (old 189), they are not necessarily directly effective. The question of whether they can also give rise to direct effects also depends on whether they satisfy the same criteria as Treaty articles (above). See the leading case of *Leonesio* v *Ministry of Agriculture* (case 93/71). Regulations are generally applicable and can therefore also obligate other individuals; they are thus capable of giving rise to horizontal direct effects.

Directives Directives have caused particular problems to the Court of Justice. At first they were thought, as a general rule, not to be precise enough to give rise to direct effects, because they were not directly applicable and only obligated the Member States to achieve an end result, thus giving rise to a wide margin of discretion. The case of *Grad*, discussed below, considered the possibility of direct effects of other forms of Community law, and the case of *Van Duyn* v *The Home Office* confirmed that directives could also give rise to direct effects, provided they also satisfy the criteria. Directive 64/221, Art 3, was held to give rise to rights directly enforceable by Miss van Duyn before the British courts against the state.

The special concerns of directives and the time limits given for their implementation were considered in *Pubblico Ministero* v *Ratti*, which concerned prosecution by the Italian authorities for breaches of national law concerning product labelling. Mr Ratti had complied with Community directives, the expiry period for implementation of one of which had not expired. The Court of Justice held he could rely on the one for which the time period had expired provided it satisfied the other requirements, but not on the directive whose implementation period had not expired.

The case of *Verbond* extended the situation to where a directive had been implemented but that implementation was not faithful to the requirement of the directive. The Court of Justice held that to deny the rights of individuals would be to weaken the effectiveness of Community obligations, and that individuals helped to ensure that Member States kept within the realms of the discretion granted.

For a considerable time the question of whether directives could be held to give rise to horizontal direct effects, and thus be enforceable against other individuals, received no answer from the Court of Justice. Arguments against horizontal effects are that directives did not have to be published, and this would have offended against legal certainty. Directives are addressed to and obligate Member States and not individuals, and therefore the latter should not be obligated by them. Arguments for horizontal effects are that Community law should be equally actionable against states and others to ensure uniform consistency throughout the Community, to avoid giving rise to two categories of rights. Treaty articles are also addressed to Member States but nevertheless obligate individuals, and directives are also published.

The Court of Justice decided in the case of *Marshall* that directives could be enforced only against the State or arms of the State and not against individuals. The result of this decision is that the scope of the concept of public service, as opposed to a private body, is crucial, as can be seen from the later case of *Duke* v *Reliance* in the UK, in which on similar facts Ms Duke lost her claim for compensation for being forced to retire earlier then men. Two further cases, *Johnston* v *RUC* and *Foster* v *British Gas*, showed that although the concept was wide enough to include nationalised industry and includes any form of State control or authority, a distinction nevertheless remains. The difficulties and limits to this approach are demonstrated in the UK case of *Doughty* v *Rolls Royce plc*, in which the Court of Appeal considered that the nationalised Rolls Royce was not a public body for the purposes of the claim to direct effects in the case. Privatisation of once nationalised companies also affects the rights of individuals. Indeed, because of this distinction a different result can occur in each Member State, where national concepts of what is a part of the State may differ. Thus, there is no uniformity in the application of Community law between public and private and employers within Member States and between Member States, because there are different concepts of what is the state and what are private and public employers. Certain individuals are thus denied rights that employees in the public sector can enforce in the face of non-compliance by Member States. The result of this decision is that the scope of the concept of public service as opposed to a private body is crucial.

Indirect Effects

However, another line of case law has developed which may provide an alternative for individuals defeated by the absence of horizontal direct effects. The first cases in this line are *Von Colson* and *Harz*, both concerning Art 6 of the Equal Treatment Directive (76/207), but in respect of a public and private employer, thus the contrast of remedies is starkly visible. Rather than highlight the unfortunate results of the lack of horizontal direct effects of directives, the Court of Justice concentrated on Art 10 (old 5) EC, which requires Member States to comply with Community obligations. The Court held that this requirement applies to all authorities of Member States, including the courts, therefore the courts are obliged to interpret national law in such a way as to ensure that obligations of a directive are obeyed, regardless of whether the national law was based on any particular directive. The effectiveness of this depends on the willingness or ability of the Member State courts to interpret national law, if it exists, to achieve the correct result.

The lack of national law has caused problems in furthering the principle enunciated in *Von Colson*. The Court of Justice held that the decision could not be applied by a Member State to support the prosecution of a Dutch firm for stocking adulterated mineral water on the basis of a breach of a Community directive which had not been specifically implemented (*Public Prosecutor* v *Kolpinghuis Nijmegen BF*). It held that to do so would breach the general principles of legal certainty and non-retroactivity. The case of *Marleasing* concerned a directive which had not been specifically implemented in Spain. The Spanish courts wanted to know whether a directive could be upheld directly against an individual. While the Court of Justice reaffirmed that directives do not give rise to effects between individuals, it also stressed it was up to the courts to achieve the result required by the directive by the interpretation of national law (in this case the Spanish Civil Code), suggesting horizontal direct effects, but now generally regarded as establishing a form of indirect effects.

State Liability

A later case has turned the attention away from horizontal direct effects to the liability of the state for its failure to implement a directive which results in harm to an individual. This is *Francovich* which concerns the claim by Italian nationals against the state for a guarantee payment granted by Directive 80/987, which had not been implemented by Italy, or for damages for failing to implement the directive in time. The Court had already held in Art 226 (old 169) proceedings that Italy had breached its obligations by its failure to implement the directive (case 22/87). The claim was made by analogy with the claim against the Community institutions under Art 288 (old 215) EEC. The Court held the directive not to be capable of direct effects because of the discretion granted to the Member States as to the result to be achieved. The Court rejected the view that the liability of the state was only a matter for the national laws. Relying heavily on the fundamental doctrines of Community law of direct effects and supremacy as outlined in *Van Gend en Loos, Costa* v *ENEL, Simmenthal* and *Factortame*, the Court determined that the duty of the Member States to ensure full application and enforcement under Arts 10 and 249 (old 5 and 189) would give rise to liability if breached. The protection of individuals would be weakened if they could not claim damages for loss caused by a Member State's failure to comply. The success of the claim, however, required that the directive must contain an individual right, which could be determined by the provisions of the directive, and that there must be a link between the breach and the damage caused.

Thus the decision in *Francovich* gives individuals rights, not from the provision of Community law but from the breach of the general obligation of the Member State to comply with its Community law obligations in Arts 10 and 249 (old 5 and 189). Hence, the case adds a remedy for individuals in the gap left where Community provisions have not been implemented by Member States or are held not to be directly effective, or because directives are effective only on the vertical and not horizontal axis. The ruling has been described by Bebr as the ultimate consequence of *Van Gend en Loos*. The 1994 judgment in *Faccini Dori* v *Recreb Srl* (case C-91/92) confirmed the Court's continued opposition to horizontal direct effects but stressed the need for national courts to interpret national law wherever possible to comply with Directives or subject the state to a liability to compensate damage caused by non-implementation. Since those cases, the Court of Justice has had the opportunity to develop the law, starting with joined cases *Brasserie du Pécheur* v *Federal Republic of Germany* (case C-46/93) and *Factortame (No. 3)* v *UK* (case C-48/93). The result of this case law is that all manner of breaches of Community law by all three arms of state could lead to liability to individuals but the focus has been moved to the seriousness of the breach. *Factortame (No. 3)* introduced the revised criteria that the breach must be analogous to that applied to liability of the EC institutions under Art 288 (old 215). This is known as the 'Shöppenstedt Formula' and in order for liability to arise on the part of the Member State, there must have been a sufficiently serious breach of a superior rule of law designed for the protection of individuals. This has provoked further case law to help decide how serious a breach is required for Member States to incur liability. *British Telecom* takes a generous view of what constitutes a breach but this can be contrasted with the *Hedley Lomas* case where a mere infringement will invoke potential liability.

Finally in this respect, the *Wagner Miret* case is important to note because it creates a bridge or link between *Marleasing* and *Francovich*. The Court says, if Member States can't construe national law to read in conformity, which is a distinct possibility as a result either of the court being incapable or unwilling, it must be assumed that Member States nevertheless intended to comply with its Community law obligations. Thus, if there is a breach, Member States must compensate according to the principles established in *Francovich*. In other words, the failure to succeed under *von Colson* failure should not be the end of the litigation line under EC law.

Decisions   In *Grad* v *Finanzamt Traunstein* the Court of Justice held that it would be contrary to the binding nature of Community law if the provisions of a decision could not be invoked by individuals. They must also satisfy the criteria discussed above and can be enforced only against those obligated.

International agreements   Although there is no statement in the Treaty that such agreements entered into by the Community or by the Member States can give rise to direct effects, the Court of Justice has held that they may also give rise to direct effects provided they satisfy the criteria previously established. These tend, however, to be more strictly applied in this regard. To this extent, an investigation of one of the GATT provisions in *International Fruit* (1971) was held not to be directly effective. However, provisions of the Yaoundé Convention and the EEC-Portugal association agreement were held to be directly effective in the cases of *Bresciani* and *Kupferberg*.

QUESTIONS

1. 'The doctrine of direct effects of Treaty provisions and directives has made a considerable contribution to protecting the rights of individuals. However, by holding that directives do not have horizontal direct effects, the Court of Justice has taken a backward step. Fortunately, some of the drawbacks of this situation may be remedied by *Von Colson* and subsequent case law.' Discuss.

First of all, this requires a definition of direct effects, followed by a brief outline of direct effects as a Community concept developed by the Court of Justice to apply to Treaty articles and directives and of how they protect individual rights, which can only be done by going through a case law history of direct effects. For example, it doesn't allow Member States to plead their own failure to implement Community law or to implement it incorrectly to defeat the rights of individuals (see the *Defrenne* v *SABENA* and the *Marshall* cases). Then discuss the *Marshall* case and why the decision was a backward step, if you agree with this. Lastly discuss the later case law which may remedy some of the undesirable effects.

A common mistake in answering this question is that direct effects are sometimes defined by reference to national legislation, in particular, the UK's European Communities Act 1972. This is trying to define a Community concept in terms of a national definition. If it is right to mention the UK Act, *any* national law would be relevant, whether Greek, Portuguese or Danish, and *all* that the national Acts said about direct effects would be equally relevant. There is no reason why the UK definition is any more correct. It is a Community established concept, hence it must be defined by reference to Community sources. Furthermore, whilst you could distinguish direct effects and direct applicability, it is not really necessary to spend a great deal of time in doing so, and it is not answering the question set.

It *is* necessary to distinguish between vertical and horizontal direct effects, which is the crux of the question. Demonstrate horizontal direct effects for Treaty articles and regulations by reference to case law, e.g. *Defrenne* v *SABENA* and *Leonesio* v *Italy*. The facts and decision in *Marshall* must be considered, but not in great detail. *Marshall* decided there could be no horizontal direct effects of directives. There should be brief discussion of the reason for this decision, but not too much as it is not directly answering the question. Directives are not addressed to individuals, therefore they should not be obligated by them.

The next part of the question to answer is whether the decision in *Marshall* was a backward step and, if so, why. The backward step is arguable because of the consequences of the *Marshall* decision. Rights contained within directives cannot be enforced by individuals against other individuals. This has the result that there is no uniformity in the application of Community law between public and private employers within Member States and between Member States, because there are different concepts of what is the state and what are private and public employers. Certain individuals are thus denied rights that employees in the public sector can enforce in the face of non-compliance by Member States. An example of the dire consequences for individuals, even where direct effects were present in the legislation, is the *Duke* case in the UK. The *Marshall* decision has thus led to an arbitrary and uneven protection of individual rights. The uniformity of Community law is undermined in important areas of law dealing with workers' rights, where many directives are relevant to private employers and the protection of individuals and their rights, e.g., Art 141 (old 119) can create horizontal direct effects but the directive providing the same rights cannot (Directive 75/117).

The question then requires you to consider the view that some of the drawbacks may have been remedied by *Von Colson* and subsequent case law. Here you need to identify cases which have helped or, to put it another way, the ways in which the Court of Justice has overcome the unfortunate consequences, by reference to example cases.

The Court of Justice has perhaps started to expand the concept of the public sector under case law (see, e.g., *Foster v British Gas*). However, although it may be considered that tinkering with the scope of what is meant by an emanation of the state will broaden the concept and protect more people, does this get to the heart of the matter? It still allows a variation as between public and private employees and between the Member States. The difficulties and limits to this approach are demonstrated in the UK case of *Doughty v Rolls Royce plc*, in which the Court of Appeal considered that the nationalised Rolls Royce company was not a public body for the purposes of the claim to direct effects in the case.

The *Von Colson* case, mentioned in the question, came before the Court of Justice with the *Harz* case because they both consider the same provision. These cases emphasised the dichotomy of the rights available to public and private employees. The Court addressed the matter by holding that Art 10 (old 5) also requires Member State courts to comply with Community law obligations by interpreting national law in compliance with Community law, rather than getting tied up with the problems of direct effects which would have helped von Colson but not Harz. The difficulty with the *Von Colson* line of argument is that it requires there to be national law to interpret, or rules the national court can comply with.

Later cases which develop the boundaries of this principle are *Marleasing*, which required the national courts to apply Community law regardless of the intent or existence of national law and *Kolpinghuis*, which held that a

Member State which has not implemented a directive cannot invoke it against an individual, i.e., direct effects may not to be used to worsen the position of an individual. Neither go as far to protect the rights of individuals as would be achieved by the extension of horizontal direct effects to directives. This denial of horizontal effects of directive by the ECJ has been confirmed in the case of *Faccini Dori* (case C-91/92).

An alternative is the use of general provisions of the Treaty, such as Arts 10 and 249 (old 5 and 189) as in *Francovich*, to impose liability on the state for the non-implementation of directives. In *Francovich*, the relevant directive was not capable of giving rise to direct effects, but the requirements of the effective and uniform application of Community law gave rise to a liability to compensate in certain circumstances where the directive conferred rights on individuals. These individual rights must be determined by the provisions of the directive alone, and there needs to be a link between the damage caused and the failure of the Member State to implement the directive. Since that case, the Court of Justice has had the opportunity to develop the law, starting with joined cases *Brasserie du Pécheur* v *Federal Republic of Germany* (case C-46/93) and *Factortame (No. 3)* v *UK* (case C-48/93). The result of this case law is that all manner of breaches of Community law by all three arms of state could lead to liability to individuals but the focus has been moved to the seriousness of the breach. *Factortame (No. 3)* introduced the revised criteria that the breach must be analogous to that applied to liability of the EC institutions under Art 288 (old 215). This is known as the 'Shöppenstedt Formula' and in order for liability to arise on the part of the Member State, there must have been a sufficiently serious breach of a superior rule of law designed for the protection of individuals. This has provoked further case law to help decide how serious a breach is required for Member States to incur liability. *British Telecom* takes a generous view of what constitutes a breach but this can be contrasted with the *Hedley Lomas* case where a mere infringement will invoke potential liability. Thus, if there is a breach Member States must compensate according to the principles established in *Francovich*. State liability is clearly a significant step forward in remedying the unfortunate consequences of the *Marshall* judgment.

2.   Explain the distinction between the concepts of direct effects and direct applicability.

OR

A distinction has been drawn between direct effects and direct applicability. What do you understand by this distinction?

For both of these questions, first of all try to define the two concepts, or at least give a working definition of them. Refer to the sections in this chapter.

(a)   Direct applicability   This is a means or mode of incorporation, or the way in which international law finds validity in national legal systems. In the EC, the phrase 'directly applicable' is specifically mentioned in Art 249 (old 189) concerning regulations, which shall have general application and shall be directly applicable. It carries an obligation not to transform Community regulations into national legislation, which does not include necessary implementation measures required to ensure the effectiveness of Community rules, e.g., *Commission* v *UK (Tachographs)*. Therefore, the special elements or criteria are that the regulation is automatically binding and general, in that it applies also to the citizens directly and not just to nation states. (Also described as a normative act.)

To what forms of legislation does the concept apply? Clearly it applies to regulations because of Art 249 (old 189), but what about other forms of Community law? It is suggested that it does not apply to the Treaties themselves, because they have been signed and ratified and have therefore been implemented in some way by the Member States. A different view may be taken in respect of Treaty articles, however, because they are not incorporated by an act or transformed but were self-executing when the Treaty was ratified, e.g., the UK did not include the text of the Treaties in the European Communities Act 1972. The Treaty provisions are therefore automatically binding and general. Directives are not directly applicable because they require further implementation and they usually give wide discretion to the Member States to whom they are addressed. Therefore they are not automatic and do not apply to all. Decisions are not directly applicable because they are not generally binding, i.e., they do not apply or bind all, but usually only named individuals.

(b)   Direct effects   'Direct effects' is the term given to judicial enforcement of rights arising from provisions of Community law which can be upheld in favour of individuals in the courts of the Member States. It describes the right to rely directly on Community law.

Direct effects can apply to articles of the Treaty, to regulations, to directives and to decisions — in fact, to any binding law in terms of Art 249 (old 189) EC, and in some circumstances outside of Art 249 (old 189), as with international agreements, provided the criteria laid down by the Court of Justice are fulfilled. The criteria are that the provisions must be clear, precise, leave no discretion, be unconditional and require no further implementation by either the Community or the Member States. Cite case law to back up all of these statements in respect of direct effects, as noted above.

In respect of directives, a further criterion is necessary. The direct effects of directives can arise only from the expiry of the period of implementation, as exampled by the *Ratti* case, or, as in the *Verbond* case, when the Member State has incorrectly implemented the obligation of the directive.

(c) The distinction between 'direct effects' and 'directly applicable'   One of the problems in looking at these two concepts is that the terminology of the Court of Justice and some of the earlier writers has been very confusing. Often the term 'direct effects' has not been used, and instead the formulation given is that the provision gives rise to effects similar to direct applicability, which can be enforced by individuals in the national courts. Direct applicability is a mode of incorporation, whereas the term 'direct effects' is a judicial development for the enforcement of rights. Another clearer difference is that direct effects can apply to all forms of Community law, whereas the term 'directly applicable' applies just to certain types. Two theorems might help prove a difference exists:

(i)   If something is directly applicable, is it then directly effective, i.e. must it follow that a directly applicable provision must be capable of direct effects? No, direct effects are not automatic. Individual provisions still have to satisfy the criteria laid down by the Court, and the term 'directly applicable' is relevant only to specific forms of provision and not to all. Back this up by looking at some forms of Community law to show that they are directly applicable but not necessarily directly effective. Regulations or Treaty articles which are directly applicable need not be directly effective. They must still satisfy the criteria, and do not do so in all instances; see, for example, the case of *Hurd* v *Jones* in which Art 5 (old 10) was held not to be directly effective. In contrast, direct effects can arise from all forms of Community legislation.

(ii)   If a provision of Community law has been held to be directly effective, does it therefore necessarily become directly applicable? In other words, does it become directly applicable by the backdoor? No, while direct effects can apply to all forms of provisions, 'directly applicable' requires generality and does not apply to all forms. The term 'direct effects' is to do with enforceability by individuals, whereas direct applicability is concerned with legal provisions which are generally binding, as with Treaty articles and regulations which apply both vertically and horizontally. For example, directives can have direct effects but are limited to the vertical axis, i.e., they are binding only on the State and not on individuals. They are therefore not generally applicable. Directives cannot obligate individuals unless specifically directed to them, and thus fail on the generality criterion, as do decisions.

Thus a real distinction between the concepts exists which can be demonstrated. Additions to this basic question may concern the suggestion that the concept of direct effects has blurred the distinction between regulations and directives. You would need to show they are still different forms of legislation for different purposes, and that regulations are still generally applicable whereas directives are not.

3.   It is now well established that the sources of Community law include a category entitled 'general principles of law'. Discuss why the European Court considered it was necessary to develop these, and how it can justify their inclusion.

The parts of this question which have to be addressed are (i) the fact that the sources of law include an established category entitled 'general principles of law', (ii) the necessity perceived by the Court of Justice to develop them, and (iii) the justification for including them.

The existence of this category can be demonstrated by the citation of cases which have involved consideration or recognition by the Court of Justice of general principles of law. See the cases noted above, such as *Hauer, R v Kent Kirk, UNECTEF, Johnston, AM & S* and *Rutili*, amongst others.

Secondly, you should consider the necessity to develop general principles of law. This part will concentrate on the moral and social requirements that any legal system in Europe must have regard for general principles of law, especially fundamental rights. An additional factor is that there would be serious clashes with Member States' constitutional law, which lead to severe strains on the Community legal system, if the Community did not take account of general principles. Also, in certain circumstances, the Treaty requires it. This part overlaps with the third part of the answer looking at the justification for the introduction of general principles.

The justification for the inclusion of general principles arises partly as a result of some Treaty articles which specifically mention them, such as one of the grounds under Art 230 (old 173), the requirement that the Court of Justice must consider them under Art 288 (old 215) and the requirement in Art 220 (old 164) that the law be observed. For further details see the relevant text in chapter 4. A further ground to justify them is the moral requirement (mentioned above) that a western legal system must include general principles, some of which serve to protect individual rights. Another argument stems from the fact that the Treaty is only a framework treaty and requires completion by reference to other laws. For the most part this is done by the specific secondary legislation of the Community, but this provides only the substantive law rules, which also often require interpretation by the Court of Justice. The Community legal order was established from scratch and does not have the traditions of the Member States' legal systems to rely on which are rich in developed principles of law. Therefore, something is needed to assist the Court of Justice in its task, and general principles, many of which are borrowed from the Member States' legal systems, do just that.

4. On 1 January 1996, the EC Council adopted a directive designed to bring about a reduction in wine, a surplus of which exists in the Community, by encouraging the export of wine outside the EU and reducing the amount produced. Article 2 of the directive provides that 'in order to assist the export of wine, export agencies shall waive all handling charges levied on wine producers'. Article 3 provides that 'the Member States shall make every effort to ensure that no individual producer is excessively prejudiced by the directive but must ensure there should not be an increase in the national wine production. Producers should be allowed to produce, in the years 1998 and 1999, up to the average amount for the last three years'. The Member States are given the power to determine how Art 3 is brought into effect.

Member States were required to implement the directive by January 1998. The directive was implemented in Germany in September 1998. The German legislation has provided for the repayment of the handling charges, less 10 per cent for administrative charges, but has not implemented Art 3.

B. Soffen, a wine producer, had two consignments of wine handled by the German Wine Export Agency (GWEA), a government export agency. One consignment was exported in February 1997, the other in March 1998. Handling charges were levied on both consignments. A second producer, Weitaugen and Beinlos (W & B), has been refused permission to increase the amount of production in 1999, even though the requested increase will only bring it up to the average for the last three years.

In an action before a German court, B. Soffen claimed, in accordance with the directive, the repayment of the handling charges levied on both consignments by the GWEA. The GWEA replied, first, that the directive had not been implemented in time and argued, secondly, that in any case the directive conflicted with the German constitution which guarantees the right to practise a trade. W & B has challenged the authorities' right to restrict its production and seeks to rely on the directive. As a part of its claim it has pleaded that the restriction also conflicts with the ECHR, which guarantees the right to the enjoyment of possessions and property.

(a) Advise the two parties as to their rights under Community law.

(b) Would your answer be any different if all export agencies were in private ownership?

This is a fairly long and complex problem, so you need to plan out your answer and the information you need to provide. First of all, work from the general to the particular. Explain generally the area or topics of law. Then deal with the material facts in turn for each of the claimants and spell out the legal issues arising. Determine the applicable legal rules which may arise from legislation or from judicial developments. Lastly, apply the law to the facts in each case and suggest a solution.

This problem concerns the late and incorrect implementation of directives and the consequences for individuals who wish to rely on them. It also has mentioned the German constitution and a provision of the ECHR which seem to have a bearing. You could briefly, by way of introduction, state that individuals can rely directly on Community law in certain circumstances because of the doctrine of direct effects, developed by the Court of Justice to ensure the consistent application of Community law throughout the Member States. Specifically, therefore, this problem is concerned with when directives can become directly effective and the criteria required.

The material facts are that a Directive, to come into force on 1 January 1998 provides for the waiver of handling charges on wine and a non-prejudicial limit on production. Germany implemented it late, with amendments and incompletely. This has given rise to problems for two wine producers. B. Soffen (BS), who was charged and W & B, who were not allowed to increase production.

The legal issues arising are what the wine producers can do to enforce the rights granted by the Directive against the German Authorities who appear to have infringed them. Furthermore there are issues of the relevance of the German constitution and the ECHR.

The applicable law which can be identified is Art 249 (old 189), which requires Member States to achieve a required result when implementing directives, and the doctrine of direct effects to allow individuals to enforce Community rights.

You can now deal with each case in turn.

The BS case   BS seeks repayment of two charges from February 1997 and March 1998. Germany argues that the late implementation (September 1998) defeats the claim. BS needs to know whether, in the absence of German legislation at the material time, it can rely on the directive directly to give it rights enforceable in its national courts.

Are they able to do this? Yes, if directly effective. Can directives be directly effective? Yes, according the Court in *Van Duyn*. Directives can give rise to direct effects providing they satisfy the criteria as laid down in *Van Gend en Loos* and subsequent cases. Additionally, in respect of directives they must satisfy the time period, this latter point is the case of *Ratti*. So, when time period expired an individual can rely on the directive if it fulfils the criteria.

With regard to the time limits, Germany should have implemented the directive by 1 January 1998. Therefore, applying the *Ratti* case, when the first charge was made the time limit had not expired, and therefore the directive could not give rise to direct effects at this time; but the time limit had expired for the second charges made in March 1998. But BS still has to consider whether Art 2 is clear and precise, etc. It is — the directive imposes a clear and unconditional obligation on Member States to ensure that they waive charges. The provision in point therefore meets the requirements for direct effect, and BS can rely on it in a national court and get repayment of the second charges. A question may be raised about whether the provision is severable from the directive. This was answered in *Van Duyn*, which held it was severable.

A further problem exists in that 10 per cent has been deducted which was not sanctioned by the directive, i.e., the German implementing legislation does not meet the requirements of the directive. Therefore there is a conflict between the directive and German legislation.

Has BS rights directly from the directive in such a case? This is demonstrated by cases to show where a Member State implemented in time but got it wrong. In *Verbond van Nederlanse Ondernemingen* the Court of Justice held that even when a directive had been implemented by a Member State, that did not necessarily prevent the directive from producing direct effects. The Court ruled that this was especially so when an individual invokes a provision of a directive before a national court in order that the latter may rule whether the national authorities, in exercising the choice of form and methods for implementation, have kept within the limits of the discretion set out in the directive.

BS would bring the claim in the national court on the basis that, whatever the national legislation says, it must be interpreted so as to give effect to directly effective provisions of the directive, as was argued in *Marshall*. Hence, BS could reclaim the whole of second charge.

In the alternative, the German authorities have argued that the directive conflicts with the German constitution. Their argument would therefore be that the German constitution must take priority to defeat the claims by BS. This is a question of supremacy which has been resolved clearly by the Court of Justice in the *Internationale Handelsgesellschaft* case. Community law prevails even over provisions of a national constitution. At the hands of the Court of Justice, therefore, the German argument would fail. National courts have not always been so quick to recognise this supremacy, however. The actual answer here lies in whether the directive does offend the German constitution, and you would not be expected to know or discuss the national legal issues but just to recognise the potential for conflict here.

The action by W & B This concerns W & B's claim against the refusal to increase production which arose after the national legislation came into force. However, the national legislation did not implement Art 3 of the directive, i.e., there is in fact no relevant national law. W & B must therefore base its claim on the directive.

The directive does not impose a clear, precise and unconditional obligation on the Member States, since it merely requires them to make every effort to introduce such provisions into their national legislation and allows them a discretion as to the method by which they do it. The ECJ cannot decide how much effort was made. The likelihood is that it cannot be said to be capable of producing direct effects, and W & B has no right to enforce the law against the Member State.

Perhaps it is with this in mind that W & B has claimed a breach of an article of the ECHR against the Member State. Although provisions of the ECHR have been held to be general principles of law to be recognised and to be upheld in the Community legal order (see *Hauer* v *Rheinland-Pfalz*), there is no case law to state that this will be upheld as a principle of Community law against the Member State's legislation. In any case, as was outlined in the cases of *Nold* and *Hauer* itself, such principles, although recognised, are not absolute, and their exercise may be restricted in the interests of the Community. There may be other alternatives, however, discussed below.

What if the export agencies were in private ownership? The Court of Justice has repeatedly emphasised that direct effects of directives only arise against the Member States and not against private individuals (see *Marshall*). However, the ECJ held in *Von Colson* that, although a directive may not be horizontally directly effective, the Member States' courts should take the provisions of the directive into account when applying national law. This principle would help BS but not W & B since there is no legislation in place. Nor would the case of *Marleasing* help because the Community law legislation is unclear as to what is required and cannot, therefore, be interpreted by the national courts.

The case of *Francovich* might apply to obtain damages for the failure to implement the directive. If an individual suffers damage as a result of the failure of a Member State, the Member State may be liable to pay damages if the directive itself defined and conferred a right on individuals, the content of which was clear. An action for damages under the *Francovich* doctrine also requires there to have been a sufficiently serious breach of a superior rule of law designed for the protection of an individual. The case for BS here is certainly clearer than for W & B. Article 2 of the directive seems to convey an individual right which if not implemented by the Member State would cause damage and may well succeed under *Francovich*. Article 3 of the directive seems far from certain and here a reference to the ECJ under Art 234 (old 177) would appear to be the only clear recommendation you could make in this case. Certainly if private employers were involved, the paths for individuals remains far more difficult but not impossible in realising their rights or compensation in lieu.

FURTHER READING

Bebr, G., Casenote on *Francovich* (1992) 29 CML Rev 557.

Brinkhorst, L., Casenote on the *Grad* and *SACE* decisions (1971) 8 CML Rev 380.

Craig, P., 'Directives, Direct, Indirect effect and the Construction of National Legislation' (1997) 22 EL Rev 519.

Duvigneau, J.L., 'From advisory opinion 2/94 to the Amsterdam Treaty: human rights protection in the European Union' (1998) LIEI 25(2), 61.

Easson, A., 'The Direct Effect of EEC Directives' (1979) 28 ICLQ 319.

Eleftheriadis, P., 'The direct effect of Community law: conceptual issues', (1996) 16 YEL 205.

Schermers, H., 'No direct effect for Directives', (1997) EPL 3(4) 527.

Steiner, J., 'From Direct Effects to *Francovich*: Shifting Means of Enforcement of Community Law' (1993) 18 EL Rev 3.

5 SUPREMACY AND RECEPTION IN THE MEMBER STATES

The supremacy or priority of Community law over the laws of the Member States can be considered from two perspectives: first, from the point of view of the Community and, secondly, from that of the Member States.

Also considered in this chapter, because it concerns the relationship between the Community and the Member States, is the principle of subsidiarity which was incorporated into the EC treaty by the TEU; see Art 5 (old 3b).

THE VIEW OF THE COURT OF JUSTICE

There is no express declaration or specific legal base for the supremacy of Community law in the treaties. It can be argued that some of the articles of the EC Treaty impliedly require primacy, e.g., Art 10 (old 5) (the fidelity clause), Art 12 (old 6) (the general prohibition of discrimination on the grounds of nationality), Art 249 (old 189) (the direct applicability of regulations) and Art 292 (old 219) (the reservation of dispute resolution). As with the doctrine of direct effects, it is through the decisions and interpretation of the Court of Justice that the reasons and logic for the supremacy of Community law have been developed. The Court of Justice's view on this is quite straightforward. From its case law, notably *Van Gend en Loos*, *Costa* v *ENEL* and *Simmenthal*, it is clear that Community law is assumed to be an autonomous legal order which is related to international law and national law but is nevertheless distinct from them.

The *Van Gend en Loos* case affirmed the Court's jurisdiction in interpreting Community legal provisions, the object of which is to ensure uniform interpretation in the Member States. The Court of Justice held that 'the Community constitutes a new legal order of international law for the benefit of which the States have limited their sovereign rights, albeit in limited fields, and the subjects of which comprise not only Member States but also their nationals'.

Further elaboration of the new legal order in *Van Gend en Loos* was given in *Costa* v *ENEL*. This case primarily concerned the payment of an electricity bill of a very low value. The case raised the issue of whether a national court should refer to the Court of Justice if it considers Community law may be applicable or, as was the view of the Italian government, simply apply the subsequent national law. The Court of Justice stressed the autonomous legal order of Community law:

> By contrast with ordinary international treaties the EEC Treaty has created its own legal system which became an integral part of the legal systems of the Member States and which their courts are bound to apply. By creating a Community of unlimited duration, having its own institutions, its own personality, its own legal capacity and more particularly real powers stemming from a limitation of sovereignty or a transfer of powers from the States to the Community the Member States have limited their sovereign rights and have created a body of law to bind their nationals and themselves.

The Court also established that Community law takes priority over all conflicting provisions of national law, whether passed before or after the Community measure in question:

> The integration into the laws of each Member State of provisions which derive from the Community, and more generally, the terms and spirit of the Treaty, make it impossible for the States, as a corollary, to accord precedence to a unilateral and subsequent measure over a legal system accepted by them on the basis of reciprocity. Such a measure cannot therefore be inconsistent with that legal system.

As additional justification, the Court of Justice also invoked the use of some of the general provisions of the Treaty: old Art 5 (now 10) (the requirement to ensure the attainment of the objectives of the Treaty) and old Art 7 (EEC) (now 12) (regarding discrimination), both of which would be breached if subsequent national legislation was to have precedence; and old Art 189 (now 249) (regarding the binding and direct application of regulations) which would be meaningless if subsequent national legislation could prevail. The Court summed up its position:

> It follows . . . that the law stemming from the Treaty, an independent source of law, could not because of its special and original nature, be overridden by domestic legal provisions, however framed, without being

deprived of its character as Community law and without the legal basis of the Community itself being called into question.

Therefore, Community law is to be supreme over subsequent national law.

In *Simmenthal* (case 106/77), the Court of Justice ruled that: 'A national court which is called upon, within the limits of its jurisdiction, to apply provisions of Community law, is under a duty to give full effect to those provisions, if necessary of its own motion to set aside any conflicting provisions of national legislation, even if adopted subsequently.' The Court of Justice ruled that directly effective provisions of Community law preclude the valid adoption of new legislative measures to the extent that they would be incompatible with Community provisions. Any inconsistent national legislation recognised by national legislatures as having legal effect would deny the effectiveness of the obligations undertaken by the Member State and imperil the existence of the Community. (This case is considered further below in respect of constitutional practices.)

Therefore, the voluntary limitation of sovereignty and the need for an effective and uniform Community law requires supremacy. To give effect to subsequent national law over and above the Community legal system which Member States have accepted would be inconsistent.

In *Factortame (No. 2)* (case 213/89), the Court of Justice, building on the principle laid down in *Simmenthal* (case 106/77), that a provision of EC law must be implemented as effectively as possible, held that a national court must suspend national legislation that may be incompatible with EC law until a final determination on its compatibility has been made. Thus national rules which prevented a national court from issuing an interim injunction while considering the existence of alleged rights under Community law, must be set aside. It was later held in case C-221/89 that the UK law breached Community law.

Finally, in this context it is worth mentioning the consequences of a Member State not giving primacy to Community law when it should have done. Liability on the part of the State will be incurred as first established by the Court of Justice in the *Francovich* case and later confirmed in *Factortame (No. 3)* and other cases. For further details refer to the previous chapter.

The Court of Justice has maintained a consistent position on supremacy, including secondary Community law, over 'ordinary' national legislation. The position of supremacy over provisions of a Member State's constitution has caused more problems.

SUPREMACY AND CONSTITUTIONAL LAW

The Court of Justice's view in respect of national constitutional law can be seen in *Internationale Handelsgesellschaft*, which concerned the claim that

Community levies were contrary to German constitutional law. The Court of Justice held that the national courts did not possess the power to review Community law:

> The law stemming from the Treaty, an independent source of law, cannot because of its very nature be overridden by rules of national law however framed, without being deprived of its character as Community law. Therefore the validity of a Community measure or its effect within a Member State cannot be affected by allegations that it runs counter to either fundamental rights as formulated by the constitution of that State or the principles of a national constitutional structure.

The Court established that if there were no violation of Community fundamental rights, the Community measures were acceptable, and there should be no reference to national constitutions to test their validity.

In *Simmenthal*, the constitutional practice existed that the power to disregard or declare invalid a provision of national law was the sole right of the constitutional court. A lower court was faced with inconsistency between a Community law provision and a national provision. The national court was aware that a reference to the Italian constitutional court would have the effect of subrogating Community law to legal practice, inconsistent with existent Community case law on the matter in *Costa* v *ENEL*. However, disregarding the national law was contrary to constitutional requirements. The Italian magistrate referred to both courts but asked the Court of Justice whether subsequent national measures which conflict with Community law must be disregarded without waiting until those measures are set aside by legislative or other constitutional means. The answer was, as noted above, that the national court should disregard the inconsistent national law.

The *Factortame (No. 2)* case represents another confirmation that national constitutional practices or rules, in this case the doctrine of parliamentary sovereignty in the UK, must not be allowed to stand in the way of a Community law right. In the case this was the clear understanding of the courts that they had no power to set aside or not apply an Act of Parliament. The Court of Justice held that even if the Community law rule was still in dispute, the national procedure should be changed so as not to possibly interfere with the full effectiveness of the Community law right. This case also starts to see a Community law incursion into national procedure, which will be taken up further below.

The above cases are just the leading cases on supremacy, those which expressly declare Community law primacy. Many other cases imply Community law supremacy, e.g., all cases which declare direct effects presuppose a supremacy. If Community law is not supreme over national law, especially subsequent law, then direct effects would be denied. Conversely if direct effects are denied where they fulfil the criteria, supremacy is therefore also denied because national law would be seen to prevail.

In summary, the Community view on supremacy is that, because of its unique nature, Community law denies the Member States the right to resolve conflicts of law by reference to their own rules or constitutional provisions. Community law obtains its supremacy because of the transfer of state power and sovereignty to the Community by the Member States in those areas agreed. The Member States have provided the Community with legislative powers to enable it to perform its tasks. There would be no point in such a transfer of power if the Member States could annul or suspend the effect of Community law by later national law or provisions of the constitutions. If that were allowed to be the case, the existence of the Community legal order and the Community itself would be called into question. A precondition of the existence and functioning of the Community is the uniform and consistent application of Community law and the Community legal order in all the Member States. It can achieve such an effect only if it takes precedence over national law. Therefore, the legal and logical consequence of this is the fact that any provision of national law which conflicts with Community law must be invalid.

Where a Community law right is involved, national procedural law must not deprive a litigant of their rights under Community law and Community nationals should be treated no less favourably than nationals, so that the general principle of Art 12 (old 6) is not breached. See for example *Levez* v *Jennings*, in which the ECJ considered a UK procedural law which limited the period of claim for damages in sex discrimination cases to a period not exceeding two years running, backward from the date of commencement of proceedings. The ECJ acknowledged that, in the absence of a Community regime on the matter, it was for Member States to determine procedural rules governing Community law rights providing they are equivalent to similar domestic actions and were effective. A limit of two years was not criticised. However, Ms Levez had been misinformed or deliberately misled by the employer as to the higher earnings of a male predecessor and had only learnt the truth on leaving her job. Under such circumstances the Court of Justice held that, if applied, the rule would serve to deprive an employee from effective enforcement of Community law because it would be almost impossible to obtain arrears of remuneration and enable employers to avoid paying damages by deceit. In such circumstances the rule would be manifestly incompatible with principles of EC law.

APPLICATION IN THE MEMBER STATES

The attitude of the Member States to international law and Community law is determined initially by the particular view the State has regarding the incorporation and the validity of such law. Two theories of incorporation of external law apply to determine the initial acceptance of Community law into the legal system — *monism* and *dualism*.

Monism basically assumes that international law and national law form part of a single system or hierarchy of laws, therefore the acceptance of international law would not require formal incorporation by legislative transformation, but after assent it would be self-executing. In other words, it would be directly applicable within the state. All that is required by such a State to achieve this is simple assent to or ratification of an international treaty.

Dualism regards international law and national law as fundamentally different systems of law which exist along side each other. In order to overcome the barrier existing between the two systems, legislation is required to transform rules of international law into the national legal system before they can have any binding effect within the State.

Community Law in the UK

The UK was not an original member of the Community, and had a number of particular problems to overcome in order to accommodate the duties of membership of the EEC in 1973. It had to accept all the previous Community legislation passed, including not only the treaties but also the regulations, directives and the judicial legal developments of this established new legal order. This is known in Community jargon as the acceptance of the acquis communautaire. It had, on the other hand, time to adjust for this. The particular difficulties of the UK legal system were (i) the largely unwritten constitution, (ii) its dualist approach to international law and (iii) the doctrine of parliamentary sovereignty. The unwritten constitution makes it difficult to alter it with any certainty. As international treaties are a prerogative of the Crown as represented by the Government in Parliament, the courts have no say in the matter, therefore, in order to apply in the UK, a provision of an international treaty must first have been enacted by the UK Parliament as an Act of national legislation. This gave rise to the question of how to convert EEC law into national law without transforming every provision, which would have been contrary to Art 249 (old 189) of the Treaty, at the same time ensuring that the EEC Treaty was not simply overruled by subsequent acts of Parliament.

The doctrine of parliamentary sovereignty   Formally, sovereignty means that there are no legal limitations on Parliament and that it has the right to make or unmake any law whatsoever. Further, no person or body is recognised as having a right to override or set aside the legislation of Parliament. The doctrine also implies that it is consequently impossible to bind future

Parliaments. Subsequent Acts can, however, expressly or impliedly override a prior Act. There is no constitutional role for UK courts, which cannot review the validity of Acts passed by Parliament. They must enforce and apply Acts of Parliament equally.

One of the problems in considering this doctrine of parliamentary sovereignty is the nature of the concept itself. It is not a rigid constitutional enactment but is really just a constitutional convention which was built up over centuries and refined by eminent jurists to the position stated by Dicey in the latter half of the last century. As a convention it is therefore also subject to the erosion of time to reflect the changing circumstances in which it must be employed. Even Dicey conceded this was not an absolute convention and that there were political, if not legal, limits to it. The fact that there has been considerable comment and publicity about the attack on parliamentary sovereignty misconceives its status. However, further consideration here is beyond the scope of this volume. Some courses may go into greater detail about the true nature and scope of the doctrine and explore the impact of other forms of international treaties and agreements. To cater for these I have included further reading at the end of the chapter.

The European Communities Act 1972   Community law implementation in the UK is primarily concerned with how the European Communities Act (ECA) 1972 observes and takes account of such well-established Community law concepts as direct effects and the supremacy of Community law, and the difficulties noted in respect of sovereignty.

In contrast to the earlier practice of incorporation, the ECA did not reproduce the whole of the treaties or subsequent secondary legislation as Acts of Parliament. If this had been done, the words of any future Act could override the prior treaties. The EEC Treaty was adopted by simple assent. The Act therefore impliedly recognises the unique new legal system and is regarded as a special form of UK legislation.

Section 2(1) recognises the legal validity and direct applicability of Community treaties and regulations already existing and provides that all such future Community legal provisions shall also be recognised as such:

> All such rights, powers, liabilities, obligations and restrictions from time to time created or arising under the Treaties, and all such remedies and procedures from time to time provided for by or under the Treaties, as in accordance with the Treaties are without further enactment to be given legal effect or used in the United Kingdom shall be recognised and available in law, and be enforced, allowed and followed accordingly . . . .

The subsection therefore recognises the doctrine of direct effects and allows for future developments by the Court of Justice. The provision continues, 'the expression "enforceable Community right" and similar expressions shall be read as referring to one to which this subsection applies'.

Section 2(2) allows for the implementation of other Community obligations which are not automatically applicable in the UK, by Orders in Council or statutory instruments. The power the executive has to make secondary legislation is subject to the limits in sch. 2 of the Act, in respect of the imposing or creation of taxation, introduction of retrospective legislation, sub-delegation and the introduction of new criminal offences with more than a two-year period of imprisonment as penalty.

Section 2(4) recognises the supremacy of Community law and therefore concerns sovereignty: 'any such provision . . . and any enactment passed or to be passed [that refers to any secondary legislation and Act of Parliament past or future] . . . shall be construed and have effect subject to the foregoing provisions of this section . . .'. That is a reference back to the entire section, and in particular to s. 2(1), and means that any future Act of Parliament must be construed in such a way as to give effect to the enforceable Community rights in existence. This is achieved by denying effectiveness to any national legislation passed later which is in conflict. This in turn is controlled by the directions to the courts concerned with the application or construction of legislation, to interpret any future Act to be consistent with Community law or, in effect, to be subordinate where inconsistency arises.

Section 3(1) instructs the courts to refer questions on the interpretation, and hence the supremacy, of Community law to the Court of Justice if the UK courts cannot solve the problem themselves by reference to previous Court of Justice rulings. This follows the *Costa* v *ENEL* ruling, and is backed up by s. 3(2) which requires the courts judicially to follow decisions of the Court of Justice on any question of Community law. This would include direct effects and supremacy although it does not expressly say so.

Therefore, it is argued that the combination of s. 2(1) and (4) with the control of s. 3(1) and (2), achieves the essential requirements of the recognition of direct effects and the supremacy of Community law for past and future UK legislation.

The ECA 1972 and parliamentary sovereignty   The view of how the ECA 1972 has affected parliamentary sovereignty is determined by what s. 2(4) actually achieves. There are two main positions in respect of this: either s. 2(4) acts as a rule of construction, or it attempts a form of entrenchment whereby it modifies the doctrine of parliamentary sovereignty.

As a rule of construction, s. 2(4) commands the courts to interpret national law to comply with Community law. The court decisions in this country generally have considered that this should apply only where the national legislation is reasonably capable of such construction, see, for example, the cases of *Macarthys v Smith* and *Garland v BREL*, considered below. Recently, however, this latter criteria is being abandoned as not actually required by the Act, see *Factortame* below.

The alternative of limited entrenchment means that s. 2(4) allows the courts to apply Community law directly over national law, regardless of the actual words or, as recently shown, existence of national law. This enables the courts to ignore implied repeals by, and the unintentional inconsistency of, future Acts of Parliament, and thus modifies the doctrine of parliamentary sovereignty in that one Parliament has been seen to bind a future one. Express inconsistency remains a problem even under this interpretation.

Community law is ultimately dependent on the national judiciary as well as national Parliaments, therefore a consideration of its reception in the courts is vital.

Judicial reception of Community law in the UK   The most important of the earlier cases is *Macarthys Ltd v Smith*, in which Lord Denning, *obiter*, thought that with regard to an express or intentional repudiation of the Treaty by Parliament, or expressly acting inconsistently, the courts would be bound to follow the express and clear intent of Parliament to repudiate the Treaty, or a section of it, by the subsequent Act. The Court of Appeal later confirmed Community law is now part of UK law, and whenever there is any inconsistency Community law has priority.

In *Garland v BREL*, the first important statement from the House of Lords, Ms Garland had complained that the practice of allowing the families of male ex-employees of BREL concessionary rail travel facilities after retirement, but not families of female ex-employees, was discriminatory. Under s. 6(4) of the Sex Discrimination Act 1975, provisions in relation to retirement were exempted from the rules on sex discrimination, and Ms Garland's claim failed. Previous UK case law had determined that s. 6(4) of the 1975 Act be given a wide interpretation, so as to discount anything to do with or connected to retirement, therefore the discrimination was lawful. Article 141 (old 119) EEC and Directive 76/207 made no such exception regarding retirement, thus UK and Community law were regarded by the House of Lords as inconsistent. The House asked the Court of Justice to give a ruling on the interpretation of Art 141 (old 119) to determine if it covered conditions in retirement. The Court of Justice held that it did. Upon return to the House of Lords, their Lordships considered themselves bound, in view of the Court of Justice ruling and ECA 1972, to interpret the Sex Discrimination Act 1975 in such a way as not to be inconsistent with the UK obligations under Community law. While the House of Lords stated the case was no occasion to pronounce on any further effects of the ECA 1972, they did state, *obiter*, that UK courts should interpret UK law to be consistent, no matter how wide a departure from the *prima facie* meaning of that law was involved. Thus the case very much follows the line that s. 2(4) allows courts to construe subsequent statutes quite widely in order to give consistency to Community law, and that it is clearly a rule of construction.

In *Duke* v *GEC Reliance*, brought at roughly the same time as the *Marshall* case, Ms Duke was required to retire at 60, earlier than men who could retire at 65. Section 6(4) of the Sex Discrimination Act 1975 was applied to render the discrimination lawful. The House of Lords considered the *Marshall* ruling, in which the Equal Treatment Directive (76/207) was held to apply to retirement itself and to have direct effects, but because this case concerned a private sector employer, the House of Lords rightly concluded that the Directive itself could not be enforced against individuals, i.e., it had no horizontal direct effects. Therefore, a head-on clash between the Community law Directive and a UK statute provision took place, with the Directive being later in time. The post-accession statute was inconsistent with a subsequent Community obligation, and thus not capable of giving effect of any intention of Parliament to comply with the Directive. Therefore, the House of Lords held there was no enforceable Community right to which the provisions of the English Sex Discrimination Act would be required to give way by virtue of s. 2(4) of the ECA 1972, and that s. 2(4) cannot apply to construe a UK statute to enforce Community directives against individuals; it can apply only to directly applicable Community law. (The House of Lords held that s. 2(4) refers to s. 2(1), which covers only directly effective Community law or directly applicable law, therefore it was not appropriate.) Ms Duke was defeated by the House of Lords, as was the view of s. 2(4) as a rule of construction.

Pickstone v *Freemans plc* involved a generous interpretation of the UK's 1983 regulations, which amended the Equal Pay Act 1970, to read consistently with Community law obligations. For the most part this was based on the intention of Parliament in passing the regulations to ensure national law complied with the Community Directive, but also was the result of a Court of Justice ruling. Section 2(4) of the ECA 1972 was used to justify the Court's interpretation of national law, but only in so far as it was reasonably possible. *Duke* was then distinguished on the basis that the Sex Discrimination Act 1975 was not intended to give effect to Community law or to be capable of doing so. This means that the intent of the UK Parliament, as perceived by the later law, becomes relevant to matters of Community law rights, rather than its intent in the ECA 1972 that Community law should take priority

Litster v *Forth Dry Dock & Engineering Co. Ltd* concerned the rights of employees on the transfer of the undertaking of a business. A number of employees were claiming unfair dismissal after a ship repairing company was transferred between owners. The relevant law was the Transfer of

Undertakings (Protection of Employment) Regulations, which purported to implement the obligations contained in EEC Council Directive 77/187 but which were considered to be somewhat ambiguous. The Directive involved did not give rise to direct effects because the case concerned a private employer. The House of Lords could not achieve a satisfactory result in keeping with the European Directive and the case law of the Court of Justice by a literal interpretation of the Regulations, therefore it concluded that it must use the Community legislation to construe the later UK legislation and imply additional words to achieve consistency with the purpose of the Directive. Here s. 2(4) is clearly being used as a rule of construction, and quite a generous one.

R v Secretary of State for Transport, ex parte Factortame Ltd (No. 2) is a particularly important statement of the view of the House of Lords on the supremacy of Community law. You may find the series of litigation in the *Factortame* cases very confusing, particularly since the case numbers are not always used consistently. To try and clarify the matter, the case proceeded as follows. In the main actions on merits, the Queen's Bench divisional court granted an interim injunction and decided to refer the substantive issue to the Court of Justice, which was given the docket number C-221/89. This is *Factortame (No. 2)*. The Crown appealed against the injunction and a second series of cases proceeded to the House of Lords, who also made a reference the Court of Justice on the procedural matter. This is *Factortame (No. 1)*, but because it was received earlier by the Court of Justice it was given the number C-213/89. Upon the return of the case to the House of Lords, full reasoning was given.

The facts are that the United Kingdom wanted to protect the British fishing quotas under the European quota system, and passed an Act in 1988 aimed at stopping the practice of quota hopping by Spanish-owned vessels registered in the UK by requiring that a minimum percentage of the directors of the a company owning fishing vessels registered in the UK be British nationals. The vessels' owners sought an interim injunction against the Crown not to apply a disputed national regulation issued pursuant to the Act. A reference was made on this procedural point to the Court of Justice by the House of Lords, and although the substantive point of Community law in relation to the UK law had not been decided at that stage, the House of Lords nevertheless considered that if Community law rights are to be found to be directly enforceable in favour of the appellants, those rights will prevail over the inconsistent national legislation, even if later. It was held, *obiter*, that: 'This [s. 2(4)] has precisely the same effect as if a section were incorporated into the national statute . . . which in terms enacted that the provisions [of an Act] were to be without prejudice to the directly enforceable Community rights of nationals of any Member State of the EEC.'

Upon the return of the procedural aspect from the Court of Justice, the House of Lords held that if a national rule precludes the court from granting interim relief, so that it can be determined whether there is a conflict between national law and Community law, the court must set aside that rule. If the injunction against the crown were not granted, the Spanish fishing companies would most probably go out of business whilst waiting for the ECJ to decide the substantive issues and for that to be returned to the QBD and decided, a process that actually took two years and seven months. Lord Bridge commented on the view that the earlier decisions in favour of Community law were an attack on parliamentary sovereignty:

> If the supremacy within the European Community of Community law over the national law of Member States was not always inherent in the EEC Treaty it was certainly well established in the jurisprudence of the Court of Justice long before the United Kingdom joined the Community. Thus, whatever limitation of its sovereignty Parliament accepted when it enacted the European Communities Act 1972 was entirely voluntary. Under the terms of the 1972 Act it has always been clear that it was the duty of a United Kingdom court, when delivering final judgment, to override any rule of national law found to be in conflict with any directly enforceable rule of Community law. Thus there is nothing in any way novel in according supremacy to rules of Community law in those areas to which they apply and to insist that, in the protection of rights under Community law, national courts must not be inhibited by rules of national law from granting interim relief in appropriate cases is no more than a logical recognition of that supremacy.

Thus, the view now of s. 2(4) of the ECA 1972 is that it is a direct rule to give priority, rather than a rule of construction which requires there to be national law to construe. The substantive matter was decided in the High Court as predicted, in favour of Community law.

The results of this case law would seem to suggest that, as far as the House of Lords is now concerned, entry to the Communities and s. 2(4) of the ECA 1972 have led to the modification of the doctrine of parliamentary sovereignty and that Community law is supreme over national law in the areas agreed by Treaty. Whether this overrides the dictum in *Macarthys Ltd* v *Smith* is open to question. It remains open for Parliament expressly to repeal the Act or pass legislation expressly in breach of Community law obligations.

I hope you have reached the conclusion that the series of *Factortame* litigation is extremely important for a number of reasons in Community law, in particular from the point of view of supremacy over national law and constitutional doctrine. I am sure you will also have appreciated that it is an extremely complicated series of cases but given its importance, it should be most carefully studied. If you can understand what is going on and the reasons for the decisions reached, then nothing else in Community law should be beyond your comprehension. It really is worthwhile taking some time on this one!

The *Factortame* case returned for final decision to the High Court (*Factortame (No. 5)*) on whether damages would be payable. It was held that the legislative failure of the UK Government would give rise to damage liability providing damage and cause were established. This was appealed to the Court of Appeal who confirmed the decision of the High Court. Finally, in October 1999, the House of Lords held that the UK Government had manifestly and gravely disregarded the limits on its discretion and that the breach of Community law was sufficiently serious to entitle the applicants to damages for losses directly caused by the breach.

In *R v Secretary of State for Employment ex parte EOC* the House of Lords confirmed the conclusion reached in *Factortame* and held that in judicial review proceedings the UK courts could declare an Act of Parliament to be incompatible with EC law, although this does not extend to being able to annul the UK Act of Parliament nor indeed command a Government to repeal the act or compel or command a minister to change the law.

The conclusion for the UK is that it has clearly and unambiguously accepted the supremacy of EC law even over UK Acts of Parliament and on the basis of the logic of Community law as espoused by the Court of Justice and not by reference to the UK ECA 1972. As such the UK seems to have gone further than some of the other Member States.

RECEPTION OF COMMUNITY LAW IN OTHER MEMBER STATES

A majority of States have not experienced any problems so far, although there is room, judicially, for this position to change. I have only provided examples and not conducted an exhaustive tour of all Member States!

Belgium

In Belgium the constitution was amended to allow for the transfer of powers to institutions governed by international law (Art 25a). However, Belgium was a dualist country, so that later laws would prevail over earlier laws including international treaties, if simply converted into national law. The courts in Belgium had no role in respect of judging the validity of international agreements but accepted Community law supremacy in its own right, as if Belgium were a monist country, and not through dependence on a Belgian statute (see *Minister for Economic Affairs v SA Fromagerie 'Le Ski'*). It was held that in the case of conflict between national law and the directly effective law of an international treaty, the latter would prevail even if earlier in time.

Germany

The *Grundgesetz* (German Constitution), Arts 24 and 25, provided for the peaceful cooperation of the German state with international organisations. Article 24 *Grundgesetz* allows for membership of international organisations and a transfer of powers to them, and was used to establish membership of the European Communities. Although Art 25 declares general rules of public international law to be an integral part of federal law and to take precedence over national law, it is silent as to the effect of international law on German constitutional law.

The discussion from the German point of view lies essentially with the relationship of international law, and in particular the membership of the Community, to the provisions of the *Grundgesetz*. Traditionally, Germany adopted the dualist approach to the reception of international law, whereby some form of transformation or adoption of international law was necessary in order for it to have any direct application in the state. There had to be a process of incorporation by statute, and once incorporated, a law would simply rank as with other *Gesetz* (Acts of the German Parliament). If a later law was in conflict with an earlier law, the later law would prevail. Following implementation under Arts 24 and 25, it is argued that there has been a shift to the monist approach.

Previously, German courts had been divided as to the effect of Community primary law and secondary law, and at times they had refused to make a reference in cases of doubt or non-acceptance, thus denying the parties to the case the chance to see whether EEC law would have affected the outcome of the case. However, the view of the Federal Constitutional Court is paramount because of its constitutional position in the German state, therefore the case law of this court must be considered.

In the *Internationale Handelsgesellschaft* case — known in Germany as 'Solange I' — the Constitutional Court held that as long as the recognition of human rights in the EEC had not progressed as far as those provided for by the *Grundgesetz*, German courts retained the right to refer questions on the constitutionality of secondary Community law to the Federal Constitutional Court, with the possible result that Community law might be ignored if it did not have sufficient regard for basic rights. This position has changed with the later rulings by the Federal Constitutional Court. In the *Wünsche Handelsgesellschaft* decision — known as 'Solange II' — the Federal Constitutional Court has accepted that Community recognition and safeguards of fundamental rights, through the case law of the Court of Justice, are now sufficient and of a comparable nature to those provided for by the

Grundgesetz. Thus, as long as EC law ensures the effective provision of fundamental rights the Federal Constitutional Court will not review Community law in the light of the rights provisions of the Constitution. The Court also stated that it would not be prepared to accept constitutional complaints from lower courts on this basis. It is argued that a reservation is still inherent in the ruling. The basis for the decision is not, however, the inherent supremacy of Community law, but the fact that Art 24 of the *Grundgesetz* allowed a transfer of powers to the Community, and the subsequent accession Act obliges the German courts to accept the supremacy of Community law.

The decision by the Federal Constitutional Court in 'Solange II' also held that the Court of Justice was a statutory court within the meaning of Art 101 *Grundgesetz*, and individuals have the right to have access to statutory courts. This effectively means that German courts can no longer refuse to make references in the last instance to the Court of Justice, as had happened in the case of *Kloppenburg*. The Federal Constitutional Court held in *Re VAT Exemption*, the follow-up to the *Kloppenburg* case, and in a separate case of *Re Patented Feedstuffs*, that German courts which are courts of last instance in terms of Art 234 (old 177) of the EC Treaty, would be in breach of the German Constitution if they failed to refer to the Court of Justice when necessary. Therefore, German courts of last instance are obliged to make a reference where a dispute as to the interpretation or application of Community law exists.

Following these cases, there would seem to be no procedural difficulty in getting Community rights at least considered in the proper forum in Germany. Any courts which refuse either to follow a previous ruling of the Court of Justice or which refuse to make an Art 234 (old 177) ruling may be subject to the review of the Federal Constitutional Court for an arbitrary breach of Art 101(1) of the *Grundgesetz*.

More recently, Germany has paid a lot more attention to the relationship between the EC and its laws and the German Constitution. In order to cater pecifically for further European integration, particularly into new areas as proposed in the Maastricht Treaty, and to take account of the increasing concern about possible infringements of the *Grundgesetz*, a new Article 23 *Grundgesetz* was added and amendments were made to other key provisions. Article 23 provides that sovereign powers can be transferred to the European Union provided the transfer has the approval of the *Bundestag* and *Bundesrat*. Joint approval is also required for the ratification of the European Union Treaty and for any future changes affecting the contents of the *Grundgesetz*.

The German Accession Act to the Treaty on European Union was passed by the German Parliament in December 1992. However, as a result of considerable criticism that there had been no real debate on Maastricht in Germany and that a referendum had not been held to test public opinion on further integration, constitutional complaints were made to the Federal Constitutional Court. In its judgment in *Brunner et al.* v *Federal Republic of Germany* [1994] 1 CMLR 57, the Federal Constitutional Court considered the changes to the Constitution, the constitutionality of the TEU and generally the relationship between the EC and the German Constitution.

Whilst it held that the transfer of powers was compatible with the principles of the *Grundgesetz*, future extensive transfers could not be made without the approval of the German Parliament and the Federal Constitutional Court would reserve to itself a right to review the compatibility of EC law fundamental rights provisions and the range of rights exercised by the EC with the German Constitution, thus appearing to backtrack on its previous judgments.

The German courts are still able to provide conflicting evidence in respect of their recognition of the supremacy of Community law. In 1996, in one of a series of cases arising from the German courts challenging the Community Banana regime preference of ACP States and not the traditional south American countries supplying Germany, the Federal Tax Court upheld German law on the basis of basic rights over the Community rules. In contrast is the German Supreme Court ruling (*Bundesgerichtshof*) in *Brasserie du Pécheur* v *Federal Republic of Germany* (case C-46/93), which accepted the principle of State liability on the part of the German State for a legislative breach. In the case, however, the Court held that the breach had not been sufficiently serious enough to impose liability.

Italy

In Italy the position, both constitutionally and judicially, was, and is, very similar to that in Germany. Both had new constitutions set up after the Second World War with strong provisions for fundamental rights. Both allowed a transfer of power to international organisations but were silent as to its effect on constitutional law (Art 11 of the Italian Constitution).

As in Germany, the focus in Italy is on the Constitutional Court. Given that two of the leading cases on supremacy, *Costa* v *ENEL* and *Simmentha* arose from Italy, it should certainly have been clear to the Italian Constitutional Court what was expected of it. Again there has been a mixed reaction, also along the lines of the German Constitutional Court.

In *Granital* v *Amministrazione delle Finanze*, the supremacy of Community law was accepted on the basis of an interpretation of Art 11 of the Italian Constitution, allowing for the limitation of sovereignty in favour of international organisations, and also by reason of the case law of the Court of Justice. The case did, however, make the reservation that Italian law should only be cast aside where directly applicable Community law exists — similar, in effect, to the judgment of the House of Lords in the *Duke* case.

A later decision in *Fragd* v *Amministrazione delle Finanze* — noted by Gaja in (1990) 27 CML Rev 93, suggests the Italian Constitutional Court is still prepared to review Community law in the light of the fundamental rights provision in the Italian Constitution.

France

French courts are divided into two hierarchies, each of which has its own appeal courts and final appeal. They have had, however, significantly different attitudes to EC law, despite the fact that both are subject to Art 55 of the French Constitution, which is monist and gives international law a rank above municipal law but is silent as to the effect on the Constitution. This is the point that has led to discrepancies between the hierarchies.

The French courts of ordinary jurisdiction   The courts of ordinary jurisdiction had no hesitation in making Art 234 (old 177) references to the Court of Justice and in giving supremacy to Community law on the basis of Art 55 of the Constitution. The French Supreme Court of Ordinary Jurisdiction (*Cour de Cassation*) has in fact gone further, and has found for the supremacy of Community law without direct reference to Art 55 of the Constitution and more on the basis of the inherent supremacy and direct effects of Community law itself. See the *Café Vabre* case, in which Art 90 (old 95) EC was held to prevail over a subsequent national statute.

These rulings have been followed consistently by the lower courts and reference to either Art 55 of the Constitution or even the above decisions is rarely made (see, for example, *Garage Dehus Sarl* v *Bouche Distribution*).

French administrative courts   These courts deal with complaints by citizens against any acts of the state administration. The Supreme Administrative Court (*Conseil d'État*) has from time to time completely denied the supremacy of Community law or the need to make reference to the Court of Justice, relying heavily on the French principle of law *'acte clair'*. This states that where a provision of law is clear, there is no need to refer to a higher court but simply apply it. See, for example, *Minister of the Interior* v *Cohn-Bendit*. Daniel Cohn-Bendit ('Danny the Red') was deported from France in 1968. In 1975 he requested re-entry but was refused. He claimed the refusal was contrary to Directive 64/221, already declared directly effective by the Court of Justice in the *Van Duyn* case. The *Conseil d'État* held individuals could not rely directly on directives to challenge an administrative Act. It declined to follow previous Court of Justice rulings or make a reference itself. The judgment of the *Conseil d'État* in the *Cohn-Bendit* case has been followed by the same court in later cases, and by lower courts.

More recently, however, two cases have demonstrated a much more cooperative attitude on the part of the French administrative courts. In

Nicolo, the *Conseil d'État* reviewed the supremacy of international law, including EEC Treaty articles, and held the latter to take precedence over subsequent national law, largely on the basis of Art 55 of the French Constitution. The submissions of the Government Commissioner were instructive in his use and observation of the decisions from the courts of other Member States and their acceptance of Community law supremacy. Secondly, in *Boisdet*, incompatible national law was declared invalid in the face of a Community regulation. In doing so, the *Conseil d'État* followed the case law of the Court of Justice.

The recent case of *Rothmans & Philip Morris Tobacco and Arizona Tobacco* has decided that not only are EC directives to be given priority over national law, even where the directive pre-dated the French statute, but also that an award of damages against the French authorities can be made where damage is suffered as a consequence of non-compliance with EC law, clearly following the lead of the ECJ in the *Francovich* case.

Previously receiving no direct mention in the French Constitution, the European Community is now referred to in a new Art 88. This was introduced by the Conseil Constitutionnel as a result of its ruling that that the move into new policy areas under the Maastricht Treaty would be incompatible with the Constitution.

THE PRINCIPLE OF SUBSIDIARITY

While there was arguably always the view that legal measures were taken centrally by the Community institutions only where necessary and, that if those measures were not suitable, Member States were allowed to regulate matters individually, the principle of subsidiarity was formally incorporated into the Community legal order in the SEA. At this time, however, it was only introduced specifically in respect of environmental measures under Art 174(4) (old 130r(4)). Essentially the Community should only take action where objectives could be better attained at the Community level than the level of individual Member State.

It was re-introduced generally into the legal order in Art 5 (old 3b) EC by the TEU. This provides that:

> The Community shall act within the limits of the powers conferred upon it by this Treaty and the objectives assigned to it therein. In areas which do not fall within its competence, the Community shall take action, in accordance with the principle of subsidiarity, only if and in so far as the objectives of the proposed action cannot be sufficiently achieved by the Member States and can therefore, by reason of the scale or effects of the proposed action, be better achieved by the Community.
>
> Any action by the Community shall not go beyond what is necessary to achieve the objectives of this Treaty.

The first sentence of the Article is simply a statement that the Community cannot act without a specific power to do so. The exact meaning of the second two sentences is, however, far from clear, particularly regarding where the line might be drawn between the competence of the Community and the competences of the Member States.

Article 1 (old A) of the TEU additionally provides that decisions are to be taken as closely as possible to the citizen and Art 2 (old B) provides *inter alia* that: 'The objectives of the Union shall be achieved . . . while respecting the principle of subsidiarity as defined in Article 5 [old 3b] of the Treaty establishing the European Community.' It is probable that the principle of subsidiarity will also join the ranks of general principles of Community law, although it is one introduced deliberately by the Member States rather than created or intoduced by the ECJ.

The difficulties with this principle may be who decides when to apply it and whether it has been observed in the decision making process. It may therefore give rise to considerable litigation to determine whether it has been adhered to correctly. Whilst the principle itself was not disturbed by the Treaty of Amsterdam, it did add a Protocol as an attempt to provide clarification of its meaning. Apart from requiring certain actions on the part of the Commission in consulting before formally proposing legislation and making reports to the European Council, the Council and the EP, it doesn't seem to have helped. The Court of Justice was asked to determine whether it had been breached in the case of *UK v Council* (*Working Time Directive*) but the ECJ dismissed this part of the action with little discussion merely to confirm that the Council had a clear power to act on working hours as an issue of health and safety of workers. Almost inevitably, the ECJ will be given further opportunities to come up with clearer and workable definitions of its meaning.

QUESTIONS

1.   'Though the Community Treaties indicate either indirectly or by implication an intention that Community law should be paramount over the law in each Member State, they contain no express provision to that effect. For the present, therefore, this question is in practice largely dependent on the constitutional law of each Member State.' Discuss.

This is a question concerned with supremacy, but it also concerns Member States' law and not just Community law.

The parts to be addressed are the indirect or implied intention of the Treaties for supremacy of Community law and the fact that there is no express provision. This requires a discussion of any Treaty articles which would lead to this conclusion and the rulings of the Court of Justice which confirm this. This is really just another formulation of the first example given.

You can quite quickly deal with the statement that there is no express provision. Clearly there is no direct expression of supremacy in the Treaty but there are indirect expressions in some of the Treaty articles from which it can be inferred or implied (see Art 249 (old 189) and regulations Art 10 (old 5) (fidelity clause), and Art 292 (old 219) (dispute resolution), amongst others). So you could infer or imply that Community law should be supreme but cannot state that the Treaty expressly or categorically requires it.

The question then suggests that because supremacy is not express, the Member States' constitutional laws determine supremacy. You are required either to confirm this with examples, or to refute it by reference to Court of Justice rulings, i.e., the issue to be addressed is whether Community law supremacy should be determined according to national constitutional laws. Your answer would be that it is dependent on the law of the Member States only if you subscribe to the theory that it is up to the Member States' laws to determine the supremacy of Community law. It is true that the Member States' courts can frustrate the requirements of the Court of Justice and the Community, although this tends to be rare. Supremacy, at the end of the day, relies on the willingness of the courts of the Member States to apply Community law.

The answer, from the Community point of view, once again lies in the case law of the Court of Justice. It claims the right to decide on the supremacy, and not the Member States, as noted above, primarily in *Van Gend en Loos* and *Costa* v *ENEL*. There are, however, cases which directly consider a conflict between Community law and national constitutional law. Only two are needed to show how this should be resolved from the Community point of view. *Internationale Handelsgesellschaft* and *Simmenthal* are clearly the leading cases to show this relationship, the view of the national courts and the view of the Court of Justice.

Thus, supremacy is not dependent on the practice in each Member State. If it were, the uniformity, and thus the legal system and Community legal order itself, would be questioned.

It must be said now that very few problems exist in the Member States in respect of granting supremacy.

You may be faced with a problem which directly considers the question of UK constitutional difficulties caused by membership of the Community, along the following lines.

2.   How, if it is possible, is the supremacy of Community law reconciled with the doctrine of parliamentary sovereignty in the UK?

The subject matter of this question is clear and it can easily be divided into three parts:

The first part would concern an explanation of what is what is meant by the supremacy of Community law. This would include the case law of the Court of Justice to confirm the legal reasoning, as given in the above answer, therefore no further details will be given here.

Secondly, a definition and the consequences of the doctrine of parliamentary sovereignty must be given. Both this part and the first part are reasonably straightforward, and would thus require fairly descriptive passages. You should try to be more concise in your description of the meaning and scope of 'parliamentary sovereignty' than for courses in constitutional law, but you could certainly employ much of the work done for this topic within that subject. Certainly you should consider the limitations which have been acknowledged in the past in constitutional law. You would have to point out that the doctrine of parliamentary sovereignty itself is subject to criticism and qualification.

The third part of the question requires more thought, especially in structuring your answer. Some sort of introduction needs to be given which will set out the issues to be tackled, e.g., an explanation that at first sight these two doctrines appear to be incompatible, hence the difficulties when one seems to impinge on the other. You should then consider the ECA 1972 and whether this has reconciled the two doctrines, or what exactly it has done. One way to tackle this is to see how the UK courts have considered this relationship. The latest cases should now be overriding the dicta of older cases, e.g., the judgment of Lord Bridge in *Factortame* or *Factortame (No. 5)* and *R* v *Secretary of State for Employment ex parte EOC* are of more use than the judgments of Lord Denning in *McCarthys Ltd* and Lord Diplock in *Garland*. Certainly, it is true that the ECA 1972 has transferred sovereignty in certain areas, as agreed, for an indefinite period, but that it has completely overruled the doctrine cannot be stated.

The real problem in trying to reconcile these doctrines is that legal reasoning is not fully reconcilable with the practical realities of Community membership. While it may be possible to repeal the ECA 1972 and leave the Communities, that is practically and politically untenable.

A question which concentrates on the practical clash of Community and national legislation puts the theories of the last question to the test.

3. Consider an inconsistency or conflict between the legal provisions in the following situations:

(a) A pre-accession (i.e., before 1972) UK statute or regulation, with an EC Treaty article and a subsequent Community regulation or directive.

(b) A post-accession (i.e., later than 1972) UK statute, with a Treaty article, an earlier regulation or directive.

(c)   A post-accession (i.e., later than 1972) UK Act or regulation, with a later Community regulation or directive.

This question covers most of the variations concerning conflict between Community and national provisions that you are likely to meet. They may not be so obviously stated as here, and may be contained within the text of a problem in which a clash of laws arises.

(a)   In the case of the pre-accession UK statute or regulation and an EC Treaty article or a Community regulation or directive, the Community provisions would overrule the UK provisions according to either (i) the UK rules that later laws overrule earlier laws, or (ii) the view of Community law as supreme, especially if the three types of provision are directly effective. The earlier UK legislation could also be challenged on the basis that the ECA 1972 allows the Treaty and the Community regulation and directive to overrule the UK law.

(b)   The second situation involves a post-accession UK statute in conflict with a Treaty article, a regulation and a directive. This involves a statute later than all three Community law provisions, and an inconsistency between the UK provision and the Community law provisions. The UK statute should, of course, be in compliance with Community law, but if this is not the case, the Court of Justice has clearly stated in case law that Community law should prevail. However, the traditional view of parliamentary sovereignty states that the UK law, as the later law, should prevail. Here you need to determine which line will be followed by application of the ECA 1972.

Section 2(1) and (4) ECA 1972 apply to ensure that future Acts of Parliament conform with prior Community law obligations. The argument is that any national legislation which is enacted after Community law must be made subject to the Community law by virtue of s. 2(4) of the ECA 1972. How would the courts regard this? According to the *obiter dicta* of Lord Denning in *Macarthys Ltd* v *Smith*, there would have to be an express intention of Parliament to overrule the pre-existing Community law. This view was confirmed by Lord Diplock (*obiter*) in the case of *Garland*, who said it would depend on the intention of Parliament as to whether there was an express intention to overrule the Treaty. If no such intention exists, then the Treaty article takes priority. A Community regulation is directly applicable, according to Art 249 (old 189). Therefore, under s. 2(4) it can overrule the UK statute, as is confirmed by case law, including Lord Templeman in *Duke*. Thus, there are few problems with Treaty articles and regulations, but directives can cause problems.

If the Community directive is directly effective, then the UK courts would also give priority to Community law on the strength of the ECA 1972, and this would be applied by the House of Lords, as held by Lord Templeman in the case of *Duke*. However, there would be a problem if the directive had been held not to be directly effective, or if the case concerned a private employer. In such a case, according to the ruling of the House of Lords in *Duke*, because directives are not directly applicable, s. 2(4) will not apply to help.

Alternatively, the House of Lords has held that s. 2(4) of the ECA 1972 applies only to allow Community law to assist the interpretation of UK legislation which is purportedly based on the Community legislation, i.e., only to later UK law. For example, in *Pickstone v Freemans*, the House of Lords went quite far to construe delegated legislation to be in compliance with Community law. *Litster v Forth Dry Dock* concerned UK regulations which purported to implement the obligations contained in EEC Council Directive 77/187. The UK regulations were considered to be somewhat ambiguous. The Directive involved did not give rise to direct effects because the case concerned a private employer. As a result of the fact that the House of Lords could not achieve a satisfactory result, in keeping with the European Directive and the case law of the Court of Justice, by a literal reading of the regulations, it concluded that it must use the Community legislation to interpret the later UK legislation, whatever the form of words used.

However, *Factortame* and later cases must now be considered, which, if it is to be read as a general statement of the law, holds that Community law is supreme regardless of the situation, because of the case law of the ECJ and the transfer of sovereign powers voluntarily undertaken by the ECA 1972 which oblige UK courts to come to this conclusion.

If, following a consideration of this previous case law, UK courts still have problems in affording Community law supremacy, they are obliged by s. 3 ECA 1972 to make a reference to the Court of Justice.

(c) The post-accession UK Act or regulation conflicting with a later Community Regulation or Directive. The case of a Community regulation or directive being imposed after a UK Act or regulation highlights the fact that the national law could not have been enacted with the Community law in mind. Community law priority would initially depend on whether the provisions have direct effects, and also on whether a public employer or private one is involved.

The Community regulation is directly applicable and would satisfy the ECA 1972, but the directive remains the problem. According to the House of Lords in *Duke*, if the directive is not directly applicable or effective, it cannot take precedence over UK law and s. 2(4) ECA cannot be used as a means to overrule or construe UK law. If the Community law is later than the UK law, then there can be no intention to comply.

Thus the question comes back to the *dicta* of Denning and Diplock that it is the intention of Parliament which will decide which law takes priority.

Another alternative is the presumption in international law that national courts must presume Parliament intended to comply with an international Treaty entered into by the State, especially so with regard to Community law. The problem with arguments about the intention of Parliament is that the courts were not able to look at *Hansard*; therefore, unless the intention to conflict is expressed and in the legislation, it would not count. There is, however, the case of *Pepper (Her Majesty's Inspector of Taxes)* v *Hart*, which has altered the strict rule about the ability to look at *Hansard*. The courts may make reference to *Hansard* provided (i) the legislation is ambiguous or obscure, or leads to an absurdity, (ii) the material relied upon consists of one or more statements by a Minister or other promoter of the Bill, together, if necessary, with such other Parliamentary material as is necessary to understand such statements and their effect, and (iii) the statements relied upon are clear.

A non-directly effective directive which conflicts with a later UK statute or regulation would clearly require the UK Parliament to amend the national law. What, however is the situation for the courts prior to the amending Act? The case of *Duke* showed that UK law took priority. This case, it is suggested, even conflicts with the *dicta* in *McCarthys Ltd* and *Garland*, because, if the intent of Parliament is all important, the words of the earlier provision will not reveal an intention to conflict with a yet to be enacted provision of Community law. In this case Community law should take priority.

An easier solution now is the case of *Factortame*, which would give supremacy to Community law because it is what Parliament intended by the ECA 1972. Section 2(4) applies to stop the implied repeal of the ECA 1972, and it doesn't even matter if Community law is later. The case of *R v Secretary of State for Employment ex parte EOC* would also be relevant to apply here to the extent that where a conflict was discovered by the Court, it would not apply the inconsistent national law but make a declaration of inconsistency which would signal the probable liability of the Member State under *Francovich*.

A question remains as to whether *Factortame* covers the very unlikely event of an express intent to breach an existing Community law obligation.

The final question in this chapter concentrates on the position in other Member States.

4. 'There is now no doubt that the primacy of Community law over any conflicting national law is fully secured in the Member States.' Comment on this statement in respect of at least two Member States.

This requires an explanation of the primacy of Community law, as in the above answers, using the logic of the Court of Justice's arguments from the

leading cases. The statement suggests that this view has been fully secured
in the Member States, and you are required to consider the position in at
least two Member States. If your course considers the position in respect of
other Member States, you may be asked to give a full answer to such a
question, but if only a brief outline is given, it should not be expected that
you go into any greater detail yourself.

The above question could appear in another form, e.g., directing you to
consider Member States other than the UK, which might have been considered
in another question, or asking you to consider the position in the UK and at
least one or two other Member States. The position in respect of other Member
States is outlined at the end of the chapter above, and will not be repeated here.

FURTHER READING

Allen, T., 'The Limits of Parliamentary Sovereignty' (1986) Public Law 614.

Craig, P.P., 'Sovereignty of the United Kingdom Parliament after *Factortame*',
(1991) 9 YEL 221.

Craig, P. 'Directives: direct effect, indirect effect and the construction of
national legislation' (1997) 22 EL Rev 519.

Emiliou, N., 'Subsidiarity: An Effective Barrier against "the Enterprises of
Ambition"?' (1992) 17 EL Rev 383.

Foster, N., 'The Effect of the European Communities Act 1972 s. 2(4)' (1988)
51 MLR 775.

Foster, N., 'The German Constitution and EC Membership' Public Law,
Autumn 1994, 392.

Gaja, G., 'New Developments in a Continuing Story: The Relationship
between EC Law and Italian Law' (1990) 27 CML Rev 83.

Maher, I. 'Community law in the national legal order: a systems analysis'
(1998) 36 JCMS 237.

Manin, P., 'The *Nicolo* Case of the *Conseil d'État*: French Constitutional Law
and the Supreme Administrative Court's Acceptance of the Primacy of
Community Law over Subsequent National Statute Law' (1991) 28 CML
Rev 499.

Mitchell, J.D.B., 'What happened to the Constitution on 1st January 1973?'
(1980) Cambrian Law Review 69.

Oliver, P., 'The French Constitution and the Treaty of Maastricht' (1994) 43
ICLQ 1.

Toth, A., 'The Principle of Subsidiarity in the Maastricht Treaty' (1992) 29
CML Rev 1079.

Wade, H.W.R., 'Sovereignty and the European Communities' (1972) 88
LQR 1.

Wade, H.W.R., 'What has Happened to the Sovereignty of Parliament?'
(1991) 107 LQR 1.

6 THE ENFORCEMENT OF COMMUNITY LAW: I

This chapter and the next will cover the enforcement of Community law which takes place before both the European Court of Justice and the national courts. It is divided roughly into the actions which are heard directly by the European Court of Justice and those heard, initially at least, by the national courts. The former are those actions taken to enforce Community law against either the Member States or the institutions of the Community and are considered in this chapter, whereas, the latter concern the enforcement of the Community law by individuals and the development of Community law remedies, both via the use of the preliminary ruling procedure under Art 234 (old 177). These will be considered in chapter 7.

ACTIONS AGAINST MEMBER STATES

In contrast to other international organisations, the European Community has a much more effective control mechanism to ensure compliance with its own laws by Member States. In the European Community, breaches of Member States' obligations are established officially by the Court of Justice following a procedure undertaken by the Commission under its duty to ensure that the Treaty and other Community measures are applied (Art 211 (old 155)). Article 226 (old 169) is the Treaty basis for Commission actions against Member States for failures to fulfil obligations under the Treaty. Article 227 (old 170) concerns actions by one Member State against another, and Art 228 (old 171) the obligation of Member States to comply with judgments of the Court of Justice.

Actions Brought by the Commission

The breach of an obligation   In order for a breach to be established, there first needs to be a duty. Membership of the Community entails many obligating duties. There are the general duties contained in the Treaties, including Art 10 (old 5), which obliges the Member States to take all appropriate measures to ensure the fulfilment of Treaty obligations, or those resulting from Community acts, and not to jeopardise the attainment of the objectives of the Treaty, and Art 12 (old 6), the duty not to discriminate on grounds of nationality. Then there are more specific duties under the various chapters of the Treaty, and the very detailed duties imposed by secondary legislation. Breaches may arise from the Treaties, secondary legislation, international agreements, decisions of the Court of Justice and general principles.

What constitutes a breach?   Article 226 (old 169) is, however, silent as to what constitutes a breach of a duty. The Court of Justice has determined that a breach can be constituted not only by an act of a Member State but also by a failure to act by a Member State. A failure to act is most often observed in the form that a Member State has failed to implement Community legislation, mainly directives, or to remove national legislation which is now in conflict or inconsistent with Community legislation. There are numerous examples to be found in the chapters of this book of breaches by a Member State.

Failure to remove inconsistent legislation also constitutes a breach even if the authorities no longer apply the national legislation and apply the Community rules in preference. For example, the French Maritime Code (*Commission* v *France*) restricted the numbers of foreign workers on French vessels but the French pleaded that the national law was not being applied. The Court of Justice held that this law, even if it was not being applied, might influence the behaviour of people who rely on the law being applied and create uncertainty.

A breach can arise from any part of a State and is not restricted to purely governmental action or inaction. For example, in *Commission* v *Belgium* (the Belgian Wood case), the Belgian Government pleaded it should not be held responsible for the negligence of the Belgian Parliament which, being out of session, was not able to implement a Community directive in time. The Court of Justice held that 'Obligations arise whatever the agency of the State whose action or inaction is the cause of the failure to fulfil its obligation even in the case of a constitutionally independent institution'.

A breach therefore may involve the action of a Member State in enacting or maintaining legislation or regulations incompatible with the Treaty or secondary Community law, or the failure to implement (or the incomplete or dilatory implementation of) Community law obligations. This includes decisions of the Court of Justice and extends to all organs of the State, not just the government, i.e., it could include breaches by the judiciary in a Member State for rendering an incorrect decision although no such action has ever commenced.

In addition to the action under Art 226 (old 169), there are further special actions which the Commission can take against the Member States in respect of specific subject matters. These are: Art 88(2) (old 93(2)) in respect of infringements of state aids provisions, Art 95 (old 100a) in respect of derogations from the internal market, and Arts 296–298 (old 223–225) in respect of emergency security measures.

The Procedure of an Article 226 Action

Article 226 (old 169) requires certain informal or administrative procedural steps to be taken before a court action can result. The first part of Art 226 (old 169) states that 'If the Commission considers that a Member State has failed to fulfil an obligation under this Treaty, it shall deliver a reasoned opinion on the matter'. This means the Commission must have concluded that the Member State is probably in breach of an obligation before it can commence an action before the Court of Justice. The matter can be brought to its attention by its own investigations and supervision of Member States' implementation, by the Member States, the EP, or by individual citizens or companies.

Having decided that a State has breached its obligations, the Commission will inform the State and give it an opportunity to answer the allegation or to correct its action or inaction before the formal procedure of Art 226 (old 169) begins. As a result of this discretion, there is no obligation to take action. Individuals have been held by the Court of Justice not to be able to force the Commission to take action (see *Lütticke* v *Commission* (1966) or *Lord Bethell* v *Commission*). Not every suspicion of infringement will even result in the initial letter being sent by the Commission to the Member State. In a report by the EP in 1982, it was estimated that only one out of every 1,000 cases suspected by the Commission resulted in a court action. The initial letter has, however, been held to be essential for the commencement of proceedings before the Court of Justice (*Commission* v *Italy (Public Works)* (case 274/83)).

In 1985, the Commission sent out 503 formal letters (1,210 in 1992 and 1016 in 1995) stating its point of view. Following the reply from the Member State, or after a reasonable time where no reply is received, the Commission will deliver a reasoned opinion which records the reasons for the failure of the Member State. This is delivered to the Member State and is registered by the Court of Justice. Many of the original complaints will have been settled informally by this stage, and the resulting number of reasoned opinions in 1985 was 233 (248 in 1992 and 192 in 1995).

If the State should fail to comply with the reasoned opinion of the Commission within a reasonable time (*Commission* v *Italy (Slaughtered Cows)*) or as stipulated by the Commission (normally two months), the Commission then has the discretionary right to bring the matter before the Court of Justice, further specifying its grounds for action. In 1985, 107 cases were brought, 64 in 1992 and 72 in 1995.

The final stage of the procedure is an action before the Court of Justice, the judgment of which is merely declaratory. It is possible, however, for the Court to order interim measures, which are considered below. After the judgment the State is required to take the necessary measures to comply with the judgment. In 1985, 23 cases were removed from the Court's register prior to judgment, the Member States having complied with Community obligations, thus judgments rendered by the Court in 1985 were only 25 (50 in 1992), the balance remained pending for judgment in 1986.

At the moment there is about a two-year delay in the Court of Justice hearing these cases, but if the matter is very important the Court will improve on this.

Defences Raised by the Member States

The Member States have raised various defences, often acceptable in international law but without success in the Community legal order, to justify their non-compliance with obligations. Some of the more common are: *force majeure* or overriding necessity in *Commission* v *Belgium* (the Belgian Wood case); Community measures being the cause of political or economic difficulties raised by the UK in *Commission* v *UK (Tachographs)* and by Italy in *Commission* v *Italy (Art Treasures)*; and reciprocity, under which the Member State claims that because the Council has failed to act (*Commission* v *Belgium and Luxembourg* (cases 90–91/63)), or because other Member States have not complied with their obligations (*Commission* v *France (Import of Lamb)* (case 232/78)), the Member State is justified in not complying.

Actions Brought by other Member States

Article 227 (old 170) is the basis for an action by one Member State against another, when one Member State considers another to have breached an obligation under Community law. As Art 292 (old 219) requires the Member States to pursue no other method of dispute resolution than that provided by the Treaty, Member States are thus obliged to use Art 227 (old 170) to resolve differences under Community law. Member States have full *locus standi* in relation to Art 227 (old 170).

Before an action can take place, the Member State must bring the matter before the Commission. The Commission will ask both states to submit their observations and then deliver a reasoned opinion on the matter. The Commission seeks to bring about a solution before court action is necessary, and may even intervene to take over the action, as it did in *Commission v France* (case 232/78) which started as an action by Ireland against France.

If a settlement or solution is not reached at this stage and three months has elapsed, or if the Commission fails to submit an opinion within three months of being informed of the matter, the Member State can take the matter before the Court of Justice. Judgment has been reached in only one of two Art 227 (old 170) actions, *France v UK* (1979), in which France successfully challenged the UK's unilateral fishery conservation measures. As an alternative to this action, Member States usually prefer to ask the Commission to bring actions under Art 226 (old 169), because this is a less politically obvious and contentious manner in which to secure compliance of Community law in the interests of the Member States concerned.

Additionally, under Art 239 (old 182), Member States may agree to refer any dispute relating to the subject matter of the Treaty to the Court of Justice for adjudication.

THE APPLICATION AND EFFECT OF JUDGMENTS

Other international tribunals are unable to enforce their judgments against miscreant Member States, for example the International Court of Justice at the Hague or the European Court of Human Rights in Strasbourg. The best that can really be achieved is the issue and discussion of a report on the failure or breach. While the initial judgment of the Court of Justice is only declaratory and carries no specific sanctions, Member States are placed under a further obligation under Art 228 (old 171) to comply with the judgment by taking the necessary measures. If they do not do this, a further action may lie against them by the Commission under Art 226 (old 169) for a breach of Art 228 (old 171). This has taken place a number of times, and increasingly so. The leading instance of this is *Commission v Italy (Second Art Treasures)*. The Commission discerned that because Italy had not complied with the Court's judgment in the first case (case 7/68), judgment should be given that Italy had also failed in its obligation under Art 228 (old 171). Despite the fact that Italy complied with the original decision prior to judgment, the Court of Justice held that Italy had also failed to comply with Art 228 (old 171). In any event, the Commission is not required to show a continuing legal interest in an action as the Court will give judgments in order to clarify the law.

The Maastricht Treaty amended Art 228 (old 171) EC to enable the Court of Justice to fine Member States for breaches of Community law. The

Commission must give its reasoned opinion of the continued failure and a time limit for compliance. If the Member State fails to comply within the time given, the Court may levy the fine. Article 229 (old 172) provides that the penalties will be determined by regulations to be adopted by the Council. A penalty calculation system has been established by the Commission (Commission Memorandum OJ 1997 C63/2.) whereby it will state what penalty, if any, it considers appropriate. The basic penalty is fixed at 500 ECU per day times factors reflecting the gravity and duration of non-compliance and the financial situation of the Member State by lump sum or penalty payment. The penalty will apply from the date of judgment in the action and not from the date of original non-compliance, hence Member States have a chance to minimise the penalty.

Interim Measures

Although interim measures are not in any strict sense a direct sanction, they can nevertheless have the effect of rectifying the alleged breach until the case has determined whether the conflicting national legislation should be removed.

Under Art 243 (old 186) EC, the Court of Justice may, in any case before it, prescribe necessary interim measures. They must be requested prior to final judgment and be applied only in urgent circumstances. A case for the requested measure must specifically be made. They have been used occasionally in Art 226 (old 169) cases. In *Commission v UK (Pig Producers)* the UK was ordered to halt subsidies to pig producers until the Court of Justice could decide whether the scheme was compatible with the rules of the common market. The Court of Justice ordered Belgium, under Art 243 (old 186), to allow access to other, non-Belgian Community nationals to vocational training in Belgian universities, in a case where non-Belgians were asked to pay enrolment fees (*Commission v Belgium (University Fees)*). It also made an interim order in *Commission v Ireland (Irish Fisheries)*, for Ireland to cease certain fishing measures which the Commission claimed were contrary to Community fishing rules. In all three cases the Member States complied immediately. In *Commission v Germany (Re Lorry Tax)*, the Court ordered that a special road tax for lorries be suspended pending the outcome of the Commission's Art 226 (old 169) action against Germany. Germany asked for a security from the Commission in the meantime, but this was held not to be required by the Court of Justice. In the *Factortame* litigation, the Commission requested, and was granted, the suspension of the alleged incompatible UK requirements.

It is often the indirect political pressure brought to bear by other Member States and actions by individuals which secure compliance by Member States, in the absence of interim measures.

Alternative Actions to Secure Member States' Compliance

While these will be considered in further detail in chapter 7, it is appropriate to mention such actions here as actions which are equally if not a lot more effective in ensuring compliance with Community law obligations by Member States.

Actions in defence or support of individuals   This is where individuals point to the breach of a Community obligation or duty by a Member State as a defence to prosecution by that Member State, or where they seek to challenge national rules which operate against their interests. It was early in the life of the Communities that the Art 234 (old 177) preliminary ruling procedure was seen to short-circuit the use of Arts 226 (old 169) and 227 (old 170). This was objected to by the Dutch Government in the *Van Gend en Loos* case, who thought that it was up to the Commission only, and not individuals, to take action or claim rights against Member States. This claim was firmly rejected by the Court of Justice, and the establishment of the doctrine of direct effects was able additionally to place the policing of Community law in the hands of private individuals, who often have more reason to bring actions.

Individuals may benefit, as well as helping to bring about the compliance with Art 226 (old 169) actions, as exampled by *Commission* v *France (Advertising of Alcoholic Beverages)*. It was held that a French ban on advertising foreign spirits was discriminatory and contrary to Community law. France failed to remove its legislation and prosecuted an importer for advertising. Waterkeyn, the advertiser, referred to the previous judgment as a defence. In *Procureur de la République* v *Waterkeyn* it was held that individuals could rely on such past judgments as a defence to protect their rights.

Actions for damages against Member States   This is where the breach by the Member State is claimed to have caused damage to individuals, who then make a claim against the Member State to recover the loss. This form of action may prove to be extremely effective in encouraging Member States to comply with Community law obligations, if they find themselves having to pay out significant damages in an increasing number of cases.

It was tried in the case of *Bourgoin* in which French turkey producers, following the Commission's Art 226 (old 169) action against the UK in *Commission* v *UK (Poultry Meat, Newcastle's Disease)*, which held a British ban was contrary to Community law, sought an action for damages against the Ministry of Agriculture which applied the ban. The claim was dismissed as showing no good cause of action unless it could be shown the Minister acted in bad faith, in which case the proper action was that for judicial review and not a tort action for damages. However, in *Bourgoin SA et al. v Ministry of Agriculture*, the case was settled out of court, and the British Government paid £3.5 million compensation to the French farmers.

The case of *Francovich* had the result that the Italian Government was obliged to pay the claimants as a result of failure to implement Community legislation. The case of *Factortame v UK* (case C-48/93) (estimated at approximately GB£80 million damages plus GB£20 million costs) and the increasing number of cases following this case are also likely to be highly effective in persuading member states to comply with Community law obligations lest they face numerous damages actions.

The next actions are those taken directly against the institutions of the Community and commencing with the action to annul acts of the institutions under Art 230 (old 173).

ACTIONS TO ANNUL COMMUNITY ACTS

An action brought before the Court of Justice under Art 230 (old 173) allows it to review the validity of acts of the Community. If the act is found to be invalid, the Court of Justice has the sole right to declare such acts void. There are two elements in respect of the action:

(a)   admissibility; and
(b)   the merits or substance of the action.

The first presents the greatest barrier to applicants in practice, and most textbooks concentrate on this aspect. The greatest problem with this topic appears to be the wide choice of cases, many of which stand in apparent contradiction to others.

Admissibility

Admissibility concerns the questions of which institutions are subject to review, which acts can be reviewed, the time limit for challenging acts and the applicants who can bring an action.

The institutions subject to review   Article 230 (old 173) states that the acts of the Commission and Council are subject to review, but case law extended this to acts of the EP (see *Luxembourg v European Parliament* in respect of its seat, *Les Verts v European Parliament* in respect of a challenge to the apportionment of election campaign funds, and *Council v European Parliament (Budgetary Procedure)*). The Court of Justice justified this extension on the basis that, as the EP's powers have grown, it can be responsible for acts which create legally binding effects in respect of third parties, and these should therefore be open to review.

Article 230 (old 173) was specifically amended by the TEU to include the review of legal acts of the EP intended to create legal effects on third parties, and acts of the ECB.

The acts which can be reviewed   The jurisdiction of the Court of Justice under Art 230 (old 173) applies to the legal binding acts of the Council and the Commission, but does not include recommendations or opinions. The privileged applicants, which are the Member States, the Council and the Commission have the right to challenge all three legal binding acts mentioned in Art 230 (old 173), i.e., Regulations, Directives and Decisions. The semi-privileged applicants can do so to protect their prerogatives but all other parties are restricted in challenging decisions only. However, the term 'Act' and the definition of what constitutes an Act or a Decision has been given a very wide interpretation by the ECJ so as to bring many actions within the scope of Art 230 (old 173) which would not on the face of it be admissible. It was held in the *Noordwijks Cement Accord* case that other acts may be subject to review. The test to apply to a particular act is whether it has binding legal effects, or changes the legal position of the applicant. Further, in *Commission v Council (ERTA)*, it was held that Art 249 (old 189) is not exhaustive, and special acts such as the minuted discussions of the Council for the European Road Transport Agreement, could also be challenged. Thus the true nature or substance of the measure is the determining factor.

As already mentioned, both the case of *Les Verts v European Parliament* and the TEU extended the list of reviewable acts to those of the EP, where they give rise to legally binding effects on the position of third parties. However, in *Commission v Italy (Re Pigmeat)* (case 7/61) it was held that the reasoned opinion given by the Commission under Art 226 (old 169) proceedings did not constitute an act which could be subject to review under Art 230 (old 173). Similarly, in *Lütticke v Commission* (1966) the applicants had requested the Commission to take action against the German Federal Republic regarding a breach of Community law. The Commission refused. Lütticke applied under Art 230 (old 173) to annul the decision not to act, but it was held that the refusal was not a legally binding act and was therefore not reviewable.

There have been, over the years, very many examples of various forms of communication, which, while not formally amounting to binding legislation, have nevertheless been held by the Court of Justice to have legal effects and thus be subject to review under Art 230 (old 173). The textbooks abound with examples. I shall provide only two here. In *French Republic v Commission* (case C-57/95), the Court ruled on a French action to annul a Commission 'Communication' which it was argued imposed new obligations on the Member States. It held that the Communication challenged, which was published in the OJ 'C' series and was not a legislative Act envisaged by Art 249 (old 189), was a measure which could be the subject of an annulment action. The content of Communication was considered and the Court thought that the Communication had 'imperative wording' and the content was the same subject matter as a withdrawn draft directive. Consequently, it held that the Communication constituted an act intended to have legal effects on its own, distinct from the Treaty provisions and an action to annul it could be upheld.

In *UK v Commission* (case C-106/96), the Council had decided not to support 'Poverty 4', a programme to combat poverty and social exclusion, but the Commission decided to fund a number of projects amounting to an expenditure of ECU six million and issued a press release to advertise this. The Court of Justice held that the Commission lacked the competence to commit the expenditure and the decision was annulled.

Time limits Article 230 (old 173) provides that the applicant has two months to challenge the act, starting from the publication of the measure or from the date of notification, or from the date it came to the notice of the addressee, regardless of the status of the applicant. The time limit for challenging a regulation has been determined to run from 15 days following publication, see Art 81 of the Rules of Procedure of the Court of Justice.

The time limits have been held by the Court of First Instance not to apply where there are such serious defects in the measure that it is to be regarded as non-existent (see *BASF v Commission and others* (case T-79/89)).

Who May Apply: Locus Standi

The question of who may apply relates to what is known as the *locus standi* of applicants. *Locus standi* means literally, the place of standing. It relates to the recognition of a legal interest in a matter which produces the right to mount a legal challenge against a legal provision. No standing means no right to challenge, hence this is absolutely crucial to a person's chances. There are now three categories of applicants: privileged, semi-privileged and non-privileged.

Privileged applicants Article 230 (old 173) names the Member States, the Council and the Commission as privileged applicants, who have the right to attack any act.

Semi-privileged applicants Initially, through the case law of the European Court of Justice, it was established that the EP and the European Central Bank have the right to challenge acts of the Council and Commission but only for the purpose of protecting their prerogatives. The term 'protection of prerogatives' is one which was essentially developed in case law and means 'where their interests are clearly affected'. See, e.g., the cases of *Maizena* v *Council* as confirmed in *European Parliament* v *Council (Chernobyl)* and more recently in *European Parliament* v *Council (Students Residence Directive)* in which the challenge to the legal base used by the Council was successful. This limited right of challenge is now confirmed in Art 173 (new 230) but strictly contained by the Court of Justice. Following its elevation to a full Community institution named in Art 7 (old 4) EC, the Treaty of Amsterdam added the Court of Auditors to this category of those allowed to bring actions to protect their prerogatives.

Non-privileged applicants   All other persons fall into this category. The details of these actions are considered next.

Admissibility for Non-privileged Applicants

Article 230 (old 173) provides three situations where non-privileged applicants can bring actions for judicial review. It provides: 'Any natural or legal person may, under the same conditions, institute proceedings against a decision addressed to that person or against a decision which, although in the form of a regulation or a decision addressed to another person, is of direct and individual concern to the former.'

(a)   Where the applicant is directly addressed   This is most likely to occur in specific circumstances where, for example, the applicant has been the subject of a decision of the Commission under the competition rules of Arts 81 and 82 (old 85 and 86) and Regulation 17 (see cases in chapter 10). For the purposes of the addressee mounting a challenge, there is no barrier to admissibility providing the time limit has been observed.

The next two categories arise from the same cause, the challenge to a Regulation or a Decision addressed to another person. Both the challenge to a Regulation *per se* and that the Regulation or the Decision must be of direct and individual concern, need to be addressed.

(b)   Where a regulation is really a disguised decision   A regulation is applicable, not to a limited number of persons, defined and identifiable, but to categories of persons viewed abstractly and in their entirety. Where the measure, although in the form of a regulation, is of direct and individual concern to the applicant, an action will be admissible but true regulations are normative acts and not open to individual challenge. See *KSH* v *Council and Commission* (case 101/76), in which a challenge to a glucose levy regulation in respect of certain producers was held not to be admissible.

In *Fruit and Vegetable Confederation v Commission* (1962), it was held that it is the nature and content of a provision that is the determining factor and not the form or label it is given. In *International Fruit Company v Commission* (1971), a group of fruit importers was held entitled to challenge a regulation prior to its adoption where the identity of the natural or legal persons affected was already known and thus fixed and identifiable. The regulation was thus the equivalent of a bundle of decisions addressed to each applicant.

Alternatively, where the applicant is named in the regulation, as in *Maizena v Council*, the action will be held to be of direct and individual concern. In the particular area of anti-dumping measures where, as a result of an investigation of individual importers a general regulation is issued to catch all imports, applicants have been more successful than normal because the regulations are regarded as hybrid regulations. For example, the Court of Justice has held that despite being measures of general application, certain individuals may challenge regulations as if they were decisions, especially when one of the articles of the regulation specifically refers to the applicant companies. See the *Japanese Ball Bearings* cases and the *Timex* case, where Timex had made a complaint allowed under an anti-dumping regulation. Once it has been demonstrated that the regulation is really a decision, the applicant is still required to satisfy the tests of direct and individual concern, considered below. It is also argued that if direct and individual concern is proved, there will be no need to demonstrate that the regulation is a disguised decision, see *CAM v Commission, Sofrimport, Extramet* and the *Timex* cases. In *Codorniu v Council*, despite the ECJ confirming that the Regulation was a legislative measure applying to traders in general, it could still be of individual concern to one of them. Codorniu had distinguished themselves by the ownership of a trademark for the term Crement from the year 1924, which the Community had tried to reserve for French and Luxembourg producers.

Finally in this context, individuals may not challenge directives *ASOCARNE v E.U. Council*.

(c)   A decision addressed to another person   In this case, in order for the application to be admissible, the decision must be of direct and individual concern to the applicant. 'Another person' has been held in *Plaumann v Commission* (case 25/62) to include the Member States and not just other individuals.

The tests of direct concern and individual concern   With direct concern, the general rule is that if a Member State is granted discretion to act under the provision, then the provision cannot by its nature give rise to direct concern. This was certainly the initial view taken by the Court of Justice in the *Plaumann* and the *Alcan* cases. However, the case of *Bock v Commission (Chinese Mushrooms)* involved authorisation for Member States to act, but nevertheless the action was held to be admissible because the number and identity of importers had already been fixed. This trend was continued in *Piraiki-Patraiki* v *Commission*, in which the French authorities were authorised to impose quotas but the Court of Justice held that, where interested parties could be identified with certainty or a high degree of probability, direct concern would be satisfied, despite the theoretical discretion on the part of the Member State.

Individual concern has been very hard to demonstrate and has often been tested by the Court of Justice, first or at the same time as direct concern to decide admissibility, as in *Plaumann* v *Commission* (case 25/62). A decision was addressed to the German Government refusing permission to reduce duties on clementines. The test was whether the decision affected the applicant by virtue of the fact that he was a member of the abstractly defined class addressed by the rule, for example because he was an importer of clementines, or did it affect him because of attributes peculiar to him which differentiated him from all other persons. Plaumann was held to be one of a class of importers and not, therefore, individually concerned.

See also *Spijker Kwasten BV* v *Commission* in which an import ban was imposed on Chinese brushes for 6 months. Spijker was the only importer in Holland and had previously requested a licence. Held the company could not be individually concerned as others could apply. The ban was prospective.

In *Töpfer* v *Commission*, it was held that the applicant must be affected alone or as a member of a fixed and closed class. Töpfer was so affected because it had applied for a licence prior to a retroactive Commission decision and was therefore identifiable, see also *CAM* v *Commission*.

In *Bock* v *Commission*, the company was individually concerned because of applications made by Bock to import chinese mushrooms, which were refused by Germany on 11 September but authorised by the Commission only on 15 September. Hence the decision was a retroactive measure in direct response to the application from Bock, who was held to have a vested legal interest.

The *Metro-SB-Grossmarkte* v *Commission* application was held to be admissible, because Metro was held to have legitimate interest in the decision aimed at another person as a result of the complaint made by Metro under the competition law regulation which led to the decision in the first place.

See also *Sofrimport* v *Commission*, concerning a decision taken to restrict the import of Chilean apples while some were in transit, a fact of which the Commission was specifically notified and required to take into account.

A Restrictive Approach

The reasons for the difficulties in demonstrating *locus standi* have been subject to much debate, and questions can concentrate on the policy factors which may be applicable. Is it the result of the deliberate policy of the Court of Justice concerned with 'floodgates' arguments, or desires to promote the Court more as a Supreme Court for the institutions and Member States and not as one directly accessible as a first instance court for individuals? To some extent the question has been answered by the establishment of the Court of First Instance primarily to handle cases under competition law and which elevates the Court of Justice into the role of an appeal court in relation to these categories of cases. Indirect alternatives are available to individuals.

Those cases held to be admissible often arise from the application of retroactive legislation. The applicants thus belonged to a fixed and identifiable group which could not be added to. Other arguments revolve around discussions about balancing the interests of the Community and individuals in the Community. The decision-making procedure in the Community is a much more complex procedure and often the result of a compromise which makes legislation more difficult to enact. The inevitable economic choices of the Community are likely to affect individuals and must be allowed to be made, otherwise the ability of the Community and Commission to operate would be undermined. Actions should not hinder the institutions' ability to operate but, on the other hand, genuinely affected individuals must be allowed recourse to challenge unlawful acts. Comparisons with the Member States may be made, in that such challenges are also subject to equally tight *locus standi* requirements. In those areas where, by contrast, individuals find it easier to achieve standing such as competition law, State aids and anti-dumping measures, it may be argued that the very often closer involvement of particular individuals makes the difference. The applicants are likely to be the ones involved in the process by informing the Commission of certain situations or can be seen clearly to be affected by the measures complained about. This then sets them apart from the many other challenges arising most frequently against legislative decisions made under the Common Agricultural Policy. However, the overall picture remains that of a restrictive *locus standi* for applicants.

Grounds for Annulment

Once admissibility has been established the grounds or substantive merits of the claim must be proved. These are laid down in Art 230 (old 173) and can often overlap in individual cases.

Lack of competence on the part of a institution to adopt a particular measure   This is really the equivalent of *ultra vires*, i.e., no power to act, and concerns the requirement that all measures must have the appropriate legal authority. Article 7 (old 4) EC requires each institution to act within the limits of the power conferred on it. *Meroni* v *High Authority* concerned the successful challenge to decisions taken by a subordinate authority where no delegated decision-making powers had been granted. The recent cases concerning the use of an incorrect legal base for a measure, as in *European Parliament* v *Council (Students Residence Directive)*, are good examples of this ground. More recently there have been further examples of this ground: *France* v *Commission* (case C-327/91), whereby the Commission exceeded its competence when it concluded an international agreement with the USA because Art 300 (old 228) EC required it to be concluded by the Council; and *French Republic* v *Commission* (case C-57/95), which was a French action to annul a Commission 'Communication', where the Court held that because the Commission had no such power to adopt an act imposing new obligations on the Member States which was not inherent in the Treaty, the Commission lacked competence and the Act was annulled. Also, see the *UK* v *Commission (Poverty Action)* case considered above.

Infringement of an essential procedural requirement Specific requirements are laid down by Art 253 (old 190) that all Community secondary law must give reasons and refer to any proposals and opinions made in respect of the provisions. The Court of Justice has held that insufficient, or vague or inconsistent reasoning would constitute a breach of this ground. It was held in *Germany* v *Commission (Wine Tariff Quotas)* that reasons must contain sufficient details of the facts and figures on which they are based.

In the *Roquette* and *Maizena* v *Council* cases, the Council failed to consult the EP as required under Art 37(2) (old 43(2)). It had asked for an opinion but did not wait long enough for the answer before going ahead with the regulation.

A measure which is not notified will deprive the applicants of the rights to protest and to have their views made known or represented to the relevant institution, as in the *Transocean* case.

In *France* v *Commission* (case C-325/91) it was held that there was a requirement to state the Treaty base, the failure to observe this leading to the annulment of the measure.

Infringement of a provision of a Community Treaty or a rule of law relating to its application This includes the breach of general principles of law, considered in greater detail in chapter 4. In the following cases, the Court of Justice recognised the general principles pleaded: the *KSH* v *Intervention Board* action considered the principle of equality; *Transocean* was concerned with the right to be heard; and *Töpfer* (case 112/77) concerned legitimate expectation and legal certainty. The *France* v *Commission* (case C-325/91) case would also be applicable here for infringing a Treaty requirement.

Misuse of power by a Community institution The basis of this ground concerns the use of power for the wrong purpose, as in *Fédération Charbonnière de Belgique* v *High Authority*, which held in respect of Art 33 ECSC that the substance of the power must be related to the end result, and as in *Giuffrida* v *Council* (case 105/75), concerning the appointment of a Community official. This category comes very close to the first one, in that the use of power as the basis of unauthorised action is the equivalent of having no lawful basis for the action undertaken or acting beyond power.

The Result of a Successful Action

Article 231 (old 174) provides that if the action is well founded, the Court of Justice shall declare the act concerned to be void. Under Art 231 (old 174), the Court shall, if it considers this necessary, state which of the effects of a regulation can be considered as definitive, and can sever parts where possible (see the *Consten and Grundig* and *Commission* v *Council (Staff Salaries)* cases). In *UK* v *Commission (Poverty 4 action)* (case C-106/96), considered above, the Court held that the Commission lacked the competence to commit the expenditure and the decision in the guise of an advertisement was annulled. However, in view of the fact that much of the expenditure had already taken place the Court decided in the interests of legal certainty to exercise the discretion given to it under Art 231 (old 174) and rule in favour of the payments made or promised.

The Court has also exercised this discretion in relation to directives — see *European Parliament* v *Council Re Students' Rights*.

Article 233 (old 176) provides that where an act has been declared void, the institutions are obliged to take the necessary measures to comply with the judgment of the Court of Justice.

Alternatives to new Article 230 (old 173)

The plea of illegality under Article 241 (old 184) As this is most likely to be raised under Art 234 (old 177) proceedings as an indirect action it is considered in chapter 7.

Action for damages under Article 288 (old 215) The action under Art 230 (old 173) only annuls the act and does not provide compensation for a damaged but successful applicant. Damages must be pursued under Art 288 (old 215), and are considered in detail below.

Preliminary rulings under Article 234 (old 177) Actions under Art 234 (old 177) avoid the strict time limits of Art 230 (old 173), but are instead subject to the national time limits. However, there needs to be an element of national law to be able to raise a matter before the national courts. For example, the *KSH* action, which had failed when raised directly before the Court of Justice, was successful when subject to an Art 234 (old 177) reference in cases 103 and 145/77 in a challenge to the Commission regulations in the UK courts.

ACTION FOR FAILURE TO ACT

Introduction

Article 232 (old 175) concerns actions against the Council or the Commission for a failure to act. It is the remedy where the unlawfulness of the institution in question is the wrongful failure to act in violation of the Treaty. This presupposes that there was a clear duty to act imposed on the institution in the first place. It complements an Art 230 (old 173) action and can be pleaded in the same action. In *Chevalley* v *Commission*, the Court of Justice held it was not necessary to state which action was the subject of the application.

There are a number of similar features between the two articles, but they were designed to cover different situations — Art 230 (old 173) illegal action, and Art 232 (old 175) illegal inaction. Both provisions, however, have as their objective the ending of a situation of illegality. Both actions are also similar in respect of the institutions which may be challenged — originally only the Commission and the Council but the TEU formally extended the right of challenge under Art 232 (old 175) to the EP and the ECB within its field of competence. Actions are heard at first instance by the CFI.

Admissibility and Locus Standi

Privileged applicants   The Community institutions and Member States have, under Art 232 (old 175), a privileged right of action which is not subject to restrictions on admissibility, and, although not express, the EP is a privileged applicant, as confirmed by *European Parliament* v *Council (Re Transport Policy)*. The privileged applicants can request general legislative acts, as well as decisions, without having to show any special interest (the 'Transport Policy' case). The ECB was given the right to take action by the TEU in areas falling within its field of competence.

Non-privileged applicants   Individuals, on the other hand, have a restricted right of *locus standi* under Art 232 (old 175), more so than under Art 230 (old 173), because there is no equivalent of 'directly and individually concerned': 'Any natural or legal person may, under the conditions laid down in the preceding paragraphs, complain to the Court of Justice that an institution of the Community has failed to address to that person any act other than a recommendation or an opinion.'

It was established by case law that to challenge under Art 232 (old 175) an individual must have been legally entitled to claim as a potential addressee: see *Lord Bethell* v *EC Commission*, involving a complaint of a failure to act on price fixing by the airlines. Any potential act would be addressed to the airlines and not Lord Bethell.

This strict view on the *locus standi* requirements has been tempered by the Court of Justice in subsequent cases and now that the requirements are analogous to the direct and individual concern of Art 230 (old 173) (see *T. Port* v *Bundesanstalt für Landeswirtschaft und Ernährung* (case C-68/95)).

Acts Subject to an Article 232 (old 175) Action

The Court of Justice has in many cases rejected applications by individuals for measures of general legislative content (see *Chevalley* v *Commission* and *Nordgetreide* v *Commission*, in which it was held that applications are restricted to decisions). Regulations cannot be requested, because by their nature they are not capable of being addressed to specific individuals.

There must be an obligation under the Treaty which is enforceable to adopt a reviewable act on the part of the institution, and a demand for an opinion is not actionable (*Chevalley* v *Commission*). *European Parliament* v *Council (Transport Policy)* holds that the acts requested need not be spelt out in detail but must be sufficiently identified.

Procedural Requirements

The invitation to act   There is a preliminary procedural step which must be taken before court action can ensue. Article 232 (old 175) provides: 'The action shall be admissible only if the institution concerned has first been called upon to act.' The applicant must request the institution to take a specific action as legally required, and advise that failure to comply will result in a court action under Art 232 (old 175). The invitation to act need not follow any precise form to qualify for the purposes of Art 232 (old 175).

Only if the institution fails to define its position within a two-month period can the matter be brought before the Court of Justice. The application to the Court of Justice must be made within a further two-month period from the end of the initial two-month period. If the institution complies with the request to act, as in *European Parliament* v *Council (Comitology)*, the Court of Justice will not allow the action to proceed.

There are two areas of Community law which give specific rights to parties to make complaints to the Commission regarding the unlawful activities of other parties. These are the competition law rules, specifically Regulation 17/62, and the anti-dumping rules. These areas have given rise to particular considerations in respect of actions under Art 232 (old 175) and Art 230 (old 173). As a result of the fact that interested parties are often specifically concerned with the result of the information passed to the Commission on the activities of other parties and the action the Commission may take, the parties will often demand that the Commission acts, failing which, the parties have attempted to take action themselves under Art 232 (old 175). They have, however, usually been defeated by the fact that the Commission's refusal to act constitutes a satisfactory definition of position for the purposes of Art 232 (old 175) and brings the matter to a close.

Definition of position   This requirement has been seen to defeat most actions, because, where the institution has explained its refusal to act, the action is inadmissible. In *Lütticke* v *Commission* (1966), the applicants had requested the Commission to take action against the German Federal Republic regarding a breach of Community law. The Commission was of the opinion that there had been no breach, so therefore refused to take action, but also notified the applicant of this. The Court of Justice declared the application inadmissible on the ground that the notification of the refusal was a definition of position. Thus a refusal to act is not itself actionable.

In *Deutscher Komponistenverband* v *Commission*, it was held that a complaint that a decision taken by the Commission was wrong, does not allow an applicant to proceed under Art 232 (old 175) on the basis that the right decision was not taken by the Commission, i.e., that it had failed to act in the right way.

In the *GEMA* v *Commission* case, a complaint was made to the Commission under Regulation 17 (competition law) about Radio Luxembourg. When the Commission failed to take any action, GEMA attempted an Art 232 (old 175) action against the Commission. It was held that the letter from the Commission to GEMA stating its decision not to take action, was a sufficient definition of position to defeat GEMA's action.

Until *European Parliament* v *Council (Re Transport Policy)*, a declaration by an institution of its unwillingness to act was regarded by some as constituting a sufficient definition of position for the purposes of the Court of Justice. However, the Court in that case stated that: 'In the absence of taking a formal act, the institution called upon to define its position must do more than reply stating its current position which in effect neither denies or admits the alleged failure nor reveals the attitude of the defendant institution to the demanded measures.'

The Substantive Action

In the 'Transport Policy' case (above), the EP had complained that the Council had failed in its Treaty obligations under old Arts 3, 61, 74, 75 and 84 (now 3, 51, 70, 71 and 80) to introduce a common policy for transport and lay down a framework for this policy, and to act on 16 specific proposals of the Commission. The Court of Justice held, with regard to the first claim, that because the Treaty requirements were so vague, they could not be said to be sufficiently specific obligations that non-implementation constituted a failure to act, despite the fact that, even as such, the obligations should have been completed long ago. The Court held, however, that the obligation in old Art 61 (now 51) of the Treaty could be identified with sufficient preciseness as to admit a failure on the part of the Council to lay down a framework.

The second claim, of failure to act on 16 proposals of the Commission, was successful only in respect of the proposals and freedom to provide services. The other measures were within the greater margin of discretion left to the Council by the Treaty.

Results of a Declaration of a Failure to Act

The institution is required under Art 233 (old 176) to take the necessary measures to comply with the judgment of the Court of Justice, within a reasonable time. A continued failure to act would, of course, be actionable under Art 232 (old 175). As with Arts 226 and 228 (old 169 and 171) actions, continued intransigence by an institution is insurmountable but politically unlikely. Article 233 (old 176) states it is without prejudice to any action for damages under Art 288 (old 215).

NON-CONTRACTUAL LIABILITY OF THE EC

Introduction

While the EC Treaty specifically refers contractual liability disputes to the jurisdiction of national courts, Art 235 (old 178) confers jurisdiction over disputes relating to claims for damages under Art 288 (old 215) of the Treaty — the so-called 'non-contractual liability' — to the Court of Justice. Article 288 (old 215) requires the Community to make good damage caused by the institutions or servants in the performance of their duties, in accordance with the general principles common to the laws of the Member States.

Non-contractual liability concerns the wrongs caused by the legislative and administrative activities of the Community, whether created by the institutions or their servants.

The Court of Justice, as in other instances when it looks to national laws for guidance and general principles, is not required to accept the lowest common denominator but makes a comparative review and selects principles of law appropriate to the situation. Therefore, a body of Community law is being built up in this area.

Admissibility/Locus Standi

In contrast to Arts 230 and 232 (old 173 and 175), there is no restrictive *locus standi* imposed by either Art 235 or 288 (old 178 or Art 215). There is a five-year limitation period on actions, which commences from the occurrence of the event causing the damage (*Schöppenstedt* v *Council*) or if not discovered until later, from when the event causing the damage is discovered (*Adams* v *Commission*).

The defendants   In an action against the Community, the appropriate institution should be named as defendant. This can be the Commission, or the Council or both, who jointly legislate in many areas of Community law, as confirmed by the Court of Justice in the *Wehrhahn* case. Member States may be sued only where they are responsible for the implementation of Community measures and are given discretion which they exceed. If there is no discretion on their part, the Commission would be the proper defendant (*Krohn* v *Commission*).

Following the TEU, the ECB is now named as a potential defendant but the EP is not which is odd given the increase in the legislative powers of the EP, especially co-decision with the Council and the extension of Art 230 (old 173) to the EP.

An Independent Action

In *Lütticke* v *Commission* (1971), damage had been suffered as a result of the Commission failing to act against Germany. The Commission argued that the action under Art 288 (old 215) was an attempt to circumvent the *locus standi* requirements of the unsuccessful Art 232 (old 175) action. The Court of Justice rejected this argument and declared that the action for damages provided by Articles 235 and 288 (old 178 and 215) was established by the Treaty as an independent form of action and whose object was to compensate a party for damage sustained and not to secure the annulment of an illegal measure. This ruling was confirmed in the *Schöppenstedt* case of 1971. Therefore, little difficulty faces applicants in respect of admissibility; the problem lies in proving that an act of the Community caused damage and was a sufficiently serious breach.

The Scope of Liability

The liability of the Community is that of a public authority, and includes not only administrative acts or omissions but also legislative acts such as regulations, directives or decisions. These would include failures of administration, the adoption of invalid acts and the negligence of employees of the institutions in the performance of their duties, but not extending to personal faults of employees. In *Sayag* v *Leduc*, Mr Sayag was employed by Euratom. While showing guests of the Community round in his own car, he was involved in an accident in which his passengers were injured. It was held that the Commission was not liable because Mr Sayag's act was not an official act of the Community. Only the necessary extension of tasks entrusted to the institutions of the Community cause liability on the part of their servants. See, for example, *Parise* v *Commission* which involved liability arising from the failure to correct an error when discovered.

All types of legislative act can be subject to an action under Art 288 (old 215).

The Requirements of the Claim

From the case law, requirements have been identified to establish liability for the purpose of Art 288 (old 215). There must be a wrongful act or omission on the part of the Community which has breached a duty, the applicant must have suffered damage, and there must be a causal link between the act or omission and the damage.

Proving liability   The act or omission of the Community must be shown to be wrongful. While a requirement of fault is not express from the Treaty, case law indicates it is necessary. In respect of actions claiming damage resulting from the wrongful adoption of legislative acts, the Court of Justice laid down a strict test in *Schöppenstedt* v *Council*, which has been repeated often: 'The Community does not incur liability on account of a legislative measure which involves choices of economic policy unless a sufficiently serious breach of a superior rule of law for the protection of the individual has occurred.' The reasoning for this is very similar to the strict requirements for *locus standi* under Art 230 (old 173), in that the high degree of discretion that the institutions need to carry out the economic tasks they must carry out necessarily affects many persons, hence then the imposition of a higher burden when choices of economic policy are involved. Therefore, it is not just unlawful conduct that will attract liability: it is the degree of conduct required under the formula developed by the Court of Justice.

This formula can, then, be divided into two parts (although in some texts it is suggested that the first element can be further divided to make three). The first element is that the rule of law must be one for the protection of the individual.

The rules of law include those general principles discussed in chapter 5, and the principles of equality/discrimination and legitimate expectation seem most often to be raised. The protection of the individual has been interpreted to include the protection of classes of persons, as with the importers in the *Kampffmeyer* case. Thus, in the *CNTA* case, the Commission was held liable to pay compensation for losses incurred as a result of a regulation which abolished, with immediate effect and without warning, the application of compensatory amounts. It was held to be a serious breach of the principle of legitimate expectation. It was held to be a serious breach of the principle of legitimate expectation. In the *Gritz* and *Quellmehl (Dumortier Freres)* cases, the ending of a subsidy was held to be a breach because it was retained on starch which was in direct competition (see also the *HNL* case, where breach of discrimination confirmed and the *Royal Scholten Holdings* case).

Secondly, the breach must be sufficiently serious. In *HNL v Council and Commission*, in which a Regulation requiring cattlefood manufacturers to use more expensive skimmed milk than cheaper soya in their foods (to use up the then 'milk lake') was invalid because it offended the principles of proportionality and discrimination (Art 34(2) (old 40(3)). However, whilst in the Art 288 (old 215) action, the breach was acknowledged, it was held not to be sufficiently flagrant. It was required to be 'manifest and grave'. This was interpreted later, in *KSH v Council and Commission*, as conduct verging on the arbitrary. In *KSH*, the damage was so extensive it caused insolvency of the company but the action was not successful because the breach of the law was not verging on the arbitrary. Factors which influence the Court of Justice in its determination of whether the breach is sufficiently serious are the effect of the measure and the nature of the breach.

The effect of the measure relates to its scope, the number of people affected and the damage caused. For example, in the *HNL* case there was little damage, and thus the action was not successful. The damage must be over and above the risk of damage normal in business. (See the *Gritz and Quellmehl* case, *Dumortier Frères v Council* and *Sofrimport*, in respect of the view that the Court requires only a small, defined and closed group of applicants to be affected.) Another important factor is whether there is a higher Community public interest involved which may be more important than the number involved because *Mulder* (cases C-104/89 and 37/90) suggests a large group need not be fatal to a claim. The presence of a large group of claimants did not defeat a claim although a serious breach still had to be demonstrated and that there was no higher public interest of the Community involved.

The nature of the breach relates to its seriousness. In the *Isoglucose* cases, the damage was extensive, causing the insolvency of one company, but the action was not successful because the breach of the law did not verge on the arbitrary. The applicants in the *Sofrimport* case were successful because of the complete failure of the Commission to take into account the interests of the applicants when specifically required to do so.

Other actions which do not challenge the legislative acts themselves, but seek only to show that the wrongful act was a failure of the administration in the implementation of the law, do not need to satisfy the formula under *Schöppenstedt*.

The damage   Having established the existence of an act or omission attributable to the Community, damage to the applicant must be proved. Damage can be purely economic, as in the *Kampffmeyer* case, involving a cancellation fee and loss of profits, but this must be specified and not speculative; or it can be moral damage and anxiety, awarded in the staff case, *Willame* v *Commission*.

The causal connection   Lastly, it must be shown that the act of the Community caused the damage. There must be a sufficiently direct connection between the act and the injury, the damages from which must be ascertainable (*Kampffmeyer* v *Commission*). It cannot, however, be too remote, as held in *Lütticke* (case 4/69) but without further specification.

In *Dumortier Frères* v *the Council (Gritz and Quellmehl)* it was held that there was no need to make good every harmful consequence especially where remote. Damage must be a sufficiently direct consequence of the unlawful conduct of the institution concerned. In *Compagnie Continentale Francaise* it was held that the causal link was only established if the misleading information given would have caused an error in the mind of a reasonable person.

Choice of Court

Where the claims are for unliquidated damages, i.e., those involving loss of profits, these should be heard before the Court of Justice (*CNTA* v *Commission*). See also the case of *Krohn*. Application of most Community legislation is by national authorities, therefore it is really only the conduct of the institutions or their servants that would require application to the Court of Justice.

Community legislative measures, especially in the agricultural sector, are actually administered by the national intervention agencies, who make payments and receive payments. Therefore, in spite of the fact it was a Community act that was wrongful, compensation must be sought from the national authorities. The appropriate remedy is thus a claim in the national courts, followed, if necessary, by a reference under the Art 234 (old 177) procedure.

QUESTIONS

1.   'In respect of the Member States, the Treaty has, in substitution for direct sanctions, devised special enforcement procedures the purpose of

which is to establish with legally binding effect whether a Member State has failed to fulfil an obligation arising from Community law.' Discuss.

This question could be taken alone, as above, or could be supplemented by other more specific variations, such as:

> Consider the effectiveness of these procedures in ensuring regard for Community law on the part of Member States.

And/or:

> Will the sanctions that have been imposed strengthen the efficacy of these actions, or what other approaches to the ECJ could be made?

The first question on its own would require a detailed but descriptive answer. I shall not provide a full answer here, but just the framework of what would be required. Clearly this concerns the Member States and the special enforcement procedures contained in the EC Treaty to establish a failure to fulfil an obligation. The question is therefore referring to Arts 226 and 227 (old 169 and 170). The focus of the question is that these procedures are a substitute for direct sanctions, and this is the part that requires discussion. First, however, you need to outline the procedures themselves. If this were the full question, you would make this a detailed description, but as part of a longer question, keep it concise.

A description of the Commission's action against Member States under Art 226 (old 169) should be given, and of the action by other Member States against a Member State under Art 227 (old 170). You could, if these were featured in your course, give an idea of how many cases reach the Court of Justice under these actions, and perhaps give reasons why you consider so very few Art 227 (old 170) actions are commenced or reach judgment. The end result of both of these actions, however, is only a declaratory judgment of the Court of Justice. According to Art 228 (old 171), Member States are required to comply with this.

The first variation would be the main focus of the question: 'Consider the effectiveness of these procedures in ensuring regard for Community law on the part of Member States.' There are no immediate sanctions under the present arrangements after the declaratory judgment. This, then, requires you to consider the merits of these arrangements and direct sanctions. The present arrangements are not coercive and rely on the goodwill of the Member States to comply with the judgment, which, in the majority of cases, they do. However, if they do not, the recourse of the Commission is to take another action against the Member States, but this time for a breach of Art 228 (old 171) for failing to comply with the earlier judgment. This time the amended Art 228 (old 171) provides that the Commission, after giving the Member State a chance to submit observations, may set a time limit for compliance and specify to the Court of Justice a fine to be paid if the Member State fails to comply.

The conclusion might be, that, despite the previous lack of direct sanctions, the procedures have been very effective, in that most states comply in time with the judgment. A hidden problem is that the cases which reach the Court of Justice are only the tip of the iceberg, because the Commission probably does not have the time and resources to take every infringement to the Court.

Next, you must speculate as to whether the new direct sanctions would be better. Specifically, the second alternative above asks you to consider whether sanctions should be imposed and to suggest other approaches which could be made to the ECJ.

Before the new procedures are discussed, you should consider whether there are any existing alternative procedures which may help to secure compliance, or at least to bring to an end, if only temporarily, the alleged breach of a Community law obligation. Here the interim measures under Art 243 (old 186) can be considered, which have been used to prevent the continued breach of Member States. Two case examples are the *Factortame* litigation in the UK and *Commission v Germany (Re Lorry Tax)*. The Commission successfully applied for interim measures in both cases, to suspend the application of the national measures alleged to breach Community law. Then you should mention that Arts 228 and 229 (old 171 and 172) now provide for sanctions, requested by the Commission, in an action to establish that the Member States have failed to comply with a previous judgment of the Court of Justice. You would need to speculate briefly whether this will be effective and better than the previous arrangement. It would still apply only to the minority of cases, and perhaps only to countries whose procedures are less efficient rather than to those that deliberately flout Community law. (One doesn't have to think too hard about which country would suffer the most in such circumstances, and against whom most of these secondary breach actions have taken place.)

It may encourage compliance, but there may be other alternatives as suggested in the question. What are these? Actions by individuals in the national courts to defend or establish their individual rights based on Community law, which are referred to the Court of Justice under Art 234 (old 177), also serve to bring to the attention of the Commission and the Court of Justice a failure by the Member State. In most circumstances the Member States amend their laws to comply with their Community obligations without the need for an Art 226 (old 169) action by the Commission. Many examples could be cited here, but leading cases are *Van Gend en Loos*, *Marshall*, or any similar case where direct effects have upheld individuals' rights under Community law, in the face of conflicting national law.

A recent development which may spur on Member States to comply far more effectively than any of the above actions, is the prospect of having to compensate in each case where an individual has suffered damage as a result of the failure of the Member State to implement a Community obligation. In the case which decided this, *Francovich*, the breach was the failure to implement a Directive, but subsequent cases have demonstrated (*Factortame*) that potentially any breach of a Community law obligation by a Member State may render it liable to compensate damage resulting from it. (See also chapters 4 and 6.) Potentially, it would appear to be at least as useful as the sanctions under Arts 228 and 229 (old 171 and 172).

Questions that involve consideration of a number of the actions for judicial review in Community law are provided next. Such questions can appear in problem or essay form. As they repeat much of the information already given above in the text, only guide notes will be provided here.

2.   On 20 October 1999, the Council adopted a regulation under which the sales of sugar beet to food manufacturers were to be subsidised in order to reduce the Community's 'sugar mountain'. Sweetness Ltd is an isoglucose manufacturer and fears that its business will suffer as a result of this subsidy.

On 10 November 1999, Sweetness Ltd wrote to the Council asking it to withdraw the regulation, on the ground that in adopting the regulation the Council had failed to observe the principle of non-discrimination in Art 34(2) of the EC Treaty.

On 5 January 2000, the Council wrote to Sweetness Ltd, saying it understood why Sweetness Ltd was aggrieved but considered there was no alternative but to adopt the regulation.

The next day Sweetness Ltd wrote to the Commission, asking it to bring an action against the Council under Art 230 (old 173). Two weeks later the Commission wrote to Sweetness Ltd, saying that it did not consider the Council to be in breach of the EC Treaty.

Can Sweetness Ltd now bring an action against either the Commission or the Council? Would it make any difference to your answer if neither the Council nor the Commission had replied to Sweetness Ltd's letters?

You should consider first whether an action under Art 230 (old 173) is possible against the Council. By the time an action under Art 230 (old 173) to annul the regulation is considered, the time limit has expired and the action would be too late. An alternative would be attempting to force the institutions to act by an Art 232 (old 175) action against either the Council or the Commission. For this to succeed an applicant must show that it was a potential addressee of the decision. To some extent this would depend on the number of isoglucose manufacturers. If only one exists, then the decision must refer to Sweetness Ltd, but if there are many, then this argument could not hold. Even if called upon to act, an explanation from the Commission, stating that by not acting it is within its discretion, would bring the action to an end.

Possible action under Art 288 (old 215) for damages should be considered (see the text above), or, lastly, if a reason arises to bring this before a national court, a reference under Art 234 (old 177) may be possible, i.e., the intervention of a national agency.

An alternative question may concern action by a Member State which affects an individual.

3.   Your client, MacDonald, is an importer of poultry products. The British Government has recently enacted measures to give effect to Council regulations implementing the common market in poultry. The effect is to prohibit the import of certain birds in which MacDonald's business specialises. MacDonald feels these national measures are contrary to Community law obligations.

On 5 March of this year he wrote to the Commission, asking them to take action against the British Government under Art 226 (old 169) EC. Last month he received a reply stating that the Commission does not intend to take action.

Advise MacDonald as to the possible remedies in both the Court of Justice and the national courts.

The same issues would need to be considered and similar information provided in the alternative essay form of this question:

4.   What remedies will an individual have, in circumstances where he or she has called upon the Commission to act under Article 226 (old 169), and the Commission has declined to do so?

An individual cannot force the Commission to take Art 226 (old 169) proceedings, as the Commission has a discretion under the terms of the article.

Before the Court of Justice the possible actions are under Art 230 (old 173) to challenge an act of the institutions, under Art 232 (old 175) to require them to act, under Art 241 (old 184) (the indirect challenge to Community regulations) and under Art 288 (old 215) (the action for damages).

The actions before the national courts could be the indirect action under Art 241 (old 184) or an action for damages. It would first have to be determined whether it is the action of the Member State which is alleged to be unlawful or the regulation itself. If it is the Member State's action, then the case must go before the national courts with a reference if necessary. If the problem is with the regulation itself, then the action must commence in the Court of Justice under Art 288 (old 215).

An individual would not be able to challenge the act under Art 230 (old 173) before the Court of Justice as the letter from the Commission is not a reviewable act unless it alters the legal position. There is a very slim chance of bringing an action before the Court under Art 232 (old 175), but the problem is admissibility, in that it must be shown that the individual, as an applicant to the Court, was a potential addressee of the measure requested. If the Commission has written and advised that it has decided to do nothing, this definition of position by the Commission would satisfy the terms of Art 232 (old 175) and the action would be dismissed. An action under Art 241 (old 184) would not arise as there is not another action in which the challenge to the regulation would be incidental. Alternatively, an action for damages may be attempted, but the criteria for Art 288 (old 215) must be proved and the breach is unlikely to be sufficiently serious.

Before the national courts, it would depend on whether there was fault on the part of the Member State, which is unclear from the facts. An action under the *Francovich* ruling would not succeed as the Member State has not breached a Community law obligation.

FURTHER READING

Arnull, A., 'Private Applicants and the Action for Annulment under Article 173 of the EC Treaty' (1995) CML Rev 7.

Cooke, J., 'Locus standi of private parties under Article 173(4)' (1997) 6 IJEL 4.

Hartley, T., *The Foundations of European Community Law* (4th edn, Oxford: Clarendon Press, 1998) chapters 10–13 and 15–17.

Hedemann-Robinson, M., 'Article 173 EC, general community measures and locus standi for private persons: still a cause for individual concern?' (1996) 2 EPL 127.

Mastroianni, B., 'The enforcement procedure under Article 169 of the EC Treaty and the powers of the European Commission: quis custodiet custodes?' (1995) 1 EPL 535.

Oliver, P., 'Interim Measures: Some Recent Developments' (1992) 29 CML Rev 7.

Rasmusson, H., 'Why is Article 173 interpreted against Private Plaintiffs?' (1980) 2 EL Rev 112.

Schermers, Heukels and Mead (eds.), *Non-Contractual Liability of the European Communities* (Nijhoff Publications, 1988).

Waelbroeck, D. and Fosselard, D., 'Case C-69/89, Codorniu SA v Council of the European Union, judgment of 18 May 1994, [1994] ECR I-1853' (1995) 32 CML Rev 257.

Wils, W., 'Concurrent Liability of the Community and a Member State' (1992) 17 EL Rev 191.

7 THE ENFORCEMENT OF COMMUNITY LAW: II

This chapter concerns actions that do not involve a direct action against either the institutions of the Community or the Member States before the European Court of Justice. The first section deals exclusively with actions that arise in the national courts, whereas the indirect challenge to Community legislation under Art 241 (old 184) can also take place before the ECJ. Neither action involves a direct challenge to Community law. The first procedure is that of the preliminary ruling procedure under Art 234 (old 177) which focuses on actions taken in the national courts and actions in which individuals predominantly have been able to assert their rights in Community law and by which a system of Community law remedies for individuals has been developed by the Court of Justice. These actions are referred to as indirect actions as they take place either in another court than the Court of Justice, i.e., the national courts, or in proceedings other than a direct action before the Court of Justice. Applications for interim relief are also considered in this chapter.

THE PRELIMINARY RULING: ARTICLE 234

Article 234 (old 177) EC has as its purpose ensuring the uniform interpretation and application of Community law. It was designed to work with the cooperation of national courts, by providing the means whereby national courts would not give their own interpretations to Community law or decide on its validity.

The preliminary ruling procedure, which is also referred to as the Art 234 reference, provides the link or bridge between the national legal systems and the Community legal system. Under Art 234 (old 177), the Court of

Justice interprets and rules on the validity of Community provisions at the request of a national court, which applies the ruling to the facts of the case. The intended relationship was of equality rather than hierarchy, therefore the Court of Justice should provide only guidelines and should not direct the municipal courts. It provides for the sharing of jurisdiction over Community law between the Court of Justice and the national courts.

The Scope of Article 234 and the Tasks of the Court of Justice

The courts of the Member States can seek a ruling from the Court of Justice on the interpretation of points of all forms of Community law, including international treaties and recommendations, and on the validity of Community secondary legislation. A request to rule on the effect of Community law is possibly, however, one of the most common questions. Article 234 (old 177) was the instrument which allowed the Court to develop the doctrines of direct effects and supremacy, vital for the development of the system of remedies under Community law which have been so helpful to individuals in getting round the restrictions placed on them by the strict *locus standi* requirements of the direct actions. Having created such doctrines, the Court receives numerable questions specifically asking whether a particular provision has direct effects. The main task of the Court of Justice is therefore to interpret and rule on the validity of Community law, so that a national court can reach a conclusion on a case involving Community law. The Court should not, however, concern itself with the application of the ruling it has made or advise the national court how to apply the ruling.

The Forums that May Make a Reference

The Court of Justice has accepted references from various bodies, including administrative tribunals, arbitration panels and insurance officers. The determination of what is an acceptable court or tribunal is a question for the Court of Justice and is not dependent on national concepts. Certain criteria have now been established by which it may reasonably be determined whether a particular body may refer to the Court of Justice for guidance under Art 234 (old 177). For example, it was clear from *Van Gend en Loos* that administrative tribunals were acceptable for the purposes of Art 234 (old 177).

While the majority of forums that decide legal matters in the Member States pose no problem, it is the peripheries of the formal legal system, and those bodies which lie either partially or entirely outside the State legal system, which raise the question of whether it is suitable for the Court of Justice to accept a reference from them. The *Vaassen* case concerned a reference from the arbitration tribunal of a private Mine Employees Social

Security Fund. The Court of Justice held that because the power to nominate members and to give approval to both the panel itself and rules changes were in the hands of a Government Minister, and because the panel was a permanent body operating under national law and rules of procedure, it qualified as a court or tribunal in the eyes of Community law. *Broekmeulen v HRC* concerned a reference made by the Appeal Committee of the Dutch Medical Professions Organisation. This was held by the Court of Justice to be acceptable, because the Committee was approved and had the assistance and considerable involvement of the Dutch public authorities, its decisions were arrived at after full legal procedure, the decisions affected the right to work under Community law, they were final and there was no appeal to Dutch courts.

In the next two cases jurisdiction was refused. In the case of *Borker*, a reference from the Paris Bar Association Council on the right of a French lawyer to appear as of right before German courts, was refused on the ground that there was no lawsuit in progress and the Council was not therefore acting as a court or tribunal called upon to give judgment in proceedings intended to lead to a decision of a judicial nature. In *Nordsee v Nordstern*, a reference from a privately appointed arbitration body was refused, despite the fact that the arbitrator's decision, based on law, including Community law, was binding. The Court of Justice held that because there was no involvement of national authorities in the process, there was not a sufficiently close link to national organisation of legal remedies, and thus the arbitrator could not come under Art 234 (old 177). Jurisdiction was also refused in the case of *Corbiau v Administration des Contributions* by a reference from the Director of Taxation because it was held that the close links between the bodies was already the issue and the administration was too close to be regarded as a court or tribunal for the purposes of Art 234 (old 177).

It is not essential if the body is a public or private body or that there is no appeal from its decision. A strong indicator is the level of involvement by national authorities. Whether these criteria remain for all cases in the future is uncertain, as the lack of an appeal may lead to instances where the national body itself has to interpret Community law without guidance if the Court of Justice is unwilling to accept jurisdiction, something which must be less desirable from a Community point of view.

The Decision to Refer

The partnership relationship requires that a ruling be given by the Court of Justice if the national court decides this is necessary to settle the matter before it. This is not always as straightforward as first appears, and questions arise as to who decides whether a preliminary ruling is necessary — the parties to the case, the national court, or the Court of Justice? The content and form of the question must also be decided, and this matter must also be considered.

Under the Art 234 (old 177) procedure, it is for the national court to decide to refer a question. The drafters of the EEC Treaty did not envisage this system as providing an individual remedy, but it is now often regarded as the initiative of one of the parties to request that a reference be made, although the national court cannot be obliged by the parties to refer.

The Court of Justice has declared that it was unable to review the facts of the case presented to it in *Simmenthal*. It has also consistently refused to rule on the validity of national laws, although it has often reformatted a question in order to give an answer to the underlying reason for the reference. In *Schwarze v EVGF*, a court requested interpretation of Community law and consideration of the validity of the national law in conflict. The Court of Justice concluded that the court was concerned more with the validity of a Community act, and it was therefore able to answer.

According to the Court of Justice in *Van Gend en Loos*, the finding by a national court that it needs to refer is not to be questioned by the Court of Justice. This position was confirmed in the *Costa v ENEL* case, in which the Court of Justice held that it is for the national court alone to judge whether a decision on the question is necessary. The Court has, however, issued guidelines in 1996 to the national courts to help them to decide whether a reference should be made. However, the Court has occasionally declined to give a ruling on questions referred to it, on the grounds that no real question arises, or that such references are an abuse or misuse of Art 234 (old 177).

Refusals to accept references   In a limited number of circumstances, the Court of Justice has refused to accept a reference from a national court.

In *SPUC v Grogan*, the case had been terminated at the national level, therefore the Court of Justice held there was no question left to be resolved.

In *Mattheus v Doego*, a contract's continuation was determinable by the entry of Spain, Portugal and Greece to the Community. The Court of Justice held it had no jurisdiction as this was a matter to be determined by the Member States and the potential new States.

The case of *Foglia v Novello (No. 1)* is of special importance. It concerned a contract for wine between a French buyer, Novello, and an Italian supplier, Foglia. Clauses stipulated the buyer and the carrier (Danzas) should not be responsible for French import duties, which were contrary to Community law. These were charged at the French border and paid by Foglia. Foglia sought to recover the duties from Novello, who denied responsibility to pay them on the basis that they were illegally charged by the French authorities. The Italian judge made a reference to the Court of Justice, asking whether the French tax was compatible with the Treaty. The Court of Justice rejected the reference on the grounds that there was no genuine dispute between the parties and that the action had simply been concocted to challenge French legislation. The Court of Justice considered this to be an abuse of the Art 234 (old 177) procedure.

Not satisfied by this, the Italian judge made a further reference, *Foglia v Novello (No. 2)*, in which he specifically pointed out that the previous case marked a radical change in the attitude of the Court of Justice to a national court's decision to refer. He requested the Court of Justice to give guidelines on the respective powers and functions of the referring court. The Court of Justice held its role was not to give abstract or advisory opinions under Art 234 (old 177), but to contribute to actual decisions, and that although discretion is given to the national courts, the limits of that discretion are determinable only by reference to Community law.

A second reference to clarify the scope of a ruling in the same case may be acceptable but not if its purpose is to challenge the validity of the first ruling; see *Da Costa en Schaake NV* and *Wünsche v Federal Republic of Germany* (case 69/85).

The more recent case in which the Court has refused jurisdiction is *Meilicke v ADV/OGA*. The Court of Justice held that as the questions raised in the reference could not be answered by reference to the limited information provided in the file, the Court would be exceeding its jurisdiction in answering what was really a hypothetical question.

A surprising refusal of jurisdiction was in the case of *TWD Textilwerke* (case C-188/92). A Commission decision addressed to Germany was not challenged within the two-month time limit under Art 230 (old 173) but instead via the national court. The Court of Justice held this to be an abuse of the procedure for not acting within the time limit. This seems to go against the promotion of Art 234 (old 177) as a vehicle for realising rights

Accepted references The decision in *Foglia v Novello (No. 1)* has been re-presented to the Court of Justice in subsequent cases. In *Vinal v Orbat* which involved Italian law in Italy, the Government claimed the case was not admissible but the Court of Justice accepted the reference.

In *Pretore di Salo v X*, there were no actual proceedings between two parties but merely the investigative proceedings of an Italian magistrate to determine whether a criminal offence might have been committed by a person or persons unknown, in the case where a river had been found to be seriously polluted. Nevertheless, when a question of a possible breach of Community law was referred to the Court of Justice by the magistrate, it was held to be admissible. The Court of Justice held it was up to the national court to decide if a reference was necessary to help it.

In two cases (*Dzodzi v Belgium* (cases C-297/88 and C-197/89) and *Leur-Bloem* (case C-28/95)), the Court of Justice has given rulings in what were essentially purely internal matters, albeit based on Community law.

Although these results would appear to be contradictory, the case of *Foglia v Novello (No. 1)* must be viewed in the light that the Court of Justice did not wish to encourage national courts to challenge the validity of laws of other Member States.

The Discretion to Refer

Does Art 234 (old 177) oblige any court to refer, and when should this reference ideally be made? This depends, first, on which paragraph of Art 234 (old 177) applies. Article 234 (old 177), paragraph two, states that any court *may* refer if it considers it necessary to reach a decision in the case; whereas Art 234 (old 177), paragraph three, states that courts against whose decisions there is no judicial remedy in national law, *shall* bring the matter before the Court of Justice. Therefore, for all courts not falling within Art 234 (old 177), paragraph three, the court is not obliged to refer and it is likely that an aggrieved party can appeal to a higher court. A problem exists, however, in deciding which courts are courts of last instance for the purpose of Art 234 (old 177), paragraph three (see further, below).

Courts that have a discretion to refer   These courts can refer at any stage of the proceedings and in any sort of proceedings (see *De Geus v Bosch* and the *Da Costa en Schaake* case). However, in *Foto-Frost v Hauptzollamt Lübeck-Ost*, the Court of Justice held national courts could not decide for themselves that Community law provisions were invalid. If a question of validity was raised but an answer was not possible from previous judgments, then national courts would be obliged to refer the question to the Court of Justice. If an appeal is still possible under national rules, it is arguable this could still be used as an alternative.

In the *Rheinmühlen-Düsseldorf litigation* (cases 146 and 166/73) the Court of Justice made it quite clear that any national court which considers that a ruling on Community will help it decide an issue has the discretion to decide regardless of any national rules of precedent or referral.

The timing of the reference   The Court of Justice has views about when a reference should be made, if considered necessary. In the case of *Irish Creamery Milk Suppliers*, it advised that the optimum time would be when facts have been established and any questions involving national law only had been settled. This does not impinge on the discretion of national courts, which ultimately can decide when to refer and the criteria necessary to decide this question.

Courts of last instance   The case law of the Court of Justice suggests that the relevant court for Art 234 (old 177), paragraph three, is the highest court for the case, rather than the highest court in the Member State. In *Costa v ENEL*, there was no right of appeal from the Italian magistrates' court because the sum of money involved was so small. The Court of Justice held that national courts against whose decisions there is no national judicial remedy, must refer a question of Community law to the Court of Justice. In most instances this is an adequate answer, and Art 234 (old 177), paragraph three, should apply to those proceedings which deny an appeal or judicial review and thus become last instance.

The situation in Member States may not be so easy to determine, for instance, UK courts which refuse leave to appeal, especially the Court of Appeal or the House of Lords Appeal Committee. This has the result that the lower court then becomes the court of last instance, and may result in a denial of the consideration of Community law to an applicant. This happened in *Magnavision* v *General Optical Council (No. 2)*, where the issue of Community law was raised in the first case under this name but was neither considered nor referred, nor was an appeal to the House of Lords allowed. The applicant then appealed to the High Court that the previous refusal meant the High Court became the court of last instance for the purposes of Art 234 (old 177). This appeal was also refused, and the High Court also refused to refer this question to the Court of Justice, thus denying a consideration of Community law points. The same situation would apply if the House of Lords refused leave to appeal and did in fact happen in the case of *Chiron Corporation* v *Murex Diagnostics Ltd (No. 8)*. It has been later held by the Court of Justice that national courts must set aside rules of national law preventing the Art 234 (old 177) procedure from being followed (*Peterbroeck Van Campenhout* v *Belgium* (case C-312/93)).

Avoiding the obligation to refer Two cases spanning a period of 20 years outline the view of the Court of Justice on the circumstances when it is *not* necessary to make a reference under Art 234 (old 177), paragraph three. It is no longer necessary where the provision in question has already been interpreted by the Court of Justice, or where the correct application is so obvious as to leave no scope for any reasonable doubt and therefore no question to be decided arises.

The *Da Costa* case raised the same question as had previously been asked in *Van Gend en Loos*. The Court of Justice referred to its previous judgment in *Van Gend en Loos* as the basis for deciding the issue, and advised that such a situation might, if the national court wished, excuse the obligation to refer.

The *CILFIT* judgment expanded the decision of *Da Costa*. In *CILFIT*, the Italian Supreme Court asked the Court of Justice directly in what circumstances it need not refer. The Court of Justice replied that, in addition to the reason given in *Da Costa*, a court might not refer if the correct application, but not interpretation, may be so obvious as to leave no scope for any reasonable doubt that the question raised will be solved. This has been argued by many writers to have positively introduced into the Community legal system the French law doctrine of *acte clair*, by which the national court need not make a reference if they consider the answer to the question on Community obvious and no doubt the controversy, will continue (you need only refer to the coverage in textbooks). However, the Court of Justice qualified this by stating that the national court must be convinced that the matter is equally obvious to courts of other Member States, that it is sure that language differences will not result in inconsistent decisions in Member States, and that Community law will be applied in light of the application of it as a whole with regard to the objectives of the Community.

These criteria would be extremely difficult to fulfil if properly followed, but arguably they are provided with the discretion not to refer so as to maintain an appearance of a bridge of equality between Community and national legal systems.

The Effect of an Article 234 Ruling

The effect on the Court of Justice   Strictly, a ruling by the Court of Justice is binding and effective in the case in point only, and there is no further binding effect on the Court of Justice. Although it is not restrained by any doctrine of precedent, the Court of Justice tends to follow previous decisions and to maintain consistency, and will cite previous judgments or parts of a judgment as the basis for a current decision. In this way the development and build-up of legal principles occurs as in common-law countries.

In other circumstances the Court has been known to overrule previous decisions, without much commotion, when it felt that the situation warranted it (see, under Art 288 (old 215), the case of *Plaumann* (case 25/62) and the later, overruling case of *Lütticke* (case 4/69)).

The effect on the national courts   The national courts are bound under Treaty obligations to apply to the facts of the case the ruling received from the Court of Justice (see *Garland v BREL*).

There have been times where the Court of Justice has made particular comments about the temporal effect of a judgment, especially when the result of the judgment would have serious economic consequences for Member States. For example the rulings in *Defrenne (No. 2)* and in the *Barber* cases were held not to be retroactive but effective only from the date of judgment and for claims already commenced. Otherwise, the effect on national courts of rulings on interpretation can be answered by reference to the *CILFIT* and *Da Costa* cases. There is no need to refer materially identical cases, but the discretion to refer remains.

On validity, the Court of Justice held in *ICC* that although a declaration of invalidity was directly addressed only to the referring court, it was sufficient reason for another court to regard the declaration as generally binding; but, again, the discretion to refer remains. However, in *Foto-Frost v Hauptzollamt Lübeck-Ost*, the Court of Justice held that if a question of validity was raised and an answer was not possible from previous judgments, the national courts were obliged to refer the question to the Court of Justice.

The future effect in the Member States' legal systems for domestic cases is a matter for domestic law, and depends on whether a strict system of precedent applies.

Interim Measures

Interim measures may also be highly relevant to Community law questions which are the subject of a reference to the Court of Justice particularly as a reference may take upwards of 18 months and more likely 2–3 years at the time of writing and in that time the lack of relief may lead to great damage and in many cases insolvency of the companies involved. The clearest leading case on this is *Factortame* (case C-213/89) in which the Court of Justice held that regardless of national rules on whether interim relief should be granted, if a right under community law were at stake pending a ruling on a reference on the substantive question, interim relief should be granted.

Article 234 (old 177) has allowed the Court of Justice to develop a system of remedies which could be secured in the Member States' courts so that so many cases need not be referred to the Court of Justice, e.g., direct effects, indirect effects and *Francovich* liability. This has, it is argued, changed the nature of relationship from a symbiotic or horizontal one more to a vertical or hierarchical relationship.

References and Interlocutory Proceedings before the English Courts

The rules in respect of UK references are determined initially by Order 114 of the High Court (and similar rules for other courts) and case law. An order referring a question on Community law to the Court of Justice may be made by a UK court on its own motion or on application by a party. The order is in the form of a court schedule, the details of which may be directed by the court. The court proceedings are then stayed to await the ruling of the Court of Justice. Copies of the order are sent to the Registrar of the Court of Justice and to the Senior Master of the Supreme Court in the UK. Orders are appealable to the Court of Appeal without leave.

It is clear that the court must be satisfied that a reference is necessary; see *R v Tymen* in which the judge refused to make a reference. While not specifically provided for in Order 114, an appeal against a refusal to make an order to refer could be made; see *Bulmer v Bollinger*.

References in the course of interim/interlocutory proceedings are discouraged as there is no final issue to be resolved and it might be that there will be no final matter to be settled. The issues giving rise to interim proceedings are often those required to be settled quickly and so a reference is not very appropriate. Nevertheless a reference may be made; see *Portsmouth CC v Richards* in the Court of Appeal. Most notable in this respect is the reference made in the course of interlocutory proceedings in the *Factortame* litigation, i.e., *Factortame Ltd v Secretary of State for Transport*, in which the injunction was refused but the House of Lords referred a question to the Court of Justice asking whether interim relief was a Community law right. The Court of Justice held that it was and this ruling was faithfully applied by the UK court. It would now seem that such references are acceptable and likely to occur in future.

THE PLEA OF ILLEGALITY: ARTICLE 241

This action provides a right to plead the illegality of a Community regulation in different circumstances from the direct challenge under Art 230 (old 173).

Article 241 (old 184) reads:

> Notwithstanding the expiry of the period laid down in the fifth paragraph of Article 230, any party may, in proceedings in which a regulation adopted jointly by the European Parliament and the Council, or a regulation of the Council, of the Commission, or of the ECB is at issue, plead the grounds specified in the second paragraph Article 230, in order to invoke before the Court of Justice the inapplicability of that regulation.

Article 241 (old 184) is not an independent or a direct cause of action to the Court of Justice. In *Wöhrmann v Commission*, the Court of Justice held that Art 241 (old 184) was available only in proceedings brought before the Court of Justice under some other action, and only as an incidental or indirect action.

Locus Standi

The Art 241 (old 184) action is available to any party, including, it is argued but without clear authority from the Court of Justice, Member States, but it is more likely to benefit individuals who are unable to meet the *locus standi* and time limit requirements of Art 230 (old 173). However, it is not designed or intended to provide a backdoor for those who fail under Art 230 (old 173). In *Commission v Belgium* (case 156/77), a Community decision was challenged directly before the Court of Justice. The Court refused Belgium the ability to plead under Art 241 (old 184) because it had allowed its right under Art 230 (old 173) to expire. It is argued that this is a denial of Member State *locus standi*, but the real basis for the Court of Justice not admitting the case was that to allow it would make a nonsense of Art 230 (old 173) time limits.

Article 241 (old 184) is designed more for those who either have no rights under Art 230 (old 173), or who were unable to meet the *locus standi* requirements, but who nevertheless are affected by the illegality of a Community regulation.

Acts that can be Reviewed

Article 241 (old 184) refers only to regulations, which can be challenged only if they form the legal basis of the subject matter of the direct action in the case (*Meroni v High Authority*). However, in *Simmenthal v Commission* (case 92/78), a decision was challenged which was based on prior regulations *and* notices. The regulations could not be challenged under Art 230 (old 173) because of the restrictive *locus standi* requirements to challenge regulations which are general acts, but could be challenged indirectly via Art 241 (old 184). Article 241 (old 184) does not, however, envisage the challenge of decisions or other forms of binding act. The Court held that it was not the form of the act which is important but the substance, therefore other acts which were normative in effect should be regarded as regulations for the purposes of Art 241 (old 184) and could be challenged under Art 241, thus applying it to notices and decisions.

Addressees of an individual act such as a decision cannot challenge it indirectly in the Court of Justice, because they should have done so directly under Art 230 (old 173) within the time limits. To allow otherwise would render the time limit meaningless, as confirmed in the *Commission v Belgium* case above.

Choice of Court

The choice of court in Art 241 (old 184) actions is particularly difficult. Non-addressees are able to use Art 234 (old 177) before the national courts, but problems exist in the challenge of individual acts addressed to other persons before the Court of Justice. They can make direct challenges under Art 230 (old 173) if directly and individually concerned. The *Simmenthal* case seemed to suggest that acts not directly and individually of concern to individuals could be indirectly challenged under Art 241 (old 184). This was confirmed in the later case of *University of Hamburg v Hauptzollamt Hamburg*, in which the university was held able to challenge a decision addressed to the German Government indirectly before the national court, because it was directly and individually concerned by it. As a result of the fact that the decision was not published, it was unable to challenge it under Art 230 (old 173).

Grounds of Review

The substantive grounds of the action are those listed for Art 230 (old 173). The *Simmenthal* case succeeded on the ground that the general measure had been used for purposes other than that for which it was intended, i.e., its proper purpose.

Effect of a Successful Challenge

The result of such an action is that the regulation is declared inapplicable in that case and not generally void (*Meroni v High Authority*). Any acts based on this voidable regulation, however, will be void and withdrawn. Also, in practice the regulation will not be applied in subsequent cases, as in Art 234 (old 177) references, e.g., the *ICC* case.

QUESTIONS

1.   Explain what you consider to be the function and purpose of Article 234 (old 177) of the EC Treaty and what is required of the European Court and national courts if that function and purpose are to be achieved. What problems, if any, have been experienced in the practical operation of Article 234 (old 177)?

This can be split for the purposes of an answer into an explanation of the function and purpose of Art 234 (old 177), the Court of Justice requirements, the national courts' requirements and then the problems in application. The problems essentially include refusals by the Court of Justice and the decision of the national courts to refer.

   (a)   State the basic purpose of Art 234 (old 177).
   (b)   Outline the functions of the Court of Justice and then the functions of the national courts.
   (c)   Consider the refusal to accept a reference by the Court of Justice and the guidelines for the national courts in making references.

These are reasonably straightforward and I shall provide only framework answers here. For further details you should refer to the relevant sections above in this chapter.

The purpose of Article 234   The purpose of Art 234 (old 177) is to act as a bridge or a link between the Community and national legal systems. It is to ensure the uniform interpretation of Community law throughout the Member States, and thus provide consistency in Community law. It provides the national courts with assistance in cases concerning Community law by obtaining rulings on the interpretation and validity of Community law.

It should be pointed out that Art 234 (old 177) is a judicial device and not part of an appeal system. Nor is it a remedy of the individual, therefore the decision to refer, as far as Art 234 (old 177) is concerned, remains that of the Member State court. The relationship is described as a symbiotic relationship.

Functions of the Court of Justice and national courts   The Court of Justice should rule on the validity and interpretation of questions of Community law submitted by the national courts. The Court of Justice must leave discretion to the Member States in deciding whether a reference is necessary.

The national court should determine the facts of a national case and decide whether a question of Community law arises which it considers must be resolved in order for it to decide the case before it. When the ruling of the Court of Justice is received, the national court must apply that ruling faithfully to the case. (A determination of when the national courts should refer has been left to the end of the answer. Generally, references should not be made until the facts have been determined.) Thus it is up to national courts to decide to refer, if they think it is necessary.

As set out above, the respective functions should be clear. National courts decide to refer, and the Court of Justice gives the ruling which is then applied.

Refusals by the Court of Justice   Initially the Court of Justice stated that it was up to the Member States to decide whether a reference was necessary, as under Art 234 (old 177), paragraph two (see *Da Costa*). Particularly in the early years of the Communities, the Court was keen to pursue an active judicial role, and encouraged references in order to enhance the status of Community law. As the number of cases before the Court of Justice increased and a considerable backlog developed, the Court of Justice may well have been prompted to start considering whether all the references were entirely necessary. Thus the Court has considered the validity of some of the references, and has on occasion refused references which in its opinion are an abuse of the system. There may be genuine circumstances, particularly where Community law proves not to be relevant, where the Court of Justice is right to refuse the reference.

In a limited number of cases, the Court of Justice has decided that there are reasons not to accept and has refused a reference. It has decided that cases which do not involve a real dispute and that concern only a theoretical consideration, which will not give an answer to a case before a court or tribunal, will not be accepted (see *Grogan*, *Borker* and *Mattheus* v *Doego*). However, if the Court of Justice goes too far, it may be infringing the discretion of the Member States. It has been argued that the most prominent case involving this issue may have gone too far in that direction. The case of *Foglia* v *Novello* has to be explained in the context of any answer looking at refusals by the Court of Justice. Was it a shot across the bows to discourage similar rulings involving the laws of one Member State being questioned in the courts of another Member State? The Court of Justice may have understandably not wished to become embroiled in such a situation, especially when better procedures, designed to determine breaches by Member States, exist, i.e., the Art 226 (old 169) action by the Commission or an Art 227 (old 170) action by the affected Member State. Further details of this case are considered in the chapter above.

The guidelines for the national courts The obligation for courts of last instance to refer on points of interpretation is covered by Art 234 (old 177), paragraph three. As they are courts from whose judgment there is no further judicial remedy, they are obliged to refer, subject to the view of the *Da Costa*, *Costa* v *ENEL* and *CILFIT* cases. The last case is often regarded as an application of the principle of *acte clair*. However, the Court of Justice has never stated that this is so. If it is *acte clair*, it is a very much restricted version of it, because it is qualified by the requirement that national courts must be aware of other States courts' understanding of the provision in question and the application of it. It would be very unlikely that national courts would be capable of this given that they would now need to be conversant with all 11 official languages, therefore *CILFIT*, like *Da Costa* previously, essentially requires there to be a materially identical question to be resolved.

Courts of last instance which require a ruling on validity are also governed by Art 234 (old 177), paragraph three, and the Court of Justice has confirmed that a declaration of validity must be referred. If a decision on validity has already been made, this may be regarded as a general ruling which all courts may follow (see the *ICC* case).

Lower national courts requiring interpretation have a discretion to refer, but would also be able to apply previous judgments of the Court of Justice. While it is not expressly stated, the application of the *Da Costa* principle would clearly be logical.

Lower courts with questions of validity also have the discretion to refer, or to allow an appeal to a higher court to decide the matter. They may not themselves rule on validity, but it was held in *Foto-Frost* that they have an express obligation to refer where an answer to a question on validity is considered necessary to decide the case at hand.

An Art 234 (old 177) question in problem form is next considered.

2.   The EC Commission addresses a directive to the Italian Government, requiring it to ensure that paid holiday schemes and sickness schemes are equalised for male and female workers. The Italian Dentists Association, a professional body to which 90 per cent of Italian dentists belong, has, with the approval of the Government, constituted its own professional arbitration tribunal to settle disputes relating to pay and conditions of work. Decisions of the tribunal are legally binding and there is no appeal from them. Angelo, a trainee dentist, claims to have received unfair treatment in comparison with female trainees, and brings a case before the tribunal.

The tribunal dismisses his claim to protection by the EC directive on the ground that he is not a worker but a trainee, despite the fact that the ECJ had recently held that the term 'worker' included trainees.

The tribunal panel does not want to make a reference under Art 234 (old 177), whereas Angelo insists it should.

Consider whether there is a duty, an ability or a right for this tribunal or Angelo to have a question referred to the Court of Justice.

The basic question is whether this tribunal can make a reference to the ECJ under Art 234 (old 177). First of all, you have to consider whether this is a court or tribunal for the purposes of Art 234 (old 177) and thus entitled to make references to the Court of Justice. Not all bodies have been so recognised. There are a number of cases considering this question, and a number of criteria have been established by which an answer may be produced:

(a)   The *Vaassen* case involved an arbitration body subject to national legal rules and bound to apply rules of law. The panel also included government appointees.

(b)   The decisions of the body in the *Broekmeulen* case did not allow for an appeal and it was not a judicial body recognised by the State. There was no practical redress before the national courts but it was established with the approval of the authorities and official assistance. The decisions were accepted as final, despite the fact that a legal remedy was in private hands.

(c)   In *Nordsee* v *Nordstern*, there was no involvement by national authorities in the case. Despite the fact that there was a legally binding decision and there was no appeal, the Court of Justice held it did not come within the jurisdiction of Art 234 (old 177).

You are therefore required to decide on a balance of factors whether the arbitration tribunal is one which is acceptable for the purposes of Art 234 (old 177). The factors in the present case are the governmental approval, the fact that 90 per cent of all potential members are included, and the legally binding decisions with no appeal. The membership figure could in fact go either way, in that it would suggest that this is not the only way in which dentists can have disputes resolved. The other 10 per cent must presumably be able to avail themselves of the ordinary national courts. On the other hand, since this body clearly is involved with Community legislation, it would defeat the uniformity of Community law if it could not refer and had to decide matters of Community law itself. Individuals such as Angelo may thus be deprived of their true rights. This, in the end, may be the most important consideration, and is certainly one that the Court of Justice would consider.

If you decide it is a tribunal for the purposes of Art 234 (old 177), the next question is whether it is obliged to refer, or whether it has a discretion to refer. It can be stated immediately that whatever the answer to that question, it is clear that Angelo has no right to a reference and that this matter comes within the discretion of the tribunal. As a tribunal against whose decisions there is no judicial remedy under Art 234 (old 177), paragraph three, the tribunal is obliged to make a reference, unless the matter to be decided by the application of Community law comes within the guidelines of the *Da Costa* or the *CILFIT* cases, in which case the obligation to refer will be excused. In the case of Angelo, you are informed that the identical question has already been resolved by the Court of Justice, who has given a ruling on the interpretation of the relevant provision that a trainee is considered a worker under Community law and is thus subject to Community rules in respect of discrimination. Therefore, there would be no need to refer, and the tribunal could simply apply the previous ruling of the Court of Justice. However, the national court retains its discretion to refer if it wishes to.

FURTHER READING

Arnull, A., 'The Evolution of the Court's Jurisdiction under Article 177 EEC' (1993) 18 EL Rev 129.

Barnard, C., and Sharpston, E., 'The changing face of Article 177 references' (1997) 34 CML Rev 1113.

Bebr, G., 'Judicial Remedy of Private Parties against Normative Acts of the European Communities: The Role of the Exception of Illegality' (1966) 4 CML Rev 7.

Bebr, G., 'The Reinforcement of Constitutional Review of Community Acts under Article 177 EEC' (1988) 25 CML Rev 684.

Hartley, T., *The Foundations of European Community Law* (4th edn, Oxford: Clarendon Press, 1998), chapter 9.

O'Keeffe, D., 'Is the spirit of Article 177 under attack? Preliminary references and admissibility' (1998) 23 EL Rev 509.

O'Neill, M., 'Article 177 and limits to the right to refer: an end to the confusion?' (1996) 2 EPL 375.

8 FREE MOVEMENT OF GOODS

INTRODUCTION

The Community policy of the free movement of goods is inextricably linked with the concepts of the common market, the internal market, and generally with the economic ideals of the Community. Free movement of goods is essential to the customs union and the common market, and is a major part of the infrastructure of the Community. One of the prime reasons for the Community, the very concept of a common European market, is to create a trading and producing bloc capable of competing with the Americans and Japanese. This has proved to be more difficult than first envisaged, in the face of Member States' attempts to protect their own national producers and industries.

The free movement of goods is described as one of the cornerstones of the Community. Its objectives are to achieve the circulation of goods without customs duties, charges, or other financial or other restrictions; to promote unlimited trade and to remove from the Member States the control over export and import matters. The internal market is defined in Art 14 (old 7a) of the EC Treaty as 'an area without internal frontiers in which the free movement of goods, persons, services and capital is ensured in accordance with the provisions of this Treaty'.

The 'common market' provides not only for the elimination of duties regarding goods originating in other Member States, but also those regarding goods originating in third countries which are in free circulation in the common market and on which customs duties have been paid. The EC is also a customs union, which concerns the external duties fixed by the Community for goods imported from outside the Community, and a common tariff is adopted in trade relations with the outside world. This aspect is now within the entire competence of the Community and is ever more tied up with world developments on customs duties, most notably GATT (General Agreement on Tariffs and Trade) and the WTO (World Trade Organisation).

FREE MOVEMENT OF GOODS

Treaty Provisions

The preamble of the EC Treaty has proved instrumental in the Court of Justice reaching decisions on cases involving the free movement of goods, as have Arts 2 and 3, Art 10 (old 5) (the fidelity clause) and Art 12 (old 6) (the prohibition of discrimination).

There are four main groups of provisions in the EC Treaty connected with the free movement of goods:

(a)   customs duties and charges having equivalent effect (Arts 23–25 (replacing old 9–17));

(b)   the common customs tariff (Arts 26–27 (old 18–29));

(c)   the use of national taxation systems to discriminate against goods imported from other Member States (Art 90 (old 95)); and

(d)   quantitative restrictions or measures having an equivalent effect on imports and exports (Arts 28–30 (old 30–36)).

The common customs tariff referred to in (b) above — also referred to as the common external tariff — imposes a single tariff for all imports which is set by the Commission. Once a product has been imported into the EU, it is then in free circulation and further tariffs cannot be imposed on the product, Art 24 (old 10).

Secondary Legislation

There is very little secondary legislation in this area of Community law, and only Directive 70/50 will be considered below. There is instead a copious amount of case law to consider. See the general comments on case law in the section in chapter 2 on the study of Community law.

THE PROHIBITION AGAINST CUSTOMS DUTIES AND CHARGES HAVING EQUIVALENT EFFECT

Articles 23 and 25 (old 9, 12, 13 and 16) EC are aimed at the abolition of customs duties and charges having equivalent effect, and at prohibiting the introduction of any such measures.

Article 23 (old 9) states that the Community shall be based on a customs union, with a common customs tariff, involving the prohibition of all customs duties on imports and exports and charges having equivalent effect. This provision covers 'all trade in goods', goods being defined by the Court of Justice in *Commission* v *Italy (Art Treasures)* as 'products which can be valued in money and which are capable, as such, of forming the subject of commercial transactions'. The definition has been extended in *Commission* v *Ireland (Re Dundalk Water Supply)* to include the provision of products within a contract for the provision of services.

Article 25 (old 12) prohibits the introduction of new customs duties or charges having equivalent effect, and equally prohibits the increase of those which are already in existence. The prohibition applies both to imports and exports. It was held to be directly effective in the leading case of *Van Gend en Loos*. The Treaty of Amsterdam has amended this by adding a second sentence to make it expressly clear that the prohibition also applies to customs duties of a fiscal nature.

A Charge having Equivalent Effect

A customs duty is usually easy to recognise, but a charge having an equivalent effect is more difficult, and this has been the subject of a considerable body of case law. In *Commission* v *Luxembourg and Belgium (Gingerbread)*, the Court of Justice held that

> a duty, whatever it is called, and whatever its mode of application, may be considered a charge having equivalent effect to a customs duty, provided that it meets the following three criteria: (a) It must be imposed unilaterally at the time of importation or subsequently; (b) It must be imposed specifically upon a product imported from a Member State to the exclusion of a similar national product; and (c) It must result in an alteration of price and thus have the same effect as a customs duty on the free movement of products.

> In certain circumstances a charge may be acceptable, e.g., if it is levied on a service rendered for the benefit of the importer, if it is specifically required by Community law or if it is part of a system of internal taxation. These criteria are all subject to further refinement by the Court of Justice.

Services rendered for the benefit of importers In *Commission* v *Italy (Statistical Levy)*, a small (10 lira) levy on imports and exports for the purpose of financing statistical surveys was held to breach Community law. While there was no discrimination between imports and exports, the Court of Justice stressed that the purpose of using the concepts of customs duties and charges having equivalent effect was to avoid the imposition of any pecuniary charge on goods circulating within the Community by virtue of the fact that they cross a frontier. The Court defined a charge having equivalent effect to include 'any pecuniary charge, however small and whatever its designation and mode of application, which is imposed unilaterally on domestic or foreign goods by virtue of the fact that they cross a frontier'. Such a charge is a charge having equivalent effect even if it is not imposed for the benefit of the Member State concerned, even if it is not discriminatory or protective in effect and even if the product on which it is imposed is not in competition with any domestic product.

Claims by Member States for charges for services rendered, such as for health inspections or warehousing fees during clearance of customs formalities, have been carefully considered by the Court of Justice. In *Commission v Belgium (Re Customs Warehouses)*, a fee fixed and levied by the municipal authorities for the use of premises to store goods pending clearance through customs, was held by the Court of Justice not to be regarded as consideration for services actually rendered to the importer when payment of storage charges is demanded solely in connection with the completion of customs formalities. In *Commission v Italian Republic (Re Customs Posts)* Italian legislation required importers at Italian customs outside normal Italian opening hours (six hours per day) to pay a fee. Article 5 of Directive 83/643 requires customs offices at frontier posts to open for normal business hours of at least 10 hours per day, Monday to Friday. Therefore, in order to comply with the Directive, Italian customs officials would have to work four hours overtime and Italian law sought to impose a charge during that four-hour period. The Italian government maintained that this was a charge for a service rendered which was commensurate to the value of the service. The Court said that it had already held on several occasions that a charge imposed on goods by reason of the fact that they cross a frontier might not be a charge having equivalent effect to a customs duty provided it constituted a benefit specifically or individually conferred on the economic operator concerned, of an amount proportional to that service. In this case the Court held the charge constituted a breach of the Treaty. In *Ford Espana v The Spanish State*, the Court rejected a claim that a charge levied by the Spanish customs for granting customs clearance at the Ford factory was a charge for services rendered and not a charge having equivalent effect to a customs duty. The charge was calculated at a rate of 0.165 per cent of the declared value of the goods. The Court of Justice held that even if the contested charge were in fact remuneration for a service rendered to the importer, the amount charged could not be regarded as proportionate to the service. The Spanish Government's argument, that in some cases the charge would be less than the cost of carrying out the inspections, only served to confirm this argument. A charge calculated on the basis of the value of the goods could not correspond to the costs incurred by the customs authorities.

Requirements of Community law   In *Commission* v *Germany (Animal Inspection Fees)*, inspection fees charged pursuant to Council Directive 81/389 were held to be acceptable because they satisfied the criteria laid down by the Court of Justice, i.e., (i) fees should not exceed the cost of the actual inspections in respect of which they are charged, (ii) the inspections in question are mandatory and uniform for all the products in question in the Community, (iii) the inspections are provided for by Community law in the interests of the Community, and (iv) the inspections promote the free movement of goods, in particular, by neutralising the obstacles which may result from unilateral inspection measures adopted under Art 30 (old 36) of the EC Treaty. The case of *Netherlands* v *Bakker Hillegom* extended these criteria to include the requirements of international conventions.

The Distinction between Internal Taxation and Charges having Equivalent Effect

This difference is crucial. If a charge imposed by a Member State on imported goods is a measure of internal taxation which is non-discriminatory, it cannot be a charge having equivalent effect, and cannot be caught by Arts 23 and 25 (old 9–16) but is governed by Art 90 (old 95) instead. Article 90 (old 95) is, however, designed to prevent circumvention of the customs rules by the imposition of discriminatory internal taxes by the Member States, and is therefore complementary to Arts 23 and 25 (old 9–16). Article 25 now specifically prohibits customs charges of a fiscal nature.

Internal taxes can never be imposed solely by virtue of the fact that the goods cross a frontier. The reason for their imposition must be that domestic products are subject to taxation and that, for competition reasons, imported goods should be subject to the same tax. It may be one thing or the other, but cannot be both. They are mutually exclusive categories.

There is a considerable body of case law of the Court of Justice on the distinction between an internal tax (to which Art 90 (old 95) might apply) and a charge having equivalent effect to a customs duty (which might be prohibited by Arts 23–25 (old 9–16)). In *Schöttle & Söhne* v *Finanzamt Freuenstadt* (case 20/76), the Court of Justice held that the purpose of Art 90 (old 95) is to remove disguised restrictions on the free movement of goods which may result from the tax provisions of a Member State. In *Steinlike und Weinlig* v *Germany*, the Court of Justice held that: 'Financial charges within a general system of internal taxation applying systematically to domestic and imported products according to the same criteria are not to be considered charges having equivalent effect.' This could be the case even where there was no domestic product similar to the imported product to which the charge applies, provided that the charge applies to whole classes of domestic or foreign products which are all in the same position no matter what their origin. *Denkavit v French State* concerned a charge on the importation of meat products which was argued to be the equivalent of a similar charge imposed on the slaughter of meat in French slaughterhouses. The Court of Justice held that in order to relate to a system of internal taxation, the charge to which an imported product is subject must be imposed at the same rate on the same product, be imposed at the same marketing stage, and the chargeable event giving rise to the duty must be the same for both products. It is not sufficient that the objective of the charge imposed on imports is to compensate for similar charges imposed on domestic products at a production or marketing stage prior to that at which the imported products are taxed. The Court of Justice held that it was bound to regard the charge in this case as a charge having equivalent effect, because (i) it was charged on imported goods by virtue of the fact that they had crossed a frontier, (ii) the tax was imposed at a different stage of production and on the basis of a different 'chargeable event', (iii) no account was taken of fiscal charges which had been imposed on the products in the Member State of origin, and (iv) to find otherwise would render the prohibition on charges having equivalent effect to customs duties empty and meaningless.

In *CRT France International v Directuer regional des impots de Bourgogne*, France introduced a new tax on the supply of CB Radio sets, none of which were produced in France. Whilst on the face of it the tax appeared to be an acceptable systematic and objective tax levied on all products using the Hertzian radio spectrum to pay for the costs of overseeing the spectrum, evidence revealed that other electronic equipment was not taxed on supply but on sale. The alternative argument that it was justified as a charge for the service of overseeing the spectrum was also rejected as this did not provide any service to importers but only to users. Hence, the ECJ concluded the charge to be contrary to old Arts 9 and 12 (new 25).

THE PROHIBITION OF DISCRIMINATORY TAXATION

Taxation was defined in *Commission v France (Re Reprographic Machines)* as a general system of internal dues applied systematically to categories of products in accordance with objective criteria, irrespective of the origin of the products.

Article 90 (old 95) provides that no Member State shall impose, directly or indirectly, on the products of other Member States any internal taxation of any kind in excess of that imposed directly or indirectly on similar domestic products. This prohibits discrimination in favour of the domestic products. Art 90 (old 95) was held to be directly effective in *Lütticke v Hauptzollamt Saarlouis* (1966) (case 57/65).

It is important to recognise that Art 90 (old 95) also requires the abolition of fiscal discrimination, i.e., the imposing of taxes by the State for the purpose of raising revenue. Where there is discrimination, a Member State may eradicate it either by lowering the tax on imported goods or by raising the tax on domestic products, or a combination of both. This is up to the Member State. The EC regime does not require it to lower import taxes only thus depriving the State of revenue.

Indirect Taxation

Article 90 (old 95) deals with taxes which are imposed directly or indirectly In *Molkerei Zentrale*, the Court of Justice ruled that the words 'directly or indirectly' in Art 90 (old 95) were to be construed broadly and embraced all taxation which was actually and specifically imposed on the domestic product at earlier stages of the manufacturing and marketing process. They are also capable of including taxes on raw materials and the assessment of the tax. In *Schottle & Sohne* v *Finanzamt Freuenstadt*, it was held that a German tax on transportation of goods for more than a certain distance, levied in this case on a lorry load of gravel, was an indirect tax on the gravel itself.

Even where the level of taxation is the same, a delay in its collection in favour of domestic goods has been held to be discriminatory and a breach of Art 90 (old 95). In *Commission* v *Ireland (Excise Payments)*, under Irish law, producers of beer, wine and spirits enjoyed an extension of four to six weeks of the period for the payment of excise duties, whereas taxes on imported beers, wines and spirits had to be paid immediately on importation or on delivery from the bonded warehouse.

In *Humblot (Michel)* v *Directeur des Services Fiscaux*, the French authorities imposed a higher tax on cars with a higher horsepower rating, none of which was manufactured in France, and the tax applied in practice only to imported cars. The Court of Justice, while recognising that a tax which tended to discriminate against a category of imported goods because no goods in that category are produced domestically, will not necessarily always be in breach of Art 90 (old 95), held that because many of the imported cars thus taxed would still be in competition with cars produced in France taxed at the lower rate, the tax was in breach of Art 90 (old 95).

In contrast is *Commission* v *Greece (Re Taxation of Motor Cars)*, in which a Greek tax on both new and secondhand cars, whether produced in Greece or imported from outside, rose steeply in respect of cars above 1800 cc cylinder capacity. The cars affected were all imported, as no cars above 1600 cc were produced in Greece. The Court held that this measure would be indirectly discriminatory only if it were shown that the taxation had the effect of discouraging Greeks from purchasing foreign cars. *Prima facie* the tax was motivated by other considerations and there was no protective effect.

Even where there may even be benefits for the imported goods, a difference in the way in which a tax is levied may be held to breach Art 90 (old 95). In *Outokumpu OY*, a flat rate tax on imported electricity from Sweden infringed Art 90 (old 95) because the tax rate on domestic electricity was calculated according to the product which was used for its manufacture for environmental reasons. The fact that only in limited circumstances would the rate of imported tax be higher was immaterial to the Court of Justice. The ease of administration in setting up a general system and that it was extremely difficult to determine precisely the method of production of imported electricity were not accepted as grounds justifying the system adopted.

Similar and Other Products

Article 90 (old 95)(2) provides that no Member State shall impose on the products of other Member States any internal taxation of such a nature as to afford indirect protection to other products. This serves to cover products that may be different but are nevertheless in competition with the domestic products.

The criteria for determining whether there is discrimination differ according to whether the case is brought under Art 90 (old 95), paragraph one (similar products) or under paragraph two (other products). If, in the case of Art 90 (old 95), paragraph one, the rates of tax on the imported product and the domestic product are the same, then *prima facie* the rule against non-discrimination has been complied with. Additionally, the basis of imposition of the taxes must not be such that differences between imported and domestic goods may result from it. The rates of tax, the basis of assessment and the rules for levying and collecting it must be non-discriminatory. In the case of Art 90 (old 95), paragraph two, to be caught by the prohibition on discrimination it has to be proved that the taxation has a protectionist effect. Direct comparisons are possible under Art 90 (old 95), paragraph one, whereas they are not under paragraph two.

In *Commission v UK (Wine Excise Duties) (No. 2)*, the Court of Justice held that the fact that the UK imposed a higher duty on table wines than on beer gave indirect protection to beer (a domestic product) over light table wines (a predominantly imported product) and contravened Art 90 (old 95), paragraph two. The UK Government had argued that wine and beer could not be regarded as competing beverages, since beer was widely consumed in public houses and wine was generally drunk only on special occasions. The Court took the view that it was necessary not only to examine the current market, but also whether market developments might lead to the two products being directly in competition with one another. The Court decided that such a relationship existed on the basis of volume, price and alcoholic strength.

A Member State may abolish discrimination, either by lowering the tax on imported goods or by raising the tax on domestic products, or may use a combination of both to remove the discrimination or protection.

Finally, in the *Fratelli Cucchi* case, the Court of Justice confirmed the mutually exclusive nature of the two regimes under charges and internal taxation; since it is often difficult to tell the difference, both Arts 25 and 90 (old 12 and 95) should be invoked together and the Court should be asked to draw the line.

THE PROHIBITION ON QUANTITATIVE RESTRICTIONS AND MEASURES HAVING EQUIVALENT EFFECT

Article 28 (old 30) lays down a general prohibition on quantitative restrictions and measures having equivalent effect.

The development of the rules on the free movement of goods reflects the general approach to the fundamental freedoms: the Court of Justice has interpreted the principle of free movement liberally in order to promote free movement, and it has interpreted the derogations allowed the Member States as restrictively or narrowly as possible. However, the Court realised that this approach was too restrictive in terms of allowing for the national diversity of products and sought to correct this in the case of *Cassis de Dijon*. The result is that, first of all there is a perfectly sound rule which seeks to ensure that there are no restrictions on the free movement of goods (Art 28 (old 30)). Then there is a rule which provides exceptions to the first rule because it is recognised that there are genuine circumstances where restrictions are justified (Art 30 (old 36)). So far, so good. Then there are guidelines and case law which help to determine how the rule applies and the circumstances which breach the rule or come within the exceptions. Additionally, there is a focus on the concepts of direct discrimination (distinctly applicable), which is easy to see, and indirect discrimination (indistinctly applicable), which starts to become complex. Then there is a very important case (*Cassis de Dijon*) which, in effect, either provides that the national rules fall outside the original rule or it permits further exceptions to those contained in Art 30 (old 36). Thus certain national rules or laws would escape the prohibition of Art 28. However, strict criteria were laid down so that Member States would not be able to exploit this new possibility. It is worth noting that Art 30 (old 36) applies to both direct and indirect discrimination but has an exhaustive list of exceptions, whereas *Cassis de Dijon* applies to indirect discrimination only, but potentially there is a much wider range of exceptions. Then, because it started to happen that every single national rule that applied to goods might be considered to come with the ambit of the *Cassis de Dijon* case, there is another important case (*Keck*). This seeks to lay down another rule or gloss on the original rules to say that certain types of law applicable to the marketing of goods should not even be considered as coming within the original rule! (If you can remember it . . . Art 28, that is.) Hence then there is a lot to consider and the route through these various aspects is not clear. I have tried to present them as they are listed above.

General Scope

In *Geddo* v *Ente Nazionale Risi*, the Court of Justice held that a prohibition on quantitative restrictions covers measures which amount to a total or partial restraint of imports, exports or goods in transit.

The most obvious examples of quantitative restrictions on imports and exports are complete bans or quotas restricting the import or export of a given product by amount or by value. These are clearly in contravention of Art 28 (old 30) and are prohibited. The cases of *Commission* v *France (Import of Lamb)* and *Commission* v *UK (Import of Potatoes)* are straightforward examples. Problems arise, however, in respect of national marketing rules which have the effect of quotas but are argued by the Member States to apply to both imports and domestic products, or to come within the justifications allowed by Art 30 (old 36) (the express derogations from Art 28 (old 30), considered below.

Each of these aspects must be considered:

(a)   the meaning of 'equivalent measures';
(b)   those that apply both to imports and domestic goods; and
(c)   the derogations in Art 30 (old 36).

The first and last are relatively easy, but the middle one causes no end of difficulty and consternation amongst academic authors, as you will clearly see by comparing treatments of this topic. The difficulty will be discussed below.

Measures having Equivalent Effect

Definition   The concept of measures having equivalent effect has been defined by secondary legislation (Directive 70/50) and by the jurisprudence of the Court of Justice. The Directive which was introduced to provide guidelines at the time when the common market was being established, continues to provide guidance as to what measures may be considered a breach of the prohibition under Art 28 (old 30).

Directive 70/50, Art 2, defines 'measures having equivalent effect' to include those which 'make imports, or the disposal at any marketing stage of imported products, subject to a condition, other than a formality, which is required in respect of imported products only'. They also include any measures which subject imported products or their disposal to a condition which differs from that required for domestic products and which is more difficult to satisfy. Basically, therefore, any measure which makes import or export unnecessarily difficult and thus discriminates between the two would clearly fall within the definition.

In *Procureur du Roi* v *Dassonville*, the term 'measures having equivalent effect' was held to include 'all trading rules enacted by a Member State which are capable of hindering, directly or indirectly, actually or potentially, intra-Community trade'. The case concerned criminal proceedings in Belgium against a trader who imported Scotch whisky in free circulation in France into Belgium, without being in possession of a certificate of origin from the British customs authorities, thus infringing Belgian customs rules. The Court of Justice held that

> the requirement by a Member State of a certificate of authority, which is less easily obtainable by importers of an authentic product, put into free circulation in a regular manner in another Member State, than by importers of the same product coming directly from the country of origin, constitutes a measure having equivalent effect.

The Court added that in the absence of a Community system to guarantee a product's origin, a Member State may take measures for the protection of consumers in the area of designation of origin of products without necessarily infringing Art 28 (old 30). However, this is subject to the further qualification that, whether or not such measures were authorised by the terms of Art 30 (old 36), they could not constitute an arbitrary discrimination or a disguised restriction on trade between Member States.

The scope of the prohibition   Measures which do not have any direct effect on imports may still be caught by the prohibition in Art 28 (old 30). In *Commission* v *Ireland (Re Buy Irish Campaign)*, the Court of Justice held that a company which is government-controlled and financed and which carries out a government policy of promoting the sale of national products by means of an advertising campaign and the use of a 'home produced' symbol, is employing a measure having equivalent effect by encouraging the purchase of domestic products, notwithstanding the fact that the government has not taken any compulsory measures but is acting by exhortation through a campaigning body. The emphasis is therefore on those rules which are capable of having an effect rather than those rules actually having an effect.

In *Apple and Pear Development Council* v *Lewis*, the ruling in the *Buy Irish* case was qualified to hold that a Member State could establish a Development Council for fruit production composed of members appointed by the Minister responsible and financed only by certain growers, as long as the activities consisted of compiling statistics, promotion, and the undertaking of research and giving technical advice.

National marketing rules often impose restrictions on the production, packaging or distribution of goods, and as a consequence infringe Art 28 (old 30). There are many examples: In *Commission* v *Belgium (Re Packaging of Margarine)*, the national rule requiring margarine to be packed in cubes, and in no other form such as tubs or rectangular blocks, was held to be in breach of Art 28 (old 30). In *R* v *Royal Pharmaceutical Society of Great Britain*, the rule of the Pharmaceutical Society prohibiting dispensing pharmacists from substituting for the product named on a doctor's prescription any other with identical therapeutical effect except under certain exceptional conditions, was held capable of coming within the operation of Art 28 (old 30). In the case itself, it was capable of being justified on the grounds of the protection of public health.

Sunday trading rules have also been brought to the attention of the Court of Justice. The case law from the UK in respect of this question has not been particularly helpful, partly as a result of the Court of Justice deciding that national courts must determine whether the reason for a rule is justified as proportionate. This has led to contradictory decisions, depending on whether the UK courts took into account the protection of workers (which would appear to justify a ban on Sunday trading) and the attempt to keep Sunday special (which appears not to justify a ban). See *Torfaen BC* v *B & Q plc* and *B & Q Ltd* v *Shrewsbury BC*.

The decisions in *Union Départmentale des Syndicats CGT de l'Aisne* v *Sidef Conforama* and *Criminal proceedings against Marchandise* are more instructive from the Community law point of view. In a request for preliminary rulings from French and Belgian courts, the Court of Justice held that national restrictions on the opening of shops on Sundays (the French *Code de Travail* provides for a mandatory day's rest on Sundays, while the Belgian *Loi sur le Travail* prohibits the employing of retail shop workers after noon on a Sunday) were not in breach of Community law. This area was a matter for the regulation of each individual Member State, and the measures considered here were not designed to control patterns of trade between Member States, nor were they applied so as to discriminate against goods from other Member States.

The Court of Justice ruled on 16 December 1992, in the case of *Stoke-on-Trent* v *B & Q*, that the UK's restrictions on Sunday trading did not conflict with Community law. It held such rules reflected 'choices relating to particular national or regional socio-cultural characteristics'. The Member States have the discretion to make such choices. Thus there is no breach of Art 28 (old 30) by Sunday trading rules.

Faced with many similar arguments by traders against national rules, the Court of Justice has re-defined its position in *Keck and Mithouard* (cases C-267–68/91). The Court considered that certain equally applicable provisions restricting selling arrangements are not to be considered a hindrance on trade (see the *Dassonville* case) provided that they affect all traders and all products (domestic and imports) in the national territory, in the same manner. Therefore, such rules are not considered to be in breach of Art 28 (old 30), nor indeed even falling within the prohibition of it. This case and subsequent cases will also considered following the *Cassis de Dijon* case below.

Exports

In *Delhaize* v *Promalvin*, a ban on the export of wine in bulk was held to breach Art 29 (old 34) which states that quantitative restrictions on exports, and all measures having equivalent effect, shall be prohibited between Member States. There was no evidence to support the contention that bottling was necessary at the source of production, especially where the wine was transported in bulk internally.

Equally Applicable Measures

Measures that apply only to imports or to exports are called distinctly applicable measures; and those which apply to both imports and domestic goods are termed equally or indistinctly applicable measures.

Article 3 of Directive 70/50 provides that measures which are equally applicable to domestic and imported goods will breach Art 28 (old 30) only where the restrictive effect on the free movement of goods exceeds the effects necessary for the trade rules, i.e., they would be disproportionate to the aim and would thus tend to protect domestic products at the expense of imports.

Procureur du Roi v *Dassonville* made no allowance for some measures introduced by Member States which applied to both imports and domestic products and might be justified on particular grounds, such as the environment. It was followed, however, by a landmark decision in Community law which seemed to address this problem — *Rewe-Zentral AG* v *Bundesmonopolverwaltung für Branntwein*, better known as *Cassis de Dijon*. This case is particularly difficult to locate within the whole scheme of measures having equivalent effect, because of the views taken of the effect of this case.

The *Cassis de Dijon* case concerned a prohibition on the marketing in the Federal Republic of Germany of spirits with less than a 25 per cent alcohol content and the ban included the liqueur Cassis de Dijon, containing only 15–20 per cent alcohol wine spirit. The prohibition applied to all low alcohol liqueurs, regardless of origin, and did not distinguish between national and foreign drinks. However, the actual result was the effective ban of French imports. The Court of Justice held that there was no valid reason why, provided they have been lawfully produced and marketed in one of the Member States, alcoholic beverages should not be introduced into any other Member State. This is one of two principles arising from the case, known as the 'principle of equivalence'. The other principle is known as the 'rule of reason' considered below.

The Derogations of Article 30

Article 30 (old 36) provides exceptions to the general prohibition of Art 28 (old 30). It states that Arts 28 and 29 (old 30 and 34) shall not apply to prohibitions or restrictions on imports, exports or goods in transit which are justified on any of the following four sets of grounds:

(a)   public morality, public policy or public security;

(b)   the protection of health and life of humans, animals or plants;

(c)   the protection of national treasures possessing artistic, historic or archaeological value; or

(d)   the protection of industrial and commercial property.

The application of these exceptions is subject to the limitation, set out in the second sentence of Art 30 (old 36), that they may not be used as a means of arbitrary discrimination or a disguised restriction on trade between Member States.

Public morality   *R v Henn & Darby* concerned a ban on the importation of pornographic magazines. The Court of Justice ruled that a prohibition that might be stricter than the laws applicable internally, was not designed to discriminate in favour of the domestic product and so was acceptable under the public morality clause of Art 30 (old 36). It was up to Member States to determine the requirements of public morality in their own State and they had, therefore, a margin of discretion in this area.

This was qualified in *Conegate v HM Customs and Excise*, the infamous case concerned with the importation of 'blow-up dolls', in which it was held that Member States did not have complete freedom to exclude all such material. A Member State might not rely on the ground of public morality to prohibit the importation of goods from other Member States when its legislation contained no prohibition on the manufacture or marketing of such goods in its own territory. The prohibition was therefore a disguised restriction on trade and a means of arbitrary discrimination, and, as such, contrary to the second sentence of Art 30 (old 36).

Public policy   The leading case in this category, *R v Thompson et al.*, considered the ban on the unlawful importation into the UK of Kruger-rands and coins, some of which were no longer legal tender and some of which were. The English coins which were no longer legal tender were goods within the meaning of Art 28 (old 30) however, because the right to mint coinage was a fundamental interest of the State; and a State which prohibits their destruction, even when they are no longer legal tender, and imposes an export ban to prevent their destruction abroad, will be justified under Art 30 (old 36) on grounds of public policy.

Public security   The leading case to deal with security is *Campus Oil*, concerning Irish rules requiring importers of petroleum products to purchase a certain proportion of their requirements from an Irish state-owned refinery at prices fixed by the Minister. The Court of Justice held that the maintenance of essential oil supplies was covered by the public security exception, but any measures taken are subject to the principle of proportionality.

The protection of the health or life of humans, animals or plants   This is a frequently argued ground for import restrictions, and virtually all goods, especially foodstuffs, have been subjected to restrictions on health grounds.

In *Commission* v *Germany (Re Health Controls on Imported Meats)*, the Court of Justice ruled that the purpose of Art 30 (old 36) is to allow national legislation to derogate from the principle of free movement of goods only to the extent justified in order to achieve one of the objectives set out in Art 30 (old 36), and not to act as a disguised restriction on trade. Hence, the systematic opening of sealed milk cartons for health checks amounted to an import restriction in *Commission* v *UK (Re UHT Milk)*. The health of consumers would be adequately protected by the necessary controls being carried out in the country of production to meet all the reasonable requirements of the country of import.

In *Commission* v *France (Re Italian Table Wines)*, systematic checks on three-quarters of each consignment of Italian wine, held up at the French border for long periods, were held not to be justified. While the Court of Justice acknowledged the right of the Member States to carry out checks, it noted that the frequency of analysis of Italian wine was considerably higher than the occasional checks carried out on French wine transported within France. The Court of Justice held that the French authorities had no right to carry out systematic checks, and, in the absence of any reasonable suspicion on the basis of specific evidence in a given case, they ought to have confined themselves to random checks.

A series of cases has now been considered by the Court of Justice, concerned with import bans on the grounds of protecting public health as a result of the content of food products, and mainly concerning food additives. In the absence of any Community regulation on the manufacture and marketing of products, Member States are free to regulate this matter as long as they do not infringe the Community provisions on the free movement of goods. The end result is that if the additives were either permitted in another product, or were allowed in another Member State and if, with regard to the results of international scientific research, in particular the work of the World Health Organisation, and to eating habits in the country of importation, the additive does not constitute a danger to public health, a ban would be a breach of Art 28 (old 30) and not justified under Art 30 (old 36). Additionally, bans would be contrary to the principle of proportionality where there was no accessible procedure by which traders were able to request that the use of specific additives be permitted. Cases include a ban on the import of beer (*Commission v Germany (Re Beer Purity Law)*), a ban on the import of sausages containing certain non-meat ingredients (*Commission v Germany (Sausage Purity Law)*), and a ban on the import of low fat cheese (*Commission v Italy (Cheese Fat Content)*). However, a ban would not infringe Art 30 (old 36) where additives are not permitted and where there is a system to allow the addition of additives to the list of permitted additives (see *Commission v Italy (Food Additives)* and *Commission v Greece (Food Additives)* (cases 95 and 293/89)).

Finally, in this category is a more recent case to demonstrate this is still a live issue. *Tommaso Morellato v Unita Sanitaria Locale* (case C-358/95) concerns the import of frozen bread which contravened national statutory limits by having a moisture content exceeding 34 per cent, an ash content of less than 1.40 per cent and containing bran. France was unable to demonstrate a threat to public health and it was easy for the Court of Justice to reach the conclusion that the national law constituted a quantitative restriction contrary to Art 28 (old 30) and was not saved by Art 30 (old 36).

An area where the public health proviso in Art 30 (old 36) is of great importance, is in the importation of pharmaceutical products, where there are often vast price differences between the retail prices of drugs in different Member States. *Schumacher v Hauptzollamt Frankfurt* concerned the ban on imports of medicinal products purchased in France for personal use. The medicines in question were available in Germany without prescription, but at four times the price charged in France. The Court of Justice held that national rules or practices which have or are likely to have a restrictive effect on importations of pharmaceutical products are compatible with the Treaty only in so far as they are necessary for the protection of health and human life. In this case the purchase of the goods in a pharmacy of another Member State in effect gives a guarantee equivalent to that resulting from the sale of the product in a pharmacy in the Member State into which it is imported. The Court held that the rule prohibiting the importation of the goods in this case contravened Arts 28 and 30 (old 30 and 36).

Artistic heritage   This ground does not justify an export tax (*Commission v Italy (Art Treasures)* (case 7/68)).

The protection of industrial or commercial property   This is to be read alongside of Art 295 (old 222), which provides that the Treaty shall in no way prejudice the rules in Member States governing the system of property ownership. This justification has been held by the Court of Justice not to extend to prevent parallel imports of products lawfully marketed in another Member State. Such a restriction of the free movement of goods would defeat the aims of the Treaty and could not be justified under Art 30 (old 36) (*Deutsche Grammophon Gesellschaft* v *Metro Grossmarkt*).

Only the specific subject matter of the property can be protected by Art 30 (old 36) when the rights have not already been exhausted by being put into circulation in the European Community (*Centrafarm* (cases 15/74 and 16/74)).

As a result of the difficulties caused by the desire to protect both trade marks and the free movement of goods, a Trade Marks Directive (89/104) and now the Trade Marks Regulation (40/94) have been passed to attempt to sort out some of the problems.

As most undergraduate courses on EC would not go into any further detail on this topic as a part of free movement of goods, nor shall I.

Cassis de Dijon and the rule of reason   In *Cassis de Dijon*, the Court of Justice stated that obstacles to the free movement of goods resulting from disparities in the national laws on the marketing of products, must be accepted as far as these provisions are necessary to satisfy mandatory requirements relating in particular to the effectiveness of fiscal supervision, the protection of public health, or the fairness of commercial transactions and the defence of the consumer. This case was a way of getting around too strict an application of the rule developed in the earlier *Dassonville* case. Thus equally applicable measures which hinder trade may be acceptable if they are in pursuit of a special interest the Member State has the right to protect. However, they must still be subject to the principle of proportionality and must constitute neither an arbitrary discrimination nor a disguised restriction on trade. (The last two terms repeat those provided in Art 30 (old 36).)

One view of the rule of reason is that it justifies measures which would otherwise have breached Art 28 (old 30). Such measures therefore fall outside the scope of the prohibition of Art 28 (old 30) in the first place. An alternative view is that the rule provides further derogations to Art 28 (old 30) and is thus analogous to Art 30 (old 36), despite the view of the Court of Justice that the derogations stated in Art 30 (old 36) were exhaustive.

One case which confirms the view of the strict scope of Art 30 (old 36) is *Commission* v *Ireland (Metal Objects)*. Irish legislation required souvenirs of Ireland which were not domestically produced to bear the designation 'Foreign'. The Commission considered the restrictions contravened Art 28 (old 30) and Art 2(3)(f) of Directive 70/50, because they were measures which lowered the value of an imported product by causing a reduction in its intrinsic value or an increase in its costs. The Irish Government argued that the measures were justified on grounds of consumer protection and therefore fell within the scope of the public policy derogation in Art 30 (old 36). The Court of Justice held that since Art 30 (old 36) constitutes a derogation from the basic rule that all obstacles to the free movement of goods between Member States are to be eliminated, Art 30 (old 36) must be construed narrowly. Neither the protection of consumers nor the fairness of transactions is included amongst the exceptions set out in Art 30 (old 36), therefore they cannot be relied on as such in connection with that article. The Court then considered whether the measures might be justified as necessary to meet mandatory requirements. However, the rules were not measures which applied to domestic and imported products without distinction; they applied only to imported products and were therefore discriminatory in nature. As a result, the measures were not covered by the decision in *Cassis de Dijon* which applies to provisions that regulate both imported products and domestic products. The rules were in breach of Art 28 (old 30).

The application of the rule of reason   In *Criminal proceedings against Karl Prantl*, the German Government argued that because criminal sanctions were attached to a measure adopted for consumer protection, the interest pursued was sufficiently important to bring it within the scope of the derogation for measures taken on grounds of public policy in Art 30 (old 36). The case concerned a provision of German law to the effect that only certain quality wines from Franken and Baden could be marketed in the bottle known as a *'Bocksbeutel'*. Anyone marketing any other wine in the *'Bocksbeutel'* committed an offence. The defendant in the main action was charged with selling quantities of Italian red wine in bottles of this type. In fact, red wine produced in the Italian Tyrol had been marketed in such bottles for at least a century, as have Portuguese wines.

The Court of Justice held that the mere fact that a national measure provided for penal sanctions in national law did not qualify it as public policy for the purposes of Art 30 (old 36). It then considered whether the national measure might fall within the scope of the rule of reason, but held that for an interest or value to be brought within the rule of reason, it has to be analogous to the derogations in Art 30 (old 36), and, secondly, there had to be no Community system covering the interest or value in question (see below). Hence the view that the rule of reason adds to the derogations in Art 30 (old 36).

Interests covered by the rule of reason   The grounds of mandatory measures, stated in *Cassis de Dijon*, are not exhaustive and have been added to by the Court of Justice. In *Commission v Denmark (Re Disposable Beer Cans)*, environmental grounds were raised. Cultural interests were invoked in *Cinéthèque SA v Fédération nationale des cinémas français*, concerning the sale of video recordings. Environmental protection and conservation of the resources of the sea were held to be interests worthy of protection in *Minister of Justice v Kramer*, and laws for the protection of workers in *Union Départmentale des Syndicats CGT de l'Aisne v Sidef Conforama* and in *Criminal proceedings against Marchandise*.

There must be no Community system covering the interest   In the *Prantl* case, above, there was a partial system of Community rules governing the types of wines which might be marketed in specific types of bottle, but these had not yet been concluded in respect of the specific bottle to rule out national competences. Therefore until Community rules were implemented, the rules adopted by the Member States could be maintained so long as they did not contravene Arts 28–30 (old 30–36). The Court of Justice held that the rules in question did in fact contravene Art 28 (old 30) and were not saved by Art 30 (old 36).

The criteria of the rule of reason   Once it has been established that the interest comes within the rule of reason and it has satisfied the first criterion that there is no Community system, the measure designed to protect that interest must meet certain further criteria:

(a)   The measure must apply to domestic and imported products without distinction. A measure meeting mandatory requirements can only be justified under Community law if it applies to imports and domestically produced goods without distinction. In *Commission v Ireland (Metal Objects)*, the rules about the labelling of souvenirs required only imported goods to bear the label 'Foreign', therefore they were distinctly applicable.

(b)   If the rules are indistinctly applicable, the measure must constitute neither an arbitrary discrimination nor a disguised restriction on trade, discussed above under Art 30 (old 36) exceptions.

(c)   The measure must be reasonable, i.e., it must meet the requirements of proportionality. In the Irish metal objects case (above), the Court of Justice took the view that the interests of consumers and fair trading would have been adequately protected if it were left to domestic manufacturers to take appropriate steps such as affixing, if they so wished, their mark of origin to their own products or packaging.

In *Walter Rau Lebensmittelwerke v De Smedt*, Belgian legislation prohibiting the marketing of margarine which did not conform to a particular shape had a clear protective effect and was an obstacle to marketing. The Belgian Government argued that the measure was necessary for consumer protection. The Court of Justice ruled that if a Member State has a choice between various measures to attain the same objective, it should choose the measure which least restricts the free movement of goods. In this case consumers might have been protected and informed that the product was margarine by other measures which would have constituted less of an interference with free movement of goods, such as labelling. Therefore, the rules contravened Art 28 (old 30). (In *Criminal proceedings against Karl Prantl*, the Court of Justice also held that the sale of a product may not be prohibited when a labelling requirement will adequately protect the consumer.)

The food additives and constituents cases are also subject to this line of argument that adequate labelling will protect consumers rather than a ban. See *Commission v Germany (Re Beer Purity Law)*, above, which provided that only malted barley, hops, yeast and water may be used in the manufacture of beer, and further that only drinks complying with those provisions could be marketed under the designation 'beer'. A further law prohibited the importation of beers containing additives, unless the additives were specifically authorised. The Court of Justice held that while it was legitimate to seek to enable consumers who attribute special qualities to beer manufactured from particular raw materials, to make their choice in an informed way, that could be done by labelling. The prohibition went beyond what was necessary for the protection of German consumers, since such protection could quite easily be ensured by the compulsory affixing of labels informing consumers about the nature of the product sold.

The case of *Cassis de Dijon* certainly allowed Member States to maintain some rules which protected an interest but it was often unclear as to whether the national mandatory requirement fell outside of Art 28 (old 30) or would be in breach of Art 28 (old 30) except for the fact it was an interest worthy of protection and thus justified (provided all other criteria were satisfied). However, it soon became seized upon by traders who had been caught infringing the national rules who claimed that their right to import goods and sell them had been infringed. The Sunday trading cases highlighted some of difficulties in that it became assumed that national laws did affect Community trade and were thus to be considered under Art 28 (old 30). In accepting this, the Court of Justice had then left it to the national courts to determine whether there was a restriction of trade which was either justified or not justified by the interest worth protecting. The interest worth protecting could, however, vary in the same case. Sunday trading concerned both the idea of 'keeping Sunday special' and the protection of workers, which allowed different national courts to reach different conclusions. Many national laws were concerned with sales and marketing rules and actually had no impact on the access of imported goods to the national market. Increasingly, however, national laws were questioned, not on the basis that they hindered imports only but they affected the volume of trade regardless of origin.

Hence, when presented with a suitable occasion, the Court of Justice was able to reconsider the case development in this area. *Keck and Mithouard* concerned the French prohibition of goods at a loss, which was argued to be a restriction of sales contrary to Art 28 (old 30). The Court emphasised that traders were using Community law to challenge laws which were not aimed at restricting imports but in fact restricted the sales of all goods without regard for origin. It then singled out selling or marketing arrangements as not coming within the concept outlined in *Dassonville* or Art 28 (old 30). Thus, providing national rules do not impede access to markets but merely regulate them without discrimination, either direct or indirect, they will be acceptable.

Subsequent cases have accepted Dutch laws concerning the times and places at which petrol could be sold (*Tankstation't Heukste* (cases C-401 and 402/92)), advertising (*Hunermund* (case C-292/92)), Belgian laws prohibiting offering products for sale at a loss of profit (*Belgapom* (case C-63/94)), but *Vereinigte Familiapress Zeitungsverlags* v *Bauer Verlag* (case C-368/95) witnessed a return to pre-*Keck* considerations. An Austrian law prohibiting the offering of free gifts linked to the sale of goods, was the basis for an Austrian publisher's suit against a German magazine containing a prize crossword puzzle. The Court of Justice repeated its position established since *Keck* that certain national rules would not breach Art 28 (old 30) unless imposing additional requirements. Austrian rules would constitute a hindrance to free movement if the content of the magazine had to be altered for the Austrian market. However, maintaining the diversity of the press was the legitimate public interest objective given by the authorities and accepted by the Court. It remains up to the national judge to determine whether the ban is proportionate, or whether less restrictive aims to reach the objective are available. Thus, this case does not involve a rule falling outside Art 28 (old 30) but restriction that could nevertheless be justified under the *Cassis de Dijon* 'rule of reason'. It seems that with this area there is more to come!

QUESTIONS

1.   'The most significant contribution to the free movement of goods has been the restrictive approach adopted by the Court of Justice to the exceptions in Article 36 (now 30) and the ruling in *"Cassis de Dijon"* ' Discuss.

By way of a brief introduction you should state that as one of the fundamental pillars of the Community, the intention of the Treaty is that goods produced in the Community and in free circulation should have free access to all Member States' markets. It is in this light that the Court of Justice has interpreted liberally the Community provisions providing for the free movement of goods. Furthermore, any exceptions or derogations allowed to the Member States have been interpreted restrictively so as to ensure the maximum support for the fundamental principles.

This question requires you to consider the case law on Art 30 (old 36), in particular the approach of the Court of Justice to that article as an exception to a general principle, therefore to be construed narrowly, the strict enforcement of the second sentence of Art 30 (old 36) and the significance of the ruling in *Cassis de Dijon*. The basic provision of Art 28 (old 30) and the exceptions allowed under Art 30 (old 36) should be outlined in the answer, and the assistance provided by Directive 70/50.

Then you must consider whether the approach has been restrictive. One view is that Art 30 (old 36) requires a narrow approach to the exceptions. Another is that the *Procureur du Roi* v *Dassonville* case serves to prohibit any Member State measure which affects trade. Furthermore, the application of the requirement of proportionality means that even if the aim of a measure is justified but the way it was achieved is not, then it breaches Community law.

Cassis de Dijon may require more detail, as it introduces involved principles of law — the principle of equivalence and the rule of reason. The so-called 'rule of reason' appeared to broaden the permitted exceptions to Art 28 (old 30). The Court of Justice stated that obstacles to the free movement of goods within the Community resulting from disparities between the national laws relating to the marketing of products, must be accepted in so far as these provisions may be recognised as necessary in order to satisfy mandatory requirements, relating in particular to:

(a)   the effectiveness of fiscal supervision;
(b)   the protection of public health; or
(c)   the fairness of commercial transactions and the defence of the consumer.

However, the Court of Justice narrowed the scope of the possible exceptions by adding the requirement that measures taken to satisfy such mandatory requirements must be indistinctly applicable and are subject both to the principle of proportionality and to the second sentence of Art 30 (old 36).

From the point of view of promoting free movement of goods, the case introduced the principle that goods lawfully produced and marketed in one Member State, which meet the public health and consumer protection standards of that State, are presumed to be marketable in the other Member States.

It thus remains to be considered whether these two developments represent the greatest contributions of the Court of Justice? To answer this, you must consider what other contributions there have been. Compare other developments, such as the cases concerned with charges having equivalent effect, and in particular in this context, the case of *Dassonville* and the way in which it was taken perhaps too literally so that any national law which in any way restricted trade came to be questioned before the Court of Justice. The Sunday trading cases serve as a very good example here. If it is true, as suggested by the Commission, that national marketing rules have been the greatest obstacle to free movement, then a strong case can be made out in support of that view. However, there is so much case law involving the *Cassis de Dijon* principle that it may be considered the Court of Justice had added an unnecessary complication against which Member States' measures must be adjudged. Finally, there is the case of *Keck* and *Mithouard* to consider, whereby national rules relating to certain selling arrangements, as opposed to requirements to be met by the goods themselves, were not to be considered as coming within the scope of Art 28 (old 30). This case would therefore appear to narrow the scope of Art 28 (old 30) as interpreted in the light of *Dassonville* and as extended, arguably, by *Cassis de Dijon*. In reining back some of the control to the Member States, *Keck* would also appear to have made a significant contribution to the free movement of goods but not necessarily in a way which ensures easier movement of goods.

2.   Healthy-Eat Ltd is a manufacturer of fruit-flavoured yoghurt and breakfast muesli. It has recently decided to try to export to the greater European market. In order to ensure the products are in good condition when they reach the shops in the Member States, Healthy-Eat Ltd markets three special European product lines. The first is 'frozen yoghurt', containing only natural ingredients. The second is unfrozen yoghurt to which preservatives are added. The third is muesli in sealed cellophane bags. All the ingredients of the products are listed on the packaging.

Healthy-Eat Ltd found that the products were particularly popular in Germany, and for four months sales boomed. Six months ago, however, the company was told that a new German consumer protection law forbade the application of the description 'yoghurt' to frozen yoghurts, and imposed a ban, justified on 'public health grounds', on the importation of any dairy product containing preservatives. Following the introduction of the law, consignments of yoghurt were turned back at the frontier. Meanwhile, consignments of muesli were subject to long delays at the German frontier while spot checks for health reasons were carried out. These involved opening half the packets in every fifth case of muesli. Payment was required for the inspections, and parking fees were imposed on the trucks.

When Healthy-Eat Ltd challenges the parking fees and charges for the health checks, it is told that they are the equivalent of an internal tax imposed on domestic food products to finance a system of factory inspection in the German food industry.

Advise Healthy-Eat Ltd as to its rights under Community law.

This problem concerns both charges having equivalent effect and measures having equivalent effect. A brief introduction to the area of law and the attitude of the Court of Justice would help to set the scene before answering the specific points in the question.

The material facts are the problems with the frozen yoghurts, the additives in yoghurts and the checks and payments for the muesli. The issues are whether the measures introduced by the German Government are in breach or are justified under Community law.

(a) First of all, the yoghurt with preservatives. Article 28 (old 30) prohibits all quantitative restrictions or measures having equivalent effect. Measures which are in breach of Art 28 (old 30) are those which meet formulae provided by the provisions of Directive 70/50 or the Court of Justice in the *Dassonville* case (case 8/74) in that they impose measures to hinder imports. The ban imposed would appear to be the case here. However, Art 30 (old 36) allows exceptions on public health grounds, and this is what Germany pleads in respect of the ban on preservatives. There is considerable case law now dealing with bans on health grounds, and any measure must be reasonable and proportional to the aim (*Commission v UK (Re UHT Milk)* and *Commission v France (Re Italian Table Wines)*). In particular, rules about preservatives have been considered in *Commission v Germany (Re Beer Purity Law)*. It was not contested that the prohibition on the marketing of beers containing additives fell within the definition of a measure having equivalent effect to a quantitative restriction in Art 28 (old 30). The justification must be based on Art 30 (old 36). The German Government argued that the measure was justified under Art 30 (old 36) on public health grounds. The Court held that the use of a given additive permitted in another Member State, having regard to the results of international scientific research, in particular the work of the World Health Organisation, amongst others, and to eating habits in the country of importation, does not constitute a danger to public health. The Court further held that the rule was contrary to the principle of proportionality because there was no accessible procedure whereby businesspeople were able to request that the use of specific additives be permitted by a measure of general application; and certain of the additives used in beers from other Member States were permitted in Germany in the manufacture of almost all drinks other than beer.

There must be a real danger to human health and the alleged harmful effects must be proved. It is unlikely, therefore, that this ban will be acceptable.

(b) The justification for the prohibition of frozen yoghurt is based on other grounds. If not excused or justified this will also be a breach of

Art 28 (old 30). This time, however, the justification for the prohibition is not made on the basis of Art 30 (old 36) but based on other grounds. As the rules appear to apply to both imports and domestic products and the justification given by the Member State is that of consumer protection, the solution lies outside Art 30 (old 36) and must be sought with help of the case law of the Court of Justice, notably the case of *Cassis de Dijon* (120/78).

Is the measure acceptable to protect the consumer, or would a more appropriate measure be preferred? *Commission* v *Germany (Re Beer Purity Law)* and *Glocken GMBH* v *USL Centro-Sud* concerning Italian pasta purity laws would be applicable here. The measure must be proportionate. Protection would be equally, if not better, served by appropriate labelling, together with an indication of the sell-by date, to guarantee consumer information. Hence, unless the measures meet the above, they will not be acceptable. In fact, there is actually a case concerned with deep frozen yoghurt in which the insistence of the French authorities that it be given a different description than yoghurt was held to be capable of infringing Art 28 (old 30); see *Smanor* (case 298/87).

(c) The aspects concerning the muesli involve a consideration of measures and charges having equivalent effect. Are these 'spot checks' for health reasons permitted under Art 30 (old 36)? Yes, provided they are only spot checks and they take place with the same frequency as checks on the equivalent domestic product. They must not constitute arbitrary discrimination or a disguised restriction on trade. They are also subject to the principle of proportionality (see *Commission* v *France (Re Italian Table Wines)* and *Commission* v *UK (Re UHT Milk)*). The checks in this case appear disproportionate and discriminatory because they are systematic.

The charges for the checks are argued to be an equivalent tax and must first be considered whether they are. If not an acceptable tax, it then needs to be considered whether they are then an acceptable or unacceptable charge prohibited by Arts 23–25 (old 9–16).

Article 90 (old 95) allows internal taxes to be imposed on imports as long as it is the equivalent of an internal tax and is not discriminatory in its application. In *Denkavit* v *France* (case 132/78), it was held that, the tax to which an imported product is subject must be imposed at the same rate on the same product, be imposed at the same marketing stage and, the chargeable event giving rise to the duty must be the same for both products. The chargeable event here is different because if a tax it would be on distribution whereas the domestic product would be taxed pre-production, and thus would not come within the provisions of Art 90 (old 95).

It must now be considered whether the fee imposed is an unlawful charge. The *Statistical Levy* case (*Commission* v *Italy*) (case 24/68) defined a charge having equivalent effect to include: 'any pecuniary charge, however small and whatever its designation and mode of application, which is imposed unilaterally on domestic or foreign goods by virtue of the fact that they cross a frontier', and which is not a customs duty in the strict sense. The Court held that: 'such a charge is a charge having equivalent effect even if it is not imposed for the benefit of the Member State concerned, even if it is not discriminatory or protective in effect and even if the product on which it is imposed is not in competition with any domestic product.'

Under certain conditions charges may be acceptable. If they are health checks with a legal basis in Community law, they may be charged for; see *Commission* v *Germany (Health Inspections)* (case 18/87). They cannot be regarded as charges having effect equivalent to customs duties, if the fees do not exceed the cost of the actual inspections in respect of which they are charged, the inspections in question are mandatory and uniform for all the products in question in the Community, the inspections are provided for by Community law in the interests of the Community and the inspections promote the free movement of goods. It would seem unlikely that Community law would be the basis of these inspections and therefore the charges in this case do not meet the criteria and thus would appear to breach Arts 23–25 (old 9–12).

The parking fees will also be held to be charges having equivalent effect to customs duties, prohibited by Art 23 (old 9); see two cases concerned with customs warehouses, *Commission* v *Belgium* (case 132/82) and *Marimex* (case 29/72).

In conclusion, none of the products could be restricted lawfully under Community law.

FURTHER READING

Steiner, J., 'Drawing the Line: Uses and Abuses of Article 30 EEC' (1992) 29 CML Rev 749.

Weatherill, S., 'After Keck: some thoughts on how to clarify the situation' (1996) 33 CML Rev 885.

Weatherill, S., 'Recent case law concerning the free movement of goods: mapping the frontiers of market deregulation' (1996) 36 CML Rev 51.

Wils, W., 'The Search for the Rule in Article 30 EEC: much ado about nothing?' (1993) 18 EL Rev 475.

9 *FREE MOVEMENT OF PERSONS*

INTRODUCTION

There is a firm legislative basis for the free movement of persons, both in primary Treaty provisions and in secondary legislation, and now in the case law of the Court of Justice. It is heralded as one of the four original fundamental freedoms of the common market. Along with the other Community free movement policies, it is broadly outlined in the Preamble and Arts 2 and 3 of the EC Treaty. Article 12 (old 6 EC) has also been very important in the development of this area of law, by outlawing various discriminatory rules and practices by Member States and organisations which did not fit easily and directly within the provisions on workers, establishment or services.

GENERAL ISSUES

General consideration of the free movement of persons involves the original reasons for inclusion in the Treaty, i.e., whether economic motives were the only or primary reason for allowing the free movement of workers, or was it the desire of the Council and Commission, concerned with human rights and the general treatment of workers. A further consideration is whether the inclusion of such rights was a reflection of the economic conclusion that it is easier to release the commodity of labour to seek capital than it is to shift capital and set up productive forces where labour surpluses exist. The arguments are finely balanced, and not all academic opinion has been in agreement. On the one hand, Wyatt and Dashwood, in their first edition, noted: 'It is significant that the macro-economic objectives of the Community are placed second to the personal rights of the Community worker to improve his standard of life by the exercise of rights by Art 48 [now 39].' On the other hand, the view of Hartley, in Green et al., *The Legal Foundations of the Single European Market*, at p. 92, was that: 'One can conclude, therefore, that the authors of the EEC Treaty regarded the Community as predominantly an economic organisation.'

Whatever your views on these points, it is arguably the case now that capital is easier to move than labour, and that rather than stimulating large scale migration from areas of high unemployment to areas of low unemployment, companies, especially multinationals, choose to establish productive capacity in lower cost countries, China being the leading example presently. Furthermore, in order to gain a place in the internal market, Japanese and other Asian capital is transferring to locate in Europe. Migration is of limited advantage to workers within Western Europe, because of the disincentives of culture and linguistics which exist and because of the limited economic gain to be achieved. The aims of the Treaty so far, then, have had limited success in promoting wholesale development of economic activity by the free movement of workers provisions. Mainly, so far, they have been of symbolic significance, although in individual circumstances the Treaty clearly brings great benefits. It is fair to say, though, that other objectives in the realms of social policy now have a greater significance in the Community, as can be observed from the content of legislation and policy outlines of the Community. Good examples are the new directives on general rights of residence not based on economic activities, and the directives that are being issued under the Social Policy Chapter. Following the Labour party victory in the 1997 General Election in the UK, this has now been properly incorporated within the EC Treaty by the Treaty of Amsterdam.

Interpretation and Application by the Court of Justice

The Court of Justice has adopted a very liberal approach to the interpretation of the free movement of workers provisions — both the Treaty principles and the further extensions of these principles in the secondary legislation — whereas the exceptions to the rights granted to the Member States are interpreted strictly.

The Internal Market

Other considerations which may impinge greatly on the free movement of persons are those relating to border controls in the Community following the establishment of the internal market, the establishment of Community citizenship and the moves towards a common Community immigration policy. Article 95(2) (old 100a(2)), introduced by the SEA, specifically excluded from the scope of Art 95 (old 100a) provisions in relation to the free movement of persons. It remains to be seen what border controls, if any, will be acceptable in respect of those wishing to take advantage of the free movement of persons provisions.

Citizenship of the Union

A new Part to the EC Treaty on 'Citizenship of the Union' was created by the TEU and confirmed by the Treaty of Amsterdam. Article 17 (old 8) establishes 'Citizenship of the Union and Art 18 (old 8a) EC has been included whereby all citizens of the Union will be entitled to move and reside freely within the territory of all the Member States. This right can be restricted by Community law limitations already in existence and future implementing measures. That this right did not translate into enforceable rights for the citizens is demonstrated by the case of *Florius Wijsenbeek* (case C-378/97). On re-entry to Holland, a Dutch national refused to show his passport, referring instead to the EC Treaty provisions, Arts 7a and 8a (now 14 and 18), on the free movement of EU citizens as removing the necessity to do so. He was prosecuted and ordered either to pay a small fine or go to prison for one day. He appealed and a reference was made to the Court of Justice. The Court held that because Art 7a (now 14) provides only that the Council may adopt provisions to facilitate the objectives of internal market, the provisions are not directly effective. The Court observed that at the time of the events in question, there were no common rules on immigration or border controls, therefore even if an unconditional right to movement was established, the Member States still retain the right to carry out identity checks and to determine whether the person entering the State is a person entitled to do so. Furthermore, Member States have the right to impose penalties for breach of the obligation to be identified, provided that such penalties are proportionate and comparable to penalties for similar national infringements. The Court considered that imprisonment would create an obstacle to free movement of persons but that the fine of NLG 65 (approximately GBP 18) appeared to be acceptable. It remains to be seen how this will affect the rights of entry and residence of those seeking work or establishment under the provisions considered below. Furthermore a new Title on Visas, Asylum, Immigration and other policies relating to Free Movement of Persons has been incorporated into the Treaty (Arts 61–69 (old 73i–73q)). Effectively it incorporates the Schengen Agreement into the EC Treaty. The Agreement was originally signed by five Member States in 1990 and now extends to all except the UK, Ireland and Denmark. This will seek progressively to remove all internal border controls and barriers to free movement for Union Citizens regardless of their economic status. For the present, however, this is in its infancy and outside the scope of most courses on EC law and most texts also. Further questions will arise relating to the granting of asylum and visas to nationals of third states but for the moment, at least, these developments lie outside the scope of this book.

This chapter is divided into two sections, dealing with workers in the first part and with establishment and services in the second part.

LEGISLATION ON WORKERS

Primary Legislation: Article 39 EC

The basic Treaty provision is Art 39 (old 48) EC, which required that the freedom of movement of workers should be secured by the end of the original transitional period. Article 39 (old 48) has been held to be directly effective in *Commission* v *France (Re French Merchant Seamen)* and in *Van Duyn* v *Home Office*.

Article 39(2) (old 48(2)) requires the abolition of any discrimination based on nationality to secure freedom of movement for nationals of the Member States. This is to apply particularly in respect of employment, remuneration and other conditions of work and employment.

Article 39(3) (old 48(3)) describes in broad terms the rights of workers, subject to those restrictions which the Member States may impose on the grounds of public policy, public security and public health. The rights are:

(a)   to accept offers of employment actually made;
(b)   to move freely within Member States for this purpose;
(c)   to remain in the Member State while working; and
(d)   to remain in the Member State after working, under such conditions as are imposed by secondary Community law.

Article 39(4) (old 48(4)) allows Members States to disregard the provisions of Art 39 (old 48) in respect of employment in the public service.

Secondary Legislation

Article 40 (old 49) EC is the empowering article for secondary legislation.

Directive 64/221 details the exclusions and restrictions allowed the Member States.

Directive 68/360 provides details on the abolition of restrictions on free movement for workers and their families.

Regulation 1612/68 details access to employment and rights as workers.

Regulation 1251/70 concerns the right to remain after work has concluded.

THE SCOPE OF LEGAL PROTECTION

Two basic definitions have to be proved in relation to questions in this area: 'nationality' and whether the person concerned is a 'worker' or otherwise entitled to remain in the Member State.

Nationality

To benefit as a worker, the person concerned must be a national of one of the Member States. It is not necessary for the members of a worker's family to be Member State nationals in order to obtain benefits, as will be seen in the secondary legislation and case law considered below.

Definition of 'Worker'

There is no definition given in the Treaty or secondary legislation, but the Court of Justice is progressively defining the scope of 'worker' in a Community context. In *Hessische Knappschaft v Maison Singer*, a German national on holiday in France was killed in a road traffic accident. A claim was made under the Community regulation related to workers. The Court of Justice held that it would not be in keeping with the foundations of the Treaty to limit the concept of worker to migrant workers strictly speaking, or to travel connected with their employment. A worker is any employed person, irrespective of whether he is wage-earning or salaried, blue collar or white collar, an executive or an unskilled labourer. In the *Hoekstra (aka. Ungar) v BBDA* case, the Court of Justice declared the reason for this view: 'If the definition of this term were a matter for the competence of the national courts it would be possible for every Member State to modify the term worker and so to eliminate at will the protection afforded by the EEC Treaty to certain categories of person.' In *Clean Car Autoservice* (case C-350/96), an employer was forbidden from appointing a manager who did not reside in Austria to manage a car hire and leasing company. The Court of Justice held that Art 39 (old 48) applies in favour of managers as well as workers but also that it applies in favour of employers who must be free to appoint managers without indirectly discriminatory condition from being applied. The term 'worker', however, does not just refer to those in employment: in certain circumstances it also applies to those who are seeking work and to those who, having lost one job involuntarily, are capable of taking another (*Hoekstra (aka Ungar) v BBDA*). (Directive 68/360, Art 7(1) states that the right of residence is not lost through involuntary unemployment.) In special circumstances, students are also included. Reference to case law is essential for clarification of these additional categories, as they are not to be perceived from the legislation.

In *Levin v Staatssecretaris van Justitie*, a British woman working in Holland for 20 hours per week and paid £30 per week, was held to be a worker. The argument that her earnings were below what was considered to be the minimum subsistence level was rejected. The Court of Justice held that factors such as part-time work, the motives for work and low wages were irrelevant to her status as a worker. Work must therefore be genuine and not so infinitesimal as to be disregarded; in other words, an activity of an economic nature. The Court ruled that work will only be disregarded if it is so minimal that it does not constitute economic activity at all.

In *Kempf* v *Minister of Justice*, it was held that despite only teaching for 12 hours per week and the fact that supplementary benefit was being claimed and received to support him, Mr Kempf qualified as a worker. The 'effective and genuine activity' as an employed person on a part-time basis qualified him as a worker. This was not defeated by the fact that his income was augmented lawfully from other means.

The Court of Justice has held in *Raulin* v *Netherlands Ministry of Education and Science* that, in considering whether work is genuine and effective, the national court should take account of all the occupational activities of the person in the host State only, and the duration of the activities. This would appear to hand the discretion to the Member States to determine who is a worker in the most difficult and unclear cases when guidance from the Court of Justice is most needed. The case concerned a claim by a French national to a grant to pursue a course in the plastic arts in the Netherlands following 60 hours work (in total) as a waitress there. She was refused the status of worker and thus the grant for the study. The Dutch court upheld this view. This case therefore casts into doubt the status of fixed-term and seasonal workers who may not benefit from the protection of the rights under the Treaty etc., e.g., grape pickers in France.

In *Lawrie-Blum* v *Land Baden-Württemberg*, the Court of Justice laid down three essential characteristics to establish an employment relationship:

(a)   the provision of some sort of service;
(b)   being directed by another person, i.e., not self-employed; and
(c)   in return for remuneration.

This was applied in *Steymann* v *Staatssecretaris van Justitie* whereby work in the Bagwhan Religious Community's commercial activities centre for remuneration paid in form of pocket money and meeting of material needs was held to qualify for the status of worker.

Work Seekers

The case of *Antonissen* helps further to define the concept and clarifies the legal status or meaning of the minutes of the Council meeting held when Directive 68/360 was passed. Increasingly, these statements had been used as a form of guideline to determine what would be reasonable in terms of the amount of time a Member State should allow a national of another Member State to remain in the country looking for work and thus be classed as a worker.

The UK wished to deport Antonissen, who had been convicted of possession of and intent to supply cocaine, and asked the Court of Justice whether it could. UK legislation gives EC citizens six months in which to find employment. Antonissen was in the country for over three years without work before his imprisonment. The Court of Justice held that Art 39(3) (old 48(3)) EC and Arts 1 and 5 of Regulation 1612/68 entail not only the freedom to enter and move freely in the host State, but also the right to stay there for the purposes of seeking employment. It also held that statements recorded in minutes regarding the acceptable time for the pursuit of work before deportation would not be allowable, have no legal significance and cannot be used to interpret the relevant legislative provisions. A Member State may deport an EC migrant worker, subject to an appeal, if he has not found employment after six months, unless evidence shows he is continuing to seek employment and that there are genuine chances of his being engaged. Therefore, after the expiry of a reasonable period, depending on the circumstances, persons may no longer be afforded the status and benefits of workers under Community law and may lawfully be deported by the Member State.

Some limits to the definition appear to have been found in *Bettray v Staatssecretaris Van Justitie*. The Court of Justice held that a national of a Member State employed in another Member State under a social employment scheme merely as a means of retraining or reintegration, cannot be regarded as a worker for the purposes of Community law as the activities could not be carried out as real and genuine economic activities. Here the position was artificially created with government money and was not therefore genuine.

The Court of Justice held in *Marie-Christine Lebon*, that those in search of work are not entitled to receive workers' benefits. Ms Lebon no longer lived with her parents, who were ex-workers, therefore she did not qualify for benefits as a dependant of a worker. She then asked if she would qualify for workers' benefits if she was looking or intended to look for work. The Court of Justice held that the benefits provided by legislation on free movement were only for those in actual employment, and not for those who migrate in search of work and have not found it. She could temporarily be classified as a worker, but not for the purposes of benefits.

Worker Training and Education

The difference between vocational training — and therefore a part of the worker training policy of the EC — and pure education — and therefore a part of the education policies exclusive to the Member States — has been considered by the Court of Justice in a series of cases.

In *Lair v Universität Hanover*, a French national employed in Germany was refused a grant by the university for a maintenance award and training fees. Ms Lair claimed she qualified as a worker because she had worked intermittently during the five years, although she was occasionally involuntarily unemployed. It was stated in the case that the period at university would lead to a professional qualification and was only a break in employment. The Court of Justice held since there was no fixed legislative definition of 'worker', there was nothing to say that the definition must always depend on a continuing employment relationship. Certain rights have been guaranteed to workers after employment has finished, e.g., the right to stay in the Member State and social security rights. This could also apply to university training, provided there was a link or continuity between work and university, in which case the university award could be considered a right under Regulation 1612/68. The status of worker was therefore retained if a link existed between the previous occupation and the studies in question. Consequently, since Ms Lair had come to Germany with the intention of working, and the course was intended to add to her qualifications, she fulfilled the criteria.

In contrast, in *Brown v Secretary of State for Scotland*, the Scottish education department refused Brown (a man of dual French/English nationality, who had been domiciled in France for many years) a university grant. He had worked for eight months in the UK prior to and in preparation for university. The Court of Justice held that university training is to be regarded as mainly vocational, and not, therefore, part of the EC worker rights, and is only covered by Art 12 (old 6) EC, generally outlawing discrimination. This covers tuition fees but not the maintenance grant, therefore a person who enters employment for eight months and does so specifically for the purpose of attending university, is not a worker for the purposes of Art 39 (old 48) and Regulation 1612/68.

The extent of the interpretation given by the Court of Justice can be judged in *Bernini v Netherlands Ministry of Education and Science*. Ms B, an Italian national and the daughter of a migrant worker, had lived in the Netherlands since the age of two. She followed an occupational training course in the Netherlands, which included 10 weeks' work as a trainee in a factory, and then began a course of architectural studies in Italy. She was refused a grant for that course by the Netherlands Ministry of Education and Science on the ground that she could not be treated as a Netherlands national as she was living not in the Netherlands but in Italy. The Court of Justice held that her work in the Netherlands, within the framework of a course of vocational training, was sufficient for her to be classed as a worker for the purposes of Art 39 (old 48), and that a migrant worker who voluntarily leaves employment in order to take up, after a certain lapse of time, a course of full-time study in their own country, retains the status as a worker, provided that there is a link between the previous occupational activity and the studies in question.

Returning to the *Raulin* case, the Court of Justice held that the 60 hours work had enabled her to claim the protection of Art 39 (old 48) EC, despite its very temporary nature. However, a migrant worker who then left that employment to begin a course of full-time study unconnected with the previous occupational activities did not retain the status as a worker for the purposes of Art 39 (old 48) EC. They did, however, have a right of residence in the host State for the duration of the course of study, regardless of whether or not the host State had issued a residence permit.

Thus definitions of what constitutes vocational training and the link to work are crucial for the determination of the status of a worker and the consequent benefits and rights.

Article 39 and Discrimination

The case of *Allué and Coonan* v *Università degli studi di Venezia*, specifically concerned discrimination and Art 39(2) (old 48(2)). The applicants, after five years of employment as foreign language lecturers, were informed that they could not be retained under a 1980 Italian decree which limited the duration of employment of foreign language lecturers. Not all the foreign language lecturers were foreign, some 25 per cent were nationals, therefore there was no dissimilar treatment, i.e., overt discrimination. The Court of Justice held that Art 39(2) (old 48(2)) also covers covert or indirect discrimination which leads to the prejudicial treatment of non-nationals. Although the rule applied regardless of the nationality, it nevertheless mainly affected the nationals of other Member States, who made up 75 per cent of such language teachers but the rule was held to be discriminatory where such limitations on the duration of employment do not exist in principle in respect of other workers.

Rights of Entry and Residence

Article 39(3) (old 48(3)) is concerned with rights to enter, move freely within, seek and take up employment in another Member State. These rights are amplified and supplemented by the provisions of Regulation 1612/68 (Arts 1–5) and Directive 68/360 (Arts 1–8).

Regulation 1612/68   This expands on the rights provided by Art 39 (old 48).

Articles 1 and 2 provide the right for nationals of Member States to take up an activity of an employed person in another Member State under the same rules as a national, i.e., without discrimination.

Article 3(1) states that the requirement of non-discrimination shall not apply where linguistic ability is necessary. This has been considered in *Groener* v *Minister of Education and the City of Dublin Vocational Education Committee*. An Irish law which required an adequate knowledge of the Irish language as a prerequisite to an appointment to a permanent full-time post as a lecturer in public vocational educational institutions, was questioned by a Dutch national. She had been appointed to a permanent position on the condition that she passed a proficiency test in the Irish language, but she had failed the exam, more than once. The Court of Justice held that such a requirement should not encroach upon a fundamental freedom; it must be proportionate to the aim pursued and should not bring about discrimination against other Member States' nationals. Due to the nature of the tasks of the position in this case, it was not unreasonable to insist on a language requirement, provided the level expected was not disproportionate to that actually required.

Article 5 of Regulation 1612/68 obliges Member States to give the same assistance to other EC nationals as to their own when seeking employment.

Directive 68/360   This directive mainly relates to the documents required in order to leave one Member State and enter another.

Article 1 abolishes restrictions on the movement and residence of nationals of Member States who enter under the provisions of Regulation 1612/68.

Article 2 provides that exit States are obliged to allow nationals to leave and to grant passports.

Under Art 3, entrance States cannot demand entry visas or equivalent documents from EC nationals but may do so in respect of members of the family who are not nationals of the Community. They can, however, require a passport or valid identity card. In *Commission v Belgium* (case C-344/95), a delay in issuing documents, the limited duration of residence permits and payments demanded in excess of that comparable for national identity cards were all measures held by the Court of Justice to breach Directive 68/360.

Article 4 requires that a residence permit be granted to any worker who produces a passport and certificate of proof of employment. The latter need not be a nationally produced or sanctioned work permit, it can be merely a letter confirming an offer of employment or job confirmation. Members of the worker's family must also be afforded a residence permit on production of a passport and relationship or proof of dependence (Art 4(3) and (4)).

These rights must not be weakened by disproportionate penalties which hinder free movement when the worker has failed to comply with the national legal requirements demanded of him or her. For example, in *R v Pieck*, Mr Pieck, a Dutch national, re-entered the UK after his original six-month entry permit had expired and he had failed to renew it. The authorities sought to deport him. The Court of Justice held that Art 4 means that a failure to obtain a permit could result in penalties for minor offences only. The administrative rules are acceptable, as is an appropriate sanction or penalty for their breach but not usually deportation which would be regarded as disproportionate. Furthermore, the residence permit is not a precondition for residence, it is merely evidence of the entitlement to enter and reside, i.e., not the right itself but merely the proof of it. Under Art 5, delays in furnishing a residence permit must not hinder taking up employment.

Further questioning, once the correct papers have been shown, regarding the purpose and duration of a stay, would be contrary to Community law (*Commission* v *Netherlands (Re Entry Requirements)*).

Article 6 provides that the permits must be valid for the whole territory of the Member State and valid for at least five years with automatic renewal. In *Rutili* v *Ministre de l'Intérieur*, Roland Rutili (an Italian) was active in trade unionism and was involved in the student riots in Paris in May 1968, but he was never convicted of any offence. He left France, but on his later return was granted entry and residence permits only on condition that he did not live in certain parts of the country (Alsace Lorraine where his family lived). France pleaded the public policy proviso and the fact that convicted nationals could be banned from certain *départements* (regions). The Court of Justice held that any prohibition could only be in respect of the whole territory. It invoked the doctrine of proportionality to compare the treatment of nationals and the nature of the penalty. A State cannot apply the measure to foreigners unless the equivalent restriction can be imposed on nationals. There was no conviction of Rutili, therefore different rules were found to apply. The Court of Justice held that conduct must pose a genuine and sufficiently serious threat to public policy or security to justify expulsion or a ban. (See further, below.)

Article 8(2) of Directive 68/360 states that Member States may require EC nationals to report their presence in the host State. The period given for this must be reasonable and the punishment for a breach of the requirement must be proportional. In *Watson* v *Belman*, Ms Watson, a UK national, was acting as an 'au pair' whilst staying with Mr Belman. Both had failed to report this to the national authorities as required and faced imprisonment and fines under national law. In addition Ms Watson was to be deported. The Italian Magistrate asked the Court of Justice if the punishments were compatible with EC law. The Court held that the failure to report did not affect the right of residence and also the doctrine of proportionality applied to limit the punishment. The use of internal rules, i.e., the requirement to report, was acceptable but the penalty must be in proportion to the offence or damage caused. i.e., a small fine. Therefore any decision to deport would be contrary to the Treaty. The Advocate General in this case considered that an 'au pair' would be a worker even if only on a board and lodge basis. In the case of *Messner*, an excessive fine for failure to report within three days was found to be contrary to the requirements of the free movement policies.

Restrictions on Entry and Residence

The restrictions on entry on the grounds of public policy, security and health under Art 39(3) (old 48(3)) are also specifically repeated in Directive 68/360, Art 10, to exempt Member States from the provisions of that directive.

The grounds of public health which justify exclusion are given in Directive 64/221, Art 4(1) and annex, and are relatively straightforward. Drug addiction is covered by the proviso of public policy and public security.

Directive 64/221 seeks to clarify the extent of the discretion given to the Member States under Art 39(3) (old 48(3)). The scope of the directive is given under Art 2(1), and includes all measures taken by the Member States to exclude EC nationals on the basis of public health, public policy and public security. The last two overlap to such an extent that they can be regarded in practice as a single category. Under Art 2(2), a ground cannot be invoked to serve economic ends.

Article 3(1) provides that measures adopted on grounds of public policy or security must be based on personal conduct. Case law excludes general categories of persons. The court held in *Van Duyn* v *The Home Office* that restrictions on the grounds of public policy must be interpreted very strictly and be subject to judicial review. In this case a Dutch woman obtained a position as secretary with the Church of Scientology in the UK, but was refused entry by the Home Office on the ground that public policy declared the church to be socially harmful. Ms Van Duyn claimed that the refusal was not made on the ground of her personal conduct but on the conduct of the group. The Court of Justice held that personal conduct must be an act or omission to act on the part of the person concerned and must be voluntary. It need not, however, be illegal or criminal in order to offend public policy. The Court further held that present association, reflecting participation in the activities and identification with the aims of a group, may be considered a voluntary act and could therefore come within the definition of conduct.

In *Adoui and Cornaille* v *Belgian State*, the Court of Justice held that the public policy justification does not allow expulsion where similar conduct by nationals does not incur a penalty or repressive measures.

In *Bonsignore* v *Stadt Köln*, the Court of Justice held that Community nationals cannot be subject to grounds extraneous to the individual case, i.e., only the 'personal conduct' of those affected by the measures is to be regarded as determinative, e.g., as a deterrent.

Under Directive 64/221, Art 3(2), previous criminal convictions shall not in themselves constitute grounds for expulsion. In *R* v *Bouchereau*, a French national had been convicted in the UK on a number of occasions for drugs possession. The UK magistrate asked the Court of Justice whether Bouchereau could be deported to stop him committing acts in the future. The Court held that it was not possible to look at a past record to decide future conduct unless it constituted a present threat and 'a sufficiently serious threat to the fundamental interests of society'. See, however, the case of *Antonissen*, considered above, where lack of employment and the lack of any serious chance of obtaining work would justify expulsion. Article 3(3) provides that the expiry of an ID card or a passport is no justification for expulsion.

Procedural Safeguards

EC law takes its example from continental administrative law, therefore specific and detailed rights have been formulated. Directive 64/221, Arts 5–9 provide rights of appeal, rights to be given reasons for deportation and judicial review of decisions:

(a) Article 5 gives the right to remain in the Member State pending a decision either to grant or refuse a residence permit.

(b) Under Art 6 the grounds for deportation must be precisely and comprehensively stated. The concerned person has a right to be informed of the grounds of refusal or deportation unless security is at stake. The cases of *Adoui and Cornaille* and *Rutili* held that the reasons must be sufficiently detailed to allow a migrant to defend his or her interests, and drafted in such a way and in such language as to enable the person to comprehend their content or effect.

(c) Article 7 provides the right to be notified of any decision to expel or to refuse a permit, and should also state the minimum period given to leave the country. This cannot be less than 15 days for a first refusal of a permit and not less than one month for expulsion.

(d) Article 8 requires that the same legal remedies shall be available as are available to nationals.

(e) Article 9 provides that there should also be a system for appeal against decisions on their merits as well on points of legality. The appeal body must be independent of the immigration service who refused entry in the first place. The case of *Gallagher* (case C-175/94) confirms this point, where Gallagher, who had been convicted of the possession of rifles for unlawful purposes in Ireland, had been deported from the UK. In questioning this decision, he was interviewed in Ireland before the case was heard by the Home Secretary. He challenged these bodies as not being independent within the meaning of Directive 64/221, Art 9. The Court of Justice held, however, that it was a matter for the national courts to decide whether the body hearing an appeal was independent but that the Directive did not specify how it should be appointed. It should, however, be genuinely independent. In *Pecastaing v Belgian State*, a French prostitute was asked by the Belgian authorities to leave on grounds of personal conduct. She claimed under Arts 8 and 9 that she should be able to stay in the country while the decision was being reviewed, which could be for up to two years during the course of an Art 234 (old 177) reference. The Court of Justice held that even under Art 234 (old 177), the right of appeal is not to be diluted, and only in cases of emergency should automatic expulsion take place; however, the urgency could finally be determined only by the Member States. Articles 8 and 9 do not grant rights to remain in the host State pending any hearing as long as the person can get a fair hearing and full facilities even while out of the country.

In *Adoui and Cornaille*, the Court of Justice held that the Art 9 appeal or review must make it possible for facts and circumstances to be examined and reasons given. The forum need not be a court, nor consist of judges, but it must be independent of the immigration service.

Rights of Workers and their Families

The rights under Art 39(2) (old 48(2)) EC are further expanded in Regulation 1612/68, notably Art 7, which has been subject to considerable judicial elucidation.

Article 7(1) reflects Art 12 (old 6) of the EC Treaty and prohibits discrimination against workers on the ground of nationality, but it specifically mentions terms and conditions of employment, dismissal and, where relevant, reinstatement. In *Ugliola*, an Italian working in Germany was recalled for military service in Italy. While German law allows for absence for military service with the German Army with no loss of benefits or loss of service in work, there was no provision made for National Service with other forces. It was held by the Court of Justice that Ugliola was entitled to the same protections as German citizens. The argument raised by the German Government was that all nationalities were treated the same if they served in the German Army, and that Germans were treated similarly if they served in foreign armies. The Court of Justice held that to treat non-nationals the same as nationals is discrimination if it results in disadvantage. Thus the concept of discrimination encompasses not only failure to treat like persons in the same way, but also failure to differentiate between unlike.

When you start a job in another country, if this the same as undertaken in the home state this does not mean that you start from day one but that previous service may count for advantages in the host State. To ignore this is to discriminate contrary to Art 7(1). In *Commission v Greece* (case C-187/96), the Court of Justice held that a Greek administrative Regulation and practice which did not take into account periods of employment in the public service of another Member State when determining seniority increments and salary grading breached Art 39 (old 48) EC and Art 7(1) of Regulation 1612/68, i.e., service elsewhere counts.

Article 7(2), which is proving to be a provision with extremely wide scope, refers specifically to equality in social and tax advantages, which also apply to the family of a worker.

In *Fiorini aka Christini* v *SNCF*, a reduced fare entitlement was claimed by the widow of an Italian SNCF worker. Widows of French workers were allowed such a family entitlement, but it was denied to the Italian. The SNCF claimed that since it was not express in the contract of employment, the benefit was not available to foreign workers. The Court of Justice held that Art 7 applies to all advantages, not just those limited to the contract of employment.

In *ONE* v *Deak*, an unemployed Hungarian national living with his mother, an Italian national working in Belgium, was refused special unemployment benefits for non-nationals on the basis that no agreement for such benefits existed between Belgium and Hungary. The Court of Justice held that special unemployment benefits were a social advantage within the meaning of Art 7 and that Deak, regardless of nationality, could derive rights as the descendant of a worker, otherwise a worker might be hindered from moving if his or her descendants were discriminated against, thus causing financial difficulty.

In the case of *Bernini* v *Netherlands Ministry of Education and Science*, previously considered under the definition of 'worker', the Court of Justice also held that the study funding granted by a Member State to the children of workers constitutes a social advantage within the meaning of Art 7(2) of Regulation 1612/68, where the worker continues to provide for the maintenance of the child. In such a case, the child may rely on Art 7(2) in order to obtain study funding under the same conditions as those applied to children of national workers, and in particular without it being possible to impose upon him any further requirement relating to his residence.

Article 7(3) provides for the same rights and access to vocational training.

Article 7(4) seeks to rule out discrimination in collective agreements. *Kalliope Schöning-Kougebetopolou* v *Hamburg* (case C-15/96) has highlighted this provision. A public service collective agreement provision which required eight years' employment to qualify for seniority promotion but which did not take account of time served in the public service of another Member State was held to be in breach of Art 39 (old 48) and Art 7(1) and (4) of Regulation 1612/68 because of detriment to migrant workers. This is regardless of the different organisation of public service in the different Member States.

Article 8 entitles workers to equality of treatment in membership of trade unions and in the exercise of any rights relating to that membership. The

Court of Justice held, in *Association de Soutien aux Travailleurs Immigrés* v *Chambre des Employés Privés*, that Art 8 applies to all workers associations, not just those in the legal form of a trade union. By maintaining legislation which denies workers who are nationals of other Member States the right to vote and to stand as candidates for membership in elections to occupational guilds, the Court of Justice has held a Member State would be in breach of Art 39(2) (old 48(2)) EC and Art 8(1) of Regulation 1612/68; see *Commission* v *Luxembourg* (case C-118/92) (exercise of trade union rights).

Article 9 provides that workers shall enjoy all the rights and benefits accorded to national workers in matters of housing, including ownership and access to local authority housing lists.

The worker's family Article 10 of Regulation 1612/68 extends the above rights to spouses and descendants and ascendants. The descendants can be any nationality, and the term includes those under 21 and adult children over 21 where they are dependent on the worker. Other members of the family not covered by Art 10(1) are subject to Art 10(2) 'Member States shall facilitate the entry of other Members' but so far there has been no judicial help on this, so it is unclear just how far this would extend beyond the boundaries of the immediate family. Dependency was defined in the *Lebon* case as a factual situation of support provided by the worker.

In *Castelli* v *ONPTS*, the Italian mother of a retired Italian worker in Belgium claimed an old age pension. Ms Castelli had never worked in Belgium, therefore her claim was based on her status as a member of her son's family. The Belgian authorities refused to pay on the grounds that she was not Belgian and that Belgium did not have a reciprocal agreement with Italy. The Court of Justice held that Ms Castelli was entitled to install herself with her son under Art 10 of Regulation 1612/68, and had the right to remain after the son's retirement and the right to the pension under Art 7.

The rights of a spouse are not dependent on residence with the entitled worker. In *Diatta* v *Land Berlin*, Ms Diatta, a Senegalese citizen, was married to a French national living and working in Berlin. She obtained work in Berlin, shortly after which the couple separated to live apart. Upon Ms Diatta's application to extend her residence permit, the German authorities refused on the ground that she was no longer a member of the family for the purposes of Regulation 1612/68. The Court of Justice ruled that the rights under 1612/68 were not dependent on how or where members of the family lived. Therefore, a permanent, common family dwelling cannot be implied as a condition of the rights granted under Regulation 1612/68.

Whether the term 'spouse' includes cohabitees was partly considered by the Court of Justice in *Reed* v *Netherlands*. Ms Reed applied for a residence permit in Holland claiming her right to remain was based on her cohabitation with a UK national working in the Netherlands. The Dutch Government refused to recognise this. The Court of Justice was aware that provisions of national laws regarding cohabitees' legal rights could be quite varied. It was unable to overcome the clear intention of Art 10, which referred to a relationship based on marriage. The Court referred instead to the 'social advantages' guaranteed under Art 7 of the regulation as being capable of including the companionship of a cohabitee, which could contribute to integration in the host country. The Court held that where such relationships amongst nationals were accorded legal advantages under national law, these could not be denied to nationals of other Member States without being discriminatory and thus breaching Arts 12 and 39 (old 6 and 48) of the EC Treaty. This is a somewhat convoluted decision but it does provide justice to free movement in the case. The cohabitee does not have rights in his or her own right, but the companionship of a cohabitee is merely regarded as one of the advantages to which workers are entitled.

Article 10(3) states that the Community law requirement on the Member States to allow entry to the family of the worker, is dependent on the worker having family housing considered as normal for national workers in the region. This requirement should not give rise to discrimination. In *Commission v Germany (Re Housing)*, the German Government had used this provision as the basis for a national law to insist that the foreign workers should maintain their housing similarly to nationals. Failure to do so would result in the refusal of (or refusal to renew) a residence permit and expulsion from Germany. The Court of Justice held that Art 10(3) applied only to initial entry of families; subsequently they must be treated the same as nationals, for whom there was no similar requirement.

Article 11 entitles the spouse and children of an entitled worker to take up any activity as employed persons. This right is to be interpreted widely to include any activity or profession, provided the appropriate qualifications and formalities are observed. The case of *Diatta v Land Berlin* is also applicable here.

Article 12 of Regulation 1612/68 gives rights to educational facilities to the children of workers, who should get equal treatment. The Court of Justice has interpreted this to include training grants for mentally handicapped people, whereby a handicapped child is to be given the same benefits and facilities as nationals (case of *Michel S*). Children of migrant workers are entitled to grants to attend educational establishments and to all benefits intended to facilitate access (*Casagrande v Landeshauptstadt München*).

The right to education continues to apply even if the worker in question has returned home, as held in *Echternecht and Moritz v Netherlands Minister for Education and Science*. Two German nationals in the Netherlands whose fathers were working, applied for study finance for a Dutch higher education establishment but were refused because the father of one of them had gone back to Germany to work, while the other's father was working for an organisation with diplomatic privileges and immunities and thus did not rely on Community law for his right of residence in another Member State. The Court of Justice held that the children of former migrant workers retained their rights under Community law, and that a Community national working in another Member State, and enjoying diplomatic status, did not thereby lose his status as a Community worker.

Article 12 applies so that the child of a Community worker, in this case an Italian working in Berlin, has the right to receive assistance from the state to pursue studies abroad where this is given to nationals, even though these studies are in the home state of the child concerned (*Carmina Di Leo v Land Berlin*).

THE PUBLIC SERVICE EXEMPTION

Article 39(4) (old 48(4)) EC exempts employment in the public service from the provisions of Art 39 (old 48). There is no Treaty definition of 'public service' which can vary considerably from State to State.

The Court of Justice has constantly stressed need for strict interpretation of the exemptions to this Article. This exemption has been held to apply to entry and not to conditions of employment. In *Sotgiu* v *Deutsche Bundespost*, Mr Sotgiu, an Italian national employed by the German Post Office, was not paid the same allowance as German nationals. This was held to be discrimination and not excused by Art 39(4) (old 48(4)). The Court of Justice has also held, in the case of *Scholz* v *University of Cagliari*, that, where Art 39(4) (old 48(4)) was not applicable to the post in question, a public service employer could not ignore previous employment experience gained in the public service of another Member State, where previous experience was a factor to be taken into account. In the *Kalliope* case it was held that Art 48(4) (now 39(4)) would not allow the Member State to justify discrimination in treatment in the public service.

The Commission has tried to obtain from the Court of Justice a strict definition of 'public service'. For example, in *Commission* v *Belgium (Re Public Employees)*, the Court of Justice held that public service applies only to typical public service posts which exercise power conferred by public law and safeguard the interests of the state, regardless of the status in Member States. The Court of Justice has on this basis excluded from the scope of Art 39(4) (old 48(4)) nurses (*Commission* v *French Republic (Re French Nurses)*); trainee secondary school teachers (*Lawrie-Blum* v *Land Baden-Württemberg*); and foreign language lecturers (*Allué and Coonan* v *Università degli studi di Venezia*).

In order to try and restrict the number of posts the Member States claim come within Art 39(4) (old 48(4)), the Commission has issued a notice (OJ 1988 C72/2) of those sectors, positions in which it thinks would rarely be covered by the public service exemption. These include public health care, teaching in State educational establishments, non-military public research and public administration of commercial activities.

THE RIGHT TO REMAIN IN THE HOST STATE

Article 39(3)(d) (old 48(3)(d)) EC is given effect by Regulation 1251/70. The right to remain in the host State after working is afforded to the worker and members of the worker's family. Additionally, the family has the right to remain in the event of the worker's death in employment.

Article 2(1) of the regulation requires workers to have worked for at least 12 months prior to retirement, or to have resided in the territory for more than two years in respect of incapacity, to qualify for the right to remain permanently.

Article 3 of the regulation concerns the rights of the family to remain in a Member State:

(a)   once the worker has acquired the right to remain, even after his death; and

(b)   if the worker dies before he has acquired the right to remain.

Workers and their families are entitled to the rights provided by Regulation 1612/68, especially Art 7, the social advantages. See the case law above, e.g., *Fiorini* v *SNCF*.

SOCIAL SECURITY PROVISIONS

Article 42 (old 51) EEC included these provisions in the Treaty to remove the disincentive which would otherwise have acted against the free movement of persons, if Community citizens were to lose out in their social security benefits by moving to another Member State.

The aims are to secure the aggregation of all periods affecting the right to benefits under the laws of several countries, and payment of benefits in the territories of the Member States. Further details of the rights to social security in a host State are provided by Regulation 1408/71. These are very detailed and are rarely the subject of courses considering Community law with the exception of very specialised courses, therefore no further coverage will be made in this volume.

FREEDOM OF MOVEMENT FOR THE SELF-EMPLOYED

Introduction

Free movement for the self-employed is broadly outlined in Arts 2 and 3 of the EC Treaty, and more specifically provided by the freedom of establishment (Arts 43–48 (old 52–58) of the EC Treaty) and the freedom to provide services (Arts 49–55 (old 59–66)). These rights of free movement are accorded on the basis of the recognition of qualifications by the host State and not the status as a worker. Thus considerations in these cases focus on the scope of the terms 'establishment' and the 'provision of services', and the progress made by the Community in providing the appropriate legislative regime to facilitate them.

Nationality   A person wishing to exercise these rights must be established in one of the Member States of the Community to establish or provide services in another. These provisions, like those applying to workers, are in favour of nationals of the Member States but likewise, family members do not have to be nationals of a Member State. Article 12 (old 6) provides the general legislative base to ensure there is no discrimination on the grounds of nationality for those establishing or providing services, rather than secondary legislation, such as Regulation 1612/68 as for workers. Clear authority for the no discrimination rule is: *Commission v UK (Re Nationality of Fishermen) (Factortame)*.

Establishment   This includes the rights to enter another Member State and stay on a long-term or permanent basis, to take up and pursue activities as self-employed persons, and to set up and manage undertakings. The concept suggests either permanent residence in the host State, or at least the establishment of a permanent professional base. It can be difficult at times to distinguish establishment from the free movement of workers, in that both concepts involve migration from one Member State to another with the intention of permanent, or at least long-term, settlement. A definition has been given in *Factortame* by the Court of Justice 'the actual pursuit of an economic activity through a fixed establishment in another Member State for an indefinite period'.

Services   The provision of services envisages a temporary state of affairs. Appearance in the host State would be for a limited period only to provide specific services, and there would be no permanent personal or professional presence in the host state or a necessity to reside. The concept of services is defined by the first paragraph of Art 50 (old 60) as those 'normally provided for remuneration, in so far as they are not governed by provisions relating to freedom of movement of goods, capital and persons'. In particular, Art 50(d) (old 60(d)) includes 'activities of the professions'.

Distinguishing the concepts of establishment and services   The distinction with 'establishment' is at times difficult to maintain. For example, the provision of services on a regular and frequent basis, with perhaps the setting-up of an office or a surgery, but with permanent residence maintained in the home Member State, is likely to take the provider of the services into the position, according to the Court of Justice, of being subject to the rules covering establishment. See *Commission* v *Germany (Re Insurance Services)*, where it was held that the provision of services which included the setting-up of offices in the host State on a long-term basis, which were staffed by their own employees, should be considered as establishment even though the legal entity remained in the home State. This is very important as the application of home rules may be stricter for establishment, and not all home rules have been found by the Court of Justice to be suitable or acceptable for the provision of services, as the case law below will show.

In *Gebhard* v *Milan Bar Council*, the Court of Justice characterised 'establishment' as the right of a community national to participate on a stable and continuous basis in the economic life of a Member State other than his or her own and 'services' by the temporary, precarious and discontinuous nature of the services which is to be determined in the light of its duration, regularity, periodicity and continuity. Hence, the setting up of chambers in Italy by a German lawyer, still practising in Stuttgart, was held to be establishment. Thus, establishment in more than one State is possible. So Gebhard, despite non-permanent presence, was deemed not to be providing services.

Scope   The provisions also apply to legal persons, most importantly to companies defined in the first paragraph of Art 48 (old 58) and Art 55 (old 66). Since the establishment of companies is the subject of study in specialised company law courses, it will not be considered further in this volume.

Derogations   There can be derogations on the grounds of public policy, public security and public health under Art 45 and 55 (old 55 and 66), and there is the equivalent of the public service exception in Art 39(4) (old 48(4)), but only on the more tightly defined ground of 'activities . . . connected . . . with the exercise of official authority' (Art 45 (old 55)). The Court held in the case of *Reyners* that the derogation was more concerned with the exercise of the prerogative power of the state rather than the preventing particular occupations from exercising rights under Community law. The derogations allowed by Arts 46 and 55 (old 56 and 66) are subject to the same considerations and restrictive interpretation given by the Court of Justice in respect of the free movement of workers, thus no further details will be given here. Directive 64/221 is also relevant as a clarification of the derogations.

Secondary legislation   Under old Treaty Arts 53, 57 and 63, the Commission was charged with the issue of directives to obtain the general objectives set out in the Treaty. A general programme was set up, and two specific instances of general legislation were enacted to facilitate free movement: Directive 73/148, concerning rights of entry and residence (which is the equivalent of Directive 68/360 for workers, considered above), and Directive 75/34 for rights of the self-employed to remain (the equivalent of Directive 1251/70). As these provide essentially the same rights as those for workers considered above the details will not be considered here.

The Court of Justice has held that the same rights of entry and residence in respect of free movement apply regardless of which form of free movement is undertaken, i.e., as a worker, a provider of services or as one wishing to establish (*Roux v Belgian State*).

The principal consideration for the provision of services and establishment is the problem encountered in the recognition of qualifications, which have hindered free movement.

Obstacles to the Freedoms

The second paragraph of Art 45 (old 55), and the third paragraph of Art 50 (old 60), subject the freedoms of establishment and to provide services to national rules, hence then the biggest impediments to the free movement of persons was the requirement of national authorities that persons were required to satisfy the conditions of the various professions. The initial approach of the Commission to get round these was the harmonisation of rules by the adoption of a general programme of Directives. These were intended to abolish the restrictions on free movement by the mutual recognition of qualifications in all sorts of self-employed trades and professions on an occupation-by-occupation basis, covering many sectors of the economy. The attempt to harmonise the conditions of the various professions proved extremely difficult and time-consuming, with the Architects Directive taking 17 years to finalise. This approach also encouraged the view throughout the Community that the only way in which these rights could be promoted was by directives and not directly from the Treaty. Thus little progress was made, and even prior to the issue of directives case law had developed the law considerably.

Two leading cases, in which Arts 43 and 49 (old 52 and 59) were held to create direct effects by the Court of Justice, radically changed the approach of the Commission in taking steps to achieve free movement. The Court of Justice was able to decide in favour of the applicants, in the absence of secondary legislation, largely on the basis of the general prohibition on discrimination, Art 12 (then 7 EEC) EC and the other Treaty Articles themselves.

Reyners v Belgian State involved the attempt by a Dutch national to get access to the Belgian Bar. The Belgian Government argued that Art 43 (old 52) was not directly effective because it was incomplete without the issue of directives required by Art 47 (old 57). The Court of Justice held that the prohibition on discrimination under Art 43 (old 52) was directly effective and declared that nationality could be no barrier to appropriately qualified lawyers entering a country to practise. The directives were simply to facilitate free movement and not to establish it, which had already been done by the end of the initial transition period of the Communities.

The *Van Binsbergen* case concerned a professionally qualified Dutch national, resident in Belgium, who was refused audience rights before the Dutch courts. The Court of Justice held Art 49 (old 59) was directly effective and was not conditional on the issue of subsequent directives in respect of the specific professions, nor on a residence requirement.

Following these two and other cases, the Commission realised that the initial approach was not the best solution and commenced work on a new approach involving providing rules for many professions across the board. This will be considered below. For the moment, it is important to consider a number of cases which highlight the problems encountered in respect of discriminatory rules, obstacles or limitations and conditions which have been imposed in the areas of establishment or provisions of services by national laws or professional rules contrary to Community law.

Establishment

Article 43 (old 52), paragraph 2, subjects establishment to the conditions laid down for nationals by the law of the country where such establishment takes place. These are mostly concerned with the professional qualifications and educational requirements of specific professions, but there are two leading cases of general application.

In *Thieffry v Paris Bar Council*, the applicant was refused access to the Paris Bar despite having obtained a Belgian diploma in law, recognised by the University of Paris as the equivalent of a French diploma, and having sat and passed the French certificate for the profession of *avocat*. The Court of Justice held that the relevant national authorities should apply any laws or practices which allow for the securing of freedom of establishment in accordance with the Community policy, even though no directives may have been enacted in that particular area. Therefore, where the competent authorities have recognised a foreign diploma as equivalent to a domestic qualification, recognition of that diploma may not be refused in an individual case solely because it is not a diploma of the host state.

In *Patrick v Minister for Cultural Affairs*, a British national had an architecture qualification which had been recognised by the French Ministry of Culture as equivalent to the French qualifications required to practise architecture in France. The Court of Justice held that Art 43 (old 52) was directly effective without the need for a specific regulation applying it to the profession of architect. The French refusal was contrary to Community law.

In the same way as will be seen for services below, also with establishment, there has been an attack on national rules which although applying to both home professionals and those establishing in the host country, are regarded as inappropriate for host professionals. The rule can survive but is only applicable to citizens, introducing therefore a form of reverse discrimination.

Lawyers   There was not a specific establishment Directive for lawyers and thus initial consideration of lawyers' rights arises from case law and starting with *Reyners* as previously considered. It was held in *Ordre des Avocats au Barreau de Paris* v *Klopp*, that the Community rules may be diminished if the effects of the national rules are unfair in application, therefore a Member State cannot exclude a lawyer on the basis that he can only have one residence and cannot refuse entry because a lawyer maintains chambers elsewhere. The Court of Justice emphasised that while Member States are entitled to require that advocates comply with professional ethics and regulate their practice in such a way as to maintain sufficient contact with their clients, their regulations should not have the effect of preventing EC nationals from exercising their right of establishment in more than one centre of activity in EC territory.

In *Vlassopoulou* v *Ministerium für Justiz*, the German authorities refused a Greek lawyer admission to the German Bar on the grounds that the applicant did not have the required German qualifications and that Art 43 (old 52) was no basis to recognise Greek qualifications as sufficient. The Court of Justice held that national rules could impede the right of establishment for lawyers if they disregarded knowledge and qualifications which had already been acquired by the person concerned in the other Member State. The German Justice Ministry was under an obligation to take account of diplomas, certificates and qualifications which the person concerned had obtained for the purpose of practising the same profession in another Member State. There was a duty to evaluate and compare qualifications to establish whether or not there was equivalence of content. However, the Court of Justice held in *Kraus* v *Land Baden-Württemberg*, that the authorities were entitled to charge an administrative fee to verify the qualifications.

In the *Gebhard* case, a German lawyer who had established a second chamber in Milan was prevented from using the title 'Avvocato'. Neither of Directives 77/249 nor 89/48 (both considered below) applied to the situation. The question was raised as to whether, the Italian rules could be imposed on him? In principle and according to the general Treaty provision

Art 43 (old 52), he was required to comply with the rules but the Court of
Justice held that national measures which hinder or make less attractive the
exercise of fundamental freedoms must fulfil four conditions. They must
be:

(a)   non discriminatory in application;
(b)   justified by imperative reason relating to the public interest;
(c)   suitable to secure the objective sought; and
(d)   proportional.

It is left to the national courts to determine whether qualifications are
equivalent and here the danger is that some will and some will not. The
consequence of this decision is that establishment is now very close to
services. Perhaps this is a fair result to achieve, i.e., that it doesn't matter
where or how you practise, either on a temporary or permanent basis,
provided qualifications are roughly equivalent. Rules which seek to prevent
this must satisfy the criteria or be struck out, at least as far as non-national
EC citizens.

Medical professions   Community measures for the medical professions include Council Directive 75/362 (OJ 1975 L167/1), which provides for the
mutual recognition of medical qualifications applicable in each Member
State, and Directive 86/457 to harmonise national training requirements.
    In *Broekmeulen* v *Huisarts Registratie Commissie*, the Court of Justice held
that a doctor who had qualified in Belgium and had a diploma recognised
by Art 3 of Directive 75/362, was entitled to registration as a general
practitioner in his native Netherlands despite the fact that if he had
qualified there, as a national, he would have had to undergo a period of
further training.

Architects   Architects are catered for by Directive 85/384 (OJ 1985 L223/15)
and Council Decision 85/385 (OJ 1985 L223/26). Directive 85/384 lays
down as a condition for professional qualification, the completion of a
course of study of at least four years. In *Conseil National de l'Ordre des
Architectes* v *Egle*, it was held that the refusal to recognise the qualifications
of a German architect, who had qualified in Germany after a four-year
course which included two semesters of practical training was contrary to
Community law.

Veterinary surgeons   Veterinary surgeons are covered by Directives 78/1026
and 78/1027 (OJ 1978 L363/7). In *Ordre Nationale des Vétérinaires de France*
v *Auer*, an Austrian national with Italian veterinary qualifications was
refused recognition by the competent authorities in France. Auer was

successful in his claim that the French rule that all practising veterinary surgeons be required to be members of the National Professional Society was an arbitrary restriction to the freedom of establishment.

The New Approach

Following this case law, especially *Reyners* and *Van Binsbergen*, the Commission decided that it was not necessary to issue directives for each individual trade and profession, especially in the case of establishment. The slow progress being made in many professions including lawyers was also a major factor in this decision. The directives that had already been worked on, and those in the pipe-line, were not rendered redundant and were, according to the Court of Justice, amplifications of or guidelines to the requirements of the Treaty articles, although work on a number was abandoned. A change of tactic was undertaken by the Commission which may overcome the problems of tackling one profession at a time. The new approach involved the enactment of general directives to apply to many professions — the Mutual Recognition Directives, considered next.

The Mutual Recognition of Diplomas Directive (89/48)   This applies to numerous professionals, except those subject to specific Community directives, who have completed a period (a minimum of three years) of post-secondary education and professional training, and who are regulated under national law or subject to the requirement of a diploma, or other similar professional qualifications the equivalent of a diploma. It applies, *inter alia*, to surveyors, chemists, town planners, chartered colourists, shipbrokers, foresters, accountants and biologists. It applies to professionally qualified persons as opposed to those who have completed only the university or college element of instruction, and includes workers, not just the self-employed.

The basic principle, contained in Art 3 of the directive, denies Member State authorities the right to refuse the rights of entry and practice of a profession on the ground that the holder does not possess the appropriate national qualifications. It does not allow absolute freedom to those who have qualified in one Member State to practise in any other Member State but subjects this right to means, under Art 4(b), by which the Member State can satisfy itself that the professional concerned is in fact qualified or experienced enough to operate in the host Member State. These means are in the form of requiring the would-be entrant to show evidence of experience and to complete either a period of supervised training in the host state (an adaptation period), or an examination of his knowledge appropriate to that required (an aptitude test) (Art 4(1)(a) and (b)). One or the other only can be required by the Member State, as they are in reality derogations from the principle of the directive where the training in the home State differs substantially from that in the host State.

The Member States remain free under the terms of the directive, to regulate the conduct and organisation of the professions as they see fit. The rules would apply to nationals of all the Member States who become members of a profession, regardless of country of origin. They will now, however, be subject to pressure for change induced by the *Gebhard* and *Säger* cases.

A clear distinction is made between the legal and other professions. The directive requires that, for professionals other than lawyers, the Member States should offer the entrant the choice of completing either the adaptation period or the test. However, Art 4(1)(b) provides that 'for professions whose practice requires precise knowledge of national law and in respect of which the provision of advice and/or assistance concerning national law is an essential and constant aspect of the professional activity, the host Member State may stipulate either an adaptation period or an aptitude test'. All Member States have provided an aptitude test for lawyers, with the exception of Denmark and in Northern Ireland.

Once the applicant has satisfied Art 4 and becomes established in the Member State, he or she is then entitled under Art 7(1) to use the professional title of the host State.

The second directive on mutual recognition   Directive 92/51, the second directive on mutual recognition of professional qualifications, was passed by the Council on 24 July 1992. It applies to occupations not covered by the first directive, i.e., those not dependent on higher educational qualifications but secondary and shorter, i.e., not degree level, post-secondary, education.

Like the first directive, Directive 89/48, it does not cover occupations already provided for by Community directives. Furthermore, it will not apply to regulated occupations covered by Directive 89/48.

A new Directive for the establishment of lawyers has now been enacted. The lawyers home title Directive (98/5 OJ 1998 L77/36) provides under Art 2 that any lawyer shall be entitled to pursue on a permanent basis, in any other Member State, under his home-country professional title as an independent or salaried lawyer. To practise, lawyers need only register with the competent authority in the host State on the basis of their registration in the home Member State (Art 3). Article 5 provides that the host lawyer may give advice on the law of his home Member State, on Community law, on international law and on the law of the host Member State. They must comply with the rules of procedure applicable in the national courts. Article 5(3) provides that activities relating to the representation or defence of a client in legal proceedings may be reserved to lawyers practising under the professional title of that State, where the host State law provides for this. The State may require lawyers practising under their home-country professional titles to work in conjunction with a lawyer who practises before the judicial authority in question and who would, where necessary, be answerable to that authority. In addition, access to supreme courts may be reserved to specialist lawyers.

Article 6 provides that in addition to the professional rules of the home State, a lawyer practising under his home-country professional title shall be subject to the same rules of professional conduct as lawyers practising under the relevant professional title of the host Member State in respect of all the activities he pursues in its territory.

Article 10 provides that a lawyer practising under his home-country professional title who has effectively and regularly pursued for a period of at least three years an activity in the host Member State in the law of that State including Community law shall, with a view to gaining admission to the profession of lawyer in the host Member State, be exempted from the conditions set out in Art 4(1)(b) of Directive 89/48/EEC. There are detailed rules on providing the necessary proof of practise, training and qualifications.

This so called third approach provides an easier way of acquiring the professional title of the host Member State and in effect circumvents the necessity under the Directive 89/48 to undertake the aptitude test to establish in another Member State. The reason given for providing this is that it was primarily directed at experienced professionals, for whom an aptitude test would constitute an obstacle on account of the time that has elapsed since they obtained their qualifications but it is hard to see how it would not be used by lawyers of any length of service.

Provision of Services

The provision of services is associated more with the areas of banking, company law, insurance and legal services. The provision of services can also be effected without having to leave the home country or enter the host country by either the provider or receiver of services as was the case of telephone sales in *Alpine Investments BV v Minister of Finance* (case 384/93). Broadcasting and information services are particularly important areas. The considerations in respect of services are the particular problems arising in respect of local requirements and their suitability to the temporary provision of services, and the scope of the term 'services', which has been held by the Court of Justice to include the recipients of services and has also impinged on the field of education and training in the Member States.

General requirements   Article 50 (old 60) of the EC Treaty states that services may be provided under the same conditions as are imposed by the State on its own nationals; but this gives rise to problems, in that some rules may not be relevant to the temporary provision of services, especially some of the professional rules.

In *Ministère Public* v *Van Wesemael*, a Belgian was prosecuted under a Belgian law for using a French employment agency and not one registered in Belgium, unless it operated in conjunction with a registered Belgian agency, to obtain the services of a variety artist in Belgium. The Court of Justice held that since the agency was registered in one Member State, it was contrary to Community law for another State to restrict its right to provide services in that country.

Local residence   In *Van Binsbergen* it was held that professional rules for the provision of services such as the requirement that advocates must be resident for professional purposes within the jurisdiction of certain courts, would be justified only if they were applied indiscriminately as between nationals and non-nationals of that Member State, and if they could be objectively justified and were proportionate to the aims.

In *Commission* v *Germany (Re Insurance Services)*, the Court of Justice held that Member States were under a duty not only to eliminate all discrimination based on nationality, but also all restrictions on the free provision of services based on the ground that the provider is established in another Member State. It also emphasised that all those national rules which apply to the self-employed permanently established in a Member State will not necessarily apply automatically to those 'activities of a temporary character which are carried out by enterprises established in other Member States'.

It has been shown in case law that a form of reverse discrimination, by which nationals are subject to the restrictive home rules but Community lawyers providing services are not, is acceptable in Community law. In the case, it was held that the residence requirement was not justified. Laws applying to the temporary provision of services must be:

(a)   justified by imperative reason relating to the public interest; and

(b)   the public interest is not already protected by the rules of the State of establishment; and

(c)   the same result cannot be obtained by less restrictive means.

Cases in respect of the directive providing for the provision of services by lawyers demonstrate this.

Directive 77/249   The directive is limited to the recognition of practising lawyers from Member States, who must be accepted on the basis that the training of lawyers in other Member States is as strict as in the host State

The directive should not interfere with the rules relating to a permanent provision of services by either home or established Community lawyers.

Article 4(1) dispenses with residence and registration requirements for 'the representation of a client in legal proceedings'.

Article 4(4) states that, where justifiable, the same rules of conduct apply to those providing services as apply to nationals.

Article 4(2) provides that lawyers providing services in judicial proceedings are required to observe both sets of rules of professional conduct, which means that lawyers must observe the rules of both the home and host States.

Article 5 subjects the right to provide services to national rules relating to the introduction of a lawyer to a particular court, and to the requirement that the guest lawyer works in conjunction with a home-admitted lawyer. Specifically it states:

> For the pursuit of activities relating to the representation of a client in legal proceedings, a Member State may require lawyers . . . to work in conjunction with a lawyer who practises before the judicial authority in question and who would, where necessary, be answerable to that authority . . . .

The requirements of Directive 77/249 were specifically considered in *Commission* v *Germany (Re Lawyers Services)*. The Court of Justice held that local rules were acceptable but could not go beyond the strict requirements of Community law so as to become a hindrance to free movement. It further held that a requirement to have local lawyers alongside at all times, and a requirement for a lawyer to live locally when only providing services were far too restrictive and therefore a breach of the Treaty.

In *Commission* v *France (Re Lawyers Services)*, similar considerations applied. In this case, provisions of national legislation requiring lawyers to act in conjunction with a member of the French College of Advocates when practising before authorities or bodies with no judicial function, and when acting in situations where French law does not require the compulsory presence of a lawyer, and rules requiring any lawyer appearing before a regional court in civil cases, where it is compulsory to be represented by a legally qualified advocate, to be a member of the Bar of that court or authorised to plead before it, were all held to be contrary to Art 59 (now 49). The rule of territorial exclusivity complained of was not justified by Art 5 of directive 77/249, and could not be applied to activities of a temporary nature carried out by lawyers established in another Member State, although they might still apply to national lawyers.

In the case of *Säger* v *Dennemeyer*, the Court of Justice has moved further in the development of a rule which prevents the restriction of services from other Member States but may still persist to limit activities of the home providers of services. Dennemeyer wished to provide patent services in Germany, something requiring a licence whose issue was restricted. His right to obtain a licence was challenged by a German Patent agent but D claimed a breach of Art 49 (old 59). The rule was non-discriminatory in that it applied to all patent agents regardless of residence. The Court held that not just discriminatory rules are prohibited, but any rules which are liable to prohibit or otherwise impede persons providing a service which they already lawfully do in the state of their establishment. To be allowed, such rules must satisfy the criteria that they be: justified, with no other rules already protecting the public interest and proportionate. It was suggested by the Court that Member States may not apply the same requirements for establishment as those providing services only, thus maintaining a distinction between these two forms of freedom, however the case of *Gebhard* considered early seems to cast doubt on this view. The rules in this area now very much resemble the rule of reason in the *Cassis de Dijon* case for the free movement of goods.

Scope

(a) *Receivers of services*   The Court of Justice has widened the scope of the freedom to provide services by holding that this freedom covers not only the provider of services, but also the recipient of services. *Luisi* v *Ministero del Tesoro* concerned a prosecution for taking money out of the country to pay for tourism and medical treatment abroad, contrary to Italian currency regulations. These were held by the Court of Justice to be payments for services, thus coming under the provisions of the EEC Treaty, payments being a fundamental freedom of the Community (Arts 49 and 50 (old 59 and 60), and Art 12 (old 6) EC).

Cowan v *French Treasury* concerned a refusal by the French Criminal Injuries Compensation Board to allow a claim for compensation in France by a British tourist who was mugged outside the Paris Metro, on the grounds that he was not French, not a resident in France and was not a member of a country which had a reciprocal agreement with France. The Court of Justice held that the protection of the person from harm on the same basis as nationals, including compensation for harm actually suffered, was a corollary of the freedom of movement. Therefore, Art 12 (old 6) of the Treaty applies directly to protect the Community citizen.

(b) *Education*   The freedom of movement may exist for persons other than workers and the self-employed as a result of other provisions of the Treaty and secondary legislation. For example, *Gravier* v *City of Liège* concerned the decision that the fee charged to foreign students for vocational training courses, but not to nationals, was contrary to Community law. The decision is unclear as to whether it was decided on the basis of old Art 59 (now 49) as well as Art 6 (now 12) of the EC Treaty.

In *Blaizot*, it was held that Community rules meant that Member States could not discriminate in favour of nationals in the payment of fees for vocational courses, which included university education. The same does not apply in favour of maintenance grants.

Belgian State v *Humbel* concerned the payment of a fee as in the case of *Gravier*, but this time for secondary education which involved elements of vocational and general study. The general education was held not to be a service as it was a part of the education policy of the Member State and therefore not subject to Community regulation. If it were part of the overall training, however, it would be considered vocational and therefore covered in respect of the fees but not the maintenance grant.

The latest case of *Wirth* seems to set the limits of this. It involved a question from a German court of whether courses available in an institute of higher education had to be classified as services under Art 50 (old 60). A German national was attempting to get a grant from German authorities to study in Holland. The Court of Justice held that courses given in a University or institute of higher education which is financed essentially out of public funds do not constitute services within the meaning of Art 50 (old 60) of the EC Treaty. Thus Member States remain able to determine their own system of grants and so discriminate against non-nationals. The conclusion would seem to be that access to institutions may be covered as are tuition fees but grants are not.

GENERAL RIGHTS OF FREE MOVEMENT

Wider general rights have been introduced with the coming into force of three directives giving general rights of residence. These are:

(a)   Directive 90/364 (OJ 1990 L180/26), which grants a general right of residence to all those not covered by existing legislation.

(b)   Directive 90/365 (OJ 1990 L180/28), which grants the right of residence to employees and self-employed persons who have ceased their occupational activity and is the equivalent of Regulation 1408/71.

These two directives are both subject to the provisions, where relevant, of Directives 64/221 and 68/360 and should have been implemented by 30 June 1992. Persons must be covered by sickness and accident insurance and must have sufficient resources from income or a pension so as not to be a burden on the social security system of the host State. They also apply to the members of the worker's family, irrespective of nationality.

(c)   Directive 90/366, on the right of residence for students. This subsequently was annulled by the Court of Justice on 7 July 1992 because it was based on the wrong Treaty article. (See the case of *European Parliament v Council (Students Residence Directive)*.) It has been re-issued under Art 7 (now 14) as Directive 93/96.

QUESTIONS

Problem questions are most frequently asked in this area of Community law, although it is quite possible to ask essay questions.

In the area of free movement of persons, the issues would typically include the status and rights of an individual as a worker in the circumstances of a deportation order for some questionable activity, such as drug abuse or prostitution, or membership of or assocation with political or otherwise radical organisations. Thus procedural rights concerning the actual deportation are important.

There might also be elements of the question concerned with the members of the worker's family who may be, and often are, any nationality under the sun. Thus, issues such as the dependency of relatives and of children (including grown-up children), their rights to stay in the country and to obtain social security or other benefits, education and or training and grants for these activities, may also need to be considered.

Hence there may be a wide variety of things to look for and to answer, and therefore the presentation of an answer is crucial. In other words 'Technique'! You've heard it before, but make a plan!

1.   'The Court of Justice has certainly interpreted the provisions of Articles 48–51 (now 39–42) EC and the implementing legislation, in a rather more liberal manner than would be dictated by a purely functional view of the Treaty based on its economic motives.' (Wyatt and Dashwood.) Discuss.

This is a very broad question and can cover a lot of ground. You must therefore plan carefully to make sure you are covering relevant material.

The answer will require you to outline:

(a)   the rights provided by Arts 39–42 (old 48–51); and
(b)   the coverage of the relevant secondary legislation, which you must therefore identify.

Then two further statements are made in the question which must be discussed:

(c)   the view that the Court of Justice has been liberal in its interpretation of the provisions; and

(d) the fact that this is clearly more liberal than taking a purely functional view of the economic motives of the Treaty.

They can be treated in the order given, but it seems best to tackle the functional economic view first and then to give examples of the Court's liberal interpretations. In this way, a form of control or basic position is established first which can be used in comparison with the later case law. Alternatively, it would be just as valid to give the examples first from the case law of the liberal interpretations and compare thse with how a purely functional view would look. Both achieve a correct end result.

The economic motives would seem to suggest that it is only the economies of the Community and the Member States that are important: the granting of individual rights is incidental and just a way of ensuring that the commodity of labour can be imported and exported to suit the demands of European capital, in order to take advantage of the free market and so that Member States can compete equally in attracting and securing labour. The personal rights given to workers are, then, secondary to the prime objectives in setting up the internal market and ensuring that business in the Member States is operating under the same rules. Under this view, it would be expected that the rights would be subject to the minimum interpretation possible to give effect to the rights granted — for example, that there would be no right to be in other Member States while unemployed and looking for work, or that the Member States have complete freedom to discriminate in the public service, or that rights would not be extended to members of the family or to students. This functional view may be opposite to the rights recognised by the Court of Justice.

The contrasting view is that of the liberal interpretation. The Court of Justice clearly interprets all parts of the Treaty in a distinct style, using the so-called teleological approach. This means that specific measures are interpreted in the light of the objectives and goals of the Community and are not just subject to a literal interpretation of the words (see, for example, the case of *Hessische Knappschaft* v *Maison Singer*). It is clear that in respect of the free movement of workers, the Court of Justice has gone far beyond a literal or functional interpretation of the provisions and has, in its judgment, sought to give the widest possible interpretation to the rights provided.

You should tackle this part of the answer by giving selective examples. Just how many you choose may depend on how many you can remember or have time to include in your answer. The following are just my examples and the list is not exhaustive. Thus you could point out that Art 39 (old 48) and the secondary legislation has been held to provide the status of worker to those who are not employed in the host state and have entered for the express reason of searching for work (see the *Antonissen* and *Lebon* cases).

The general prohibition on discrimination was considered in the case of the two language teachers employed by the University of Venice (*Allué and Coonan v Università degli studi di Venezia*). This was held also to apply in circumstances where a rule was being imposed on both nationals and other Community citizens, and thus there was no direct discrimination. The public service provision in Art 39(4) (old 48(4)) has been restricted in two ways. First, once employed in the public service, there can be no discrimination in respect of the conditions of work and employment. Furthermore, entry is not restricted to levels of the public service which do not exercise power conferred by public law and safeguard the interests of the state. Such restrictions on the Member States' ability are not to be perceived from a functional view of the provision.

When we turn to the secondary legislation, even more surprising interpretations can be put forward. While it may be possible to perceive that a non-Community national spouse has the right to stay in a Member State after separation from the Community worker, as in *Diatta*, it is unlikely that one would realise from the legislation that the rights to the same treatment in social matters would include the right to the companionship of a cohabitee (see *Reed v The Netherlands*). The case law on Art 7(2) of Regulation 1612/68 has certainly demonstrated the very liberal interpretations that can be achieved by the Court of Justice. These include the right to many benefits for members of the family.

Finally, by way of example, is the extension of the term 'worker' to apply in specific circumstances to students? This is not to be perceived from a reading of the appropriate provisions, and took place even before the directives granting rights of residence were passed by the Council.

Thus there are clear indications that the Court of Justice has interpreted in a far more liberal manner than is dictated by a functional view.

2.   Arni and his girlfriend, Bertha, both German nationals, left Germany following convictions for the possession and supply of marijuana and came to the UK to look for work. After serious but unsuccessful attempts for six months to find work, Arni was so depressed that he started taking drugs again. He was caught and convicted of the possession of cocaine and sentenced to six months' imprisonment. On his release he was issued with an order for immediate deportation.

Bertha, in the meantime, had obtained work as a model for an art college, but because this was only for six hours a week and the income derived therefrom was minimal, she found it necessary to apply for social security assistance. Her application was, however, refused. Bertha was also issued with an order for immediate deportation.

The grounds given for the two deportations were the past and present convictions for drug offences and that their presence in the UK was contrary to public policy.

Advise Arni and Bertha of their rights under Community law.

In the case of free movement of workers problems, reference to the Treaty Preamble and Art 2 and, in particular, Art 3(c) (the reference to the abolition, as between Member States, of obstacles to freedom of movement for persons), would be a useful introduction to the area covered. The Court of Justice often uses these to determine the position of the Community in respect of the issues before it. Then it would be useful to outline briefly the scope of rights given by Art 39 (old 48) EC and secondary legislation (Regulation 1612/68 and Directives 64/221 and 68/360). There is usually no need to rewrite in full the actual provisions. A summary of their scope which sets out the context of the Community legal regime in this area should be acceptable.

Addressing the issues   The issues arising from the facts are the immediate deportation orders, the convictions of Arni and whether he is entitled to stay in the UK, the part-time work of Bertha and her right to claim social security.

Point-by-point answer   Both are German nationals, thus Community nationals, so they can avail themselves of the procedural rights in respect of entry into and deportation from a Member State. These rights apply to Community persons and do not specify Community workers (see Arts 5–9 of Directive 64/221).

Their procedural law rights in the face of the orders for immediate deportation are of first and immediate importance to Arni and Bertha. These should be dealt with before you decide whether they are workers, otherwise they will be deported and the substantive rights may be undermined. The deportations appear to be contrary to Community law. According to Directive 64/221, Art 7, the minimum period of notice for deportation for those already in the country is one month. Furthermore, they have rights of appeal or review of these decisions under Arts 8 and 9. Unless there is an immediate threat to the state, they have the right to stay in the country to await the result of the appeal. The cases of *Adoui and Cornuaille* and *Pecastaing* are relevant. In the case of Bertha, those decisions would clearly be applicable; whereas with Arni, his right to await the result of the appeal is less likely, due to his recent conviction for the possession of cocaine. Provided he is no serious and immediate threat, however, he should be allowed the period of one month before deportation.

Having averted the immediate deportations, you can now turn to the substantive issues of the problem. In order to avoid deportation following a consideration of the merits of the case, Arni must show a right to stay in the UK, which will be the case if he can be regarded as a worker. Is he a worker? He is not employed, but in limited circumstances those seeking work can be regarded as workers and obtain rights under Community law.

According to the *Antonissen* case, the Court of Justice held that Art 39(3) (old 48(3)) EC and Arts 1 and 5 of Regulation 1612/68 entail not only the freedom to enter and move freely in the host State but also the right to stay there for the purposes of seeking employment. But there are acceptable time limits to this right to seek work. Six months was held to be reasonable and unless there is a genuine chance of employment, the Member State may deport a person. It is likely that Arni will not be classified as having a right to continue to look for work because of his inability to find work in the past, his recent imprisonment and the unlikely possibility of finding work now. Therefore, deportation would seem to be justified under Community law.

Does Bertha have the right to stay? If she is a worker she can stay. She has only part-time work and needs social security, but this does not present a problem for the status of worker, according to the Court of Justice in the cases of *Levin* and *Kempf*. As a worker she is therefore afforded the rights, under Art 7 of Regulation 1612/68, to the same social and tax advantages as nationals. This has been held to include social security benefits in *Fiorini, Castelli*, and others. Therefore, unless there are compelling reasons for her deportation she has the right to stay as a worker.

Despite the fact that it is likely that Arni does not have his own right to stay, Bertha, as a worker, also derives rights in favour of her family and dependants under Community law (Regulation 1612/68, Arts 10–12). Can Arni benefit from these? They are not married and he is not part of the family or a dependent relative. As her boyfriend, can he obtain rights? The Court of Justice held in the *Reed* case that no direct rights as a cohabitee arise, but Bertha may be able to claim the companionship of Arni as one of her rights under Art 7(2) of Regulation 1612/68. Therefore, they will both be able to stay unless the grounds for deportation are nevertheless acceptable and override Bertha's right.

The reasons given for deportation are the convictions and presence contrary to public policy. Directive 64/221 has given further explanation to the grounds given to Member States of public policy grounds. Under Art 3(1), past convictions are not a sufficient ground for deportation unless the person is a seriously sufficient present threat (see *R v Bouchereau*). On this basis, Bertha has past convictions only and should not be subject to deportation. Arni, however, has recent convictions, and on balance it would probably be acceptable under Community law to deport him, considering the seriousness attached to the use of cocaine. If there is doubt, a reference under Art 234 (old 177) EC should be made to the Court of Justice, as this would be breaking new legal ground.

The final question in this chapter concerns the freedom to provide services. This may appear as a part of a longer question combined with issues concerning the freedom of workers.

3.   Boris runs a veterinary surgery in Luxembourg part-time, and has also set up a surgery in Trier, where he is self-employed in premises rented from the local authority. While the German authorities were investigating his protest that he was being charged more than German nationals renting similar premises from the local authority, they discovered that he had failed to register his practice as required, and also that he continued to practise in Luxembourg. They have now ordered that he should cease practising and have issued a deportation order. Boris holds all the appropriate Luxembourg qualifications for veterinary practice. Advise Boris as to his rights under Community law.

As with question 2 above, the first aspect to consider is that concerning the procedural rights to prevent the unlawful deportation before Boris's substantive rights can be considered. For the freedom to provide services and establishment, this is covered by Directive 73/148. As this provides the same rights as those relating to workers, refer to the comments in the question above. Thus, once his immediate deportation has been avoided, you can now consider what rights, if any, Boris has under the provisions relating to the free movement of persons.

At first sight, it is not entirely clear which set of provisions will be applicable to Boris. He is clearly self-employed, but both the freedom of establishment and the freedom to provide services seem to be relevant here. He has established a professional presence in the host state but continues to maintain his professional base in Luxembourg. Thus, on the face of it, there is no permanent establishment in Germany. It is clear, however, that he is providing services in Germany. The conclusion reached is important in order to determine exactly which rules of the host state and profession may be applicable and enforceable against Boris, and because the application of home rules may be stricter for establishment and not all home rules have been found by the Court of Justice to be suitable or acceptable for the provision of services.

The *Commission* v *Germany (Insurance Services)* case may be helpful in this respect. There it was held that the provision of services which included the setting-up of offices on a long-term basis and staffed by nationals of the host state, should be considered as establishment, even though the legal entity remained in the home state. The likely solution in this case is that Boris will be considered to be established in Germany, and may thus be subject to stricter home rules requirements. Article 43 (old 52) subjects establishment to the conditions laid down for nationals by the law of the country where such establishment takes place. However, as a result of the more recent cases of *Gebhard* (case 55/94) and *Säger* (case 76/90), and almost regardless of whether the provision of services or establishment is involved, any rules which hinder or make less attractive the exercise of the fundamental freedoms will be subject to the following four conditions. They must be:

   (a)   non-discriminatory in application;
   (b)   justified by imperative reason relating to the public interest;
   (c)   suitable to secure the objective sought; and
   (d)   proportional.

Whilst this is a matter for the national courts to decide, it is arguable the requirements do not meet the criteria and a reference to the Court of Justice might be necessary to settle the matter.

The other issues to consider are the higher rent charged for his premises, the failure to register and the order to cease practising. These will be taken in reverse order, as his right to practise is the most important, i.e., if he has no right to establish he need hardly be concerned with the failure to register and will no longer need to rent premises.

Apart from the fact that directives for the mutual recognition of veterinary qualifications have been passed (Directives 78/1026 and 78/1027), Art 43 (old 52) has been held in similar cases to be directly effective. In *Patrick* v *Minister for Cultural Affairs*, a British national had an architecture qualification which had been recognised by the French Ministry of Culture as equivalent to French qualifications required to practise architecture in France. The French refusal was contrary to Community law. Boris's right to establish must therefore be recognised.

The failure to register and the prohibition from practising in Germany because he continues to practise in Luxembourg, should not prevent Boris's establishment in Trier. In *Ordre Nationale des Vétérinaires de France* v *Auer*, an Austrian national with Italian veterinary qualifications was refused recognition by the competent authorities in France. Auer was successful in his claim that the French rule that all practising veterinary surgeons be required to be members of the National Professional Society was an arbitrary restriction on the freedom of establishment. This would therefore suggest that the failure to register should not prevent his right to establishment.

As far as maintaining two premises, it was held in *Ordre des Avocats au Barreau de Paris* v *Klopp*, that the Community rules may be diminished if the effects of the national rules are unfair in application, therefore a Member State cannot exclude a lawyer on the basis that he can only have one residence and cannot refuse entry because a lawyer maintains chambers elsewhere. The Court emphasised that while Member States are entitled to require that advocates comply with professional ethics and regulate their practices in such a way as to maintain sufficient contact with their clients, their regulations should not have the effect of preventing EC nationals from exercising their right of establishment in more than one centre of activity in EC territory. Boris therefore cannot be prevented from establishing in Germany because he continues his surgery in Luxembourg.

The higher rent being charged is clearly discriminatory, but is it a breach of Community law? Article 12 (old 6) EC generally prohibits discrimination on the grounds of nationality. In *Steinhauser v Biarritz*, Art 43 (old 52) in combination with old Art 7 EEC (now Art 12 EC) was interpreted to provide for the pursuit of establishment in the widest sense. In that case it applied to the renting of a hut which was refused to the applicant. In the case of Boris, it would certainly apply to the discrimination in the amount of rent being charged.

FURTHER READING

Bernard, N., 'Discrimination and Free Movement in EC Law' (1996) 45 ICLQ 82.

Daniele, L., 'Non-discriminatory Restrictions to the Free Movement of Persons' (1997) 22 EL Rev 191.

Foster, N., 'European Community Law and the Freedom of Lawyers in the United Kingdom and Germany' (1991) 40 ICLQ 607.

O'Keefe, D., 'The Free Movement of Persons and the Single Market' (1992) 17 EL Rev 3.

Plender, R., 'The Treaty of Amsterdam and the free movement of persons' (1998) 9 EBLR 400.

Roth, W., 'The European Community's Law on Services: Harmonisation' (1988) 25 CML Rev 35.

10 EC COMPETITION LAW

INTRODUCTION

Competition law is a necessary and an integral part of the Community and its policies. It is constructed to ensure the maintenance of the common market. One of the aims of the internal market is to establish and maintain European-wide competition to stimulate the entire economy of the Community for both the domestic and world markets. In order to retain fair competition, more so in a free market, some form of intervention on the part of the state is required. The Community is distinctly interventionist and increasingly so in order to outlaw abuses of industry to the detriment of consumers and the market. However, too much intervention hinders growth and results in inefficient small scale production which cannot benefit from the economies of scale. Therefore the Community must tread a middle path.

This chapter considers the competition rules of Arts 81 and 82 (old 85 and 86) and the relationship between these two articles. It is also concerned with the mergers policy of the Community and briefly examines the procedural law of competition law and merger law.

POLICY OBJECTIVES

The broad policy objectives are to maintain, and even encourage, competition for the benefit of the Community, to achieve a single market and the integration of the Community, to encourage economic activity among small- and medium-size enterprises and to maximise efficiency by allowing the free flow of goods and resources. At the same time it must be ensured that companies do not become too competitive so as to be able to eliminate competition and thus start to dominate a market. Action is concentrated on the larger players in the market rather than the small- and medium-size business enterprises.

EC competition rules are generally designed to intervene to prevent agreements which fix prices, or conditions or the supply of products, to prohibit agreements which carve up territories, and to prevent abuses of market power, which have the effect of removing real competition, and controlling mergers, which would also remove competition.

The Broad Legislative Outline

The Preamble of the EC Treaty refers to the 'removal of existing obstacles [which] calls for concerted action in order to guarantee steady expansion, balanced trade and fair competition'.

Article 2 includes 'by establishing a common market and an economic and monetary union and by implementing the common policies . . . referred to in Articles 3 and 4 (old 3a), to promote . . . a harmonious and balanced development of economic activities'.

Article 3(g) of the EC Treaty lists among the activities of the Community, 'a system of ensuring that competition in the internal market is not distorted'.

Article 10 (old 5) has also been pleaded with Art 3(g) and Art 81 (old 85) as a general principle of law supporting the argument that competition law also applies in respect of the Member States and not just undertakings, so that they are prohibited from encouraging or requiring acts or conduct by companies which may distort competition in the Community.

These basic provisions are expanded in three sets of rules: one relating to the activities of legal persons, i.e., the business undertakings; one relating to anti-dumping measures; and one relating to the activities of the Member States. This chapter will be concerned only with the private undertakings, to which two provisions are applicable: Art 81 (old 85), for agreements between cartels involving more than one entity; and Art 82 (old 86), concerned with dominant positions, dealing predominantly with one entity but also applicable to one or more undertakings.

Application and Interpretation

The Commission is given the task of ensuring that competition in the Community is not distorted by companies setting up their own rules and obstacles to trade, thus replacing the national rules and obstacles which the Community is trying to abolish with the free movement of goods provisions, which seek to prevent the creation of artificial barriers to trade on the national boundaries. The two go hand in hand, you can't have one without ensuring you have the other. To have prevented the Member States, on the one hand, from restricting the movement of goods just to allow private companies to do it by their agreements and practices, would defeat the objectives of the first policy. Some companies are in better positions to divide the market than are some Member States, because their turnover is the same as, or greater than, the GNP of some of the EU Member States.

The application of the rules by the Commission and the interpretation of the rules of the Court of Justice have not been done in isolation by looking at the provisions alone, but have been carried out in the light of the objectives of competition policy, which are applied in the light of the general objective of the Treaty. In *ICI Commercial Solvents* v *Commission* the Court of Justice held:

> The prohibitions in Articles 85 and 86 [now 81 and 82] must be interpreted and applied in the light of Article 3(f) [now 3(g)] of the Treaty which provides that the activities of the Community shall include the institution of a system ensuring that competition is not distorted, and Article 2 of the Treaty which gives the Community the task of promoting 'throughout the Community harmonious development of economic activities'.

Metro v *Commission* is also a good example, whereby the Commission, in pursuit of a goal, was forced to rely on Art 2 EEC to justify particular decisions reached. The agreements in this case were deemed to satisfy competition rules because they helped to maintain employment.

ARTICLE 81

Article 81 (old 85) EC deals with restrictive practices. It sets out the prohibitions and the consequence of failure to observe them. It also provides a framework by which exemptions from the prohibitions can be obtained.

Article 81(1) (old 85(1)) prohibits agreements between undertakings, decisions by associations of undertakings and concerted practices which may affect trade between the Member States and which have as their object or effect the prevention, restriction or distortion of competition within the common market.

Article 81(2) (old 85(2)) provides that any agreements or decisions prohibited pursuant to Art 81 (old 85) shall automatically be void.

Article 81(3) (old 85(3)) concerns the exemptions.

Article 81 (old 85) has been subject to some considerable definition in the jurisprudence of the Court of Justice, and was held to be capable of producing direct effects in *BRT* v *SABAM*.

Article 81(1)

'Agreements between undertakings' The term 'undertakings' includes both natural and legal persons as independent or complementary economic actors. According to the Commission decision in *Polypropylene Cartel Community v ICI*, this includes any entity engaged in economic or commercial activities.

The term 'agreements' is not limited to legally enforceable agreements. It is not the form of the agreement that is important from the Commission's point of view but its effect on competition. Therefore a broad interpretation is given to the term 'agreements', and includes non-binding agreements, as in, for example, the *Polypropylene* decision. The term applies to both horizontal agreements (where the parties are at the same level of the economic process) and vertical agreements (where the parties are at different levels of the economic process), as is illustrated by the rulings of the Court of Justice in *Consten and Grundig v Commission*, and *Société Technique Minière v Maschinenbau Ulm* (the 'STM case').

'Decisions by associations of undertakings' This has been held to include a trade association held liable for behaviour by its members in *AROW v BNIC*, where the Bureau National Interprofessionel de Cognac was fined because it had fixed a minimum distribution price for cognac, arguing that this was necessary to guarantee quality. The Commission decided that, given all the other quality control measures which existed in the cognac industry, this argument could not be sustained.

Non-binding recommendations made by trade associations may also amount to decisions, as held in *Vereeniging van Cementhandelaren (Cement (Association) v Commission*.

'Concerted practices' This term is interpreted widely in *ICI v Commission (Aniline Dyes)*. ICI was the first among a number of undertakings, accounting for 85 per cent of the market, to raise prices. The companies all said that the price coordination was simply a reflection of parallel behaviour in an oligopolistic market, where each producer followed the price leader. The Court of Justice held that this was a concerted practice arising out of coordination, which became apparent from the behaviour of the participants and which was designed to replace the risk of competition and the hazards of competitors' spontaneous reactions.

In *Suiker Unie v Commission*, the Community's main sugar producers had made deliveries in Holland only with the assent of the producers in that country, so as to weaken considerably the competitive pressure which unrestricted sugar imports would have engendered. They said they had not agreed to any plan to that effect, and hence there was no concerted practice.

The Court of Justice held that there was no need for an actual plan, and a concerted practice included:

> Any direct or indirect contact between such operators, the object or effect of which is either to influence the conduct on the market of an actual or potential competitor or to disclose to such a competitor the course of conduct which they themselves have decided to adopt or contemplate adopting on the market.

However, in *Ahlström Oy et al.* v *Commission* (cases C-89, 104, 114, 116-7/85 and C-125–9/85) (Woodpulp Cartel cases) the Court of Justice held that the burden be placed on the Commission to prove a concerted practice by establishing 'a firm, precise and consistent body of evidence' that a concerted practice existed. Parallel price increases would not satisfy this unless there was no other plausible explanation for them. Agreements which were taken by the parties within their trade association to fix recommended prices were upheld as restricting competition contrary to Art 81(1) (old 85(1)).

Even unilateral conduct on the part of a manufacturer has been deemed by the Court of Justice to be capable of amounting to an agreement or a concerted practice. In *Ford* v *Commission*, the refusal of Ford Germany to supply right-hand drive cars to Britain was held to form part of the contractual relations between the undertaking and its dealers.

Types of prohibited agreements Article 81(1) (old 85(1)) lists particular examples of agreements, etc., which have as their object the restriction of competition. These include:

(a) price-fixing arrangements (see for example, the *Cement Association* and *AROW* v *BNIC* cases);

(b) market sharing agreements (see for example, the *Consten* and *Grundig* case);

(c) agreements which apply dissimilar conditions to equivalent transactions with other trading parties, thereby placing them at a competitive disadvantage (see for example, the *Metro* case); and

(d) requirements that the conclusion of contracts is subject to the acceptance by other parties of supplementary obligations, which, by their nature or according to commercial usage, have no connection with the subject of such contracts.

An example of the last of the conditions listed would be the imposition by a producer on a distributor of an export ban. See, as an example, the *Suiker Unie* case.

The Object or Effect of Restricting Competition

Object   Even if, as a result of considering the terms of the agreement, it is
clear that the object is to restrict competition, it is still necessary to consider
the economic effects of the agreement to determine whether it is caught by
Art 81(1) (old 85(1)), as it may fall within the *de minimis* doctrine, or it may
have no effect on trade between the Member States (see the *STM* case).

Effect   If it is not established that the object of the agreement or practice is
to restrict or distort competition, it is necessary for the Commission to
undertake an examination of the effect of the agreement on the market.

In *Brasserie de Haecht SA v Wilkin*, the Court of Justice said that the
agreement, decision or concerted practice had to be examined in the context
of the market in which it operated, and in the context of the effects
surrounding its implementation. This entails scrutiny of the relevant product market and the relevant geographical market, the impact of national
laws upon competition, the existence of intellectual property rights, and the
level of competition on the rest of the market and the behaviour of other
competitors.

The Commission therefore has to pay close attention to the definition of
the market for the purposes of competition law. As a result of the case law
of the Court of Justice the Commission has now presented its methodology
in a 'Notice on the Definition of the Relevant Market' (OJ 1997 C372/5).

'Which may affect trade between the Member States'   'Trade' is given a wide
definition and encompasses the production and distribution of goods, trade
in agricultural produce, and the services sector (including banking, insurance and professional services). Even opera singers have been held to be
involved in trade.

Consten and Grundig v Commission was concerned with exclusive territorial sales licences which served to encourage the volume of trade. The
Court of Justice held that the contract between Grundig and Consten, on
the one hand by preventing undertakings other than Consten from import-
ing Grundig products into France, and on the other by prohibiting Consten
from re-exporting those products to other countries of the Common
Market, indisputably adversely affected the flow of trade between the
Member States.

Brasserie de Haecht SA v Wilkin concerned an agreement which stipulated
that Wilkin were obliged to obtain all their supplies of liquor, beer and soft
drinks for the café and for their own personal use exclusively from the de
Haecht brewery, in return for loans. The agreement was held, when viewed
in the light of a combination of the objective, factual or legal circumstances,
to appear to be capable of having some influence, direct or indirect, on

trade between Member States, of being conducive to the partitioning of the market, and of hampering the economic competition sought by the Treaty.

In *Vereeniging van Cementhandelaren* v *Commission*, the Court of Justice upheld the Commission decision declaring that an agreement of a Dutch national cement dealers association extending over the whole of the territory of a Member State, by its very nature has the effect of reinforcing the dividing of markets on a national basis.

Exemptions from Article 81(1)

Apart from the justifications considered below under Art 81(3) (old 85(3)), certain agreements have been deemed by the Court of Justice and Commission not to fall within the category of a 'restriction of competition'. These judicial exemptions from the application of Art 81 (old 85) are also referred to as coming within an type of 'rule of reason' in competition law.

Objective necessity   There are cases where the restrictions are objectively necessary for the performance of a particular type of contract, as in franchising agreements. In *Pronuptia de Paris* v *Schillgalis*, the Court of Justice held that the compatibility of distribution franchise agreements with Art 81(1) (old 85(1)) depended on the clauses contained in the agreements, and on the economic context in which they are included.

Clauses which are indispensable to prevent the know-how and assistance provided by the franchisor benefiting competitors, and clauses which implement the control necessary for the preservation of the identity and reputation of the organisation represented in the trade mark, do not constitute restrictions on competition within the meaning of Art 81(1) (old 85(1)). However, clauses which fix prices or which effect a partitioning of markets between franchisor and franchise or between franchises, and which are capable of affecting trade between Member States, constitute restrictions on competition contrary to Art 81(1) (old 85(1)).

High commercial risks   The Court of Justice has held that where the commercial risk undertaken by a distributor, licensee or franchise is great, some exclusivity may be conferred on him to induce him into the market. In *Société Technique Minière* v *Maschinenbau Ulm*, the French company, La Technique Minière, purchased 37 levelling machines, and were given exclusive sales rights for the territory of France. Maschinenbau were not to compete. The Court of Justice held that due to the high cost of the product and its specialised nature, the agreements would not offend Art 81 (old 85).

Quality control   Cases involving selective distribution systems, such as in *Metro* v *Commission* to ensure the quality of sales and service, to benefit the consumer in terms of safety of electrical goods and to maintain employment in an important industry, would not breach Art 81 (old 85).

The de minimis doctrine   The doctrine of *de minimis* means that some agreements which affect competition may nevertheless not be caught by Art 81 (old 85) because they do not have an appreciable affect on intra-Community trade. It was first formulated in *Völk v Vervaecke*, involving an exclusive dealership to Vervaecke for 80 washing machines monthly. The Court of Justice held that an exclusive dealing agreement, even with absolute territorial protection, may, having regard to the weak position of the persons concerned on the market in question in the area covered by the absolute protection, escape the prohibition, i.e., as having too small an effect really to affect trade.

The Commission issued a Notice on Agreements of Minor Importance (OJ 1997 C372/13) setting out the criteria which will be used in determining whether a practice may affect trade between Member States. The basic criteria are that the undertakings have less than a 5 per cent market share in the Community as a whole. In line with a general concern which has arisen and has been responded to by the Commission about vertical agreements, the threshold for vertical agreements has been raised to 10 per cent of market share. It remains 5 per cent for horizontal agreements. Market shares below this remove agreements from the scope of Art 81 (old 85), unless they are serious or intended breaches of the competition rules or they fix prices. Even above these thresholds, small- and medium-size enterprise agreements will be considered leniently by the Commission. Although such notices are not binding law and certainly cannot amend the Treaty provisions, they are a clear indication that providing an agreement falls within the exception allowed, the Commission will not take action under the competition rules. The general concern about the rigidity of the present application of the rules to vertical agreements (see *Consten and Grundig*) will most probably lead to the issue of an umbrella block exemption replacing the individual ones presently applying and which are briefly mentioned below.

Article 81(2)

Article 81(2) (old 85(2)) provides that: 'Any agreements or decisions prohibited pursuant to this article shall be automatically void.' In the *STM* case the Court of Justice held that this provision applies only to those parts of the agreement affected by the prohibition in Art 81(1) (old 85(1)), or to the agreement as a whole if those parts are not severable from the agreement itself.

Article 81(3)

Article 81(3) (old 85(3)) provides:

> The provisions of paragraph 1 may . . . be declared inapplicable in the
> case of:
> — any agreement or category of agreements between undertakings;
> — any decision or category of decisions by associations of undertakings;
> — any concerted practice or category of concerted practices;
> which contributes to improving the production or distribution of goods
> or to promoting technical or economic progress, while allowing con-
> sumers a fair share of the resulting benefit, and which does not:
>   (a)   impose on the undertakings concerned restrictions which are not
> indispensable to the attainment of these objectives;
>   (b)   afford such undertakings the possibility of eliminating competi-
> tion in respect of a substantial part of the products in question.

The parties to such agreements must make an individual notification to
the Commission under Art 81(3) (old 85(3)) and Art 4 of Regulation 17/62
considered below. Failure to notify means that the agreement would be
void and the parties would be liable to fines. Once notified, the Commission
will consider whether the agreement can be exempted and issue an official
decision which can be challenged under Art 230 (old 173) before the Court
of First Instance.

In order to avoid unnecessary work for all involved, common agreements
may be exempted from the prohibition in Art 81(2) (old 85(2)) by virtue of
a block exemption for typical types of agreement, sometimes within certain
industries or areas. In such cases there is no need to apply for individual
notification.

Block exemptions   These set out types of restrictions or provisions which do
not infringe Art 81(1) (old 85(1)) or which would be exempted. The
following are examples of such exemptions. It would not be usual to learn
the details of these.

* Regulation 1983/83 (OJ 1983 L173/1) on exclusive distribution agreements.
* Regulation 1984/83 (OJ 1983 L173/5) on exclusive purchasing agreements.
* Regulation 123/85 (OJ 1985 L15/16) on distribution agreements in
respect of motor vehicles.
* Regulation 417/85 (OJ 1985 L53/1) on specialisation agreements.
* Regulation 418/85 (OJ 1985 L53/5) on research and development
agreements.

- Regulation 4087/88 (OJ 1988 L359/46) on the application of Article 85(3) (now 81(3)) to categories of franchise agreements.
- Regulation 240/96 (OJ 1996 L31/2) on technology transfer agreements.

Comfort letters   Instead of taking every individual application for negative clearance or exemption through to a decision, the Commission frequently settles cases informally by way of a so-called comfort letter. A comfort letter is simply a notification to the parties that, in the Commission's opinion, the agreement does not infringe Art 81(1) (old 85(1)), or that it qualifies for exemption. The Commission then closes the file after sending the comfort letter.

These comfort letters do not bind the national courts or produce legal effects in national law. This was made clear in a series of cases involving perfume manufacturers: *Guerlain SA, Rochas SA, Lancôme SA, Lanvin SA* and *Nina Ricci SA*. Obviously, a statement of this nature from the Commission would be of persuasive authority, but a national court would not necessarily be bound by it. In the action by French shops who were unable to get supplies from Lancôme and Guerlain, the Court of Justice rejected the view that the comfort letters provided a defence to such actions against the refusal to supply.

The case of *Koninklijke Vereeniging ter Bevorderung van de Belangen des Boekhandels* v *Free Record Shop BV*, Free Record Shop Holding NV concerns competition agreements which were concluded prior to Regulation 17 and notified to the Commission prior to the deadline of 1 November 1962. Normally such agreements would carry provisional validity until the Commission had either given positive clearance or had taken a negative decision holding them to be contrary to EC law. Many agreements, similar to this one about the retail price maintenance for books, have continued in this legal limbo ever since. The Commission is simply unable to investigate all of them and many are left without interference. The agreement in question, however, had been challenged as contrary to Art 81 (old 85) EC by a shop selling below the imposed retail price. Having lain dormant for so long, questions about the continued validity were raised by the national court. The Court of Justice held that until the Commission decides one way or the other the agreement remains provisionally valid even if it has been amended but only in so far as the amendments render the agreement less restrictive. More restrictive amendments would end the validity unless these were severable from the original agreement.

Conflict of Community Law and National Law

The question of the resolution of potential conflicts between EC and national competition law and the problem of double jeopardy, were addressed in *Walt Wilhelm* v *Bundeskartellamt*. The Federal Cartel Authority in Germany and the Commission had instituted proceedings against Walt Wilhelm for breach of competition rules. Walt Wilhelm submitted that the Bundeskartellamt could not maintain proceedings for an offence which was at the same time the object of investigation by the Commission. The Court of Justice ruled that conflicts between Community law and national law in the matter of cartels must be resolved by applying the principle that Community law takes precedence.

In order to clarify the procedure and assist national courts in considering cases which involve issues of EC competition law, the Commission has issued a Notice to National Courts on the Application of Articles 85 and 86 (now 81 and 82) (1993 OJ C39/5) setting out the procedure which should be followed. The notice also indicates that national courts should take notice of 'comfort letters' although they remain non-binding.

ARTICLE 82

Article 82 (old 86) applies where individual organisations have a near monopoly position or share an oligopolistic market with a small number of other companies, and take unfair advantage of this position to the detriment of the market, other companies and the end consumers. Article 82 (old 86) provides that the abuse by one or more undertakings of a dominant position within the common market or in a substantial part of it is prohibited, in so far as it affects trade between Member States. The Court of First Instance confirmed in the *Re Italian Flat Glass* (cases T-68, 77-8/89) that Art 82 (old 86) could apply to activities of more than one undertaking where the companies together could constitute a dominant position. Oligopolies may also find their activities being considered under the Merger Regulation, considered in the text below. The requirements are, a dominant position, abuse of it and the effect between Member States. Article 82 (old 86) then goes on to give specific examples of such abuse.

A Dominant Position

For Art 82 (old 86) to be applicable, there must be domination of the common market or a substantial part of it. This requires a definition of the relevant market by reference to both the product and the geographical area.

The Court of Justice, in *United Brands* v *Commission*, defined a dominant position as:

> a position of economic strength enjoyed by an undertaking which enables it to hinder the maintenance of effective competition on the relevant

market by allowing it to behave to an appreciable extent independently of its competitors and customers and ultimately of consumers.

Defining the relevant product market The test for the relevant product market concerns itself with the interchangeability of the products or product substitution. A number of factors can influence this. For example:

(a)   Cross elasticity, i.e., if the price of one product rises, will consumers change to another, e.g., lager for beer, frozen vegetables for fresh vegetables, margarine for butter, artificial sweeteners for sugar.

(b)   Physical characteristics which are similar. These are factors which may mean a product is not unique and incapable of being replaced by something else. Recently, the Commission has published a Notice on the Definition of the Relevant Market (OJ 1997 C372/5) which provides a summary of the case law and Commission methodology for determining the relevant markets.

In *Europemballage and Continental Can* v *Commission*, the Court of Justice stressed the crucial importance of defining the relevant product market, and because the Commission had failed to define the product market properly the decision was quashed. The Commission had said that the companies had a dominant position in the market for cans for meat, cans for fish, and metal tops. It did not explain why these markets were separate from each other, or from the general market in cans and containers. The Court of Justice held it necessary to identify the 'characteristics of the products in question by virtue of which they are particularly apt to satisfy an inelastic need and are only to a limited extent interchangeable with other products'.

The *United Brands* v *Commission* case is probably the most useful to learn with regard to Art 82 (old 86), as it covers just about every topic for that provision. The case arose out of a complaint by a number of banana importers. The Commission considered the case under Regulation 17 and imposed a fine of 1 million units of account (the forerunner of the ECU/EURO).

UBC had been found to have infringed Art 82 (old 86), in that it had required its distributors not to sell bananas while still green (the green banana clause) and had charged distributors in different Member States different prices, sometimes by as much as 138 per cent without objective justification. UBC had also refused to supply a Danish company with Chiquita bananas because they had advertised another brand. UBC sought the annulment of the decision and the fine. The Court had to examine the definition of the relevant product market. Although they controlled 40–50 per cent of the banana market, UBC argued that the market in bananas was only a small part of a larger market in fresh fruit, and that although they might occupy a dominant position in the banana market, they did not occupy a dominant position in the fruit market as a whole.

The Court of Justice considered the special characteristics of the banana (*sounds like a music hall joke!*) and stated the relevant product market turned on whether the banana could be:

> singled out by such special features distinguishing it from other fruits that it is only to a limited extent interchangeable with them and is only exposed to their competition in a way that is hardly perceptible.

There existed a special market for old, young and infirm people who rely on them, and other fruits were not substitutable; therefore the relevant product market was the banana market.

In *ICI Commercial Solvents* v *Commission*, ICI were found to have a dominant market in one possible product, raw material used for the manufacture of drugs. Although others were available, the Court held the difficulty of substitution was a deciding factor in determining a dominance.

The concept of non-interchangeability is an important test which is applied by the Commission in identifying the relevant product market (see, for example, the *Hoffman la Roche* case).

The same product may in fact be classified into different markets; for example in *Michelin* v *Commission* (case 322/81), replacement tyres were held by the Court of Justice to constitute a different market from the same tyres when supplied to the car production factories.

The market share   The market share is also an important but not definitive consideration. In the cases considered above, Hoffman la Roche had market shares of 70–80 per cent in some drugs, Continental Can had a 70–80 per cent share of the can market in Germany, ICI had a virtual monopoly of the raw material, and in *Suiker Unie* v *Commission*, the Sugar Union commanded 85 per cent of the Belgian production. United Brands had only a 40–45 per cent share of the banana market, but the share of the competition becomes relevant. In this case the next share was only about 16 per cent. Other factors were also critical in the *United Brands* case, such as the company's control of the production and shipping of bananas. However, the Commission has suggested in its 10th Report on Competition Policy that in the case of a highly fragmented market, a share of 20–40 per cent might constitute dominance.

Dominance, or in the case near total domination in one market for drinks containers, may be enough to lead to abuse in an associated markets, even though dominance in that associated market has not been demonstrated or exists, where the products, manufacturers and consumers were largely the same in both markets (*Tetra Pak International* v *Commission*).

Defining the relevant geographical market   In the *United Brands* case, the Court of Justice held that consideration was required of the opportunities for competition, 'with reference to a clearly defined geographical area in which the product is marketed and where the conditions are sufficiently homogeneous for the effect of the economic power of the undertaking concerned to be able to be evaluated'.

A substantial part of the Community is required, but whatever market is demonstrated, it must be drawn to show market dominance. In a narrowly drawn geographical market, a firm which operates on a comparatively localised basis might possess adequate market power to occupy a dominant position, but if the market is too narrowly drawn, it will not be sufficiently large to be a substantial part of the common market. This latter problem should be seen in the context of the decision in *Suiker Unie*, where the Court of Justice held that dominance of the sugar market in Belgium and Luxembourg, approximately 10–15 per cent of the Community, was dominance of a substantial part of the common market. In *Tetra-Pak* v *Commission* (case T-83/91) the geographical market was defined as the whole Community.

The abuse of the dominant position   Article 82 (old 86) gives four specific examples of such abuse, including:

(a)   directly or indirectly imposing unfair purchase or selling prices or other unfair trading conditions, e.g., unfair low prices, loss leaders or unfair high prices as in *United Brands* or *Hoffmann la Roche;*

(b)   limiting production, markets or technical development to the prejudice of consumers, e.g., restrictions on exports in the *Suiker Unie* cases, restrictions on resale in *United Brands*, refusal to supply which might eliminate competitors in *ICI Commercial Solvents;*

(c)   applying dissimilar conditions to equivalent transactions with other trading parties, thereby placing them at a competitive disadvantage, as in *United Brands;* and

(d)   making the conclusion of contracts subject to acceptance by the other parties of supplementary obligations which, by their nature, or according to commercial usage, have no connection with the subject of such contracts, for example, the green banana clause in the *United Brands* case.

Oscar Bronner GmbH & Co. KG v *Mediaprint Zeitungs-und Zeitschriftenverlag GmbH & Co.* (case 7/97) helps define perhaps in a more positive way the boundaries of what may be regarded as the abuse of a dominant position, in that this was not found to be the legal position from the facts. A media undertaking holding a clear dominant position (46.8 per cent circulation) in one market was not obliged to allow access to a home delivery scheme, the only one in the market, to a smaller rival newspaper who could not economically set up their own scheme. There was, in other words, no breach of Art 82 (old 86) although there was a dominant position in the market. The case stresses that the exploitation of the advantages achieved by reaching a dominant position does not necessarily amount to unlawful abuse.

These examples are not exhaustive. In *Continental Can*, the Court of Justice held that the acquisition of a position of dominance through takeover or merger might amount to an abuse of a dominant market position. The Court held: 'Abuse may therefore occur if an undertaking in a dominant position strengthens such a position . . . that the degree of dominance reached subsequently fetters competition.'

Intellectual property rights may also infringe Arts 81 and 82 (old 85 and 86). The ownership of these would not, but the exercise of the rights must be done with the principles of Arts 81 and 82 (old 85 and 86) in mind. Further details will not be included here, as this tends to be more of a specialised area of study.

'May affect trade between Member States' The principles developed in Art 81 (old 85) cases also apply here. In *ICI Commercial Solvents*, the Court of Justice held that the expression could not be interpreted so as to limit the sphere of application of the prohibition to the industrial and commercial activities supplying the Member States. Article 82 (old 86) therefore covers abuse which may directly prejudice consumers, as well as abuse which indirectly prejudices them by impairing the effective competitive structure.

The Commission must therefore consider all the consequences of the conduct complained of, without distinguishing between production intended for sale within the market and that intended for export. When an undertaking in a dominant position within the common market abuses its position so that a competitor within the common market is likely to be eliminated, the area of trade is unimportant, once it has been established that this will have repercussions on the competitive structure within the common market.

THE ENFORCEMENT OF COMMUNITY COMPETITION LAW

Council Regulation 17/62

Regulation 17 empowers the Commission to carry out its function of ensuring that the provisions of the EC Treaty are applied, to address to undertakings decisions and recommendations for the purpose of bringing to an end infringements of Arts 81 and 82 (old 85 and 86), and to enforce these by way of fines and periodic payments.

Much of the law arising from Regulation 17 is concerned more with the rights of parties to be heard and present their view of matters, and they will not be considered here. It would be rare to be asked details of this in an ordinary Community law course. Courses specialising on competition law may do so.

The regulation's main stipulations are as follows:

Under Art 2, parties may apply to the Commission for a declaration of negative clearance.

Articles 4–8 and 25 allow agreements to be notified to the Commission for the purpose of achieving individual exemption under Art 81(3) (old 85(3)). A notification for exemption under Art 81(3) (old 85(3)) gives the parties to any agreement interim protection from fines (Art 15(5)).

The Commission, under Art 3, can, on its own initiative or on a complaint by an individual or a Member State, take decisions requiring the undertakings concerned to bring any infringement to an end. The penalties are non-criminal in nature (Art 15(4)).

The Commission is able to make an informal request for information which, if unsuccessful, will be followed by the formal procedure provided in Art 11. This imposes a duty on governments and competent authorities of Member States, and on undertakings, to cooperate with the Commission in investigations and to comply with requests for information.

Article 14 empowers the Commission to carry out investigations necessary for its enforcement duties. Under this provision, the Commission can examine the books and other business records of companies under investigation. While the investigation is being conducted the procedure is essentially administrative, but once the Commission has issued an objection, the proceedings become quasi-judicial and the Commission is required to observe Community law procedural rights (see the *Transocean* and *Hoffman la Roche* cases in respect of the right to be heard). (See also the *National Panasonic* case in respect of lawyer–client secrecy.) The investigations authorised under this provision include the infamous 'Dawn Raids' on the premises of companies under investigation. In *Hoechst* (cases 46/87 and 227/88) the authority to raid was challenged on the ground that it lacked precision but the Court of Justice held that it was acceptable providing the Commission indicated clearly its suspicions rather than have to supply full information.

Article 15 provides that for intentional or negligent breaches of Arts 81 or 82 (old 85 or 86), the penalty may be anything up to 10 per cent of the previous year's turnover of the undertaking. In 1991 in the *Tetra-Pak Rausing* case, Tetra-Pak were fined 75 million ECUs (c. GB£55 million) for pricing policies. The fine was confirmed by the CFI in case T-83/91. More recently, the Commission has fined Volkswagen 102 MECU which is roughly GB£67,000,000 (Decision 98/273, OJ 1998 L124/60).

In requests for information or access, the Commission is required to state the legal basis of the request and to remind undertakings of its power to impose penalties for supplying incorrect information or refusal to supply information or allow investigations (Art 15(1)(b)).

Article 16 provides for the imposition of daily penalties to compel undertakings to put an end to an infringement of either Art 81 or 82 (old 85 or 86). Before imposing a fine for failure to cooperate with an investigation, the Commission must consult the Advisory Committee on Restrictive Practices and Monopolies (the committee is composed of officials from each Member State competent in the matter of restrictive practices and monopolies) (Art 10(4)).

Article 19 relates to the rights of undertakings, associations of undertakings and third parties to be heard. Before taking any decision under the regulation (Arts 2, 3, 6, 7, 8, 15 and 16), the Commission is required to give the undertakings or associations affected the right to be heard on the matters to which objection has been taken. It may also hear other natural or legal persons where it considers it necessary, and is required to grant applications on behalf of such persons to be heard where they show a sufficient interest. Further details on these rights and hearings procedures are detailed in Commission Regulation 99/63.

Article 20 requires that information acquired shall be used only for the purposes of the relevant investigation, and under Art 20(2), information normally covered by the obligation of professional secrecy shall not be disclosed.

United Brands is a good example of the enforcement of Art 82 (old 86). The Commission considered the case under Regulation 17 and imposed a fine of one million units of account.

All decisions taken by the Commission under Regulation 17 are subject to review by the Court of First Instance under Art 230 (old 173) EC. Art 17 of the regulation states that the Court may cancel, reduce or increase any fine or periodic payment imposed by the Commission.

THE RELATIONSHIP BETWEEN ARTICLES 81 AND 82

Community Merger Control

It is in the area of mergers and acquisitions, or, as they are termed in the Community, concentrations, that the relationship of Arts 81 and 82 (old 85 and 86) with each other has come under closest scrutiny. Originally the Commission was of the view that Art 81 (old 85) would not apply to concentrations. Thus, if competition was restricted or distorted by a concentration of companies, Art 82 (old 86) was the appropriate measure with which to tackle it. This policy was pursued by the Commission in the case of *Continental Can*, where the Commission tried to remedy an abuse of a dominant position which had been achieved by takeovers and substantial holdings in European companies by an American company. It was the first attempt at merger control by the Commission. It was not successful, mainly because the Commission failed to establish the relevant markets, rather than through a failure to show abuses by the concentration. The Court of Justice's views in the case were, however, instructive in respect of the relationship of Arts 81 and 82 (old 85 and 86) and the restrictive approach to the problem adopted by the Commission, that by refusing to consider the use of Art 82 (old 85) as well for mergers, it had handicapped itself. The Court of Justice held:

> Articles 85 and 86 [now 81 and 82] seek to achieve the same aim on different levels, *viz.* the maintenance of effective competition within the common market. The restraint of competition which is prohibited if it is the result of behaviour falling under Art 85 [now 81], cannot be permissible by the fact that such behaviour succeeds under the influence of a dominant undertaking and results in the merger of the undertakings concerned. In the absence of explicit provisions one cannot assume that the Treaty, which prohibits in Art 85 [now 81] certain decisions of ordinary associations of undertakings restricting competition without eliminating it, permits in Article 86 [now 82] that undertakings after merging into an organic unit, should reach such a dominant position that any serious chance of competition is practically rendered impossible. Such diverse legal treatment would make a breach in the entire competition law which could jeopardise the proper functioning of the common market.

The Court further held Arts 81 and 82 (old 85 and 86) cannot be interpreted in such a way that they contradict each other, because they serve to achieve the same aim.

In *Tetra-Pak* v *Commission* (case T-51/89), Tetra-Pak were found to be in breach of Art 82 (old 86) following the acquisition of another company which held an exclusive licence to manufacture sterilised milk cartons. Whilst the acquisition itself did not offend Art 82 (old 86), the consequent dominant position which was immediately abused did.

The difficulties in dealing with the realities of complex commercial cross-holding were highlighted by *BAT and Reynolds* v *Commission*. In this case the Court of Justice had to consider the Commission decision that the acquisition of a minority holding in a competing company was not an infringement of Arts 81 and 82 (old 85 and 86). Two applicant, competitive companies objected to this decision. The original companies remained independent after the agreement, therefore Art 81 (old 85), which the Court of Justice considered could apply to mergers, was considered first. The Court of Justice upheld the Commission decision that no anti-competitive object or effect had been established and there was no control, thus there was no case under Art 82 (old 86) either. However, although an acquisition itself may not restrict competition, it may influence conduct to restrict or distort competition. The case is an example of the need to consider both in such complex situations.

The Mergers Regulation

It was following the *Continental Can* case that the Commission realised that a new approach was required to tackle the problems of concentrations. The Commission put forward a proposal for a regulation on merger control, but it was 16 years later, on 21 December 1989, that the Council adopted Regulation 4064/89 on the control of concentrations between undertakings This now provides the legal foundation of Community policy control of mergers and acquisitions, and entered into force on 21 September 1990 as amended up to 1997. The concept of a concentration has been outlined in a Commission Notice (OJ 1998 C66/2).

The regulation establishes a division between large mergers with a European dimension, over which the Commission will exercise supervision, and smaller mergers which will fall under the jurisdiction of national authorities. The Commission's jurisdiction under Arts 81 and 82 (old 85 and 86) and Regulation 17 is repealed in respect of concentrations.

Article 1 states that the regulation applies to mergers and takeovers with a Community dimension, defined in Art 2 as those with an aggregate worldwide turnover of all the undertakings of more than 5,000 million ECU, and an aggregate Community-wide turnover of each of at least two of the undertakings of more than 250 million ECU. A new Art 1(3) provides that a Community dimension may nevertheless pertain, if:

(a) the combined aggregate world wide turnover of all the undertakings is more than 2,500 million ECU;

(b) in each of at least three Member States, the combined aggregate turnover of all the undertakings is more than 100 million ECU;

(c) in each of at least three Member States, the aggregate turnover of each of at least two of the undertakings concerned is more than 25 Million ECU; and

(d) the aggregate Community wide turnover of each of at least two of the undertakings concerned is more than 100 million ECU.

However, if each of the undertakings concerned achieves more than two-thirds of its aggregate Community-wide turnover within one and the same Member State, a concentration will fall outside the scope of the regulation, and the merger will be subject to national rather than Community control.

Article 2 provides the power of review to determine whether mergers are compatible with the common market. The creation or strengthening of such a position will be declared incompatible with the common market where it would significantly impede effective competition in the common market as a whole or in a substantial part of it. In making this appraisal, the Commission is required to take into account the following matters:

(a)   the general competitive situation in the market concerned, including the need to preserve and develop effective competition within the common market (similar to the general requirement imposed by Art 3(g) EC), the structure of all the markets concerned (product and geographic markets), the actual or potential competition from undertakings located within or without the European Community (% share); and

(b)   the position of the undertakings concerned within that market, which includes the concepts of market position and economic and financial power, suppliers' and users' access to supplies or markets, legal barriers to entry into the market, supply and demand trends for the relevant goods and services, the interests of intermediate and ultimate consumers, and the development of technical and economic progress provided that it is to consumers' advantage and does not form an obstacle to competition.

The last requirements are similar to the exemptions under Art 81 (old 85) EC.

Where a merger is found by the Commission not to impede effective competition, it will be declared compatible with the common market (Art 2(2)). The Member States, however, retain the right in such circumstances to veto mergers in particularly sensitive ares of their economies, provided this is compatible with the general requirements of Community law.

Article 3 defines a concentration to include mergers, acquisitions of direct or indirect control of undertakings by persons already controlling at least one undertaking, partial mergers and merger-like joint ventures. However, it excludes from the scope of the regulation, coordination of market behaviour of firms which remain independent of each other. Such coordination, if adverse to competition in the common market, would fall within the scope of Art 81 (old 85) EC and Regulation 17, as in the *BAT* case. However, a recent case would seem to contradict this view. In joined cases *France* v *Commission* (case C-68/94) and *Société Commerciale des Potasses et de l'Azote (SCPA)* v *Commission* (case C-30/95), the Court of Justice determined that the merger Regulation applies also to collective dominance. The case concerned a proposal that potash companies in Germany be concentrated, thus creating a *de facto* monopoly in the German market and a dominant position with the French Company SCPA in the Community market. To obtain Commission approval, the parties agreed to certain conditions relating to cooperation between the dominant firms and the distribution of products in the markets identified. France objected to the Commission decision before the Court of Justice and SCPA, before the CFI. As they both concerned the same decision, the CFI declined jurisdiction and the whole matter was referred to the Court of Justice. The decision is important because it is the first time the Court of Justice has clearly stated the Merger Regulation to be applicable to collective dominance, despite the lack of express words to that effect in the Regulation and the doubts of the Member States when the Regulation was enacted that it would apply to oligopolies. The Court of Justice, on the other hand, thought that there was nothing in the regulation to exclude its application. That collective dominance was not sufficiently established by the Commission in the case itself does nothing to upset this.

The effect of the regulation is described as one-stop-shopping, in that only one authority (Commission or national) need take action depending on the area of dominance. It provides for the operation of a so-called 'principle of exclusivity' whereby all decisions on Community-wide mergers are taken by the Commission, Member States having undertaken not to apply their national competition rules to such cases (Art 21(1) and (2)), although there is provision for referral to national authorities in certain cases. See the new Commission Notice on Cooperation between National Competition Authorities and the Commission (OJ 1997 C313/1).

Enforcement of Regulation 4064/89

Article 4(1) of Regulation 4064/89 requires a concentration with a Community dimension to be notified to the Commission within one week after the conclusion of the agreement, the announcement of the public bid, or the acquisition of a controlling interest, whichever of these shall occur first. Fines for a failure to notify can be imposed up to a maximum of 50,000 ECU (Art 14(1)).

Article 7(1) provides that a concentration with a Community dimension shall not be put into effect before notification or in the three weeks following notification. The validity of transactions in securities on stock exchanges is not affected (Art 7(5)).

Under Art 10(1), the decision to open proceedings referred to in Art 6(1) must be taken within one month of the day following receipt of the notification. Article 6 provides that the Commission is under a duty to examine all notifications as soon as they are received, and to notify its decision to the undertakings concerned and the national authorities without delay. If the Commission considers that the proposed concentration falls outside the scope of the regulation, it must record that finding by way of a decision. Where it finds that the proposed concentration has a Community dimension but does not raise serious doubts as to its compatibility with the common market, it must decide not to oppose it and must declare it compatible with the common market. Where the concentration both falls within the scope of the regulation and raises serious doubts as to its compatibility with the common market, the Commission must decide to issue proceedings.

Article 10(3) requires that a decision that a concentration is incompatible with the common market must be taken within four months of the decision to open proceedings. During this period the parties to the proposed concentration will be free to propose changes to their merger in order to avoid a negative decision.

Where the Commission has found a proposed concentration to be incompatible with the common market, it may require the separation of the undertakings brought together, or the cessation of joint control, or any other action that may be appropriate to restore the conditions of effective competition (Art 8(4)). So far the proposed merger of Aerospatiale, Alenia and de Havilland (MO53) has been prohibited under the Regulation and following this first blocking by the Commission, another seven mergers have been blocked.

Article 13 confers the power to undertake 'all necessary investigations' on the Commission, including the power for officials to examine and take copies of or extracts from books and other business records, to ask for oral explanations on the spot, and to enter any premises, land or means of transport of the undertakings concerned.

The regulation also allows for the imposition of fines and periodic payments for failure to notify, for supplying incorrect or misleading information, and for obstructing an investigation by Commission officials (Arts 14 and 15). Where the parties intentionally or negligently fail to comply with an order to suspend the concentration, or disregard a decision to stop a merger or undo a merger, the Commission may impose a fine of up to 10 per cent of the aggregate annual turnover of the undertakings (Art 14(2)).

QUESTIONS

Questions on competition law can be both essay questions looking generally at its role, or problem questions which, due to the complexity of the subject matter, tend to be long and factually involved.

1.   What is the function of competition law within the goals and general policies of the EC? To what extent do the Preamble and introductory articles of the Treaty define the application of that function?

To answer this question, you must briefly outline the goals and general policies of the Community, then define the function of competition law within this framework, before moving on to the more specific second part of the question, which asks if the application of its function is defined by the Preamble and Arts 2 and 3.

The goals of the Community are generally to be determined from the Preamble and Arts 2 and 3 of the Treaty. These are, to create a common market of the Member States, to create a closer union, to improve the economic and social progress of the Member States by the elimination of barriers, to harmonise the economic policies of the Member States, to promote a harmonious development of economic activities, and to provide for balanced trade and fair competition. In particular, Art 3(a) to 3(t) spell out the individual policies which are to be pursued. If you can, summarise rather than reproduce these in your answer.

Now you can consider the function of competition law. A competition law policy is one of the fundamental policies of the Community, and is necessary to satisfy one of the elements of the Preamble to the Treaty. Furthermore, Art 3(g) of the EC Treaty lists among the activities of the Community, the inclusion of 'a system ensuring that competition in the internal market is not distorted'.

Competition law is designed to combat anti-competitive behaviour undertaken by companies in the Community. It is vital to the establishment of the common market and the integration of the Community. By its prevention of abusive monopolies, it encourages economic activity among small- and medium-sized enterprises, and allows the free flow of goods and resources. At the same time it must be ensured that companies do not become too competitive and start to dominate a market. Competition law seeks to promote equality, which should result in fair competition. Competition law is necessary if the other general aims of the Community are to be achieved. In particular, it closely complements the provision on the free movement of goods in the Community. Without either one of these, there would be little point in having the other, i.e., without laws which prevent unfair competition, businesses could enact artificial barriers to trade, usually along national boundaries, to frustrate the free movement of goods. This is done by various sorts of agreements and practices whereby markets are divided or prices inflated to the detriment of the single market in the Community and to the consumers. Thus competition law is fundamental to the achievement of the single market and the Community.

Finally, you need to consider the influence of the Preamble and Arts 2 and 3 on the application of competition law. The Preamble states that 'removal of existing obstacles calls for concerted action in order to guarantee steady expansion, balanced trade and fair competition'. The introductory provisions set out in Arts 2 and 3 contain conflicting ideologies of why or even of how, this aim is to be achieved. On the one hand, a market orientated approach defines the problems of competition as barriers to free trade which must be removed. This approach presupposes there is formal equality of all individuals or undertakings in the market and the Commission is merely interested in the regulation of the market and not any particular interest. On the other hand, a structural approach concerns changes to the market structure because the inequality of the actors has been recognised. Therefore, the Commission is entitled to regulate and structure the market in order to achieve the goals set by the inclusion of competition policy in the Community.

Article 2 refers to 'establishing a common market and an economic and monetary union' and to promoting 'harmonious . . . development of economic activities'. See the case of *Metro* at p. 252 above.

Article 3(g) of the EC Treaty lists among the activities of the Community 'a system ensuring that competition in the internal market is not distorted'. Article 3 is of growing importance in the Community legal order, and appears to be being promoted by parties as a general principle of Community law. It has been pleaded in Art 230 (old 173) actions as a rule of law with which Community legislation should comply. As yet there have been no cases where this has been successful, but time will tell. See the test in respect of *ICI Commercial Solvents* above at p. 252.

Article 10 (old 5) has also been pleaded closely with Art 3(g) EC and Art 81 (old 85) as a general principle of law supporting the argument that competition law also applies in respect of the Member States and not just undertakings, so that they are prohibited from encouraging or requiring acts or conduct by companies which may distort competition in the Community.

Thus the Preamble and introductory articles allow the court to be aware of the general aims in looking at specific situations and that competition law must be applied in the light of the wider general aims of the Community. The factual circumstances which arise must be construed in this legal framework.

An example of a long and complex problem question follows.

2.   Yves Eaux is a French company which makes designer eau-de-Cologne, accounting for 25 per cent of the Community market. Yves Eaux sells only to retailers, but insists that retailers sell at 100 EUROs per 50ml bottle. Yves Eaux sells to them at 80 EUROs per 50ml bottle, with a discount of 20 per cent for orders of 500 bottles, and another discount of 20 per cent if the buyer stocks only products purchased from Yves Eaux.

Yves Eaux appoints an approved retailer in each town, who must devote an agreed minimum retail floorspace exclusively to the sale of Yves Eaux's products, must employ at least two sales staff who have been trained at Yves Eaux's factory, and must promote Yves Eaux's products in accordance with Yves Eaux's instructions. Buyers who meet these requirements are allowed a further 20 per cent discount, which is Yves Eaux's estimation of the cost to the approved retailer of meeting Yves Eaux's requirements. All purchasers, whether approved retailers or not, are contractually bound not to resell to any other retail outlet, or to engage in sales outside their own town or Member State.

Superchem own a UK chemist, and already buy in quantity from Yves Eaux, reselling the product at 80 ECU per 50ml. Superchem approach Yves Eaux to become an approved dealer and thus obtain all discounts. Superchem say that they already employ two sales assistants who, although not trained by Yves Eaux, have been fully trained. Yves Eaux refuses Superchem's application, claiming that the training of Superchem's assistants is inadequate, that Superchem do not provide enough space to Yves Eaux's products and promotions and that they refuse to sell at the recommended price. A further ground for the refusal is that there already is an approved retailer in Superchem's town.

The managing director of Yves Eaux recently attended the annual convention of French perfume manufacturers and met the directors of two other companies accounting for 10 per cent and 15 per cent of the market. Over drinks, they agree, informally, not to sell their products to approved retailers of the other makers.

Superchem have now complained to the EC Commission of Yves Eaux's policies, in particular regarding the refusals to appoint Superchem an approved retailer, to allow the same discounts as to an approved retailer and the ban on resales other than to consumers. Superchem have also discovered, from the sales representatives of the other two companies, who are trying to make up sales in non-approved retailers, of the 'hands off' approach to approved retailers, and also complain of this to the Commission.

You are required to determine whether any of the activities of Yves Eaux breach Community competition law.

This, as you will appreciate, is a very long question and incorporates a great deal of factual information. I doubt that you would come across any longer questions. With such questions it is vital that you plan ahead and identify what needs to be answered, so that you do not waste time discussing aspects of the question which are not really answering it.

This question clearly concerns competition law, and as an introduction you could state the basic aim of competition law in the Community, i.e., to prevent the distortion of competition by one or more firms by agreement or the abuse of a dominant position. This is primarily achieved by Arts 81 and 82 (old 85 and 86).

The issues to be addressed in the above question are outlined for the most part in the complaints made to the Commission. (You might not

always have these spelt out for you and may be required to work these out
for yourselves.) Thus the matters to be addressed are, the various refusals,
the ban on reselling outside the retailer's town, the insistence that a resale
price is maintained, and the agreement with the other perfume houses. You
have to decide which Treaty articles apply to each of the activities. This is
not obvious, because some activities can attract the application of both Arts
81 and 82 (old 85 and 86). This problem involves both these provisions. The
relationship between Yves Eaux and its approved retailers may be considered to constitute an agreement under Art 81 (old 85), or as the abuse of
a dominant position under Art 82 (old 86). If Art 81 (old 85), it may be
exempt under a block or individual exemption. The clearest matter is the
agreement made at the convention which concerns Art 81 (old 85), and thus
I would advise tackling this issue first. State the basic aim of Art 81 (old
85), i.e., to prohibit anti-competitive agreements. The agreement here,
although informal, seeks to carve up the markets. Even as a non-binding
agreement or concerted practice, it would come within the scope of Art 81
(old 85) (see the *Polypropylene* Commission decision and *ICI* (*Aniline Dyes*)
case). The matters agreed would come within the types of prohibited
agreements under Art 81 (old 85), such as market sharing, price fixing, and
bans on exports. Even the conditions imposed on Superchem may come
within agreements according to the *Ford* v *Commission* case. If not, these can
still be considered under Art 82 (old 86). The agreements could easily be
shown to have an object or effect of distorting trade in the Community (see
the *Consten and Grundig* case and the *STM* case).

The remaining issues are all concerned with the policies of Yves Eaux in
respect of the refusals to supply Superchem as an approved retailer. These
would appear to be covered by Art 82 (old 86), because they appear to be
an abuse of the strong position of Yves Eaux. However, the biggest problem
which you may have seen immediately, is the fact that Yves Eaux commands only 25 per cent of the Community market. Nevertheless you should
briefly run through the requirements of Art 82 (old 86) to assure yourself
that this would not apply in this case. First of all you are required to show
a dominant position. This is defined by product and geographic market.
The product is clear, eau-de-Cologne, and the market share is 25 per cent.
Is this enough? Certainly, shares above 45 per cent would almost certainly
be considered dominant, as in the case of *United Brands*, but below this is
unlikely. While there is no clear word from either the Commission or the
Court of Justice on this point, the Mergers Regulation states that concentrations whose market share does not exceed 25 per cent would not be
considered to impede competition. The Commission has suggested in its
10th Report on Competition Policy that in the case of a highly fragmented
market, a share of 20–40 per cent might constitute dominance. Whether the
Court of Justice would agree is a different matter. In this case we know that

three companies between them have 50 per cent of the market and the gap between them is not great. Dominance would also suggest the ability to ignore what other firms are doing because of the market strength, however, the agreement itself is evidence that they are not able to do this. It is likely that any action under Art 82 (old 86) might not succeed. You should therefore consider the policies under Art 81 (old 85).

Do the conditions imposed on the approved retailers constitute agreements in breach of Art 81 (old 85)? The contracts between Yves Eaux and retailers certainly come within the definitions of agreements between undertakings, and it would seem to be clear that the object of most of the conditions imposed on retailers would appear to fall within the express type of activities deemed incompatible with the common market by Art 81 (old 85), i.e., those fixing the purchase and sales prices, those limiting or fixing the market by banning further sales outside the town or country, those applying dissimilar conditions. They would appear to breach Art 81 (old 85) unless there are any other considerations which would excuse them.

These agreements are in effect forms of exclusive or selective distribution agreements, certain types of which have been exempted from Art 81 (old 85) by the Commission. Individual clearances have been given by the Commission, and there is also the block exemption granted by Regulation 1983/83 (exclusive distribution agreements). Although perfume products have not been expressly catered for in the legislation, the Commission has issued similar agreements with comfort letters to state that it does not consider the types of agreement to be in breach of Art 81 (old 85) (see the perfume cases, case 99/79). It may be argued that these letters might serve to protect the agreements in the case above. However, the Commission did state that certain types of clauses would not satisfy Art 81 (old 85), and these were removed from the agreements. These related to the fixing of resale prices and limiting the ability to resell, especially on national lines.

The Court of Justice has also considered these types of agreements in the *Pronuptia* case, the *Metro* case and the perfume cases themselves. It held that if the clauses went beyond the objective criteria and instead merely imposed limits to restrict the quantity of retailers with nothing to do with quality, they may breach Art 81 (old 85). Thus, in *Pronuptia*, it held that clauses which fix prices or which effect a partitioning of markets between franchisor and franchisee, or between franchises, and which are capable of affecting trade between Member States, constitute restrictions on competition contrary to Art 81(1) (old 85(1)).

Thus, the insistence that retail prices are adhered to and the prohibition on further sales outside the town and country, would appear to breach Art 81 (old 85). The training and space requirements could be linked to quality and thus objectively be justified.

3.   'Even though Article 85 [now 81] is meant to cover concerted actions as opposed to abusive conduct covered by Article 86 [now 82], both provisions need to be interpreted in conjunction with each other.' (Van Bael and Bellis, *Competition Law of the EEC*.)

The scope of Articles 81 and 82 (old 85 and 86) might also have allowed their application to mergers and acquisitions, however, in practice this proved impossible and other measures proved necessary.

Discuss these statements in the light of legislative activity on the part of the Community and case law arising from decisions of the Commission.

This question requires you to consider the relationship of Arts 81 and 82 (old 85 and 86) to each other, and their application to the area of mergers.

First of all, outline the basic legislative regime under the Treaty and relevant secondary legislation, i.e., the Preamble, Arts 2, 3 and 10 (old 5), Arts 81 and 82 (old 85 and 86), Regulation 17 and the Mergers Regulation. Then briefly outline the area covered by both Arts 81 and 82 (old 85 and 86). Next, the relationship between these articles must be considered, especially in respect of their attempted application to mergers. Lastly the introduction and scope of the Mergers Regulation need to be outlined.

As the first two parts are straightforward and considered in the answers above, I will provide guidelines on the last two parts of the answer only.

The relationship of Arts 81 and 82 (old 85 and 86) is highlighted in a case concerned with the difficulties in dealing with the realities of complex commercial cross-holdings. In *BAT and Reynolds* v *Commission*, the Court of Justice had to determine whether the Commission decision that the acquisition of a minority holding in a competing company was not an infringement of Arts 81 and 82 (old 85 and 86), was correct. Two applicant and competitive companies had objected to the decision. The companies, whose activities were the subject of the complaint, had remained independent after their agreement to establish cross-holdings, therefore 81 (old Art 85) was considered first. The Commission decision that no anti-competitive object or effect had been established was upheld by the Court. Furthermore, no control had been proved, therefore there was no case either under Art 82 (old 86). Generally, the Court of Justice held that although an acquisition itself might not restrict competition, it may influence conduct to restrict or distort competition. Therefore, it becomes necessary to consider the application of both articles in such complex situations.

It is in the area of mergers and acquisitions, or, in Community jargon, concentrations, that, prior to the Mergers Regulation 4064/89 coming into effect, the relationship of Arts 81 and 82 (old 85 and 86) with each other has come under closest scrutiny. Originally the Commission was of the view that Art 81 (old 85) would not apply to concentrations. Thus, if competition was restricted or distorted by a concentration of companies, Art 82 (old 86) was the appropriate measure with which to tackle it. This policy was pursued by the Commission in the case of *Continental Can*, where the Commission tried to remedy an abuse of a dominant position which had been achieved by takeovers and substantial holdings in European companies by an American company. It was the first attempt at merger control in this way by the Commission. It was not successful, mainly because the Commission failed to establish the relevant markets, rather than through a failure to show abuses by the concentration.

The view of the Court of Justice in the case was, however, instructive in respect of the relationship of Arts 81 and 82 (old 85 and 86) and the restrictive approach to the problem adopted by the Commission. By refusing to consider the use of Art 81 (old 85) as well for mergers, the Commission had handicapped itself. See the quote from the case on p. 267.

Thus firms could avoid Art 81 (old 85) by establishing close connections which did not constitute full merger, and thus be caught by Art 82 (old 86). This would allow market partition and a defeat of the aims of the Community. Therefore, Arts 81 and 82 (old 85 and 86) cannot be interpreted in such a way that they contradict each other, because they serve to achieve the same aim.

It was following this case that the Commission realised that a new approach was required to tackle the problems of concentrations. Hence the long road to a Mergers Regulation was embarked on. The details of this are as outlined above in this chapter. Note, however, that the Merger Regulation rather than Art 82 (old 86) might apply to situations of collective dominance as highlighted by the cases of *France* v *Commission* (case C-68/94) and *Société Commerciale des Potasses et de l'Azote (SCPA)* v *Commission* (case C-30/95).

FURTHER READING

Art, J-Y. and Van Liedekerke, D., 'Developments in EC competition law in 1996: an overview' (1997) 34 CML Rev 895.

Cook, J. and Kerse, C., *EC Merger Control* (Sweet and Maxwell, 2nd edn., 1996).

Goyder, D., *EC Competition Law* (2nd edn, Oxford: Clarendon Press, 1993).

Korah, V., An Introductory Guide to EC Competition Law and Practice (6th edn, Hart Publishing, 1997).

Levitt, M., 'Access to the File: The Commission's Administrative Procedures under Articles 85 and 86' (1997) 34 CML Rev 1413.

Turnbull, S., 'Barriers to Entry, Article 86 EC and the Abuse of a Dominant Position: An Economic Critique of European Community Competition Law' (1996) ECLR 96.

Winckler, A. and Hansen, M., 'Collective Dominance under the EC Merger Control Regulation' (1993) 30 CML Rev 787.

11 SEX DISCRIMINATION

INTRODUCTION

This area of Community law developed later than the other areas considered, because of the less extensive provision for it in the Treaty, the delays by
the Member States in implementing the principle of equal pay, and the
delays by the Commission in introducing secondary legislation. Article 141
(old 119) was the sole original provision for the European Community to
concern itself with sex discrimination. There now exists a considerable
body of Community law on the subject, in the form of primary and
secondary legislation and the very many progressive decisions of the Court
of Justice and the recent additions introduced by the Treaty of Amsterdam.

As with the free movement of persons, there are a number of general
issues to be considered in respect of sex discrimination. These concern the
reason for the inclusion of sex equality rights in the first place, and the role
of the Commission, Council and Member States in promoting equality. It
may be suggested that the EC would seem an unlikely source of women's
equality rights, because it is primarily a vehicle to promote the economic
integration and development of the Member States rather than a body
committed to equality between the sexes, which is really more of an
internal matter for the Member States. Social considerations would seem to
have little place in this development, and it is now generally accepted that
the immediate reason for including old Art 119 (now 141) in the EEC Treaty
was not to promote social justice but to meet economic considerations. The
article was allegedly included principally at the request of the French,
whose legislation purported to provide for equality between male and
female workers. It was feared that French industry would be at a disadvantage if equal pay were not a principle enforced in the other Member States.

Thus the aim is to ensure similar economic conditions apply in all the Member States.

In *Defrenne* v *SABENA (No. 2)*, however, the Court of Justice declared that:

> Article 119 [now 141] also forms part of the social objectives of the Community, which is not merely an economic union, but is at the same time intended, by common action, to ensure social progress and seek the constant improvement of the living and working conditions of their peoples, as is emphasised by the preamble to the Treaty. . . . This double aim, which is at once economic and social, shows that the principle of equal pay forms part of the foundations of the community.

LEGISLATION

The EC Treaty

Although Art 141 (old 119) provided originally the only specific mention of equal treatment in the EC Treaty, it has formed the basis upon which the principle has been expanded into areas beyond equal pay, and has become a fundamental social principle of the Treaty. So while the initial concern may have been for economic reasons, continued concern is arguably more genuine, as demonstrated by the issue of directives by the Commission and the pronouncements of the Court of Justice and evolving Community policies.

Its status as a general principle of law in the Community legal order has been considerably strengthened by changes introduced by the Treaty of Amsterdam. The Treaty of Amsterdam has introduced as one of goals outlined in Art 2 EC 'equality between men and women' and has added a new final sentence to Art 3 EC which reads: 'In all the activities referred to in this Article, the Community shall aim to eliminate inequalities, and to promote equality, between men and women.' Furthermore a new enabling power has been introduced in new Art 13 EC which provides that the Council, acting unanimously, and in consultation with the EP, may take appropriate action to combat discrimination based on sex or sexual orientation, amongst others. Finally, the Treaty of Amsterdam has amended and added two sentences to Art 141 (old 119) which locate within a treaty base, the principles of equal pay for work of equal value and positive discrimination previously contained in directives only. Being contained in the latter meant that they could not give rise to direct effects against other individuals (no horizontal direct effects of directives — see the case of *Marshall* below).

Secondary Legislation

The European summit meetings of 1972–3 requested the Commission to produce proposals for a social action programme. Since then the following directives have been adopted:

(a)   the Equal Pay Directive 75/117 (OJ 1975 L45/19);
(b)   the Equal Treatment Directive 76/207 (OJ 1976 L39/40);
(c)   the Social Security Directive 79/7 (OJ 1979 L6/24);
(d)   Directive 86/378 on equal treatment in occupational pensions (OJ 1986 L225/86);
(e)   Directive 86/613 on equal treatment of the self-employed and protection of self-employed women during pregnancy and motherhood (OJ 1986 L359/86);
(f)   The Pregnancy and Maternity Directive 92/85 (OJ 1992 L348/1).
(g)   The Parental Leave Directive 96/34 (OJ 1996 L145/9);
(h)   The Burden of Proof in Sex Discrimination Cases Directive 97/80 (OJ 1998 L14/6);
(i)   The Part-time Workers Directive 97/81 (OJ 1998 L14/9). (While this latter directive is not directly aimed to address sex discrimination, it will have this effect as it aims to reduce the inequality between full-time workers and part-time workers, the majority of which are women.)

While the amount of legislation is limited, it has been subject to very liberal interpretations by the Court of Justice, far beyond a literal reading of the provisions, in cases more often brought by individuals rather than by the Commission in Art 226 (old 169) actions (see the *Garland*, *Defrenne* and *Marshall* cases considered below).

THE TREATY OBLIGATION

Article 119 (new 141) provided that 'During the first stage Member States shall ensure and subsequently maintain the application of the principle that men and women should receive equal pay for equal work'. New Art 141 has amended this to remove the reference to the transitional period, it now refers also to equal pay for work of equal value, first introduced by Directive 75/117 (discussed below) and has included a new paragraph 4 concerned with positive discrimination also previously introduced by a Directive (76/207) (also discussed below).

Article 141(1) (old 119(1)) provides: 'Each Member State shall ensure that the principle of equal pay for male and female workers for equal work or work of equal value is applied' and, secondly, attempts to define what 'equal pay' actually means. Article 141(2) (old 119(2)) narrowly defines 'pay' as 'the ordinary basic or minimum wage or salary and any other consideration, whether in cash or in kind, which the worker receives directly or indirectly, in respect of his employment, from his employer'.

Article 141(2) (old 119(2)) defines 'equal pay without discrimination' to mean:

(a)   that pay for the same work at piece rates shall be calculated on the basis of the same unit of measurement; and

(b)   that pay for the same work at time rates shall be the same for the same job.

In *Defrenne* v *Sabena (No. 2)* (case 43/75), a claim for compensation was made for the damage suffered from February 1963 until February 1966 because Gabrielle Defrenne was paid at a substantially lower rate than her male colleagues for the same work. The Court of Justice stated that the forms of direct discrimination covered by Art 141 (old 119) included those arising from legislation or collective labour agreements but that Art 141 (old 119) did not apply to equal treatment other than equal pay, and that it was limited to cover only remuneration based on the relationship between employer and employee. Furthermore, the principle of equal pay was sufficiently clear and precise to have direct effects, but only prospectively in cases where the discrimination complained of could be identified solely by employing the criteria of equal pay for equal work. It held that Art 141 (old 119) had been horizontally directly effective since January 1962, and not from 1957 because of the unforeseen economic consequences of this.

THE EQUAL PAY DIRECTIVE (75/117)

The Equal Pay Directive added little to the interpretation of Art 141 (old 119), but had extended the principle of equal pay to 'work to which equal value is attributed' and extends to 'all aspects and conditions of remuneration' (Art 1).

Although many of the cases decided by the Court of Justice were originally raised in respect of Directive 75/117 alone or in combination with Art 141 (old 119), the Court was able to answer them by reference to Art 141 (old 119). Therefore, no distinction will be made here between those cases, and reference will be made to the actual provision where appropriate. The case law concerns a number of different issues, including the direct effects of Art 141 (old 119), the scope of the principle of equal pay, and the meaning of the term 'pay' and the phrase 'equal work', especially in relation to part-time work.

The Concept of Pay

In *Defrenne v Belgium (No. 1)*, although the job content was identical, until 1966 air hostesses working for SABENA were paid at a lower rate than stewards, and were required to retire at 40 instead of 55. The lower retirement age for hostesses meant that they were unable to take advantage of a special pensions scheme. The Court of Justice held, in respect of the retirement pension, that the definition of 'pay' contained in Art 141 (old 119) was not wide enough to include social security schemes 'directly imposed by law without any element of consultation within the industry or undertaking concerned and which cover all workers in general, the employer's financial contribution being a public law rather than a contractual duty'.

Defrenne v SABENA (No. 2), involved an action to claim compensation for the damage suffered by virtue of the fact that, from February 1963 until February 1966, Defrenne was paid at a substantially lower rate than her male colleagues for the same work. The Court of Justice stated that 'among the forms of direct discrimination which may be identified solely by reference to the Article 119 (now 141) criteria are included those which have their origin in legislation or in collective labour agreements'. It held that Art 141 (old 119) did not apply to equal treatment other than equal pay, and that it was limited to cover only remuneration based on the relationship between employer and employee.

The concept of pay under Art 141 (old 119) has since been held to include concessionary rail travel facilities for the family of an ex-employees in *Garland v British Rail Engineering*, rules by which seniority/loyalty payments are achieved in favour of full time employees in *Nimz v Hamburg*, sick pay, even though part of a statutory scheme in *Ingrid Rinner-Kuhn v FWW Spezial-Gebaudereiningung*, a severance grant in *Kowalska v Hamburg* and compensation for lost wages for attendance on training course for works council members in *Arbeiterwohlfahrt der Stadt Berlin v Monika Botel*.

The Concept of Pay and its Relationship to Pensions

Although the first *Defrenne* case seemed to rule out the inclusion of benefits enjoyed during retirement within the concept of 'pay' in Art 141 (old 119), a number of cases make it clear that the decisive criterion in that case was the fact that the pension rights in question related wholly to a state social security scheme. At the time, however, pensions were not considered to be pay. There is now a number of cases which consider this complicated relationship between pay, pensions and social security. They are often difficult to understand, therefore careful reading is required.

This area is becoming increasingly complex not just because the concept of pay is being stretched but because it has brought it into the very grey area of the boundary between the jurisdiction of the Member States and that of the Court of Justice. Article 7 of Directive 79/7 stipulates that Member States have the right to exclude from equal treatment the determination of pensionable age for the purposes of granting old age and retirement pensions and the possible consequences for other benefits. The thinking originally was that pensionable age could be equated with retirement age and thus anything to do with the pension age, which can be set by the State, is not within the jurisdiction of the EC, but the Member States. However, if pension schemes involve a private or contractual element, the Court of Justice has held that this can be regarded as pay. However, many schemes are hybrid and have both a government and private involvement. Coupled with increasing privatisation of pensions, further complicates this area.

In *Worringham & Humphries* v *Lloyds Bank*, the bank operated an arrangement whereby male workers under 25 were paid five per cent more than their female counterparts, which sum went towards a pension scheme. The total, however, formed the basis of calculation of other social advantages and welfare benefits. The Court of Justice ruled that a contribution to a retirement benefit scheme which is paid by employer on the employee's behalf by means of an addition to gross salary, is pay within the meaning of Art 141 (old 119). Amounts which determine other benefits linked to salary were also part of the pay of the employee, even if they were deducted at source by the employer and paid into a pension fund on behalf of the employee.

Liefting v *University of Amsterdam* confirmed that any payment, even if relating to pensions and required by statute, which resulted in a difference in the amount by which other benefits are calculated, is pay for the purposes of Art 141 (old 119).

In *Bilka Kaufhaus* v *Karin Weber Van Harz*, it was held that where supplements were made under contract by the employer to the State social security scheme in respect of a pensions scheme, they were thus linked to pay and were held to be pay for the purposes of Art 141 (old 119).

Redundancy payments, even though compulsory, were held in *Barber* v *Guardian Royal Exchange*, to be a form of payment made after the termination of the contract of employment and therefore covered by Art 141 (old 119), because, even though they reflected considerations of a Member State's social security policy, they were a part of the employment relationship.

The deciding factor in the light of these cases appears to be whether the rules of the specific scheme are a part of the employment contract by voluntary inclusion of the employer. Schemes which are entirely compulsory state security schemes will not be covered by Art 141 (old 119). What brings a benefit within pay is that it is received from the employer by reason of the existence of the employment relationship — this therefore includes statutory redundancy pay. The Court emphasised the importance of the fact that the occupational pensions scheme was funded without any contribution being made by the public authorities.

The *Barber* decision caused severe problems as it was not expected that pensions should be pay, because they were linked to retirement and this had been different for men and women as most schemes set up on the basis that women would retire earlier. Actuaries knew they would live longer so they were necessarily different, i.e., there would be differences based on the different ages in the schemes. As a result of the *Barber* judgment, this would mean that there would be unlawful discrimination not previously thought to be the case, for which huge amounts of compensation, not previously contemplated, would be payable. This would not have been taken account of in the actuarial schemes and the pensions schemes would have had severe difficulties in making payments not previously foreseen. Hence the Court of Justice declared Art 141 (old 119) to be directly effective for pensions only from date of judgment, i.e., 17 May 1990.

There are a number of points to note in relation to *Barber*:

1.   Protocol 2 to the Maastricht Treaty states that the benefits arising from social security schemes shall not be considered as remuneration in respect of periods of employment prior to 17 May 1990 with the exception to those who had instigated proceedings prior to that date. This, like the judgment was to overcome the economic effect on employers in the case of a retroactive application of the ruling of the Court of Justice, i.e., the period of earnings before judgment do not give rise to a claim. The protocol clarified the judgment. The *Barber* case, however, sparked off many more cases seeking to establish its exact meaning and consequences.

2.   The time limit in *Barber* and Protocol 2 do not apply to discrimination in relation to the right to join, i.e., access to an occupational pension scheme, which is governed by the judgment in *Bilka Kaufhaus*. See, for example, *Vroege* v *NCIV Instituut* (case C-57/93).

Other cases continue to consider the ramifications of *Barber*, for example *Neath* v *Hugh Steeper* (case C-152/91). Inequality in employees' *contributions* arising from actuarial factors such as life expectancy, which differed according to sex would not be caught by Art 141 (old 119). This was a conversion of a periodic pension payment to a lump sum scheme. Whilst benefits and payments must be equal, this is not the case for the contributions as other factors other than a simple difference in sex are involved. The funding system to provide the amount of pension to be available does not come under Art 141 (old 119). The amount needed for a pension is determined by actuaries who base their figures on the fact that women live longer after retirement and have a right to a pension at an earlier age thus they need more capital available to supply this. If they work the same time, they must pay more. This becomes quite clear when converted to a lump sum. Women will get more. In this case, the male applicant got less and according to the Court of Justice, there was no discrimination.

There are still very many cases concerned with this very complex relationship between different treatment for different circumstances. It is complicated because there remains a lawful discrimination on the part of Member States as to when females and males receive state pensions. Any difference which relates to the access to pensions or the amount paid in or out to achieve this is in law entirely acceptable unless, according to *Barber*, it has become part of the contractual relationship by the intervention of an agreement between the employer and employee. It is then pay, comes within Art 141 (old 119) and the employer cannot discriminate. If ever there was something to boggle the mind then this is it!

Implementing the Equal Pay Principle: Equal Pay for Equal Work and for Work of Equal Value

Directive 75/117 extended the principle of equal pay to 'work to which equal value is attributed' and to 'all aspects and conditions of remuneration' (Art 1) but this has now been incorporated into Art 141 (old 119).

Article 1 of the Directive also provides that where a job classification scheme is used for determining pay, it must be drawn up so as to exclude discrimination based on sex. The Equal Pay Directive requires Member States: 'to provide recourse to legal action for employees who feel themselves wronged' (Art 2); 'to abolish all discrimination arising from laws, regulations and administrative procedures which is contrary to the principle of equal pay' (Art 3); 'to declare null and void or amend all provisions in collective or individual agreements or wage scales which are contrary to the principle of equal pay' (Art 4); and 'to protect complainants from unfair dismissal on the grounds that they have complained' (Art 5).

Equal Pay for Equal Work: The Basis for Comparison

The scope of the concept of equal pay for equal work could not be restricted by a requirement by Member States that the persons whose work was being compared be contemporaneously employed. In *Macarthys Ltd v Smith*, Smith was employed from March 1976 at a salary of £50 per week, and complained of discrimination because her predecessor, a man, had received a salary of £60 per week. The Court of Justice held that comparisons are confined to parallels, which may be drawn on the basis of concrete appraisals of the work actually performed by employees of different sex within the same establishment or service and who need not be employed at the same time. However, the Court was careful to point out that: 'It cannot be ruled out that the difference in pay between two workers occupying the same post but at different periods in time may be explained by the operation of factors which are unconnected with any discrimination on grounds of sex.' This is a question of fact for the national courts to decide. In this case the court therefore expressly left open the possibility of a genuine material factor defence.

Work of Equal Value

Although many of the cases decided upon by the Court of Justice were originally raised in respect of Directive 75/117 alone or in combination with Art 119 (now 141) but the Court was able to answer them by reference to Art 119 alone. This was largely to do with avoiding the issue of having to pronounce on HDE (Horizontal Directs Effects) of Directives.

In *Mary Murphy* v *An Bord Telecom Eireann*, the Court of Justice ruled that while it is true that Art 119 (now 141) applies only in the case of equal work, if that principle forbids workers of one sex engaged in work of equal value to be paid a lower wage than workers of the opposite sex on grounds of sex, it certainly prohibits such a difference in pay where the lower paid category of workers is engaged in work of higher value.

Discrimination

Article 141 (old 119) and Directive 75/117 clearly outlaw direct discrimination, where a distinction is drawn between the rights of men and women overtly on the basis of sex. Indirect discrimination, however, is more difficult to determine. It covers cases where a class of persons is mainly or entirely constituted of women, and a difference is drawn between that class and other persons which operates in a discriminatory manner against women. Whether the discrimination offends legislation is often dependent on the motives behind it. The Court of Justice has considered this in a number of cases concerning pay differences between full-time and part-time workers.

Part-time work   In *Jenkins* v *Kingsgate*, the employers paid full-time workers 10 per cent more per hour than part-time workers, in order, it was claimed, to discourage absenteeism and to achieve a more efficient use of their machinery. All but one of the part-time workers were women. The Court of Justice held that a difference in rates of remuneration between full- and part-time employees is acceptable provided the difference is attributable to factors which are objectively justified and do not relate directly or indirectly to discrimination based on sex, for example, to encourage the recruitment of full-time employees. However, where there is no plausible explanation to account for the difference in pay, it is likely to be discrimination contrary to Art 141 (old 119).

Objective justification   The Court of Justice has accepted that the policy of paying part-timers less can be justified as long as it is established that the means to achieve the objective correspond to a real need of the employer and are appropriate and necessary in order to achieve the objective of employing as few part-time workers as possible.

In *Bilka Kaufhaus* v *Karin Weber Van Harz*, a store gave full-time employees a non-contributory pension on retirement, while part-timers qualified only if they had been employed permanently for at least 15 years. The undertaking claimed they needed to pay full-timers more to attract them in sufficient numbers. The Court of Justice held there was indirect discrimination, contrary to Art 141 (old 119), unless the employer had taken the action on the ground of objectively justified factors unconnected with discrimination based on sex. In order to show that the discrimination is objectively justified, the employer must show that the measures giving rise to the difference in treatment:

(a)   correspond to a genuine need of the enterprise;

(b)   are suitable for attaining the objective pursued by the enterprise; and

(c)   are strictly necessary for that purpose, i.e., proportional.

National legislation which gives rise to the discrimination will not justify it in terms of Community law. In *Ingrid Rinner-Kuhn*, the legally supported refusal to pay sick pay to workers who worked a normal week of fewer than 10 hours, or 45 hours per month, was held by the Court of Justice to breach Art 141 (old 119) where such a measure affected a far greater number of women than men, unless the Member State could show that the legislation was justified by objective factors unrelated to any discrimination on grounds of sex.

The severance grant in *Kowalska* v *Hamburg*, paid only to full-time civil servants, when 90.2 per cent of all part-time civil servants were women, would be unlawful discrimination unless objectively justified. Such schemes must treat two classes of workers the same way, in proportion to hours and other factors, according to Art 141 (old 119).

In *Arbeiterwohlfahrt der Stadt Berlin* v *Monika Botel*, the failure to recompense part-timers for all the hours spent on a training course would amount to discrimination unless objectively justified.

In *Enderby* v *Frenchay Health Authority* (case C-127/92), the Court of Justice held that it was for the national court to determine, if necessary by applying the principle of proportionality, whether and to what extent the shortage of candidates for a job and the need to attract them by paying higher pay constituted an objectively justified ground for the difference in pay between jobs of equal value. This aspect should be relatively easy to prove, other aspects are not so easy, for example, the relative number of full-time to part-time vacancies.

A more recent case extends the same principles of indirect discrimination to a relatively more recent situation of job sharing or percentage jobs, i.e., an activity more likely to be taken up by women than men. In *Hill and Stapleton* v *Revenue Commissioners* (case C-243/95), it was held it would be discrimination to appoint job sharers, who transfer to full-time work, to a lower salary scale point than they enjoyed under job share on the basis of the actual time worked where a majority of women are job sharers unless such a rule can be justified by objective criteria unrelated to any discrimination on grounds of sex.

Job evaluation schemes   The UK was found to have breached the Equal Pay Directive by failing to compel employers to undertake job evaluations, for the purpose of enforcing equal pay for work of equal value (*Commission* v *UK (Re Equal Pay for Equal Work)*). Member States must endow an authority with the requisite power to decide whether work has the same value as other work, after obtaining such information as may be needed (see now the Equal Pay (Equal Value Amendment) Regulations 1983 (SI 1983 No. 1754), in respect of the UK).

In *Rummler* v *Dato-Druck*, a job evaluation scheme which was based on muscular effort, fatigue and physical hardship was held by the Court of Justice not to be in breach of Art 1 of Directive 75/117 as long as the following condition was met, i.e., it must, in so far as the nature of the tasks carried out in the undertaking permitted, take into account criteria for which workers of each sex showed particular aptitude. The Court of Justice said that criteria based exclusively on the values of one sex contained a 'risk of discrimination'.

Burden of proof   In the *Dansk (Danfoss)* case, different pay was justified by the firm on the basis of seniority and flexibility payments. The Court of Justice held that where the criteria were not transparent the burden was placed on the employer to prove they were objectively applied.

The increasingly difficult issues of proof have to some extent been tackled by the Court of Justice in its case law, by insisting, for example, that the employer be required to justify certain actions rather than the employee having to prove, with a lack of or difficulty in gaining the knowledge, that certain practices infringe EC law. However, Directive 97/80 (OJ 1998 L14/6) has been passed now which consolidates the case law on this matter of proof. The previous attempt to enact this Directive to assist claimants in difficult proof issues in sex discrimination cases was vetoed by the UK Conservative Thatcher Government in 1989.

THE EQUAL TREATMENT DIRECTIVE (76/207)

Directive 76/207 aims to put the equal treatment principle into effect for men and women as regards access to employment, including promotion, vocational training and working conditions (Art 1(1)). It was enacted under Art 308 (old 235) rather than Art 141 (119) as it goes well beyond the original scope of the article.

Article 1(2) states that later provisions (Directive 79/7 and 86/378) will define the substance, scope and implementation of the principle in the field of social security.

Under Art 2(1), there must be no discrimination whatsoever on grounds of sex either directly or indirectly by reference, in particular, to marital or family status.

Article 1 refers to equal treatment for men and women whereas Art 2 refers to no discrimination on the grounds of sex. Are these the same or similar or overlapping concepts or does the second mean more than the first? Two cases have considered the scope of the protection provided for by these provisions in so far as what is meant by the right to equality within the framework agreed by the Member States and interpreted by the Court of Justice. *P v S and Cornwall County Council* involves a male-to-female transsexual who was dismissed from employment in an educational establishment following the submission of a proposal to the employers to undergo gender re-assignment. The Court held that this was unlawful discrimination on the grounds of sex because it was 'based, essentially if not exclusively on the sex of the person concerned'. Whilst there is no comparator as such, all other workers be they male or female become the point of comparison. If they are not subject to the same treatment, i.e., dismissal, then P is discriminated against on grounds of sex. Hence the Directive is not limited to discrimination on the grounds of gender. By that it is meant, not so much the difference between genders but rather more it seeks to remove any discrimination where sex is a decisive factor.

The question which was raised after this case: was has the concept of no discrimination on the grounds of *sex* transmuted into no discrimination on the grounds of *sexuality* or even no 'sexual orientation discrimination', i.e., no discrimination in respect of what some would consider a person's *lifestyle choice*. The answer was 'no', as a same-sex cohabitee's case determined the boundaries of EC law. In *Grant v South West Trains*, SW trains regulations specifically excluded benefits from same-sex partnerships. Whereas opposite-sex partners (not necessary to be married but a stable relationship had to be established) received rail travel benefits same-sex partners did not. The Court of Justice held this was not discrimination based on sex, as the rule would apply also to same-sex male relationships; rather, this was discrimination based on sexual orientation. The Court then discussed a number of points in connection with this. It stated that in some Member States such a relationship would, but only for a limited range of rights, be treated the same as an opposite-sex relationship and in some not recognised in any particular way. The Court referred to the new Art 13 (old 6a) by which the Member States can take action to outlaw sexual orientation discrimination. It held that the present state of law in the EC does not equate same-sex relationships with opposite-sex ones therefore the discrimination in respect of sexual orientation, although present, is lawful (i.e., not contrary to Art 141 (old 119) or the Directive). The Court seems to have decided to leave this issue to the Member States.

Direct Effects

Various articles (Arts 3(1), 4(1), 5(1) and 6) of the Directive have been declared to be directly effective in *Marshall v Southampton Area Health Authority* and *Johnston*. However, in line with other Directives, this is only vertically and other means of enforcement must be pursued if a private employer is involved.

Requirements of the Directive

Articles 3–5 specify with regard to each of the three spheres of operation of the Directive the exact goals which the Member States are required to achieve with regard to each.

- Article 3 — access to employment and promotion,
- Article 4 — access to training vocational guidance and advanced vocational guidance, and
- Article 5 — working conditions, including conditions governing dismissal).

In each sphere the Member States must:

(a) Abolish any laws, regulations and administrative provisions which are contrary to the principle.

(b) Make provision for the annulment or amendment of any provisions contravening the principle of equal treatment found in any individual contracts of employment, collective agreements, internal rules of undertakings, or in any rules governing the independent occupations or professions.

(c) Take the measures necessary to ensure that with regard to those laws, regulations and administrative provisions which contravene the principle of equal treatment, when the concern which originally inspired them is no longer well founded, they shall be revised. And when they are contained in collective agreements, labour and management shall be requested to take the necessary revision. This applies to access to employment and promotion, and to working conditions, but not to vocational training.

Derogations from the Equal Treatment Principle

Article 2 of Directive 76/207 provides for a number of exceptions to the principle of equal treatment.

Article 2(2) provides Member States with the right to exclude activities and, where appropriate, training for which the sex of the worker constitutes a determining factor. *Commission* v *UK (Re Equal Treatment for Men and Women)* concerned an exemption for employment in a private household and for firms employing fewer than six staff. The Court of Justice held that while such exemption under Art 2(2) might be available in an individual case, under circumstances where the sex of the worker was a determining factor, Art 2(2) did not justify a blanket exclusion. The restriction of access of males to midwifery was held to be acceptable, but Member States are required, however, where they do exempt certain occupations, to assess them periodically in order to decide, in the light of social developments, whether there is justification for maintaining the exclusions concerned. They must notify the Commission of the results of this assessment (Art 9(2)).

In *Commission* v *Germany (Re Equal Treatment Directive)*, the Court of Justice ruled that Member States were obliged to provide the Commission with a list of the occupations so exempted, to review the list periodically in accordance with Art 9(2) of the Directive, and to inform the Commission of the results of reviews when completed.

In *Johnston* v *Chief Constable of the RUC*, a claim by the RUC that failure to renew the contracts of a number of female police officers was justified, was dismissed. They argued it was based on the derogation of Art 2(2) and, by analogy, to the public policy derogations of Art 39 (old 48) EC, because of a policy decision that women could not carry firearms. The Court of Justice held that the exception allowed by Art 2(2) might apply to certain activities carried out by police officers, but not to police activities in general. The Member States might therefore restrict such specific activities, and the training leading thereto, to men, provided that the situation was reviewed regularly to ensure that the restrictions remain justified, and that the restrictions complied with the principle of proportionality. The Court of Justice questioned whether the refusal to renew Ms Johnston's contract could not be avoided by allocating to women duties which, without jeopardising the aims pursued, could be performed without firearms.

In *Commission* v *France (Re Discrimination in the French Civil Service)*, the Court of Justice further stated that the derogations in Art 2(2) could only cover specific activities, that there should be an element of transparency enabling effective supervision by the Commission and that they should, in principle, be capable of adjustment to meet social developments. In this case, the system of separate recruitment, which entailed the fixing of the percentage of posts to be allocated to men and women respectively, did not satisfy the Court of Justice. The percentage was not governed by any objective criterion laid down in legislation or regulations, and there was no transparency, therefore the Commission could not supervise the system and this was a further breach of the directive.

The derogation was considered further and accepted in *Sirdar* v *The Army Board*. Ms Sirdar was made redundant from her post as chef for the Commando Regiment of the Royal Artillery for economic reasons but was offered a post as a chef for the Royal Marines. However, she was then informed that she was ineligible. The Royal Marines exclude women from their regiment on the ground that their presence is incompatible with the requirement of interoperability, i.e. every marine, regardless of specialisation, must be capable of fighting in a commando unit. The Court of Justice accepted that the Royal Marines differed fundamentally from other units in the British army, being a small force in the first line of attack, and it was established that chefs are also required to serve as front line commandos. All members are engaged and trained for that purpose without exception. The Court held, therefore, that the competent authorities were entitled to exclude women providing the decision was proportionate.

Pregnancy and Maternity

Article 2(3) provides that the directive shall be without prejudice to provisions concerning the protection of women, particularly as regards pregnancy and maternity. In other words, a different legal regime can apply here, specifically to protect women, but these provisions should not be used to disguise discrimination.

The directive recognises the legitimacy of protecting women's needs in two respects:

(a)   to ensure protection of a woman's biological condition during pregnancy and thereafter until physiological and mental functions have returned to normal; and

(b)   to protect the special relationship between mother and child in the immediate period after child birth and to prevent it from being disturbed by pressure of work.

In addition there is also now Art 10 of Directive 92/85 for the protection of pregnant workers, which designates the period of protection as from the beginning of pregnancy to the end of maternity leave (14 weeks leave minimum) in which women are protected from dismissal for any reasons connected to pregnancy. They can be dismissed in the normal course of events, e.g., for theft. After that special protection is lost. Case law had, however, already reached this position ahead of the directive coming into force.

In *Johnston* v *Chief Constable of the RUC*, the RUC sought to rely on Art 2(3) as a defence. The Court of Justice held that Art 2(3) did not apply to allow women to be excluded from a certain type of employment on the ground that public opinion demanded that women be given greater protection than men against risks which affected men and women in the same way.

In *Hoffman* v *Barmer Ersatzkasse*, a father claimed that the refusal to grant six months' paternity leave following the birth of his child while the mother went back to work, was discrimination contrary to Arts 1, 2 and 5(1) of the Equal Treatment Directive. The Court of Justice held that the directive was not designed to settle questions concerned with the organisation of the family, or to alter the division of responsibility between parents, and that parental leave may therefore be reserved to the mother by the Member States by virtue of Art 2(3).

In *Commission* v *France (Re Protection of Women)*, French legislation allowing certain privileges for women, including extended maternity leave, a reduction in the working hours of women aged 59, bringing forward retirement age, time off for sick children, an extra day's holiday each year per child, a day off on the first day of a school term and others, was held by the Court of Justice not to be justified by Art 2(3) and that the reasons given for the protection applied equally to male and female workers.

In *Dekker* v *VJM Centram*, VJM refused to employ Ms Dekker because she was pregnant and this would mean that Insurance law, which did not recognise pregnancy as a reason for paying insurance money would not reimburse the employers during her maternity leave. As a social institution, they claimed they could not afford to hire a replacement for her. The Court held that the employer was in direct contravention of Arts 2(1) and 3(1) of the Directive by their refusal to employ even though national rules forced this situation. In the *Thibault* case, promotion was assessed on the basis of the six months previous work presence. This discriminated against women on maternity absence who lost the chance to be assessed for promotion and was held to unlawfully discriminate. The Court held Arts 2(3) and 5(1) require substantive and not just formal equality.

Dismissal During or After Pregnancy

The protection of pregnant women from dismissal received its strongest support in the case of *Webb* v *EMO Air Cargo (UK) Ltd* (case C-32/93). In this case a women taken on, on an indefinite contract to replace her predecessor, who herself was on pregnancy and maternity leave, was dismissed when it was discovered that she was pregnant. The Court of Justice held that to be discrimination contrary to Arts 2(1) and 5(1) of Directive 76/207. In future cases on these and similar facts will be considered under Directive 92/85 specifically enacted to cover such situations.

The limits of the directive for protection in respect of pregnancy can be noted in *Hertz* v *Aldi*. Ms Hertz was dismissed because of repeated absence due to illness originating from pregnancy. The Court of Justice held that although pregnancy-related discrimination was a form of direct discrimination, the Directive did not apply to dismissals due to illness-related absence outside of the maternity leave time granted. It was necessary to look at national legislation to consider whether there was any direct or indirect discrimination in the grounds of dismissal.

In *Habermann-Beltermann* v *Arbeiterwohlfahrt* (case C-421/92), HB was employed on a permanent nights contract and was dismissed when discovered to be pregnant on the basis of a national law prohibiting the night time work of pregnant women. While the prohibition was allowed by the Directive, it was not permitted to justify dismissal. It was held that, neither existing national legislation in respect of night time work nor employment contract rules could render void an employment contract by reason of the fact that the female worker was found to be pregnant.

The case of *Larsson* v *Dansk Handel & Service*, however, confirms the previous position adopted by the Court of Justice in the *Hertz* case that, Directive 76/207 does not prevent dismissals for absences due to illness attributable to pregnancy even where the illness arose during pregnancy and continued during and after maternity. The Directive only prevents dismissal during the period of protected maternity leave. The dismissal after the leave period is not specifically catered for by EC law and the situation to determine unlawful discrimination reverts to comparing dismissal due to illness on a direct basis with the dismissal of a man for illness. Directive 92/85 had not at the time of the facts of this case been adopted but arguably would not have helped as it only protects dismissal from the beginning of pregnancy to the end of maternity leave as confirmed in *Brown* v *Rentokil* (dismissal during the protected pregnancy period is unlawful). Absences due to illnesses thereafter are treated in the same way as any other illness and may constitute grounds for dismissal according to provisions of national law.

The Promotion of Equal Opportunity by Removing Existing Inequalities Affecting Women's Opportunities

Article 2(4) states that the Directive shall be without prejudice to measures to promote equal opportunity for men and women, in particular by removing existing inequalities which affect women's opportunities in the areas covered by the Directive. However, the extent to which the authorities of the Member States can provide legislation or indeed private employers discriminate positively in favour of women by, for example, shortlisting or interviewing only female candidates or if dismissing only males is a difficult question. In *Re Protection of Women: Commission v France*, considered above, it can be seen that not all measures will be considered to be fair by the ECJ. In *Kalanke*, the ECJ ruled that national rules (which provided that, where equally qualified men and women were candidates for a position with fewer women, women are automatically to be given priority) involved discrimination on the grounds of sex and according to the Court of Justice, the rules had gone beyond promotion and had overstepped the exception provided for in Art 2(4). This ruling by the Court was subject to criticism.

However, there has now been a refinement of this position both in the subtlety of approach by the Member State authorities and the interpretation by the Court of Justice in the case of *Marschall* (C-409/95). *Marschall* involved an application for a teaching post by a qualified man being rejected by the local authority pursuant to a law which provided that women should be given priority in the event of equal suitability. However, in contrast to *Kalanke*, the existence of a 'saving clause' which provides that if a particular male candidate has grounds which tilt the balance in his favour, women are not to be given priority, enabled the Court to reach a more balanced conclusion that the provision was one which could fall within the scope of Art 2(4) of the Directive and did not offend the prohibition of discrimination. There were, however, two safety mechanisms (or, if you prefer, complications) to the process, which should be set up, first to avoid discrimination against men and then to stop the pendulum from swinging against women. The Court considered that such clauses are acceptable provided the candidates are objectively assessed to determine whether there are any factors tilting the balance in favour of a male candidate but that such criteria employed do not themselves discriminate against women. Somewhat convoluted, but it does appear to strike the balance.

The new Art 141(4) will provide the Court of Justice with greater power to pursue the more liberal approach adopted in *Marschall* (C-409/95). It seeks further to remove discrimination but the limits to what is acceptable positive discrimination is as yet unknown.

Access to Employment

Article 3(1) provides that there shall be no discrimination whatsoever on the grounds of sex in the conditions, including selection criteria, for access to all jobs or posts, whatever the sector or branch or activity and to all levels of the occupational hierarchy. In *Dekker v VJM Centram*, VJM refused to employ Ms Dekker because she was pregnant, and this would mean that insurance law, which did not recognise pregnancy as a reason for paying insurance money, would not reimburse the employers during maternity leave. As a social institution they could not afford to hire a replacement. The Court of Justice held that the employers were in direct contravention of Arts 2(1) and 3(1) of the Directive by their refusal to employ, even though national rules forced this situation.

The case of *Von Colson and Kamann v Land Nordrhein-Westfalen*, considered below, is an example of the application of the equal treatment principle to access.

See also the *Hill and Stapleton* case, considered previously, whereby it would be discrimination to appoint part-time job sharers who transfer to full-time work to a lower salary scale point than they enjoyed under job share on the basis of the actual time worked where a majority of women are job sharers unless such a rule can be justified by objective criteria unrelated to any discrimination on grounds of sex.

Working Conditions and Dismissal

Article 5 of Directive 76/207, on working conditions and conditions governing dismissal, has been subject to much judicial interpretation, especially in cases referred from UK courts.

Member States can, under Art 7 of Directive 7/79, exclude from the Equal Treatment Directive the determination of pensionable age for the purposes of granting old age and retirement pensions and the possible consequences thereof for other benefits.

Burton v British Railways Board concerned equal access to a voluntary redundancy scheme. The Court of Justice held that the principle of equal treatment contained in Art 5 of the Equal Treatment Directive applied to the conditions of access to voluntary redundancy benefit paid by an employer to an employee wishing to leave his employment. However, the actual requirement of which Mr Burton had fallen foul was not caught by the provision. The Court ruled that:

> the fact that access to voluntary redundancy is available only during the five years preceding the minimum pensionable age fixed by national social security legislation and that age is not the same for men as for women, cannot in itself be regarded as discrimination on grounds of sex within Article 5 of the Equal Treatment Directive.

The question of the meaning of the term 'dismissal' and the relationship between the two directives was to come before the Court of Justice in further references from UK courts. Specifically, in *Roberts v Tate and Lyle*, it was held that access to a redundancy scheme was concerned with dismissal, and therefore was covered by Art 5 and not excluded by Art 7 of Directive 79/7, because it was not linked to the state security system. In these circumstances, the grant of a pension to persons of the same age who are made redundant amounts merely to a collective measure adopted irrespective of the sex of the workers in order to guarantee them the same rights. It was held that Art 5(1) must be interpreted as meaning that a contractual provision which lays down a single age (55) for the dismissal of men and women under a mass redundancy involving the grant of an early retirement pension, whereas the normal retirement age is different for men and women, does not constitute discrimination on grounds of sex contrary to Community law.

The cases of *Habermann-Beltermann* and *Webb*, above, also concern unlawful discriminatory dismissal contrary to Art 5(1).

Article 5 and Retirement Ages

In *Marshall* it was held that enforced earlier retirement for women than for men is not justified by Art 7 of Directive 79/7 and is therefore direct discrimination.

Remedies

Article 6 of Directive 76/207 provides that Member States must introduce into their own legal systems such measures as are necessary to enable all persons who consider themselves wronged to pursue their claims by judicial process.

Von Colson and Kamann concerned the reimbursement of travel expenses as damages for discrimination. The Court of Justice ruled that full implementation of the directive entails that sanctions must be such as to guarantee real and effective judicial protection, and must therefore have a real deterrent effect on the employer. Where a Member State chooses to penalise the breach of the prohibition on discrimination by the award of compensation, that compensation must be adequate in relation to the damage sustained and amount to more than purely nominal compensation. Article 6 is not, however, itself directly effective (see also *Johnston* v *Chief Constable of the RUC*).

In the second *Marshall* case, it was held that damages mean full damages not limited by national statutory rules. This ruling of the Court of Justice has proved very controversial also. Despite the fact that the Directive does not specify the damages required, the Court held the Directive gave a right to full compensation from date of breach and it was not to be subjected to a national limitation period for damages.

In the most recent case of *Draehmpaehl* v *Urania*, a job was offered only to females, contrary to EC law and German law as well. In the consequent claim for damages due to discrimination, damages were limited by German statute to a maximum of three months' salary, but this was dependent on proving fault on the part of the employer. If more than one claimant sued, the total compensation payable was limited to six months' salary. The Court of Justice held liability to compensate cannot be made dependent on fault and that compensation itself must guarantee real and effective judicial protection, have a real deterrent effect on the employer and be adequate in relation to the damage suffered. Limits such as three months' salary are acceptable where the employer can prove that, notwithstanding the discrimination, a better qualified person was appointed and the complainant would not have been appointed in any event. However, an aggregate award ceiling regardless of the number discriminated against is not acceptable under Directive 76/207 as it might have the effect of dissuading applicants so harmed from asserting their rights. The problem with this latter aspect is that not every one could be appointed to the position, only one person. What if there were 50 male applicants who were thus discriminated against? This was not considered in the case itself.

Subsequent cases may clarify these points. *Coote v Granada* (case C-185/97) represents an extension of the law in Directive 76/207. The Court of Justice held that Art 6 would be undermined if employees who wished to pursue legal actions were refused references in future as happened in this case.

Article 7 requires Member States to take the necessary measures to protect employees against dismissal by the employer as a reaction to a complaint within the undertaking or to any legal proceedings aimed at enforcing compliance with the principle of equal treatment.

THE SOCIAL SECURITY DIRECTIVE (79/7)

Article 1 states as its purpose 'the progressive implementation . . . of the principle of equal treatment for men and women in matters of social security'.

Scope

Article 2 of Directive 79/7 provides that it applies to the working population, which includes self-employed persons, workers and other people whose activity is interrupted by illness, accident or involuntary unemployment and persons seeking employment, and to retired or invalided workers and self-employed persons.

It was confirmed in *Drake v Chief Adjudication Officer* that Art 2 includes persons who have been working but whose work has been interrupted by one of the risks referred to in Art 3 (see below). Ms Drake had given up work solely because of one of the risks listed in Art 3, namely the invalidity of her mother. It was held she must therefore be regarded as one of the working population for the purposes of the Directive.

The limits of this scope were considered in *Achterberg et al.*, concerning claims from three women who were voluntarily unemployed. The Court of Justice held that the Directive did not apply to those who were unemployed but not seeking work or suffering from one of the risks listed. Furthermore, in *Jackson and Cresswell v Chief Adjudication Officer* (case C-63–4/91) the Court of Justice confirmed that the Directive only applies to the types of social security which replaced a worker's wage and not general schemes to relieve poverty.

Article 3(1) provides that it applies to:

(a)   statutory schemes which provide protection against sickness, invalidity, old age, accidents at work and occupational diseases or unemployment; and

(b)   social assistance, in so far as it is intended to supplement or replace the schemes referred to in (a).

It is limited to statutory schemes; contracted out schemes come under Directive 86/378.

In *Drake v Chief Adjudication Officer*, Ms Drake had given up her job to look after her mother but her application for benefit was turned down. It was held that Art 3(1) must be interpreted as including any benefit which in a broad sense forms one of the statutory schemes referred to, or a social assistance scheme designed to supplement or replace such a scheme. The fact that the benefit which forms part of a statutory invalidity scheme is paid to a third party and not to the disabled person, does not place it outside the scope of the Directive.

In *R v Secretary of State for Social Security, ex parte Smithson*, a claim in respect of loss of housing benefit due to the operation of British social security rules was held by the Court of Justice not to be within the scope of Directive 79/7, which applied only to statutory schemes providing protection against certain named risks, including old age and illness, but not need of financial help with accommodation costs. This is regarded as a surprisingly restrictive interpretation of the provision, given the Court of Justice's attitude to other provisions on equal treatment.

Family credit, however, because it is a means to enable (in this case) a single mother to go to work, is in the view of the Court of Justice in *Meyer v Adjudication Officer* (case C-116/94) within the scope of the Directive. Article 3 provides for social assistance for the persons covered by Art 2 which include 'persons seeking employment'. Article 3 has also been held to include prescription charges in this context as in the UK the exemptions from these were linked to old age pensions and thus discriminatory. The Court held that they were part of a statutory scheme providing protection against sickness and were thus covered (see *R v Secretary of State for Health, ex parte Richardson* (case C-137/94)).

Discrimination

Article 4 of Directive 79/7 defines the principle of equal treatment as meaning:

no discrimination whatsoever on grounds of sex either directly, or indirectly by reference in particular to marital or family status, in particular as concerns:
— the scope of the schemes and the conditions of access thereto,
— the obligation to contribute and the calculation of contributions,
— the calculation of benefits including increases due in respect of a spouse and for dependants and the conditions governing the duration and retention of entitlement to benefits.

Article 4(1) was held to be directly effective in *McDermott v Minister for Social Welfare*, where an Irish rule granting social security supplements for dependants to married men without requiring them to prove that the persons in respect of whom they were claiming were in fact dependent on them, but requiring such proof in the case of married women, was in breach of the Social Security Directive.

In *Drake*, it was held the refusal of benefit for women living with wage-earning husbands constituted discrimination prohibited by the Directive.

Integrity v Rouvroy concerned exemptions from social security payments for low-wage-earning women. The male plaintiff had earned very little in the past but was not allowed the same exemption. This was held by the Court of Justice to be contrary to Art 4(1) of Directive 79/7.

A case which echoes the concerns in the equal pay cases about indirect discrimination against part-time, and thus predominantly women, workers is *Ruzius-Wilbrink v Bestuur van de Bedrijfsvereniging voor Overheidsdiensten*. A Dutch law granted entitlement to a disability allowance to insured persons aged 17 or over who become incapable of working. The benefit was calculated on the basis of past earnings which discriminated against those being paid less than the minimum weekly wages, i.e., part-time workers. Official statistics showed that 75 per cent of part-time workers were women, and the plaintiff, who received a lower rate of benefit as an ex part-time worker, claimed that the criteria were discriminatory on grounds of sex. The Court of Justice held that in circumstances like this there is effective discrimination against workers of one sex, and the differentiation will be in breach of Art 4(1) of Directive 79/7 unless objectively justified. The fact that persons could now receive more in benefits than they had received in wages was not an objective justification in the eyes of the Court.

Maternity

Article 4(2) of Directive 79/7 provides that the principle of equal treatment shall be without prejudice to the provisions relating to the protection of women on the grounds of maternity and the payment of maternity benefits.

Remedies

Article 5 of the directive requires the Member States to take the necessary measures to abolish any laws, regulations or administrative provisions which are contrary to the principle of equal treatment.

Article 6 is the exact equivalent of Art 6 of the Equal Treatment Directive. It requires the Member States to provide recourse to judicial process so that individuals may enforce the principle of equal treatment in the national courts.

In *R* v *Secretary of State for Social Security, ex parte Eunice Sutton* (case C-66/95), it was held that in contrast to the position taken in *Marshall (No. 2)*, Art 6 of Directive 79/7, which is almost identical to Art 6 of Directive 76/207, does not oblige the Member State to pay interest on the payment of benefits when the delay was the result of unlawful discrimination. The reason given was that the payments are made under social security benefits and not compensation for damage sustained. The Court of Justice did hold, however, that post-*Francovich*, a Member State must make good loss to an individual the result of a breach of Community law, but that it was up to the national courts to decide that question.

Derogations

Article 7 empowers the Member States to exclude from the scope of Directive 79/7 a number of reserved areas. These include most notably the determination of pensionable age for the purposes of granting old age and retirement pensions and the possible consequences thereof for other benefits, and the granting of old age or invalidity benefit by virtue of the derived entitlements of a wife.

The approach of the Court of Justice to the exception in Art 7(1)(a) has restricted it to old age pensions and retirement pensions and consequences therefrom but not to dismissal and its consequences. (As noted in *Burton* v *British Railways Board*, *Roberts* v *Tate and Lyle*, *Marshall* v *Southampton Area Health Authority* and *Beets-Proper* v *F. Van Lanschot Bankiers NV* above.)

The judgment in *Barber* has had considerable consequences on the scope of this derogation as many of the pension schemes which might otherwise have been excluded from equal treatment are now outside the derogation. Contracted out pension schemes were held to provide deferred pay and thus fall outside Art 7(1) of Directive 79/7. Further details of the *Barber* judgment and the follow up Protocol and case law are noted above.

It was held in *R* v *Secretary of State for Social Security, ex parte EOC* (case C-9/91), that the different periods of contribution for retirement pensions for men and women in the UK was acceptable, because it was necessarily linked to the different pensionable ages allowed by Art 7.

DIRECTIVE 86/378

This Directive extends equal treatment to occupational, as opposed to statutory, pension schemes and applies similar rules to Directive 79/7. It did not come into effect fully until 1 January 1993. The wide definition given to 'pay' in some of the earlier case law includes some of the schemes covered by this Directive. Whilst the case of *Newstead* confirms that contracted out pensions schemes in the UK will be considered under this directive employers' contribution could nevertheless be regarded as pay under Art 141 (old 119) (see, for example, the cases of *Worringham* and *Bilka Kaufhaus*). As a result of the *Barber* judgment, much of this Directive would seem to be redundant as the schemes concerned by it, with the exception of those relating to the self-employed, have been decided to constitute deferred pay and thus be covered by Art 141 (old 119) EC. There are proposals to amend and consolidate the law in this area.

DIRECTIVE 86/613

This provides for equal treatment of the self-employed to complement Directive 76/207, especially in respect of women during pregnancy and motherhood. It came into force on 30 June 1991.

DIRECTIVE 92/85

Directive 92/85 is now in place and should have been implemented by the Member States by 19 October 1994. Essentially it expands on the pregnancy exception in Art 2 of Directive 76/207 and specifically with the dismissal of pregnant women from employment from the beginning of pregnancy to the end of maternity leave. It also covers part-time workers.

The Directive has now been considered by the Court of Justice in case law coming before the Court. The Directive provides for a minimum 14 week maternity leave, protection from dismissal (Arts 8 and 10) and under Art 11, employment rights during the maternity leave must be secured including payments and allowances, at least the equivalent as those payable to workers on sick leave.

In *Boyle et al v Equal Opportunities Commission* (case C-411/96), the Equal Opportunities Commission, set up to promote and defend equal rights, was accused of unlawful discrimination. Boyle and five colleagues raised a number of questions about the maternity scheme run by the EOC. This reflected the UK civil service maternity scheme. It had been agreed in the employment tribunal and accepted by the Court of Justice that for the purposes of direct effects of the Directives, the EOC was an emanation of the State.

The Court decided as follows:

A clause requiring repayment of maternity payments over and above the statutory minimum if a woman did not return to work following maternity leave when she had undertaken to return, was not contrary to the Directive. Although, there was no similar clause applying to those receiving higher rate sick leave payments, this was not discrimination against women according to the Court, as maternity leave under Directive 92/85 was a special provision not to be compared with that of a man or woman on sick leave. Higher rate sick leave pay would apply to both women and men.

In answer to a question about the commencement of maternity leave, the Directive specified only the minimum number of weeks to be granted and left it to Member States to lay down provision as to when it should commence.

A clause which prohibited a women from taking sick leave during the minimum period of 14 weeks' maternity leave under Art 8(1) of Directive 92/85 unless she elected to return to work and thus terminate her maternity leave, was contrary to EC law. However, a similar clause in respect of supplementary maternity leave is compatible with Directives 76/207 and 92/85 as EC law does not apply to supplementary maternity leave. Thus a woman can be restricted to maternity or sick leave but not both.

Article 11(2)(a) of Directive 92/85 requires maternity leave rights in the 14-week minimum period to be at least the same as minimum statutory rights when on sick leave. A clause which limited the period during which annual leave accrues to that 14-week period was compatible with EC law. Outside of that period no annual leave would accrue. There was no discrimination, direct or indirect, according to the Court of Justice, as all employees on unpaid leave accrued no annual leave entitlement. A right to supplementary leave over and above the protection provided by the Directive and which was available to women only could not constitute less favourable treatment.

In contrast, in answer to the fifth question, a clause which restricted the accrual of pension rights to the 14-week period and denied it during the supplementary unpaid period of leave was held to be contrary to Directive 92/85. Although, under Art 11(4), entitlement to benefits could be subject to workers satisfying national legislation this was not possible where the pension scheme was wholly occupational and governed by the employment contract. Therefore, accrual of pensions rights was not dependent on receiving pay during the supplementary period.

This meant a part success for the applicants. Moreover, the offending clauses cannot now be enforced either by the EOC or other employers with the same contractual clauses.

Directive 92/85 was also considered in *Handels-og Kontorfunktionaererernes Forbund I Danmark v Faellesforeningen for Danmarks Brugforeninger (Pedersen et al)* (case C-66/96). Danish law provided that women who were unfit for work as a result of the pregnancy before or after the maternity leave period could not receive full pay but rather benefits instead from the local authority. Workers who were medically attested ill, received full pay from their employers. Secondly, employers were also permitted not to provide employment for a pregnant employee, even if not unfit, if they considered there was no work available. With regard to the first provision, it should be of no surprise that the Court of Justice held that the discriminatory treatment based on the pregnancy was contrary to Art 119 (now 141) and Directive 75/117 and that the second provision led to unequal treatment of women in breach of Art 5 of Directive 76/207. The argument that the rule was for the protection of pregnant women in line with Art 2(3) of Directive 76/207 and Directive 92/85 was rejected by the Court which considered it to preserve the interests of the employer. The failure to pay in full when the employee was sent home was thus contrary to those Directives.

Although there are a number of future proposals for Directives or action on the part of the Commission, they will not be discussed here as they are far too speculative and are best left to treatment in the textbooks and courses.

QUESTIONS

1.   Assess the contribution of the Court of Justice to the promotion of equal employment rights for women and men.

This requires you to concentrate on the jurisprudence of the Court of Justice in cases concerning equal rights, and how the Court has helped the promotion of these rights. Thus, rather than looking at all such cases where equal rights have been secured, you should concentrate on those cases in which the Court of Justice has, by a liberal interpretation, advanced the cause of equal rights in the Community.

Cases coming into this category include the *Defrenne* litigation and any cases involving the generous and wide interpretation of Art 141 (old 119), including the concept of pay in *Garland* and indirect discrimination in *Bilka Kaufhaus*. The Court has been particularly instrumental in securing equal pay and rights of part time workers in such cases as *Jenkins*. The Equal Treatment Directive has also been interpreted generously in cases such as *Marshall*, *Barber* and most recently in *Webb*. The Court has even advanced the cause of equal rights through procedural means, so that an effective remedy should be given by the Member States in cases where rights have been breached (the *Von Colson* case, the second *Marshall* case and *Johnston* v *RUC*). The definition of what constitutes discrimination has also been given a generous interpretation in *P* v *S and Cornwall County Council*.

According to your own view of what the Court of Justice has done or what it should do, your conclusion may range from considering that the

Court of Justice has contributed significantly, to the view that it has only done what was to be expected.

An extended version of the above question and answer comes in the form of the second question, where the second part repeats the requirements for the answer of the first question.

2. Given that the Community is essentially an economic community, social concern would seem to have little place in its development. Explain the appearance in the EC Treaty of provisions for the abolition of sex discrimination and the consequent attitude displayed by the Court of Justice when faced with cases concerned with these provisions.

The aspects of this question which are required to be addressed are (i) the suggestion that the Community is essentially an economic community, (ii) the limited place that social concern had or has in its development, and (iii) the attitude the Court of Justice has displayed in case law. Since the third part repeats the last answer, I will not consider it here.

The first part requires you to consider the original aims of the Community and the reason for the inclusion of social rights, and the second part the development of the Community and the development of the provision of social rights. As outlined above, this area of Community law is a later developer than the other areas because of the less extensive provision for it in the Treaty, and the delays by the Member States in implementing the principle of equal pay and by the Commission in introducing secondary legislation. Art 141 (old 119) was the sole original provision for the European Community to concern itself with sex discrimination.

The main aim of the Community is undoubtedly the harmonisation of specific aspects of the Member States' economies, principally, at first, creating the single market. Social policy would not seem greatly to assist the achievement of this result. However, it is suggested that the immediate reason for including Art 141 (old 119) in the EC Treaty was not to satisfy social justice, but out of economic considerations. The article allegedly was included at the request of the French, whose legislation purported to provide for equality between male and female workers. It was feared that French industry would be at a disadvantage if equal pay were not a principle enforced in the other Member States. Thus the aim was to ensure similar economic conditions applied in all the Member States. A consideration which supports this view is the fact that Art 141 (old 119) applies only to equal pay and not to all discrimination on the grounds of sex. See the quote from *Defrenne* v *SABENA (No. 2)* set out on p. 280 above.

While the economic goals of the Community originally were undoubtedly paramount, if not exclusive, developments to date, including the directives on equal treatment and the considerable body of Community law on the subject, might lead to an amended conclusion. Thus you need to outline these developments as discussed above in the answer to question 1.

3.   Karen and Bev work for Fullworth, a high street retail store. Bev works as one of 20 part-time sales assistants, 18 of whom are female and two male. All of them are paid 15 per cent less per hour than male full-time sales assistants. There are no female full-time sales assistants. When Bev complained to the management that this was discrimination, they justified it on the ground that because they required male workers to sell certain items, such as men's clothes, and in order to attract male workers to the low paid retail sector, they were forced to pay a premium. Bev had never noticed that there was such a specific division of functions among the sales assistants.

Karen was employed at Fullworth as a secretary but was recently promoted to the position of a buyer. She has discovered that a male office worker, employed as a clerk, receives more money than she does, even after her recent increase. When she complained, she was informed that the different duties justified the difference in wages.

As a result of poor sales, Fullworth decided to make some redundancies, and Bev and Karen were chosen as the first two to be dismissed, despite their longer service with the company than many of their female and male counterparts. Furthermore, their redundancy payments were also lower than those of male workers with the same length of service made redundant at another branch three months previously. They have both complained to an industrial tribunal. The company has refuted the alleged discrimination in pay for the reasons previously given, and has also stated that any discrimination in respect of redundancy is acceptable, as this is excluded from the scope of Community law which does not relate to retirement and pensions.

As a general introduction to this problem on discrimination, you could state the narrow Treaty base for Community law, but that a number of directives have now been issued and that the Court of Justice interprets these liberally, to give the maximum protection to the rights provided.

The issues in this problem are (i) the difference in pay of the female part-time workers as compared with male full-time workers, (ii) the comparison of Karen's pay with the male office worker, (iii) the redundancies and the redundancy payments, and (iv) the rights to pursue these claims before the national tribunals. It is to be noted that this last issue is particularly important because they are employed by a private employer, which may affect their rights to remedy in the national courts if they are dependent on the direct effects of Directives. However, unless you are advised on a particular course that a full discussion of the procedural aspects of the case must be given, a brief statement of the problems and possible solutions should complete an answer in a question which essentially concerns sex discrimination. Article 141 (old 119) is the primary legislative provision in this area.

First of all, Bev is not claiming that she has been directly discriminated against, but indirectly compared to full-time workers, despite the fact that she is paid the same as male part-time workers. The cases of *Jenkins* v *Kingsgate* and *Bilka Kaufhaus* confirm that this will be regarded as indirect discrimination, when the disadvantage falls on a category which is predominantly female, unless it can be justified objectively. The *Bilka Kaufhaus* case also provides three guidelines to determine whether a difference in pay is objectively justified. The measure employed must correspond to a real need on the part of the undertaking, be appropriate to achieve the objective and be necessary for that objective. Thus it is a question of fact. Given that the reason put forward might be an objective justification if it were true, the facts of the case, if proved, would appear to contradict this, i.e., there is no discrimination of functions and no shortage of applicants for full time positions has been demonstrated. The difference in pay is likely to breach Art 141 (old 119). See also the case of *Dansk* (*Danfoss*) in which the burden is placed on the employer to prove that the difference is justified.

Karen is concerned with a claim of work for equal value under Directive 75/117, but the claim is also capable of being made under Art 141 (old 119) especially now as the Treaty of Amsterdam has expanded Art 141 to include equal value claims. In this case she is comparing her wages with those of a male worker whose work is arguably of lesser or equal value, but she receives lower wages. Should the company refuse to carry out a job evaluation scheme to test this, it can be imposed on them through court proceedings. Following the *Mary Murphy* v *An Bord Telecom Eireann* case, this claim is also likely to succeed.

The final claims are made by both, in respect of redundancy payments and the redundancies themselves. The redundancies would be included under the terms of Directive 76/207, Art 5 (conditions governing dismissal). The company claim, that these are linked to pensions and thus excluded by Art 7 of Directive 79/7, would be dismissed on the basis of the *Marshall* case, i.e., that they were not linked to the State pensions arrangements and were purely concerned with dismissal. Thus, the redundancies would fall to be considered under Directive 76/207, but a problem persists in that Bev and Karen are complaining that it is the basis on which they were chosen that is discriminatory.

While there is no direct case on this aspect, *Worringham* v *Lloyds Bank* would seem to be helpful because it stated that conditions of access to redundancy schemes come under Directive 76/207. If the basis of choice is a condition of access to a scheme, it may cover this situation. The employer is likely to claim the right to choose who to make redundant and not be forced by old custom and practice to choose the last in. If the national court is unable to decide, or decides against Karen and Bev, they will be unable to rely directly on the directive because a private employer is involved and there are no horizontal direct effects.

The only remaining aspect of this issue to be considered is the lack of direct comparison between Bev and Karen and their male colleagues because the comparators were made redundant three months previously from another branch. This should not, however, stand in the way of the claim, following the case law of Court of Justice. *Macarthys* v *Smith* (case 129/79) held that a contemporaneous comparator was not required and *Murphy* v *Irish Telecom* (case 157/86) allowed comparisons with employees in the same company, i.e., not employed directly beside the complainants. Further support that a much wider basis of comparison should be allowed arises from the cases of *Defrenne (No. 2)* (case 43/75) and *Commission* v *Denmark* (case 143/83) although the statements made in these cases are not unequivocal.

A reference to the Court of Justice would probably be needed to resolve the matter, which the tribunal should make. In the event that it does not, you would be taken into the area of Art 234 (old 177) and direct effects. It may be that your question will also ask you to consider these aspects, but I shall just refer you to the appropriate chapters, where these issues have been considered in questions in those chapters.

Also, consider the difference in the amount of redundancy payments. It has been held that redundancy payments are a part of the concept of pay, and this aspect could therefore be considered under Art 141 (old 119) and Directive 75/117 (hence no difficulty with direct effects, see the *Worringham* and *Bilka* cases). As pay, the amount should be equal.

The final aspect concerns the difficulties which might arise in respect of pursuit of the claims in the national tribunals. If the national court is unable to decide or decides against Karen and Bev on any of the issues, the result will differ according to the provision relied on and the action taken by the Member State in respect of implementing the Directives. Any claims made under Art 141 (old 119) will be safe in all circumstances because this was held to be directly effective in *Defrenne (No. 2)* (case 43/75) (both vertically and horizontally). It can be observed that all of the claims, except that against the unfair redundancy conditions, can be made relying on Art 141 (old 119), therefore only one may present difficulties. However, if the Member State has accurately implemented the Equal Treatment Directive, 76/207, then the applicant can invoke national law before the national court to uphold her rights. However, if it has not been implemented or incorrectly implemented, the claimants will be unable to rely directly on the Directive because a private employer is involved and there are no horizontal direct effects; see the *Marshall* case. The result in such a circumstance would depend on whether the national court could interpret any national law in compliance with Community law, thus following *Von Colson* (case 14/83) and *Marleasing* (case C-106/89). If this is not the case, a further possibility exists in that a claim may be made against the State, in accordance with *Francovich* (case C-6/90), for a failure to implement the Directive with the result that the claimant has suffered damage.

FURTHER READING

Armstrong, K., 'Tales of the Community: sexual orientation discrimination and EC law' (1998) 20 J Soc Wel & Fam L 455.

Dashwood, A. and O'Leary, S., *The Principle of Equal Treatment in the EC Law* (Sweet & Maxwell, 1997).

Docksey, C., 'The Principle of Equality between Men and Women: a Fundamental Right under Community Law' (1991) 20 ILJ 258.

Ellis, E., *European Community Sex Discrimination Law* (OUP, 1991).

Fredman, S., 'Reversing Discrimination' (1997) 113 LQR 575.

Hervey, T. and O'Keefe, D., (eds), *Sex Equality Law in the European Union* (Wiley, 1996).

Nielsen and Szyszczak, *The Social Dimension of the European Community* (3rd edn, Copenhagen: Handelshojskolens Forlag, 1997).

Prechal, S. and Burrows, N., *Gender Discrimination Law of the European Community* (Dartmouth, 1990).

BIBLIOGRAPHY

Brown and Kennedy, *The Court of Justice of the European Communities* (4th edn, London: Sweet & Maxwell, 1994).

Charlesworth and Cullen, *European Community Law* (London: Pitman, 1994).

Collins, *European Community Law in the United Kingdom* (4th edn, London: Butterworths, 1990).

Craig and De Búrca, *EC Law, Text, Cases and Materials* (2nd edn, Oxford: Oxford University Press, 1998).

Edwards, *European Community Law — An Introduction* (2nd edn, London: Butterworths, 1995).

Ellis, *Public Law of the European Community: Text, Materials and Commentary* (London: Sweet and Maxwell, 1995).

Foster, *EC Law (Questions and Answers)* (2nd edn, London: Blackstone Press, 1998).

Foster (Ed), *EC Legislation* (10th edn, London: Blackstone Press, 1999).

George, *Politics and Policy in the European Union* (3rd edn, Oxford: Oxford University Press, 1996).

Goyder, *EC Competition Law* (2nd edn, Oxford: Clarendon Press, 1993).

Green et al., *The Legal Foundations of the Single European Market* (Oxford: Oxford University Press, 1991).

Hartley, *The Foundations of European Community Law* (4th edn, Oxford: Clarendon Press, 1998).

Kapteyn and van Themaat (Gormley (Ed)), *Introduction to the Law of the European Communities* (3rd edn, Deventer: Kluwer, 1998).

Lasok and Bridge, *Law and Institutions of the European Communities* (6th edn, London: Butterworths, 1995).

Nielsen and Szyszczak, *The Social Dimension of the European Community* (3rd edn, Copenhagen: Handelshojskolens Forlag, 1997).

Pinder, *The Building of the European Union* (3rd edn, Oxford: Oxford University Press, 1998).

Plender and Usher, *Cases and Materials on the Law of the European Communities* (3rd edn, London: Butterworths, 1993).

Pollard and Ross, *European Community Law: Text and Materials* (London: Butterworths, 1994).

Steiner and Woods, *Textbook on EC Law* (6th edn, London: Blackstone Press, 1998).

Swann, *Economics of the Common Market* (7th edn, London: Penguin, 1992).

Tillotson, *European Community Law: Text, Cases and Materials* (London: Cavendish, 1994).

Ward, *A Critical Introduction to European Law* (London: Butterworths, 1996).

Weatherill, *Law and Integration in the European Union* (Oxford: Oxford University Press, 1995).

Weatherill, *Cases and Materials on EC Law* (4th edn, London: Blackstone Press, 1998).

Weatherill and Beaumont, *EU Law* (3rd edn, London: Penguin, 1999).

Wyatt and Dashwood, *European Community Law* (3rd edn, London: Sweet & Maxwell, 1993).

A few of the most important internet homepage addresses are:

Europa, the European Union's Server
  http://europa.eu.int/index-en.htm

The European Parliament
  http://europa.eu.int/index-en.htm

The Council of Ministers
  http://ue.eu.int/en/summ.htm

The Commission
  fttp://europa.eu.int/comm/index_en.htm

The Court of Justice
  http://curia.eu.int/en/index.htm

The Official Journal, L series
  http://europa.eu.int/eur-lex/en/oj/index.html

INDEX

TITLES IN THE SERIES